Explaining Terrorism

This volume comprises some of the key essays by Professor Crenshaw, from 1972 to the present-day, on the causes, processes and consequences of terrorism.

Since the early 1970s, scholars and practitioners have tried to explain terrorism and to assess the effectiveness of government responses to the threat. From its beginnings in a small handful of analytical studies, the research field has expanded to thousands of entries, with an enormous spike following the 9/11 attacks. The field of terrorism studies is now impressive in terms of quantity, scope, and variety. Professor Crenshaw has studied terrorism since the late 1960s, well before it was topical, and this selection of her work represents the development of her thought over time in four areas:

- defining terrorism and identifying its causes;
- the different methods used to explain terrorism, including strategic, organizational, and psychological approaches;
- how campaigns of terrorism end;
- how governments can effectively contribute to the ending of terrorism.

This collection of essays by one of the pioneering thinkers in the field of terrorism studies will be essential reading for all students of political violence and terrorism, security studies, and IR/politics in general.

Martha Crenshaw is a Senior Fellow at the Center for International Security and Cooperation (CISAC) and the Freeman Spogli Institute for International Studies, and Professor of Political Science, by courtesy, at Stanford University. She is also Professor of Government Emerita at Wesleyan University. She is a lead investigator with the National Consortium for the Study of Terrorism and Responses to Terrorism (START) at the University of Maryland.

Routledge series on political violence
Series editors: Paul Wilkinson and David Rapoport

This book series contains sober, thoughtful and authoritative academic accounts of terrorism and political violence. Its aim is to produce a useful taxonomy of terror and violence through comparative and historical analysis in both national and international spheres. Each book discusses origins, organisational dynamics and outcomes of particular forms and expressions of political violence.

Aviation Terrorism and Security
Paul Wilkinson and Brian M. Jenkins (eds.)

Counter-Terrorist Law and Emergency Powers in the United Kingdom, 1922–2000
Laura K. Donohue

The Democratic Experience and Political Violence
David C. Rapoport and Leonard Weinberg (eds.)

Inside Terrorist Organizations
David C. Rapoport (ed.)

The Future of Terrorism
Max Taylor and John Horgan (eds.)

The IRA, 1968–2000
An analysis of a secret army
J. Bowyer Bell

Millennial Violence
Past, present and future
Jeffrey Kaplan (ed.)

Right-Wing Extremism in the Twenty-First Century
Peter H. Merkl and Leonard Weinberg (eds.)

Terrorism Today
Christopher C. Harmon

The Psychology of Terrorism
John Horgan

Research on Terrorism
Trends, achievements and failures
Andrew Silke (ed.)

A War of Words
Political violence and public debate in Israel
Gerald Cromer

Root Causes of Suicide Terrorism
Globalization of martyrdom
Ami Pedahzur (ed.)

Terrorism versus Democracy
The liberal state response, 2nd edition
Paul Wilkinson

Countering Terrorism and WMD
Creating a global counter-terrorism network
Peter Katona, Michael Intriligator and John Sullivan (eds.)

Mapping Terrorism Research
State of the art, gaps and future direction
Magnus Ranstorp (ed.)

The Ideological War on Terror
World-wide strategies for counter-terrorism
Anne Aldis and Graeme P. Herd (eds.)

The IRA and Armed Struggle
Rogelio Alonso

Homeland Security in the UK
Future preparedness for terrorist attack since 9/11
Paul Wilkinson et al. (eds.)

Terrorism Today, 2nd Edition
Christopher C. Harmon

Understanding Terrorism and Political Violence
The life cycle of birth, growth, transformation, and demise
Dipak K. Gupta

Global Jihadism
Theory and practice
Jarret M. Brachman

Combating Terrorism in Northern Ireland
James Dingley (ed.)

Leaving Terrorism Behind
Individual and collective disengagement
Tore Bjørgo and John Horgan (eds.)

Unconventional Weapons and International Terrorism
Challenges and new approaches
Magnus Ranstorp and Magnus Normark (eds.)

International Aviation and Terrorism
Evolving threats, evolving security
John Harrison

Walking Away from Terrorism
John Horgan

Understanding Violent Radicalisation
Terrorist and jihadist movements in Europe
Magnus Ranstorp (ed.)

Terrorist Groups and the New Tribalism
Terrorism's fifth wave
Jeffrey Kaplan

Negotiating With Terrorists
Strategy, tactics and politics
I. William Zartman and Guy Olivier Faure (eds.)

Explaining Terrorism
Causes, processes, and consequences
Martha Crenshaw

Explaining Terrorism

Causes, processes, and consequences

Martha Crenshaw

LONDON AND NEW YORK

First published 2011
by Routledge
2 Park Square, Milton Park, Abingdon, Oxon, OX14 4RN

Simultaneously published in the USA and Canada
by Routledge
711 Third Avenue, New York, NY 10017

Routledge is an imprint of the Taylor & Francis Group, an informa business

Typeset in Baskerville by Swales & Willis Ltd, Exeter, Devon

British Library Cataloguing in Publication Data
A catalogue record for this book is available from the British Library

Library of Congress Cataloging-in-Publication Data
Crenshaw, Martha.
Explaining terrorism : causes, processes and consequences / Martha Crenshaw.
p. cm.
1. Terrorism. I. Title.
HV6431.C756 2010
363.325—dc22
2010017264

ISBN13: 978–0–415–78050–6 (hbk)
ISBN13: 978–0–415–78051–3 (pbk)
ISBN13: 978–0–203–84056–6 (ebk)

Contents

Preface and acknowledgments

I am often asked how I came to study terrorism, which was an obscure and not entirely respectable subject when I began my academic career as a graduate student in 1967. When I started research on what became my Ph.D. thesis on the use of terrorism by the Front de Libération Nationale (FLN) during the Algerian war, I found perhaps three or four relevant books or monographs, a chapter in an edited book, and a few articles in military journals assessing terrorism as an initial stage of insurgency, with particular reference to the ongoing war in Vietnam. My choice of what was then an unusual topic was inspired by a short mention in a small book published in 1962, *Guerrillas in the 1960s*, by Peter Paret and John W. Shy. In the conclusion the two authors observed that "terrorism has received less systematic analysis than any other component of irregular war."[1] They noted that it was essential to study the effectiveness of terrorism under different circumstances and to differentiate among the various forms of terrorist activity. It so happened that just at that time I needed a topic for a graduate seminar paper. I had taken courses in Russian history as an undergraduate at Newcomb College (then the women's college of Tulane University) and was fascinated by the nineteenth-century Russian revolutionary movement, but I did not speak Russian, and anyway I was drawn to explore a more contemporary example. I chose the Algerian war as a case study in part because I spoke French and knew something of French politics and in part because I was intrigued by its complexities and the important part terrorism seemed to have played in the FLN's winning strategy against the French. The classic film *The Battle of Algiers*, which opened in 1966 to critical acclaim and public controversy, had compellingly dramatized urban terrorism, although in French political and scholarly circles the war was largely a taboo subject. I was fortunate that Edward Kolodziej, my dissertation adviser at the University of Virginia, encouraged my unorthodox pursuits. I was also fortunate that most of my colleagues at Wesleyan University, where I taught in the Government Department from 1974 to 2007, thought that my research program held academic promise. I am grateful to all my students at Wesleyan over the years. I tested most of my ideas on those who took my course on "The Politics of Terrorism."

From its inauspicious beginnings in the early 1970s, the research field of terrorism has expanded to thousands of entries, with an enormous surge in production following the September 11, 2001 attacks on the World Trade Center and the Pentagon. It has become such an established and prominent field that a graduate student in sociology at the University of California Berkeley wrote her Ph.D. thesis on its development.[2] The online program of the 2010 Annual Convention of the International Studies Association listed a total of 79 papers on terrorism. After the 9/11 shock terrorism was transformed from a backwater issue in international politics, rarely considered important to the power or interests of states, into the focal point of American foreign policy and the motivating force behind two long wars, in Afghanistan from 2001 and Iraq from 2003. What has become the interdisciplinary field of "terrorism studies" is now impressive in terms of quantity, scope, and variety, although the level of theoretical development remains inconsistent and uneven and there is still acute need for a solid empirical foundation.

I was pleasantly surprised when Andrew Humphrys at Routledge suggested that I assemble a volume representing my contributions to the field. The invitation presented me with the opportunity to try to show that at least a small degree of intellectual coherence links my discrete and varied projects. The selection of my work in this volume is meant to illustrate the development of my thought over time, from my first publication in 1972 to the present, in four areas.

Part I addresses the now familiar conundrum of defining terrorism and identifying its causes and forms. Can terrorism be distinguished from other forms of political violence? Is it possible to generalize about terrorism, or are we restricted to particular explanations bound to time and place? Can there be a neutral definition, without pejorative implication? These are questions that I attempted to answer in 1972. What are the origins of this form of political violence? In 1981 I argued that three interrelated levels of analysis are necessary to explaining the causes of terrorism: societal conditions, group decisions, and individual dispositions. This conceptual framework is now widely accepted among scholars and forms the basis for much of my subsequent work. In Part I I also dispute the argument proposed after the 9/11 attacks that the terrorism of the twenty-first century is fundamentally different from everything that has gone before and that our past understanding of the meaning of terrorism and why and how it happens is irrelevant at best, harmful at worst. I stress similarities in ends, means, and forms of terrorism and trace continuity over time.

Part II builds on my work on the causes of terrorism and analyzes in more depth the different approaches to explaining terrorist behavior: strategic, organizational, and psychological approaches. All three approaches focus on the group as the relevant actor, but they employ different perspectives or lenses to examine collective behavior. The articles included here argue that group dynamics matter more than individual motivations and that there is no generic "profile of a terrorist." Groups using terrorism resemble other political organizations, so that over time organizational maintenance may supersede ideological purpose, rivalries among groups in competitive environments may drive behavior, different roles and structures within organizations may matter to outcomes, and organizations may offer their members selective incentives, not just the pursuit of common ends. At the same time terrorism is purposeful and instrumental at the level of the collectivity, as I argued at the outset of my career with reference to the use of terrorism as a means of national liberation during the Algerian war.

Part III considers government policies toward terrorism. The essays discuss the feasibility of a "grand strategy" of counterterrorism, the usefulness of coercive diplomacy as a policy instrument, and the politics of the counterterrorism policy process. Coercing nonstate actors presents formidable difficulties that defending governments may not be able to overcome. Formulating a public strategy, formalized for the first time under the Bush Administration in the 2003 and 2006 National Security Strategies for Combating Terrorism, is inherently difficult.

Part IV, by way of conclusion, asks how campaigns of terrorism end. Organizational and psychological explanations of terrorism imply that it is difficult for both groups and individuals to abandon the practice and that it is in some sense self-perpetuating, yet some campaigns of terrorism do come to an end without the defeat of the sponsoring organization. The puzzle is to understand how, why, and when. Knowing the causes of terrorism may not help, since the reasons for the onset of terrorism are not necessarily the same as the reasons for its decline. I ask not only why groups abandon terrorism, but why some opposition groups that are capable of using terrorism and aware of its salience and potential utility decide not to adopt the method.

The contents of Part I of this volume include "The Concept of Revolutionary Terrorism," originally published in the *Journal of Conflict Resolution*, XVI, in 1972, and "The Causes of Terrorism," from *Comparative Politics*, 13, 1981. "The Debate over 'New' vs. 'Old' Terrorism," was published in *Values and Violence: Intangible Aspects of Terrorism, Studies in Global Justice*, Volume 4, Dordrecht: Springer Netherlands, 2009.

Part II contains the following essays: "An Organizational Approach to the Analysis of Political Terrorism," *Orbis*, 29, 1985; "The Subjective Reality of the Terrorist," in *Current Perspectives on International Terrorism*, edited by Robert O. Slater and Michael Stohl, London: Macmillan, and New York: St. Martin's, 1988; "The Logic of Terrorism: Terrorism as the Product of Strategic Choice," in *Origins of Terrorism: Psychologies, Ideologies, Theologies, States of Mind*, edited by Walter Reich, Cambridge: Woodrow Wilson International Center for Scholars and Cambridge University Press, 1990; and "Decisions to Use Terrorism: Psychological Constraints on Instrumental Reasoning," in *Social Movements and Violence: Participation in Underground Organizations*, edited by Donatella della Porta for *International Social Movement Research*, Volume 4, Greenwich, CT: JAI Press Inc., 1992.

Part III contains three essays. Two are book chapters: "Coercive Diplomacy and the Response to Terrorism," in *The United States and Coercive Diplomacy*, edited by Robert J. Art and Patrick M. Cronin, Washington: United States Institute of Peace Press, 2003; and "Terrorism, Strategies, and Grand Strategies," in *Attacking Terrorism: Elements of a Grand Strategy*, edited by Audrey Kurth Cronin and James M. Ludes, Washington: Georgetown University Press, 2004. The third is "Counterterrorism Policy and the Political Process," from *Studies in Conflict and Terrorism*, 24, 2001.

Part IV includes two analyses from the 1990s: "How Terrorism Declines," from *Terrorism and Political Violence*, 3, 1991; and "Why Violence is Rejected or Renounced: A Case Study of Oppositional Terrorism," in *The Natural History of Peace*, edited by Tom Gregor, Nashville, TN: Vanderbilt University Press, 1996.

These materials have been edited for the present publication. Every effort has been made to contact copyright holders for permission to reprint material in this book if such permission was necessary. Permission was granted in all requests and the author acknowledges and thanks the publishers cited above. The publishers of this volume would be grateful to hear from any copyright holder who is not appropriately acknowledged here and will undertake to rectify any errors or omissions in future editions. All views and opinions presented in this book are those of the author, who assumes full responsibility.

I would also like to thank the institutions that helped fund my research program over many years. They include the Woodrow Wilson Foundation, the National Endowment for the Humanities, the Russell Sage Foundation, the Harry Frank Guggenheim Foundation, the Ford Foundation, the United States Institute of Peace, the John Simon Guggenheim Memorial Foundation, the U.S. Department of Homeland Security (grant awarded to the National Consortium for the Study of Terrorism and Responses to Terrorism at the University of Maryland), and the National Science Foundation. The views and conclusions contained in this volume are mine and should not be interpreted as representing the official policies, either expressed or implied, of the U.S. Department of Homeland Security, START, or any other institution or government agency.

Introduction

Definitions, approaches, responses, and trajectories

The purpose of this essay is to integrate the chapters that follow into a discussion of unresolved analytical questions as well as contemporary developments in the study of terrorism. I aim to set out the intellectual framework in which my arguments can be placed and to engage some of the current debates that animate scholars and practitioners in the field.

The analysis of terrorism has never been the exclusive province of scholars or the preserve of a single academic discipline.[1] An inescapable fact of life is that its study has always been driven by events and policy interests. Terrorism research takes place in a mixed and messy world of academics, think tanks, government analysts, journalists, and pundits. Neglect of the subject has been punctuated by high-profile crises that draw immediate attention from media, government, and public. In the most prominent instance, the 9/11 attacks on New York and Washington, terrorism reoriented American foreign policy and led to war in Iraq and Afghanistan. The 2004 and 2005 bombings in Madrid and London similarly brought the threat of a mix of domestic and imported terrorism to the top of the policy agenda in Spain and Great Britain. Scholarship is unavoidably "policy relevant."

Since its beginnings in the early 1970s, the study of terrorism has slowly entered the mainstream of social science disciplines.[2] In the field of international relations and foreign policy, it was only after the 9/11 attacks that many scholars thought that the threat of terrorism mattered to the power and interests of states or to international security. Some scholars still do not consider terrorism a major threat, but even the most skeptical find it hard to avoid taking terrorism seriously in light of American conceptions and policy preferences. In 2009, for example, President Obama justified escalation of the war in Afghanistan in terms of the continuing danger to the American homeland from Al Qaeda. The threat of nuclear terrorism is America's foremost national security concern, as expressed in the 2010 Nuclear Posture Review:

> The most immediate and extreme threat today is nuclear terrorism. Al Qaeda and their extremist allies are seeking nuclear weapons. We must assume they would use such weapons if they managed to obtain them.[3]

Defining terrorism

In 2004 the U.N. Secretary-General's High-level Panel Report defined terrorism as

> any action . . . that is intended to cause death or serious bodily harm to civilians or noncombatants, when the purpose of such act, by its nature or context, is to intimidate a population, or to compel a Government or an international organization to do or to abstain from doing any act.[4]

However, the U.N. itself has not succeeded in defining terrorism, and the task remains problematic. In my view, the basic outline of the concept that I proposed in 1972, and which is included in Chapter 2, still applies.[5] This definition grew out of my study of the Algerian war, and thus it is relevant to the use of terrorism during an insurgency or civil war as well as in peacetime settings. Terrorism is a form of violence that is primarily designed to influence an audience. Its execution depends on concealment, surprise, stealth, conspiracy, and deception. Terrorism is not spontaneous, nor does it involve mass participation. The act itself communicates a future threat to people who identify with the victims. The choice of time, place, and victim is meant to shock, frighten, excite, or outrage. Psychological impact is central to both the aspirations of its users and its effectiveness. It is an asset to those who challenge authority, in part because it maximizes effect while minimizing effort. Its inherent transgressiveness makes it attractive to those out of power, who see in disorder the path to future gain and who often wish to do away with the norms that they violate.

When the Cold War ended, it seemed likely that a definitional consensus would finally emerge as charges of ideological bias faded. Immediately after the 9/11 attacks there appeared to be little doubt about what terrorism was, and most of us working in the field probably concluded with some relief that the concept was no longer contested and that each presentation of our findings need no longer be accompanied by an argument about how to define terrorism. However, the Bush Administration's declaration of a "global war on terror" raised familiar and long-standing concerns about labeling and stereotyping opponents as well as puzzlement about just what and who the enemy was. How could the United States go to war against a method of violence (terrorism) or an emotional state (terror)? The stretching of the concept of terrorism to encompass all violent extremism contributed further to a loss of precision.

Why is it so hard to reach a commonly accepted and analytically useful definition of terrorism? This puzzle is not just an "academic" question about establishing the attributes and boundaries of a variable: what we call things matters.[6]

The dilemma is to arrive at a "neutral" definition of a method rather than a moral characterization of the enemy, since the use of the term is not merely descriptive but as currently understood deprives the actor thus named of legitimacy. Since the early use of the term in the latter half of the nineteenth century, it has not been possible to escape a pejorative connotation. Does the use of terrorism delegitimize the cause it serves? Kofi Annan argued that it did, but those charged with being "terrorists" respond that whatever action they undertook was not terrorism because its end was just. From this point of view, violence in the service of "national liberation," for example, cannot by definition be terrorism.

In addition, for purposes of empirical as opposed to normative appraisal, it is difficult to draw a hard and fast line between terrorism and other forms of political violence, particularly when terrorism occurs in the context of civil war, insurgency, or other manifestations of wider violence that mobilize large numbers of people and blur the boundaries between combatants and noncombatants. We typically think of oppositional terrorism as violence that is not intended to control territory, but in the context of an insurgency opposition groups use terrorism to seize and hold territory, by intimidating the inhabitants and driving the government out. We think of terrorism as aimed at the power of the state, but in the context of sectarian or communal conflict it is directed against local communities of a rival faith.

How useful is the combatant-noncombatant distinction?[7] In practice the distinction is not always obvious. Are prison guards, for example, military or civilian targets? What about the person who sells goods and services to the prison guard? What about the body guard of the oppressive leader? Who is a "collaborator"? In the best of circumstances it is not always easy to say that "civilian" targets do not have military value since undermining enemy morale is a typical military objective. Actors using terrorism against civilians typically claim that the victims played a military role and were thus legitimate targets. If it is accepted that attacks on civilian targets in a peacetime setting by nonstate actors constitute terrorism, how should we classify attacks on military personnel in exactly the same context, such as the 9/11 Pentagon attack involving a hijacked civilian airliner? The suicide bombing of the U.S. Marine Barracks in Beirut in October, 1983 was an attack on a military target, but American forces were engaged in a peacekeeping mission and consequently their rules of engagement prevented them from defending themselves more vigorously.

All these questions are still vexing, but one way of addressing the problem is to look at both intention and context. If the purpose of the act of violence is to create a psychological effect in a watching audience rather than to destroy an asset of military value, and if the attack occurs in the context of a systematic campaign of similar threatening actions, then the attack can be presumed to be terrorism. A single act of violence is interpreted in light of the pattern of actions of which it forms a part. Its place in the pattern helps permit inference.

As we have known from the beginning of the study of terrorism, we need to know intent or motivation in order to judge whether or not an attack represents terrorism, as well as to understand the phenomenon itself, but the task is not simple even in an age where communications technology makes it easy for nonstate actors to explain themselves. Merely uncovering the facts of what happened, never mind who did it, and then deciding whether the act was politically motivated and premeditated are complex tasks for research. As a case in point consider the 2009 Fort Hood shootings: if Major Hasan was mentally deranged and acted without direct assistance from Al Qaeda, the shootings would not generally be defined as terrorism. However, if he was not logistically linked to the organization but inspired at a distance by the call to jihad was the attack terrorism?

In contrast to the early days of terrorism studies, we now have extensive databases of terrorist incidents, and methods for analyzing statistical data on terrorism have grown increasingly sophisticated. But aggregate analysis is still at the mercy of the database compiler's definition of terrorism and how it guides the coding of incidents. A highly politicized example of the consequences of changing definitions in mid-database occurred in 1981, when U.S. government statistics on international terrorist incidents were revised to include threats as well as actual acts of violence. The change approximately doubled the number of terrorist incidents included in the count of the preceding twelve years.[8]

A critical omission in incident databases, even the most comprehensive Global Terrorism Database (GTD), is that they do not consistently include failed and foiled attempts.[9] We cannot fully understand the intentions behind terrorism without considering what was planned as well as what was accomplished. Uncompleted attacks, however, are inherently difficult to study. Information in the public domain may be scarce, and governments may have an incentive to avoid disclosure. If a plot is disrupted at an early stage, it may appear far-fetched and the danger exaggerated. Yet in a post-9/11 world police and intelligence services are pressured to intervene well before plans can come to fruition.

The term "terrorist organization" is also contentious, although I use it in my work. Its use can imply that the organization in question uses terrorism exclusive of other means, which is rare (the Abu Nidal organization may be a case in point, however). The designation can be a way of labeling a group so as to exclude them from normal politics and/or subject them to sanctions and reprimands. Government designation lists, such as the U.S. State Department's list of Foreign Terrorist Organizations, can be considered operational forms of defining terrorism and labeling terrorist actors.[10] In 1998, when Clinton Administration special envoy Robert Gelbard publicly called the Kosovo Liberation Army a terrorist group, the Serbian government used his remarks as justification for repression of the Albanian majority in Kosovo.[11]

Another complicating factor in defining terrorism is the question of whether states can be considered terrorists as opposed to third-party sponsors of the use of terrorism by proxy nonstate actors. My view is that the identity of the actor does not matter to the specification of the method. However, in general the vastly greater power and presumed legitimate authority of states as compared to nonstates makes it difficult to explain their behavior in the same terms, since the state has many other means of exercising influence or controlling behavior. Nevertheless, when states use tactics such as placing explosives on airliners (Libya), death squads at home (Argentina during the "Dirty War"), hit teams to assassinate dissidents abroad (Libya or South Africa under the apartheid regime), or deployment of state agents to organize local cells (Iran in Lebanon), they are not unlike nonstates. Similarly, when oppositions use terrorism to control populations (for example, by assassinating rival leaders or designated "collaborators") they are not unlike states. In failing and failed states, government and opposition may be close to equal in power and authority.

The causes of terrorism

If we could agree on what terrorism is, what are the "independent variables" or causal mechanisms? What factors or conditions make terrorism likely or unlikely? Are these variables observable or measurable? These questions, too, are unresolved.[12]

In my 1981 article on the causes of terrorism, included here as Chapter 2, I proposed a conceptual framework based on three levels of analysis: the individual, the group and its strategy, and environmental conditions. I also distinguished between two types of causal influence, direct and permissive, concepts that I borrowed from Kenneth Waltz's classic *Man, the State, and War*.[13]

Research on the aggregate level, which has become an important part of the causal analysis of terrorism, focuses on underlying conditions such as poverty, levels of education, or repression in part because these attributes can be coded and quantified and then correlated with counts of incidents of terrorism. Although this approach can produce rigorous analysis and encompass large numbers of cases, it is problematic to link the behavior of small numbers of people to conditions that affect large numbers or attitudes held by vast majorities. There is an enormous disproportion between the number of people who hold similar beliefs or who experience the same conditions and the number of those who not only act but act by using terrorism. Campaigns of terrorism can be quick to emerge or decline, whereas change in the environment tends to be incremental. Interpretations based on underlying economic, social, political, or cultural conditions obscure the role of agency.

It is also essential to ask not just what causes terrorism in a generic sense but what causes particular forms of terrorism. Researchers also need to compare the selection of a specific tactic of terrorism to alternatives, both violent and nonviolent. Groups in the same conflict system or social movement sector behave differently. How do groups choose between different forms of political expression and within a range of violent options, opt for terrorism? Why not nonviolent protest? Then, having adopted a terrorist strategy, why do some groups target the general public with relative indiscrimination (terrorism is never purely random) as opposed to pinpointed attacks on elites? Why would some groups but not others seek to cause mass casualties by bombing markets, trains, buses, or even funeral processions? Why do only some groups resort to "suicide terrorism"?

It is also important to consider the type of conflict in which terrorism occurs. Terrorism in the context of an insurgency or civil war may have different causes and consequences than terrorism in a peaceful and orderly setting where violence is the exception rather than the rule.

Interest in the individual level of the causation dynamic also remains strong. The process by which individuals become "radicalized," particularly in democratic settings, is a key concern for contemporary researchers as well as governments.[14] Radicalization, which I define as willingness to use or support violence as opposed to the peaceful pursuit of radical change, is a mix of psychological, sociological, political, and economic processes. It is distinct from recruitment to the ranks of an organization, although it is often assumed that the two always go together. Not all those who are recruited into militant groups have radical beliefs, and not all "radicals" are recruited or join. In fact, a point of dispute is whether individuals (primarily male and young) "self-radicalize" or whether their beliefs grow more extreme because they are socialized in a group of like-minded militants and/or fall under the influence of a strong leader. Both developments may happen, of course, if an individual first becomes attracted to the cause through exposure to internet and video sources, and then seeks out a group or institution that embodies the newly-acquired values.

Types of terrorism

Another research ambition is to develop a meaningful typology of terrorism. It is simplest to construct a set of categories based on the assigned group's ideology or purpose: thus groups can be classified as left-revolutionary, nationalist-secessionist, far right, single-issue, religious, or a hybrid mix. What difference does this distinction among ends make? Are particular tactics or forms of organization associated with different aims? Do causes or consequences vary by type?

The answer given by proponents of the view that there is a fundamentally "new" terrorism is that religious groups are intrinsically different in method and structure as well as intention, an argument that I challenge in Chapter 3. As I note, we should ask what anomaly or puzzle requires a shift to a new paradigm, using the classic terminology of Thomas Kuhn.[15] What is the problem that cannot be solved without a new understanding? In my view, the puzzle that is really at the heart of the debate over old vs. new terrorism is the apparent willingness, if not eagerness, of some groups to cause mass casualties. What is the cause of indiscriminate lethality? Is such lack of restraint or inhibition new? Is terrorism growing more lethal? Attempts to establish a firm causal connection between religious beliefs and mass casualties or fatalities have not so far been successful. Secular groups and states have been and still are willing to kill large numbers of innocent people in the service of a political cause, whether the violence in question is genocide, unintended "collateral damage," or terrorism. Mass casualty terrorist attacks are still comparatively rare.

Another way of looking at the issue of how terrorism develops over time is to consider the 9/11 attacks as an example of strategic innovation: a significant point of novelty in the historical development of terrorism, one that offers a new conception of strategic effectiveness but does not alter the nature of the phenomenon itself. What changes is the strategic conceptualization of terrorism, meaning the way in which ends are related to means. Innovation is best considered a form of problem solving, in which new logical connections are discovered or problems are redefined to reach a new solution. From this perspective, innovation is a result of learning and effort, not sudden insight or illumination.

In many ways the 9/11 attacks represented a new way of resolving an old problem for Al Qaeda: how to inflict major devastation on the U.S. homeland. The failure to bring down the towers in the 1993 bombing of the World Trade Center was an instructive precedent. The 2001 attacks, expanded in scope, combined hijackings with suicide bombings by using aircraft as the explosive device, to an extraordinary destructive effect that may not have been anticipated (even if wished for). Yet the plot's complexity, length of planning time, number of participants, technical requirements (ability to pilot a commercial aircraft at a minimal level for the leaders, martial arts training for the followers), and ability of the conspirators to remain secret for so long in a foreign country without a popular support network were also exceptional and have not been duplicated since. These skills had very little, if anything, to do with religion.

Hijackings, the first component, were in themselves an innovation in the late 1960s and early 1970s, initiated by the Popular Front for the Liberation of Palestine against Israel in 1968. Their purpose was to bargain with governments, with release of prisoners a typical demand. Hijackings were one tactic in a general strategy of hostage taking, which included embassy takeovers as well as kidnappings. The practice of hijackings fell into disuse because of enhanced airport security measures, improvement in government rescue capacity, and the unwillingness of potential host governments to provide refuge and asylum for hijackers. Midair bombings offered a substitute, beginning in the mid-1980s, but security measures quickly made it difficult to place a bomb in checked luggage or bring it on board (particularly after the downing of Pan Am 103 in 1988). Governments, however, remained wedded to the idea that the lives of hostages were a useful bargaining chip for hijackers, who would not expend them carelessly. Possibly Al Qaeda leaders understood and exploited this preconception. Nobody expected that hijackers could pilot a commercial aircraft, which was a startling development not just because of the acquisition of the skill but the extent of planning and forethought involved in doing so.

A second component of the plot was a suicide mission. This tactic of terrorism was also an innovation when it began in Lebanon in the early 1980s. By 2001 it was a well-established practice, having "migrated" to other conflict theaters, notably Israel-Palestine and, more geographically distant, Sri Lanka. Al Qaeda had used the tactic previously with the 1998 East Africa embassy bombings and the attack on the USS Cole in Yemen in 2000. It has since become a hallmark of the organization.

The third element, which was not so innovative, was the deliberate aim of killing large numbers as well as hitting iconic economic, political, and military targets within the U.S. Mass casualties are most easily caused by explosions, which typically require the construction of explosive devices and detonators (now called IEDs or *improvised* explosive devices, although this distinction seems unnecessary). In order to cause extensive damage, a bomb must be large, and sizable bombs are most easily transported by truck, car, boat, or other vehicle. The car-bomb technique had been tried unsuccessfully in 1993 with the first World Trade Center bombing organized by Ramzi Youcef, the nephew of Khalid Sheikh Mohammed (KSM), who became the planner and project manager of the 9/11 attacks. As noted, midair explosions were also a well-known and accessible element of the terrorist repertoire, and in the 1990s Youcef and his uncle had planned a simultaneous assault on American airliners over the Pacific. The plot was foiled, but the intention was clear.

Al Qaeda leaders thus conceived of hijackings as suicide missions employing the aircraft itself, loaded with fuel for a transcontinental flight, as the explosive device. The implementation of the inventive scheme required operatives with special skills, and in many ways it was unlucky chance that led Mohammed Atta and his coconspirators from Germany to Al Qaeda's camps. Judging by the number of failed or foiled attacks against the American homeland, Al Qaeda remains fixed on this general ambition and on the specific tactic of exploiting air travel but incapable of repeating its 9/11 accomplishment.

Projections of a "new terrorism" often imply not just "catastrophic" terrorism that causes large numbers of deaths and injuries but terrorism involving "weapons of mass destruction," or "WMD." In many ways the term is an unfortunate catch-all, tossing into the same basket methods that are actually different in terms of likelihood and potential consequence: nuclear, chemical, biological, and radiological. These diverse methods are unusual, rarely employed, likely to kill, injure, and/or panic large numbers of people, and prohibited for states in warfare because they fall under a normative and legal taboo. Some "WMD" may not be more destructive in a physical sense than "ordinary" weapons although they may indeed be more shocking, in part because we have made them so by publicizing our apprehensions. It is not clear, for example, that an explosion involving chlorine gas is fundamentally different from one using fertilizer or triacetone triperoxide. One way of reframing the research question is to ask why WMD terrorism has happened so infrequently, if indeed Al Qaeda has persistently tried to acquire and use such weapons.[16] Over twenty years after the establishment of Al Qaeda, Aum Shinrikyo remained the only terrorist organization to have conclusively crossed the WMD threshold.

Integrating approaches to understanding terrorism

In 1985 I argued that groups that use terrorism should be considered a subset of political organizations, not sui generis or unique (see Chapter 4). Since then a general scholarly consensus has emerged that violent organizations can be analyzed in the same terms as other political or economic organizations. Groups using terrorism have, for example, been compared to transnational activist networks.[17] Other research emphasizes internal structures and dynamics that are common to terrorist groups or to certain types of groups, such as those motivated by religious beliefs,[18] organizational learning and adaptation,[19] decision making,[20] and social network theory.[21]

While there is substantial agreement that research should focus on the group as the actor in the process of terrorist violence, scholars are divided as to whether terrorism is strategic or inner-directed.[22] I have argued that terrorism exhibits strategic logic in relating ends to means (see Chapter 6), but I have also analyzed terrorism as a way of maintaining organizational cohesion and satisfying emotional demands from members and constituencies (see Chapters 4, 5, and 7). I suggest that terrorism is the product of an interplay or interaction between instrumental and "subjective" thinking.

These explanations are not necessarily alternatives; they can reasonably be combined as two facets of the same reality. Priorities will be weighted differently, depending on the group's preferences and circumstances. Terrorism can be calculated for external effect but still influenced by demand and by internal considerations such as need for external resources or organizational strength. Terrorists seek critical public support and organizational vitality as well as political change. If an organization is not prepared to spend time and effort on self-maintenance, it cannot effectively pursue ideological objectives or take advantage of strategic gains.

Actors employ terrorism for five basic and interrelated reasons, regardless of specific political objective or ideology: to set the political agenda in a conflict, to undermine the authority of the government or governments they oppose, to provoke overreaction from the government or from the targeted population, to mobilize popular support at home or abroad, and to coerce compliance. Terrorism can be expected to accomplish these purposes more effectively than other methods. Groups may pursue all of these uses of terrorism simultaneously or sequentially because they are not mutually exclusive or incompatible. Most groups will pursue a pragmatic mix of internal and external considerations.

This is not to say that the end goal is irrelevant. There would be no need to take the risks associated with the use of terrorism if social solidarity were all that mattered. Surely a mountain-climbing or sky-diving club would serve psychological needs just as well, offering action, risk, danger, adventure, cohesiveness, and bonding. It has not been shown that killing people as part of a group promotes more of a sense of belonging than other collective activities. It is especially hard to explain suicide terrorism as a search for solidarity, since the benefit accrued will not be enjoyed for long.

In terms of agenda-setting, terrorism is famously useful for advertising a cause, more so than other less visible and shocking forms of violence. It attracts attention not just to the act of violence itself but to the issues those responsible wish to contest and to what is at stake in a conflict. Attention will be negative in some quarters, but inevitably positive in others, depending on audience position and predisposition. Raising issues puts them on the table for public discussion, perhaps even bargaining. Terrorism can frame grievances, for example, through the choice of target. This framing can be amplified and clarified through verbal communications explaining actions, but the actions also speak for themselves. Terrorism thus demonstrates power and in doing so can secure public recognition for the actor behind it. It helps shape identity and image.

A puzzle is why so many acts of terrorism are unattributed or unclaimed. Almost half the incidents in the GTD cannot reliably be attributed to any specific group. If terrorism is meant to advertise a cause and gain recognition, why would its users not take credit? Plausible deniability might be one reason, part of an effort to avoid opprobrium or punishment. If there is no credible claim, government intelligence agencies may not be able to attribute responsibility with sufficient assurance and credibility to justify a forceful response. However, a second strategy of terrorism may better explain this puzzle: terrorism undermines the government's authority by revealing its weakness. The identity of the actor is less important than the demonstration that the government cannot defend its citizens from terrorist attack and often cannot even protect its own security forces (hence a reason for attacks on police and military targets that do little material damage). Terrorism spreads insecurity, undermines public confidence, and sometimes weakens the economy, which inflicts a material blow but also degrades the government's international reputation.

I treat provoking overreaction as a separate purpose because it is a form of leverage that turns the government's power against itself. Provocation can contribute to the erosion of government authority and competence, especially if the government is shown to be incapable of controlling the security forces or the reaction of the majority public. It can help mobilize popular support if the government's response is indiscriminate but not so repressive that the public cannot resist. Provocation can exploit the "glass house" effect: a government's overreaction can damage its international reputation and standing and even stimulate third-party intervention. Provoking the government and its supporters can also augment the spoiler effect in peace processes.[23]

Terrorism is useful for mobilizing popular support at all levels, from the outer ring of a concentric circle of sympathizers to the inner ring of active members (although by stating this I do not mean that terrorist groups are social movements). An organization cannot expect to achieve its long-term political goals – the establishment of a Caliphate, the overthrow of a government, the expulsion of a foreign occupier, control over territory, or secession from a larger state – without the support of some constituency. We can assume that terrorists will seek support, whether they get it or not. Support can be voluntary or coerced. Voluntary support may be ideational, when supporters sympathize with the group's ideological objectives, or material, when supporters expect to gain resources, or both. In some cases, people may support the terrorist organization as the lesser evil. As noted, provocation of an indiscriminate government response can push some portion of the public to the side of the opposition. Terrorists are constrained, however, because the population may be intimidated rather than enraged and alienated. Demonstrations of power may also draw support, if the public is simply waiting to see which side will win before committing. Terrorism against a hated enemy can serve to bolster feelings of honor and pride, overcome humiliation, and satisfy demands for vengeance. In all these ways terrorism can assist in recruitment and organizational maintenance.

Because terrorism seems advantageous in building the organization and extending its influence, like-minded groups are likely to compete with each other for support, money, and recruits.[24] Rivalry is not the only form of interaction, however, since groups also cooperate, sometimes to the extent of merging into a single organization. Al Qaeda in particular has shown a preference for transnational alliances and mergers. The causes and consequences of different patterns of interactions require further investigation.

Another disputed issue is whether terrorism is successful at compelling the withdrawal of occupying powers (states or international institutions such as the United Nations or NATO). Robert Pape contends that campaigns of suicide terrorism work very well against democracies of a different religion, and his critics counter with equal conviction that suicide terrorism is not unique and/or that it does not succeed nearly as well as he predicts.[25] Compelling withdrawal is actually a subset of a larger purpose of coercing compliance on the part of the adversary. For example, in the 1970s Palestinian hijackings of civilian airliners were intended to coerce the U.S. and Europe into withdrawing support for Israel, as well as to advertise Palestinian discontent and sense of injustice. But whether or not terrorism actually compels compliance does not matter as much as whether groups believe that it is a useful tactic. Terrorists operate in an information-scarce and uncertain environment. Their perceptions of time may not be the same as that of their government adversary. It is the perception that terrorism will work over the long term that matters, and partial success can be encouraging because it represents movement toward the end goal. Terrorism can certainly inflict pain; whether or not it is acute enough to cause a policy shift is a different question, the answer to which depends on many other factors. Terrorism can also be a form of deterrence or bargaining for incremental concessions. Whatever the purpose of terrorism, it is extremely difficult to judge its effectiveness alone or even as one element in a mix; it is almost always used in conjunction with other methods that undoubtedly contribute to success or failure.[26] In other words it is hard to isolate terrorism as a causal mechanism in long-term political outcomes. It is easier to judge its short-term effects, which are by definition its intermediate objectives.

A test of competing hypotheses for explaining terrorism would ask whether groups ever sacrifice one type of goal for another. Have groups mounted attacks that clearly undermined their strategic interests because of internal or internecine considerations, or vice versa? Is there evidence of tension between external and internal drives and pressures? In this respect, I suggest that the "new" jihadist terrorists are not motivated differently from others.[27]

How governments respond to terrorism

A central question regarding counterterrorism policy concerns the effectiveness of force and threats of force. The case study included here (see Chapter 8) asks how well a strategy of coercive diplomacy worked from the inauguration of the Clinton Administration in 1993 to the beginning of the war in Afghanistan in 2001. Another issue is whether or not a cohesive counterterrorist strategy or grand strategy is possible. Chapter 9 considers this question with respect to the Bush Administration's declaration of a "war on terror." A third important topic is how well the American government is organized to combat terrorism, which is addressed in Chapter 10.

With regard to the use of force, instructive lessons about effectiveness and unintended consequences can be drawn from the American experience prior to the onset of the twenty-first century wars in Afghanistan and Iraq, as Chapter 8 claims. For example, the Reagan Administration's retaliatory bombing of Libya in 1986, which was followed by the midair bombing of Pan Am 103 in 1988, has important implications for the pursuit of a strategy of deterrence of terrorism. When American threats and shows of force failed to deter Libya, U.S. implementation of the threat provoked more terrorism. It is not clear whether Libya doubted the credibility of the threat or believed that the U.S. would not be able to link the regime to the La Belle disco bombing in Berlin. Fear of further reprisals did not subsequently deter Libya from a mass casualty attack on civilians.

Similar frustration surrounded American efforts to induce the Taliban to turn over Bin Laden between 1998 and 2001. In 2010 Abdul Salam Zaeef, a former senior member of the Taliban, published his autobiography.[28] He argued that before 9/11 he at least did believe that the U.S. would go to war, but that the Taliban could not turn over Bin Laden for a number of principled reasons: no extradition treaty with the U.S. due to absence of legal recognition by the U.S. of the Taliban regime, defense of sovereignty and the fairness of Islamic justice, rejection of American efforts to "control the world," and no evidence of Bin Laden's complicity in terrorism. Bin Laden, in his view, was merely a scapegoat and an excuse for the U.S. to invade the Muslim world. Zaeef claimed that after 9/11 he tried desperately to open a dialog with the U.S. in order to avert certain war. However, the head of the Pakistani intelligence services (ISI) reportedly told him:

> We both know that an attack on Afghanistan from the United States of America seems more and more likely. We want to assure you that you will not be alone in this *jihad* against America. We will be with you.[29]

Zaeef explains that he condemned this pronouncement as hypocritical and understood full well that Pakistan would support the U.S. offensive. At the same time other Pakistani officials were assuring the Taliban that the U.S. would not attack, and Mullah Omar and his advisers agreed that that the U.S. was not likely to go beyond threats. The Taliban leaders rejected the U.S. claim that Bin Laden was responsible for the 9/11 attacks and did not appear to have given any consideration whatsoever to the prospect of complying with American demands.

A related and persistently confounding policy issue concerns attribution of responsibility. The case of the Taliban shows that the defending state can be satisfied that the perpetrators of terrorism are identified, but that the adversary, the recipient of the deterrent threat, will not be convinced – or will not admit to being convinced. Since 2008, U.S. policy has been to deter nonstate actor acquisition or use of WMD terrorism through threat of retaliation. However, the ability to detect who is behind such an act of terrorism remains weak. Two examples from the pre-9/11 period further suggest that states seeking to deter terrorists face significant obstacles because of attribution difficulties: the Khobar Towers bombing in Saudi Arabia in 1996 and the bombing of the USS *Cole* in Yemen in 2000. If a government cannot retaliate immediately after the adversary crosses the red line because of uncertainty about responsibility, circumstances are likely to change so as to make it hard to retaliate later, even if attribution is decisive. Timing of response is important.

Another controversial issue related to the use of force is whether or not "decapitation" of a terrorist leadership works to defeat the organization. The tactic became a mainstay of American policy in Afghanistan and Pakistan, as numbers of drone attacks mounted under the Obama Administration. Clearly the U.S. government found the practice effective and was willing to take large risks, such as inflicting civilian casualties (a consequence that has always troubled the U.S., as seen in President Clinton's response to Sudan in 1998) and alienating Pakistani public opinion. But the outcome of removing leaders is disputed.

The larger problem is crafting a coherent grand strategy or overarching conception of national policy that links different elements of the response to terrorism, including both soft power and "kinetic" or military force. A critical underlying question is what we mean by an effective counterterrorism policy. The Bush Administration first sought the elimination of terrorism as a threat to the American way of life. The goal then expanded to ending tyranny and spreading *effective* democracy around the world, based on the assumption that establishing democracy would end terrorism and in fact all violent extremism. The Obama Administration, taking a more modest approach, refrained from ambitious claims about spreading democracy and ending tyranny, but it placed the defeat of Al Qaeda at the top of the national security agenda. Both administrations tied the goal of ending terrorism to the parallel objective of containing the spread of nuclear weapons and preventing terrorist access to them.

To implement such long-term goals, governments must choose the level at which their actions will best influence the course of terrorism to produce an intermediate outcome. They must also decide which actions are compatible components of the higher strategy; often governments appear not to see the whole, only the parts (for bureaucratic reasons – each agency has its own strategy or at least its own tactic). Nor do they always anticipate the unintended consequences of counterterrorism outside the domain to which it was supposed to apply.[30] The effects on democratic institutions and norms can be severe and irreversible.

Do governments want the group or organization to cease to function (e.g., by banning political parties that have terrorist wings or ensuring military defeat of the organization)? Or would they accept the continued existence of the opponent if terrorism was renounced and the group converted to peaceful means (as the U.S. did with the PLO)? Do they want to woo away the individuals that compose the group through deradicalization programs, offers of amnesty, or social reinsertion policies? Do governments wish to reduce critical popular support for terrorism by delegitimizing the practice? Do they want to influence the states that support or might support terrorism? For example, U.S./Afghan policy toward Taliban in Afghan included both "reconciliation" with the organization and "reintegration" of its members. However, while President Hamid Karzai wanted to focus on the former, the U.S. wanted to focus on the latter, and without American support for reconciliation, Taliban leaders might not find the offer sincere.[31]

In contrast, Spain banned Basque Euzkadi ta Askatasuna (ETA) and its political wing Batasuna but practices "social re-insertion" of ETA militants. This apparently benevolent and conciliatory measure is not without its attendant problems:

friends and relatives of victims object to killers walking down the street. Released or "deradicalized" prisoners may return to violence. Both responses to terrorism raise the delicate issue of rewarding violence.

Although the institutional reforms the U.S. government undertook after the 9/11 attacks were sweeping – and unimaginable before 9/11 – the policy-making and implementation process is still far from perfect. Many criticisms of the process offered before 9/11, such as those presented in Chapter 12, still apply. In 2004 the National Counterterrorism Center (NCTC) was established to coordinate the work of multiple intelligence agencies with terrorism accounts. Although the NCTC was meant to solve the organizational problems pointed out by the 9/11 Commission, it did not succeed in integrating and directing a national effort. In February 2010 the Project on National Security Reform, a nonpartisan research and policy organization in Washington, financed by Congress, issued a critical report.[32] The authors of the report observed a familiar and longstanding tension between the NCTC, the State Department, and the CIA. The decision-making process has remained decentralized, with many competing loci of authority and responsibility. The establishment of a Department of Homeland Security added another player to an already crowded field, although its purpose was consolidation.

An important question, unfortunately one that is unlikely to be particularly amenable to empirical investigation, is whether or not an improved policy-making process would yield better policy substance. The assumption behind criticisms of process appears to be that it would. Frank Foley concluded that processes matter to policy outcomes: Britain and France adopted different responses to similar threats of terrorism because of different institutions and norms.[33] However, he did not argue that one government was more effective than the other. Would an improved American process of policy-making and implementation produce a better result? Would the U.S. intelligence community be better able to put the dots together if the government had more efficient institutions, coordination, and information flow? Is the problem with counterterrorism bureaucratic inertia or deficiencies in policy conception? Perhaps we should reverse the question: would a strong and coherent national policy based on a clear conception of counterterrorism effectiveness produce a more efficient process?

Trajectories and endings

In a study coauthored with two criminologist colleagues, we found that the attack patterns of about half of the groups that targeted American interests since the 1970s followed a distinct trajectory of escalation and decline within about a ten-year period.[34] Their trajectories exhibited a cyclical pattern, which is an important finding. But we also discovered that the cyclical groups represented only about half of the ones we analyzed. The others were much more unpredictable and erratic. Some groups lasted for some time but attacked sporadically during their lifespan; other groups were transitory and short-lived with limited ranges of activity. Why are some groups short-lived and others long-lived? What determines duration or longevity? By 2008 Al Qaeda had passed the twenty-year mark; how did the organization survive for so long?

As I noted in the research that is the foundation for Chapters 11 and 12, the reasons for decline are not necessarily the reasons for the onset of terrorism. It is not unreasonable to suppose that the longer the lifespan of the group, the greater the distance between the two sets of causal explanations.

Based on a survey of groups active from 1968 through 1989, Chapter 11 describes different pathways or exits from terrorism, including defeat by the government, a voluntary decision to abandon terrorism, and organizational disintegration. For example, groups sometimes bring about their own demise by exceeding the bounds of tolerance of watching, even potentially sympathetic, audiences. Consider Fareed Zakaria's explanation of why the Obama Administration's post-surge policy in Pakistan showed promise in persuading the Pakistani army to take the threat of terrorism seriously:

> The militants in Pakistan, like those associated with al-Qaeda almost everywhere, went too far, brutally killing civilians, shutting down girls schools and creating an atmosphere of medievalism. Pakistan's public, which had tended to play down the problem of terrorism, came to see it as 'Pakistan's war.' The army, reading the street, felt it had to show results.[35]

In 2005, Ayman al-Zawahiri recognized the risk of antagonizing supporters in his letter to Abu Musab al-Zarqawi, then head of Al Qaeda in Iraq. Referring to the unacceptability of attacks on ordinary Shia and the "slaughter" or beheading of hostages, Zawahiri warned that "the mujahed movement must avoid any action that the masses do not understand or approve."[36]

Chapter 12 analyzes decision making in terrorist organizations and asks not only why groups might abandon a strategy of terrorism but also why they might reject it as an option at the outset of a struggle. I used the frameworks developed in Part II to consider abandoning terrorist as a strategic choice, as a result of organizational pressures, and as the outcome of psychological processes. I found that groups may reject terrorism at the beginning of a campaign to bring about political change for four reasons: it is an elitist strategy that does not involve the masses; its costs are too high; it is hard for leaders to control; or it is morally wrong, especially if it involves attacks on civilians. Groups also seemed to abandon terrorism under a specific set of circumstances: it had worked to accomplish its purpose, such as gaining international recognition; its costs increased or its benefits declined, or both; or new more attractive options appeared for the pursuit of objectives. Interestingly, in no case did groups abandon terrorism because they changed their ideological orientation or long-term goals.

The general neglect of the subject that I noted in my work has since been remedied by Audrey Kurth Cronin's comprehensive study of decline and demise.[37] She emphasizes that there is no single way out for each type of group; instead combinations of pathways are common. As she notes, we should ask exit from terrorism to what? Do groups disappear from sight by dissolving or succumbing to

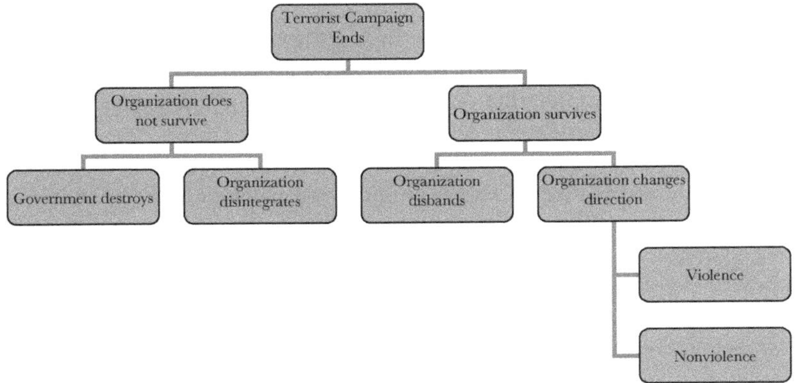

Figure 1 Outcomes of terrorism

government pressure, or do they switch directions? If so, is the shift to nonviolence (e.g., forming a political party), intensified violence (e.g., moving to full-fledged insurgency), or alternative forms of violence (e.g., crime)?

One model of outcomes of terrorism follows. Terrorism can end with either the organization's destruction or its survival. If the organization no longer exists, it may have been crushed by the government, with most or all of its members and certainly its leadership in prison or killed.[38] The alternative to defeat by external force is disintegration from within, when the organization collapses and members disperse. If the organization survives intact it may voluntarily give up terrorism and disband. Note that in the cases of both collapse and abandonment individual members of the organization survive. On the other hand, the group may collectively abandon terrorism and move to a substitute form of action. The change of direction may be toward another type of violence or toward nonviolent political participation, such as establishing a political party or joining a social movment.

This model inevitably simplifies the reality of how terrorism ends, but it provides a basic outline of possible paths. Further research should introduce more complexity. Outcomes can be mixed or partial, as when decapitation of the leadership produces demoralization and subsequent collapse. The model needs to accommodate mergers, splits, and factions. If an organization dissolves from internal pressures or disbands voluntarily, its members may form a new group or join an existing rival. The phenomenon of latency should be accounted for: how long should an organization be inactive before we decide that it has abandoned terrorism? How easy is it to return to terrorism? An organization that the government has destroyed may regenerate in the establishment of a new replacement organization if demand for terrorism persists. If so, the government's victory will be short-lived. A more complicated model would also include the timing of outcomes in terms of the group's lifespan and relate outcomes to organizational structure and strength. Are older groups, for example, less likely to disintegrate because they are better institutionalized than younger organizations? Are centralized hierarchical groups more likely to dissolve than decentralized or networked organizations? Although size is difficult to estimate, do bigger groups behave differently than smaller groups?

We need to understand not just how but why these outcomes occur. Endings will be influenced not only by conciliatory or coercive government responses and extent of popular support but by the number of groups and the relationships among them. A group that has a monopoly over violent opposition to the state is likely to behave differently than a group that has powerful rivals. Cause and effect relationships are not straightforward. For example, increased popular support for a terrorist organization is not necessarily the route to continued violence. To the contrary: growing support might encourage a shift to nonviolence if the group thinks it can win enough votes to gain power through elections (assuming the opportunity is offered). However, an organization might also adopt a mixed strategy, continuing violence while also engaging in the political process. The Irish Republican Army (IRA) is a case in point.

The case of the Italian Red Brigades demonstrates how outcomes can be mixed and how different factors interact to produce them. The Red Brigades alienated the public by actions such as kidnapping and murdering Aldo Moro, disillusioned followers by killing dissidents, and provoked the state into reorganizing the security forces and implementing restrictive legislation. At the same time, the Italian government offered a way out at the individual level through policies of "repentance" or plea-bargaining. A number of different factors thus coincided to produce a tipping point. Similarly, in 2010 the U.S. government believed that applying more force to the Taliban collectively would make individual members more susceptible to offers of reintegration and thus erode the organization from within.

It is also important to compare groups that end to those that do not. At a minimum we should compare short-lived to long-lived groups. Cronin found the median life-span of durable terrorist groups to be five to nine years. In her dataset of 457 terrorist organizations active since 1968, nineteen had life spans longer than forty years.[39] The Armed Revolutionary Forces of Colombia (FARC), ETA, and IRA are prominent among them.

Counterterrorism policy makers should ask which outcomes are preferable, and how they might best be reached. It is critical to distinguish between groups that might abandon terrorism either by quitting or joining the political process and those unlikely to shift course. American policy in Afghanistan in 2010 appeared to reflect a consensus that Al Qaeda had to be destroyed. However, signals were mixed about the possibility of negotiating with the Taliban, or with some moderate elements of the Taliban. The discussion of "counterinsurgency" vs. "counterterrorism" approaches to the war obscured as much as it clarified what the U.S. hoped to accomplish. Despite long experience in dealing with the threat, policy makers still need clear analytical guidance to inform the expectations about the adversary upon which counterterrorism strategy will be based.

Part I

What and why?

1 The concept of terrorism

In a classic article, Giovanni Sartori stresses the importance for comparative politics of the construction of basic concepts that are discriminatory and "classificatory," enabling one to study "one thing at a time and different things at different times."[1] Sartori emphasizes the need for precise conceptual connotation; only by making the definitional attributes of a concept more exact, rather than by increasing their number to extend the range of the concept, does one retain the possibility of empirically testing the concept. He concludes that the most needed concepts are on a middle-level of abstraction, combining high explanatory power with precise descriptive content.[2]

In 1972, at the outset of the academic study of terrorism, a review of theoretical literature on the subject revealed the absence of a concept of terrorism defined in accordance with Sartori's requirements. In fact, there were very few studies of terrorism at all. What follows is my early effort to define terrorism, which in my view has not lost its relevance, particularly since my analysis considers the use of terrorism in the context of an insurgency or revolutionary war, in this instance the struggle of the Algerian Front de Libération Nationale (FLN) against the French.

In 1939 a study of the treatment of terrorism by the League of Nations explained that the term "terrorism" was formed from the Latin word "terror," which originally meant physical trembling and later came to include the emotional state of extreme fear.[3] Terrorism thus means "system of terror" and was coined to condemn the Reign of Terror during the French Revolution.[4] My analysis retains the original distinction between "terror" and "terrorism," although many authors use the terms interchangeably. Waciorski mentions the 1937 definition of terrorism proposed by the League of Nations Convention for the Prevention and the Repression of Terrorism, prompted by anarchist activities: acts of terrorism are criminal acts directed against a state and which aim, or are of a nature, to provoke terror.[5] In conclusion Waciorski proposes a different definition: "Terrorism is a method of action by which an agent tends to produce terror in order to impose his domination."[6] In 1948 the *Encyclopaedia of the Social Sciences* defined terrorism as a tool of nonstate actors: "a term used to describe the method or the theory behind the method whereby an organized group or party seeks to achieve its avowed aims chiefly through the systematic use of violence."[7]

Unfortunately most 1960s analyses of "internal warfare," when they defined "terror" or "terrorism" at all, did not improve on the older attempts and often sacrificed clarity for brevity: "the attempt to govern or to oppose government by intimidation,"[8] "the threat or the use of violence for political ends,"[9] "a peculiar and violent type of political struggle,"[10] or something used against people, not things.[11] Only one student of internal war, Thomas P. Thornton, considered terrorism in detail and defined it in a manner that could constitute a basis for further theoretical development: "a symbolic act designed to influence political behavior by extranormal means, entailing the use or threat of violence."[12]

Outside the scope of studies devoted to internal war, an interesting definition was found in Walter's analysis of "regimes of terror" or the governmental use of terrorism.[13] Walter, like Thornton, pointed out that insurgent and governmental terrorism are basically similar phenomena and that the same type of concept could define both.[14] Walter describes a "process of terror" that involves three elements: (1) an act or threat of violence, which (2) causes an emotional reaction, and (3) produces social effects. A similarly structured "siege of terror" is the attempt to destroy an authority system by creating extreme fear through systematic violence.[15]

None of these authors clearly sets out the essential attributes of the concept of terrorism. They do not distinguish between the qualities data *may* have and properties they *must* have in order to be classified under the concept of terrorism. From the comparative study of these definitional efforts and from the investigation of a particular case of what all observers agreed to be "terrorism" in the activity of the FLN during the Algerian Revolution, 1954–62, my analysis proposed an alternative definition of the concept, intended to be an improved "data-container" and a more useful guideline for interpretation and observation.[16]

This definition applies to oppositional terrorism; thus the concept here defined is not necessarily applicable to the use of violence by governments to maintain control or to implement policies. I considered revolutionary terrorism as a part of insurgent strategy in the context of internal warfare: the attempt to seize political power from the established regime of a state, if successful causing fundamental political and social change. Violence is not revolution's unique instrument, but it is almost always a principal one. Such internal war is often of long duration and high intensity of violence.[17]

Certain essential elements of the definition of terrorism are thus situational constants. It is a method or system used by a revolutionary organization for specific political purposes. Therefore neither one isolated act nor a series of random acts is terrorism.

The form of the individual acts that make up the terrorist strategy is violent; they are acts of emotionally or physically "destructive harm."[18] Terrorism differs from other instruments of violence in its "extranormality": it "lies beyond the norms of violent political agitation that are accepted by a given society," states Thornton.[19] In my opinion terrorism is socially as well as politically unacceptable, as the following description of the ways in which acts of terrorism may be extraordinary should demonstrate. Acts of terrorism are often particularly atrocious and psychologically shocking, such as throat-cutting or physical mutilation of victims. It usually occurs within the civilian population; both the victims and the scene of violence are unaccustomed to it and it occurs unexpectedly. The act is not only unpredictable but often anonymous. This arbitrariness of terrorist violence makes it unacceptable and abnormal.

Many definitions of terrorism refer to the use *or* the threat of violence.[20] Actually the single act of terrorism within its context is a combination of use and threat; the act implies a threat. There may be written or verbal threats as well, but the violent act is essential. This duality of the act of terrorism issues from the fact that the revolutionaries select for attack objects that are not obstacles to be eliminated, but symbols of certain groups or forces in the state.[21] Since the victims are examples of the groups they represent, the act of terrorism is a threat to the other members. The act must convey the message "you may be next" to a particular group. This is one of the reasons for terrorism's apparent irrationality: the individual attacked is usually not personally dangerous or offensive. A consistent pattern exists of choosing victims among groups whose political behavior or attitudes are important to the outcome of the conflict.

The insurgents deliberately intend to create a psychological effect through these acts. This effect may range from terror or extreme fear in direct target groups (among whom there are victims) to curiosity, sympathy, or admiration in groups not directly threatened.[22] This emotional response is intended in turn to influence political behavior and attitudes in order to further the revolution's chances of success. The most important target group is therefore the mass of the civilian population among whom there will be the most victims.

Summarizing the basic components of a definition of the concept of terrorism produces the following list of essential properties that empirical examination of data must reveal:

(1) Terrorism is part of a revolutionary strategy – a method used by insurgents to seize political power from an existing government.
(2) Terrorism is manifested in acts of socially and politically unacceptable violence.
(3) There is a consistent pattern of symbolic or representative selection of the victims or objects of acts of terrorism.
(4) The revolutionary movement deliberately intends these actions to create a psychological effect on specific groups and thereby to change their political behavior and attitudes.

This definition can be illustrated by considering the activity of the FLN in Algeria. Terrorism was an important element of the FLN's eight-year struggle against French rule. Although resistance to French authority even in the form of armed bandits attacking the French military was relatively normal and considered perfectly honorable in many areas, FLN terrorism was definitely extranormal. Throat-cutting, a frequent FLN method, was previously used only in animal sacrifices. The FLN also cut off victims' noses, the nose being regarded as a symbol of honor and dignity in Algerian society.[23] Normal tribal violence in rural Algeria, particularly in the Berber regions, was highly ritualized, symbolic, strictly regulated by custom, and involved little bloodshed.[24] Sometimes a murderer could atone for his crime by paying a fine to the victim's relatives. In urban areas the FLN tended to explode bombs or grenades in crowds; the unusualness of such violence needs no further explanation.

The individual victims of FLN terrorism were most often members of identifiable politically relevant groups (e.g., the European minority, Muslim local or tribal authorities, Muslim elected or nonelected officials in the French administration, Muslims who disobeyed FLN orders on a variety of subjects, policemen, French administrators, Muslims who cooperated socially, politically, or economically with the French, and French military officers responsible for dealing with the Muslim community). On some occasions the FLN attacked farms, animals, or economic installations as psychological threats.

It is not possible to prove FLN intent in each individual act of terrorism. While it is logical that when the FLN chose Muslim municipal officials as victims, the subsequent large number of resignations of these officials was a deliberate aim, specific evidence may be lacking. However enough data do exist to indicate that in general acts of terrorism were part of a calculated strategy. The FLN often issued warning tracts or left explanatory messages on the bodies of their victims.[25] According to the FLN the only victims of their violence were "traitors" or "enemies," but their definition of these categories was highly flexible. The FLN journal *El Moudjahid* sometimes explained motivations. An article once boasted that the action of FLN *fidayine* had caused panic, insecurity, disarray, disorientation, *bouleversement*, and fear in the enemy camp.[26] Another time the FLN claimed that their activities in metropolitan France against police and economic objectives created an "incontestable psychological shock" and enumerated the specific political effects thereby gained.[27] Other than such primary sources, journalist Yves Courrière's four-volume history of the Algerian war is an invaluable account of the FLN's internal deliberations.[28] Demonstration of intent is thus not of overwhelming difficulty in this case.

The concept of terrorism defined in this chapter not only identifies cases of terrorism, but it also aids in explaining the empirical and theoretical significance. The reason for the frequency of terrorism is that it is an effective strategy; its benefits outweigh its costs.

The revolutionary movement's decision to use terrorism should be considered as a choice among violent means, not between violence and nonviolence, because peaceful means of political protest were denied by the regime. An FLN leader explained, "Urban terrorism like guerrilla warfare is the only method of expression of a crushed people."[29] The cost of terrorism is much lower than the expense of forming, arming, and supplying guerrilla bands. Insurgent weakness may thus make terrorism the only alternative. A terrorist organization, whether urban or rural, requires few militants who need little training, no uniforms, no special equipment, and minimal logistical support and who do not even require individual weapons. The same firearm may be used for several operations.[30] In fact knives suffice. Bombs are relatively easily produced. A terrorist can support himself financially, since he does not have to leave civilian life to join the maquis. Individuals not groups usually perform acts of terrorism, although a support organization is necessary. The basic requirements for terrorism are secrecy, discipline, and thorough organization, none of which requires heavy financial investment.

The attractiveness of terrorism to insurgents who lack means is the reason it is often called the "weapon of the weak," and many strategic models of insurrection situate it as the first phase in the conflict, followed respectively by guerrilla and then conventional warfare as the insurgents grow stronger.[31] Such schemes can be unnecessarily rigid in assigning terrorism to the outbreak of the insurrection. Although the FLN used terrorism early in the Algerian war, its later use although perhaps illustrative of military weakness did not signify impending defeat. Physical weakness does not always imply political weakness, and the single-cause interpretation of terrorism is gravely misleading. Thornton's is the most flexible model: the insurrection is a continuum with terrorism, guerrilla activity, and conventional warfare respectively taking precedence at each stage. The last phase of warfare is then a mixture of all three forms.[32]

Terrorism's value to revolutionary movements is not proportional to its expense, but to its psychological effectiveness. The most extreme but not the only reaction to acts of terrorism is emotional terror. Psychologists commonly define the psychological condition of terror as extreme fear or anxiety. Following Freud they conceive of normal fear as rational appreciation of a real danger, whereas anxiety is abnormal fear, an irrational response to a vaguely perceived unfamiliar menace.[33] Acts of terrorism are an original type of menace. Terrorism poses a real not imaginary danger, and thus it is hardly fair to label the fear it causes "abnormal." Nor is such fear *necessarily* irrational. However the reaction to the terrorist menace tends to be anxiety because the stimulus although real is vague, incomprehensible, and totally unexpected: the qualities of the anxiety-producing situation. Persons confronted with terrorism feel helpless, which contributes to their anxiety, but this feeling is usually based on actual impotence. Terrorism appears irrational to the threatened individual, who therefore cannot respond rationally. The members of direct target groups (and perhaps indirect targets, if they feel some affinity with the direct target) feel vulnerable, and investigation of people who experienced air raids during World War II shows that one of the most important causes of anxiety is a feeling of extreme helplessness and the consequent breakdown of the sentiment of personal invulnerability. When an individual feels that he has barely escaped serious danger, his psychological defenses are shattered and he feels future threats more acutely.[34] Furthermore studies of concentration camp prisoners suggest that the unpredictability of danger in such an environment is the most psychologically damaging factor.[35]

Terrorism affects the social structure as well as the individual; it upsets the framework of precepts and images upon which members of society depend and trust. Since one no longer knows what sort of behavior to expect from other members of society, the system is disoriented. The formerly coherent community dissolves into a mass of anomic individuals, each concerned only with personal survival. "The *sine qua non* of a society . . . is the possession of mutual expectations by members of society, allowing them to orient their behavior to each other."[36] Terrorism destroys the solidarity, cooperation, and interdependence on which social functioning is based, and it substitutes insecurity and distrust.

The following excerpts from the personal diary of Mouloud Feraoun, an Algerian novelist and schoolteacher who lived in Fort National, Kabylia, eloquently express the consequences of terrorism:

> Again a market day. . . . Toward noon I made a rapid tour of the town. People seem brittle, ready for any madness, any anger, any stupidity. I felt through the crowd an impression of horror, as though I were living in the midst of a nightmare. An undefinable curse reigns over us. I found myself in the center of the hell of the damned, on which the bright Algerian sun shone. I hurried home, shaken. I do not know where this comes from, this is the first time I feel such suffering. Perhaps it is that, fear, the panicky fear without a precise object, without foundation.[37]
>
> My [French] colleagues are truly mad, they are pitiable and I would like to reassure them. But when one believes himself persecuted, he accepts only menace, he understands only danger, he imagines only scenes of carnage, he thinks only of death.[38]
>
> At each execution of a traitor or pretended such [by the FLN], anguish takes over the survivors. No one is sure of anything, it is truly terror. . . . Terror which rules mysterious and unexplainable. Nerves are on edge.[39]
>
> Each of us is guilty just because he belongs to such a category, such a race, such a people. You fear that they will make you pay with your life for your place in the world or the color of your skin, you are afraid of being attacked uniquely because nobody has attacked you yet; you wonder why you don't do anything when you are almost sure of not being able to do anything – even sincerely mourn the victims, mourn them totally in the shadow of that secret and inadmissible joy which is that of the escapee.[40]

Jacques Soustelle, Governor General of Algeria in 1955, described the social effects of terrorism: rather than stimulating cooperation among the threatened, it led to division and strife.[41] Shops were closed and people were afraid to leave their homes; Soustelle feared a total collapse of economic life and social structure.[42]

The success of terrorism in producing fear or terror is not absolute, and if it causes fear in the immediate, political action may not result from it. Terrorism may produce a psychological tolerance, a numbed passivity on the part of the target, which is often a precursor of hostility. This anger may eventually erupt into overt aggression against the insurgents. In some cases the revolutionary movement may intend to create a mixture of fear and hostility, for example in an unpopular minority. But if terrorism should lead to passive bewilderment or anti-insurgent aggression from the mass population, the revolutionary cause would suffer seriously.

The tolerance of violence seems to be influenced by two factors. The first is the duration and magnitude of the terrorist threat. Sustained intense relentless terrorism is more likely to numb the target than is sporadic terrorism.[43] This finding corroborates the conclusion that terrorism's psychological effectiveness is based to a large degree on its unpredictability. Revolutionary movements usually lack the power to carry out sustained terrorism except in limited areas, but there they do risk the overuse of violence. Feraoun, referring to Kabylia in 1956–7, comments:

> For many, all these murders finish by losing their former significance. One wonders, in effect, if all those who fall are traitors. Little by little, doubt and lassitude invade consciences; despair gives way to anger. If this continues each one will accuse himself of treason and all the traitors, reunited, will revolt against the killers, who will expire cruelly in their turn.[44]

Minor rebellions against the FLN did occur occasionally, usually in the form of supporting French self-defense programs.

The second factor in the use of terrorism that affects the popular reaction is communication. There is some indication that if the revolutionary movement provides positive recommendations to its targets on how to relieve the condition of stress caused by terrorism, there is less danger of inaction.[45] In Kabylia and in many other areas the FLN issued puritanical and unreasonably excessive negative orders: the populations were forbidden to consult doctors, lawyers, midwives, or pharmacists or to smoke, drink alcohol, amuse themselves, or cooperate with Europeans in any fashion. These orders, in addition to private acts of vengeance carried out under the guise of FLN directives, made the FLN unpopular with the populations under its control. But even complying with revolutionary demands does not provide complete relief, for there is no immunity. There is a boundary line in terrorism between too much clarification and too much obscurity. Overstepping the line in the first direction makes terrorism lose its unpredictability and thus its power to terrify. Going too far in the second direction may cause the target to revolt.

Hostility inspired by terrorism may not always lead to behavioral aggression against the insurgents. Psychological theories now consider hostility and aggression as reactions to frustration.[46] Revolutionary terrorism and the fear it may cause are frustrating situations, but the resulting hostility may be "displaced": frustrated people often aggress against those they blame for their unpleasant experiences, *but they do not always blame those who actually are most contiguous with those events*.[47] Frustrated individuals and outside observers do not necessarily perceive the same "frustrating agent;" therefore attribution of blame may be irrational.[48] People may transfer their aggression to an available and acceptable object that they consider less likely to punish.[49] For example, the Janis air war studies found that citizens blamed their own governments for not protecting them against raids, rather than the countries actually responsible for the bombings.[50]

Revolutionary propaganda can increase the regime's attractiveness as an object for popular aggression. The FLN usually found this persuasion task simplified by the division in Algerian social and political life between the dominant European minority and the estranged Muslim mass of the population. French counterinsurgency methods also helped them. By bidding for Muslim support as the champions of nationalism and independence and by constantly vilifying the French, the FLN increased the likelihood of the phenomenon of displacement of aggression. It is also probable that the Muslim population feared FLN violence more than they did the French, since they were virtually unprotected against the terrorism that they dreaded more. The FLN possessed local knowledge that the French did not.

If terrorism arouses anger or aggressive behavior, the revolutionaries, if they consider this a drawback, can deny guilt in the matter. In intense conflicts it is difficult to establish facts; opinion is usually so polarized – a condition that terrorism helps to create – that most people believe only the arguments of the side with which they are ideologically sympathetic. Hence vehement denial may substitute for proof. The FLN used this tactic on several occasions, of which the most spectacular was the Melouza massacre in 1957. The FLN ordered the execution of all male inhabitants of a village, Melouza, that had rebelled against FLN terrorism, supported a rival nationalist movement, and also cooperated with the French army. When the gruesome details of the massacre became known, even the FLN's customary supporters abroad joined in the universal condemnation. The FLN then denied their responsibility and accused the French of staging the incident in order to discredit the FLN; they lent credibility to this thesis and gained international publicity by sending telegrams pleading innocence to world leaders and calling for a United Nations investigation. Although outside of Algeria most people accepted the French version, in Algeria most Muslims believed the FLN – after all, the French did not have a reputation for honesty in Algeria. Thus credibility became a key factor in interpretation.

Ted Gurr argued that although terrorism may cause immediate behavioral change, it is not advisable for insurgents because it does not result in wholehearted long-run ideological support: "support given under coercion is unlikely to develop into a more enduring allegiance unless it can be systematically maintained over a long period."[51] Leites and Wolf disagreed with the "hearts-and-minds" approach to revolution: "the only 'act' R [rebellion] needs desperately from a large proportion of the populace is *nondenunciation* (that is, eschewing the act of informing against R) and noncombat against it."[52] Fear, lack of enthusiasm for the authorities, and "commercial" motives that calculate the possibilities of reward all are as powerful in prompting popular support for the insurgents as is sympathy or conviction.[53] And since the active supporters of the revolution are always a small minority, little active mass support is required. Leites and Wolf concluded that it is popular behavior, not attitudes, that counts: "thorough organization and effective coercion can enjoin or engender particular modes of behavior by the population, notwithstanding popular preferences that would lead to different behavior if a purely voluntary choice could be made."[54]

The Algerian case falls somewhere between these two positions. Certainly ideological preferences are not the only motives that prompt popular behavior, but it is difficult to conceive of a revolutionary minority coercing a determinedly opposed population. There must be a combination of ideological affinity, realistic calculations of the insurgents' chances, and coercion.

Terrorism is a form of coercion that influences behavior and attitudes. It causes a polarization of opinion; confronted with terrorism it is impossible to be neutral or uninvolved:

> It is fair . . . to say that the very violence of terrorism has made no small number among us leave our ease and our laziness in order to reflect. Each one has been obliged to bend over the problem, to make an examination of his conscience, to tremble for his skin because the skin of the Kabyle is not worth much in the eyes of the terrorist.[55]

Terrorism also affects the attitudes of indirect targets. When the direct target is an unpopular minority, attacks on that group may arouse admiration and respect for the insurgents among the general population. In Algeria many Muslims approved of FLN terrorism when Europeans were the victims, and many considered the FLN terrorists in Algiers (the center of anti-European terrorism), as heroes of the revolution.[56] In fact indignation caused by the French execution of FLN prisoners encouraged the Algiers FLN to avenge the Muslim population by bombing Europeans; the FLN was "*obliged* (to manifest their presence and their community of sentiment with the mass of the people) to mark their reaction by an act."[57] It was cruelly ironic that the leader of the Algiers FLN, convinced that the Melouza killings were the work of the French, ordered acts of terrorism in retaliation.[58]

Tillion described the cycle of violence and counter-violence that terrorism, with its simultaneous and complicated psychological consequences, sets into motion. The Europeans of Algiers, maddened by FLN terrorism and under the pressure of fear and horror, called for repression against the Muslim population as an antiterrorist measure and refused any political reforms. Governmental action against Muslims – the arrests, the torture, and the executions – directly contributed to the growth of terrorism. Muslims, who almost unanimously regarded the condemned prisoners as national heroes, became angry and desperate each time there was an execution. The FLN then reacted with acts of terrorism, appeasing the Muslims and infuriating the Europeans. Tillion accused both sides of trying to outbid the other in violence.[59]

The importance of the governmental response to terrorism cannot be underestimated. If the insurgent organization is weak, official repression may destroy it when terrorism demonstrates its existence, and terrorism is likely to incite more severe measures than other forms of less spectacular violence. In Algeria the French destroyed much of the FLN organization immediately after the opening of the revolution on November 1, 1954, but they were unable to halt guerrilla activity and clandestine terrorism against Muslims in inaccessible areas. If, as the accounts of terrorism in Algiers indicate, the revolutionary movement survives the regime's initial reaction, repression is likely to further revolutionary goals by alienating the civilian population from the government, and in the Algerian case from the Europeans. From any viewpoint an efficient response to terrorism is difficult. Protection of the population and isolation of the guilty are hopeless tasks when the terrorists are indistinguishable from the mass, which happens when the population is either afraid or unwilling to inform on the insurgents. Without intelligence the government cannot make the crucial distinction. Hence to the government the entire population is suspect and all are guilty at least of complicity with the enemy. However strongly tempted by circumstances, the regime should avoid antiterrorist measures that are illegal and indiscriminate. Policies such as interning suspects without trial, widely practiced during the Algerian war, create popular sympathy for the insurgents; if interned suspects are not members of the revolutionary movement at the time of their seizure, they are likely to be on their release. Repression is also self-defeating because it increases insecurity and disorder, thereby contradicting the government's most basic function. If terrorism is successful, it is a symptom of disarray in the body politic. It may mean that dissidents are given no opportunities for peaceful protest or that the population is dissatisfied with the regime. The causes of terrorism are political, but the response to it is usually based on military force.

The regime's response to terrorism is to some degree predictable, through consideration of its history of reactions to crises. The French in Algeria always responded forcefully to Muslim expressions of dissent. The FLN risked provoking another severe repression, such as that near Sétif in 1945, when Muslim anti-European riots provoked a French retaliation that left at least 15,000 Muslims dead. But it was unlikely that in 1954 the Fourth Republic, burdened with the Indochina defeat, the problems of the European Defense Community, and nationalist agitation in Tunisia and Morocco, would be capable of anything but its characteristic indecisiveness and inefficiency.

Another problem in analyzing the relative advantages and disadvantages of the use of terrorism is the question of its consequences for the internal organization and its members. Frantz Fanon's view, based on his Algerian experience, is that violence is therapeutic and beneficial. It is a "cleansing force" for individuals, freeing natives from their inferiority complexes in regard to the colonialists and giving them self-respect.[60] The former FLN leader Ouzegane agrees:

> Urban terrorism, our liberating terrorism, functioned as a safety valve. It permitted patriots ulcerated by the unequal struggle, revolted by French injustice . . ., to liberate themselves from an unconscious psychological complex, to keep cool heads, to respect revolutionary discipline.[61]

Ouzegane suggests that terrorism controls militant impatience and relieves the tension caused by inaction. According to Fanon violence also binds the individual to the revolutionary cause; the FLN leaders' trust in their subordinates was "proportional to the hopelessness of each case. You could be sure of a new recruit when he could no longer go back into the colonial system."[62] These bonds in turn serve individual personality needs by reintegrating persons alienated by the colonial system into the revolutionary community.[63] A critic of these ideas points out that Fanon himself, a psychologist, listed cases of Algerians traumatized by French violence; French doctors could add cases of Frenchmen traumatized by having killed or tortured:

> Therefore if one means by violence terrorism with all its implications, nothing can affirm that it really possesses this disalienating effect. On the contrary, everything leads one to think that violence, suffered or performed, contains a part, more or less large, of traumatization. This traumatization . . . can then only result in a repetition of the violent act . . . One could point to Frenchmen, having suffered German violence, echoing it in Indochina and from there into Algeria. It has also been said that the first terrorists of 1954 were the sons of those shot in 1945 [at Sétif]. In turn what will become of the children of these terrorists?[64]

Ouzegane does not support this view: "One must differentiate between 'violence that liberates and violence that oppresses.'"[65]

Although Ivernel correctly assumed that the events at Sétif greatly influenced the 1954 movement, his traumatization theory is seriously challenged by the fact that many Frenchmen who suffered from the Germans were sensitized by their experience and many (Germaine Tillion being a notable example) attempted to halt the violence from both sides in Algeria.[66]

Other studies dispute Fanon's position that violence is psychological therapy. Janis and Katz, for example, note three "corrupting effects" of the use of violence: guilt, the weakening of internal superego controls, and "contagion effects," or unrestrained imitation. Violence with use becomes more frequent, extreme, and uncontrollable.[67] Another view corroborates Fanon's conclusions but not his logic: despite the revolution's moral sanctioning of violence, its use causes guilt that encourages future violence by binding the anxiously guilty followers to their leaders.[68]

Revolutionary leaders usually treat the moral problem of terrorism as one in which the ends justify the means. They excuse terrorism as a last resort in an attempt to express political opinion and blame the regime for forcing them to take such desperate measures. "It's our only way of expressing ourselves," explained Saadi Yacef, head of the Algiers terrorist organization.[69] These justifications do not appear to exorcise all guilt; Yacef disguised himself as a woman to inspect the results of a bombing he had ordered and was deeply moved when he discovered the body of a personal friend, a European. He wept when Tillion reminded him of the deaths for which he was responsible and when she called him an assassin.[70] A female member of the bomb network was mentally unbalanced by having performed acts of terrorism.[71] A bomb-maker, Taleb, also had moral qualms and insisted that his bombs be used only on material targets.[72] However another less sensitive terrorist claimed that the role of the terrorist was no different from that of the technician or the ordinary soldier.[73] It is true that terrorism is often a strictly disciplined form of violence.

One can only conclude that emotional guilt caused by terrorism is a purely personal matter. The majority of FLN terrorists did not feel so guilty that they refused to commit acts of terrorism. There can be no general rules, and there is no evidence to indicate that the internal effects of terrorism have long-term consequences on either the individual or the society of which he forms a part.

Conclusions

Summing up, terrorism's attractiveness and significance for revolutionary organizations are due to the combination of economy, facility, and high psychological and political effectiveness. From the insurgent viewpoint there are certain foreseeable risks in employing a terrorist strategy: (1) the danger of creating hostility rather than fear in the population; (2) the possibility that the governmental response will destroy the organization; and (3) the risk that the use of terrorism may emotionally harm the terrorists themselves. Of these three potential obstacles to terrorism's efficiency, the first is subject to the influence of propaganda and ideology and is thus partially a communication factor. Because of this risk of psychological backfiring, it is difficult to conceive of a situation where a minority using terrorism could impose a solution on a majority unless the minority's goal was acceptable to the majority. The second factor, the government's response, is external to the organization, but it is predictable that if the revolution is seriously trying to obtain some degree of popular sympathy, regime repression will work in its favor. The insurgents can ignore the third problem, since arguments for and against violence cancel each other out. Here also communications that justify terrorism on moral grounds may modify its psychological effects. One may conclude that the effectiveness of terrorism is increased by nonviolent persuasion. Paradoxically terrorism, which must appear irrational and unpredictable in order to be effective, is an eminently rational strategy, calculated in terms of predictable costs and benefits.

Terrorism occurs when it appears useful to insurgents or those who seek radical change; terrorism seems to be the appropriate means to ends such as general insecurity and disorientation, control of the civilian population, demoralization of the adversary, or publicity. Terrorism is particularly attractive when alternative means of reaching goals are absent. Thus terrorism is, as revolutionary propaganda often proclaims, a measure of desperation and is likely where political expression is denied to opponents of the regime. That is not to say that revolutionary perceptions may not be false; in reality terrorism may be dysfunctional to the revolution or it may occur in states that permit opposition. Furthermore once a terrorist strategy is under way, it gains a momentum of its own, and insurgents may find themselves trapped in a cycle of terrorism and repression, unable to abandon terrorism because of militant and popular pressures.

One of the general conditions for the success of a terrorist strategy is obviously the accuracy of insurgent calculations. If insurgent perception of the situation and estimate of the psychological and political responses of selected targets to particular acts are correct and technical efficiency is high, then terrorism is likely to succeed. Governmental response is an opposing variable and may cause the failure of terrorism. The balance of these two factors determines the outcome, which is judged by the degree of discrepancy between insurgent intentions and actual consequences. It is more difficult to estimate the effectiveness of terrorism as compared to other violent or nonviolent methods, such as guerrilla warfare, strikes, boycotts, or propaganda. In cases of successful revolution or national liberation, as Algeria, one may ask whether or not the insurgents would have won without terrorism, but cases where terrorism succeeded but the revolution failed, or vice versa, are difficult to assess.

2 The causes of terrorism

Terrorism occurs both in the context of violent resistance to the state as well as in the service of state interests. If we focus on terrorism directed against governments for purposes of political change, we are considering the premeditated use or threat of symbolic, low-level violence by conspiratorial organizations. Terrorist violence communicates a political message; its ends go beyond damaging an enemy's material resources.[1] The victims or objects of terrorist attack have little intrinsic value to the terrorist group but represent a larger human audience whose reaction the terrorists seek.

The study of terrorism can be organized around three questions: why terrorism occurs, how the process of terrorism works, and what its social and political effects are. Here the objective is to outline an approach to the analysis of the causes of terrorism, based on comparison of different cases of terrorism, in order to distinguish a common pattern of causation from the historically unique.

The subject of terrorism inspired a voluminous literature in the years between 1972 and 1981, when this analysis was first published. However, nowhere among the highly varied treatments does one find a general theoretical analysis of the causes of terrorism. This may be because terrorism was often approached from historical perspectives, which, if we take Laqueur's work as an example, dismiss explanations that try to take into account more than a single case as "exceedingly vague or altogether wrong."[2] Certainly existing general accounts in 1981 were often based on assumptions that were neither explicit nor factually demonstrable. Judgments centered on social factors such as the permissiveness and affluence in which Western youth were raised or the imitation of dramatic models encouraged by television. Alternatively, political explanations blamed revolutionary ideologies, Marxism-Leninism or nationalism, governmental weakness in giving in to terrorist demands, or conversely government oppression, and the weakness of the regime's opponents. Individual psychopathology was often cited as a culprit.

Even the most persuasive of statements about terrorism were not cast in the form of testable propositions, nor were they broadly comparative in origin or intent. Many were partial analyses, limited in scope to revolutionary terrorism from the Left, not terrorism that is a form of protest or a reaction to political or social change. A narrow historical or geographical focus was also common; the majority of explanations concerned modern phenomena. Some focused usefully on terrorism against the Western democracies.[3] In general, propositions about terrorism lacked logical comparability, specification of the relationship of variables to each other, and a rank-ordering of variables in terms of explanatory power.

Constructing a general explanation of the sources of terrorism is not a simple task, but it is possible to make a useful beginning by establishing a theoretical order for different types and levels of causes. I approach terrorism as a form of political behavior resulting from the deliberate choice of a basically rational actor: the terrorist organization. A comprehensive explanation, however, must also take into account the environment in which terrorism occurs and address the question of whether broad political, social, and economic conditions make terrorism more likely in some contexts than in others. What sort of circumstances lead to the formation of a terrorist group? On the other hand, only a few of the people who experience a given situation practice terrorism. Not even all individuals who share the goals of a terrorist organization agree that terrorism is the best means. It is essential to consider the psychological variables that may encourage or inhibit individual participation in terrorist actions. The analysis of these three levels of causation will center first on situational variables, then on the strategy of the terrorist organization, and last on the problem of individual participation.

This chapter represents only a preliminary set of ideas about the problem of causation; historical cases of terrorism are used as illustrations, not as demonstrations of hypotheses. The historical examples referred to here are significant terrorist campaigns since the French Revolution of 1789; terrorism is considered as a facet of secular modern politics, principally associated with the rise of nationalism, anarchism, and revolutionary socialism.[4] The term "terrorism" was coined to describe the systematic inducement of fear and anxiety to control and direct a civilian population, and the phenomenon of terrorism as a challenge to the authority of the state grew from the difficulties revolutionaries experienced in trying to recreate the mass uprisings of the French Revolution. Most references provided here are drawn from the best-known and most-documented examples: Narodnaya Volya and the Combat Organization of the Socialist-Revolutionary party in Russia, from 1878 to 1913; anarchist terrorism of the 1890s in Europe, primarily France; the Irish Republican Army (IRA) and its predecessors and successors from 1919 to the present; the Irgun Zwai Leumi in Mandate Palestine from 1937 to 1947; the Front de Libération Nationale (FLN) in Algeria from 1954 to 1962; the Popular Front for the Liberation of Palestine from 1968 to the present; the Rote Armee Fraktion (RAF) and the 2nd June Movement in West Germany since 1968; and the Tupamaros of Uruguay from 1968 to 1974.

The setting for terrorism

An initial obstacle to identification of propitious circumstances for terrorism was the absence of significant empirical studies of relevant cross-national factors (a defect since remedied). By 1981 there were a number of quantitative analyses of collective violence, assassination, civil strife, and crime,[5] but none of these phenomena is identical to a campaign of terrorism. Little internal agreement existed among such studies, and the consensus found was not particularly useful for the study of terrorism.[6] For example, Ted Robert Gurr found that "modern" states are less violent than developing countries and that legitimacy of the regime inhibits violence. Yet, Western Europe was experiencing high levels of terrorism. In the 1961–70 period, out of 87 countries, the United States was ranked as having the highest number of terrorist campaigns.[7] Although it is impractical to borrow entire theoretical structures from the literature on political and criminal violence, some propositions can be adapted to the analysis of terrorism.

To develop a framework for the analysis of likely settings for terrorism, we must establish conceptual distinctions among different types of factors. First, a significant difference exists between "preconditions," factors that set the stage for terrorism over the long run, and "precipitants," specific events that immediately precede the occurrence of terrorism. Second, a further classification divides preconditions into enabling or permissive factors, which provide opportunities for terrorism to happen, and situations that directly inspire and motivate terrorist campaigns. Precipitants are similar to the direct causes of terrorism.[8] Furthermore, no factor is neatly compartmentalized in a single nation-state; each has a transnational dimension that complicates the analysis.

First, modernization produces an interrelated set of factors that is a significant permissive cause of terrorism, as increased complexity on all levels of society and economy creates opportunities and vulnerabilities. Sophisticated networks of transportation and communication offer mobility and the means of publicity for terrorists. The terrorists of Narodnaya Volya would have been unable to operate without Russia's newly established rail system, and the Popular Front for the Liberation of Palestine could not indulge in hijacking without the commercial jet aircraft. In Algeria, the FLN only adopted a strategy of urban bombings when they were able to acquire plastic explosives. In 1907 the Combat Organization of the Socialist-Revolutionary party paid 20,000 rubles to an inventor who was working on an aircraft in the futile hope of bombing the Russian imperial palaces from the air.[9] Today we fear that terrorists will exploit the potential of nuclear power, but it was in 1867 that Nobel's invention of dynamite made bombings a convenient terrorist tactic. The use of explosives continues to dominate terrorism.

Urbanization is part of the modern trend toward aggregation and complexity, which increases the number and accessibility of targets and methods. The popular concept of terrorism as "urban guerrilla warfare" grew out of the Latin American experience of the late 1960s.[10] Yet, as Hobsbawm has pointed out, cities became the arena for terrorism after the urban renewal projects of the late nineteenth century, such as the boulevards constructed by Baron Haussman in Paris, made them unsuitable for a strategy based on riots and the defense of barricades.[11] In preventing popular insurrections, governments have exposed themselves to terrorism. P. N. Grabosky has recently argued that cities are a significant cause of terrorism in that they provide an opportunity (a multitude of targets, mobility, communications, anonymity, and audiences) and a recruiting ground among the politicized and volatile inhabitants.[12]

Social "facilitation," which Gurr found to be extremely powerful in bringing about civil strife in general, is also an important permissive factor. This concept refers to social habits and historical traditions that sanction the use of violence against the government, making it morally and politically justifiable, and even dictating an appropriate form, such as demonstrations, coups, or terrorism. Social myths, traditions, and habits permit the development of terrorism as an established political custom. An excellent example of such a tradition is the case of Ireland, where the tradition of physical force dates from the eighteenth century, and the legend of Michael Collins in 1919–21 inspired and partially excused (in the eyes of its supporters) the much less discriminate and less effective terrorism of the Provisional IRA in Northern Ireland from the 1970s to the 1990s.

Moreover, broad attitudes and beliefs that condone terrorism are communicated transnationally. Revolutionary ideologies have always crossed borders with ease. In the nineteenth and early twentieth centuries, such ideas were primarily a European preserve, stemming from the French and Bolshevik Revolutions. Since World War II, Third World revolutions – China, Cuba, and Algeria – and intellectuals such as Frantz Fanon and Carlos Marighela[13] have significantly influenced terrorist movements in the developed West by promoting the development of terrorism as routine behavior.

The most salient political factor in the category of permissive causes is a government's inability or unwillingness to prevent terrorism. The absence of adequate prevention by police and intelligence services permits the spread of conspiracy. However, since terrorist organizations are small and clandestine, the majority of states can be placed in the permissive category. Inefficiency or leniency can be found in a broad range of all but the most brutally efficient dictatorships, including incompetent authoritarian states such as czarist Russia on the eve of the emergence of Narodnaya Volya as well as modern liberal democratic states whose desire to protect civil liberties constrains security measures. The absence of effective security measures is a necessary cause, since our limited information on the subject indicates that terrorism does not occur in efficient and ruthless dictatorships; and certainly repressive military regimes in Uruguay, Brazil, and Argentina crushed violent oppositions. For many governments, however, the cost of disallowing terrorism is too high.

Turning now to a consideration of the direct causes of terrorism, we focus on background conditions that positively encourage resistance to the state. These instigating circumstances go beyond merely creating an environment in which terrorism is possible; they provide motivation and direction for the terrorist movement. Here the focus is on reasons rather than opportunities.

The first condition that can be considered a direct cause of terrorism is the existence of concrete grievances among an identifiable subgroup of a larger population, such as an ethnic minority discriminated against by the majority. A social movement develops in order to redress these grievances and to gain either equal rights or a separate state; terrorism is then the resort of an extremist faction of this broader movement. In practice, terrorism has frequently arisen in such situations: in modern states, separatist nationalism among Basques, Bretons, and

Québeçois has motivated terrorism. In the colonial era, nationalist movements commonly turned to terrorism.

This is not to say, however, that the existence of a dissatisfied minority or majority is a necessary or a sufficient cause of terrorism. Not all those who are discriminated against turn to terrorism, nor does terrorism always reflect objective social or economic deprivation. In West Germany, Japan, and Italy, for example, terrorism was the chosen method of the privileged, not the downtrodden. Some theoretical studies have suggested that the essential ingredient that must be added to real deprivation is the perception on the part of the deprived that this condition is not what they deserve or expect, in short, that discrimination is unjust. An attitude study, for example, found that "the idea of justice or fairness may be more centrally related to attitudes toward violence than are feelings of deprivation. It is the perceived injustice underlying the deprivation that gives rise to anger or frustration."[14] The intervening variables as we have argued lie in the terrorists' perceptions. Moreover, it seems likely that for terrorism to occur the government must be singled out to blame for popular suffering.

The second condition that creates motivations for terrorism is the lack of opportunity for political participation. Regimes that deny access to power and persecute dissent create intense dissatisfaction. In this case, grievances are primarily political, without social or economic overtones. Discrimination is not directed against any ethnic, religious, or racial subgroup of the population. The terrorist organization is not necessarily part of a broader social movement; indeed, the population may be largely apathetic. In situations where paths to the legal expression of opposition are blocked, but where the regime's repression is inefficient, revolutionary terrorism is doubly likely, as permissive and direct causes coincide. An example of this situation is czarist Russia in the 1870s.

Context is especially significant as a direct cause of terrorism when it affects an elite, not the mass population. Terrorism is essentially the result of elite disaffection; it represents the strategy of a minority, who may act on behalf of a wider popular constituency who have not been consulted about, and do not necessarily approve of, the terrorists' aims or methods. There is remarkable relevance in E. J. Hobsbawm's comments on the political conspirators of post-Napoleonic Europe:

> All revolutionaries regarded themselves, with some justification, as small elites of the emancipated and progressive operating among, and for the eventual benefit of, a vast and inert mass of the ignorant and misled common people, which would no doubt welcome liberation when it came, but could not be expected to take much part in preparing it.[15]

Many terrorists are young, well educated, and middle class in background. Such students or young professionals, with prior political experience, are disillusioned with the prospects of changing society and see little chance of access to the system despite their privileged status. Much terrorism has grown out of student unrest; this was the case in nineteenth-century Russia as well as post-World War II West Germany, Italy, the United States, Japan, and Uruguay.

Perhaps terrorism is most likely to occur precisely where mass passivity and elite dissatisfaction coincide. Discontent is not generalized or severe enough to provoke the majority of the populace to action against the regime, yet a small minority, without access to the bases of power that would permit overthrow of the government through coup d'état or subversion, seeks radical change. Terrorism may thus be a sign of a stable society rather than a symptom of fragility and impending collapse. Terrorism is the resort of a discontented elite when conditions are not revolutionary. Luigi Bonanate has blamed terrorism on a "blocked society" that is strong enough to preserve itself (presumably through popular inertia) yet resistant to innovation. Such self-perpetuating "*immobilisme*" invites terrorism.[16]

The last category of situational factors involves a precipitating event that immediately precedes outbreaks of terrorism. Although it is generally thought that precipitants are the most unpredictable of causes, there does seem to be a common pattern of government actions that act as catalysts for terrorism. Government use of unexpected and unusual force in response to protest or reform attempts often compels terrorist retaliation. The development of such an action-reaction syndrome then establishes the structure of the conflict between the regime and its challengers. There are numerous historical examples of a campaign of terrorism precipitated by a government's reliance on excessive force to quell protest or squash dissent. The czarist regime's severity in dealing with the populist movement was a factor in the development of Narodaya Volya as a terrorist organization in 1879. The French government's persecution of anarchists was a factor in subsequent anarchist terrorism in the 1890s. The British government's execution of the heroes of the Easter Rising set the stage for Michael Collins and the IRA. The Protestant violence that met the Catholic civil rights movement in Northern Ireland in 1969 pushed the Provisional IRA to retaliate. In West Germany, the death of Beno Ohnesorg at the hands of the police in a demonstration against the Shah of Iran in 1968 contributed to the emergence of the RAF.

This analysis of the background conditions for terrorism indicates that we must look at the terrorist organization's perception and interpretation of the situation. Terrorists view the context as permissive, making terrorism a viable option. In a material sense, the means are placed at their disposal by the environment. Circumstances also provide the terrorists with compelling reasons for seeking political change. Finally, an event occurs that snaps the opposition's patience with the regime. Government action is now seen as intolerably unjust, and terrorism becomes not only a possible decision but a morally acceptable one. The regime has forfeited its status as the standard of legitimacy. For the terrorist, the end may now excuse the means.

The reasons for terrorism

Significant campaigns of terrorism depend on political choices. As purposeful activity, terrorism is the result of an organization's decision that it is a politically useful means to oppose a government. The argument that terrorist behavior should be analyzed as a calculated choice is based on the assumption that terrorist organizations possess internally consistent sets of values, beliefs, and images of the environment. Terrorism is seen collectively as a logical means to advance desired ends. In short, the group's reasons for resorting to terrorism constitute an important factor in the process of causation.[17]

Terrorism serves a variety of goals, both revolutionary and subrevolutionary. Terrorists may be revolutionaries (such as the Combat Organization of the Socialist-Revolutionary Party in the nineteenth century or the Tupamaros of the twentieth century), nationalists fighting against foreign occupiers (such as the Algerian FLN, the IRA of 1919–21, or the Irgun), minority separatists combatting indigenous regimes (such as the Corsican, Breton, and Basque movements and the Provisional IRA), reformists (the bombing of nuclear construction sites, for example, is meant to halt nuclear power, not to overthrow governments), anarchists or millenarians (such as the original anarchist movement of the nineteenth century and modern millenarian groups such as the Red Army faction in West Germany, the Italian Red Brigades, and the Japanese Red Army), or reactionaries acting to prevent change from the top (such as the Secret Army Organization during the Algerian war or the Ulster Defence Association in Northern Ireland).[18]

To state that extremist groups resort to terrorism in order to acquire political influence does not mean that all groups have equally precise objectives or that the relationship between means and ends is perfectly clear to an outside observer. Some groups are less realistic about the logic of means and ends than others. The leaders of Narodnaya Volya, for example, lacked a detailed conception of how the assassination of the czar would force his successor to permit the liberalization they sought. Other terrorist groups are more pragmatic: the IRA of 1919–21 and the Irgun, for instance, shrewdly foresaw the utility of a war of attrition against the British. Menachem Begin, in particular, planned his campaign to take advantage of the "glass house" that Britain operated in.[19] The degree of skill in relating means to ends seems to have little to do with the overall sophistication of the terrorist ideology. The French anarchists of the 1890s, for example, acted in light of a well-developed philosophical doctrine but were much less certain of how violence against the bourgeoisie would bring about freedom. It is possible that anarchist or millenarian terrorists are so preoccupied with the splendor of the future that they lose sight of the present. Less theoretical nationalists who concentrate on the short run have simpler aims but sharper plans.

However diverse the long-run goals of terrorist groups, there is a common pattern of proximate or short-run objectives of a terrorist strategy. Proximate objectives are defined in terms of the immediate reactions that terrorists want to achieve in their different audiences.[20] The most basic reason for terrorism is to gain recognition or attention – what Thornton called advertisement of the cause. Violence and bloodshed always excite human curiosity, and the theatricality, suspense, and threat of danger inherent in terrorism enhance its attention-getting qualities. In fact, publicity may be the highest goal of some groups. For example, terrorists who are fundamentally protesters might be satisfied with airing their grievances before the world. Today, in an interdependent world, the need for international recognition encourages transnational terrorist activities, with escalation to ever more destructive and spectacular violence. As the audience grows larger, more diverse, and more accustomed to terrorism, terrorists must go to extreme lengths to shock.

Terrorism is also often designed to disrupt and discredit the processes of government, by weakening it administratively and impairing normal operations. Terrorism as a direct attack on the regime aims at the insecurity and demoralization of government officials, independent of any impact on public opinion. An excellent example of this strategy is Michael Collins's campaign against the British intelligence system in Ireland in 1919–21. This form of terrorism often accompanies rural guerrilla warfare, as the insurgents try to weaken the government's control over citizens and territory.

Terrorism also affects public attitudes in both a positive and a negative sense, aiming at creating either sympathy in a potential constituency or fear and hostility in an audience identified as the "enemy." These two functions are interrelated, since intimidating the enemy impresses both sympathizers and the uncommitted. At the same time, terrorism may be used to enforce obedience in an audience from whom the terrorists demand allegiance. The FLN in Algeria, for example, claimed more Algerian than French victims. Fear and respect were not incompatible with solidarity against the French.[21] When terrorism is part of a struggle between incumbents and challengers, polarization of public opinion undermines the government's legitimacy.

Terrorism may also be intended to provoke a counterreaction from the government, to increase publicity for the terrorists' cause and to demonstrate to the people that their charges against the regime are well founded. The terrorists mean to force the state to show its true repressive face, thereby driving the people into the arms of the challengers. For example, Carlos Marighela argued that the way to win popular support was to provoke the regime to measures of greater repression and persecution.[22] Provocative terrorism is designed to bring about revolutionary conditions rather than to exploit them. The FLN against the French, the Palestinian nationalists against Israel, and the RAF against the Federal Republic all appear to have used terrorism as provocation.

In addition, terrorism may serve internal organizational functions of control, discipline, and morale building within the terrorist group and even become an instrument of rivalry among factions in a resistance movement. For example, factional terrorism frequently characterized the Palestinian resistance movement in the 1970s. Rival groups competed in a vicious game where the victims were Israeli civilians or anonymous airline passengers, but where the immediate goal was influence within the resistance movement rather than the intimidation of the Israeli public or international recognition of the Palestinian cause.

Terrorism is a logical choice when oppositions have such goals and when the power ratio of government to challenger is high. The observation that terrorism is a weapon of the weak is hackneyed but apt. At least when initially adopted, terrorism is the strategy of a minority that by its own judgment lacks other means. When the group perceives its options as limited, terrorism is attractive because it is a relatively inexpensive and simple alternative, and because its potential reward is high.

Weakness and consequent restriction of choice can stem from different sources. On the one hand, weakness may result from the regime's suppression of opposition. Resistance organizations lacking the means of mounting more extensive violence may then turn to terrorism because legitimate expression of dissent is denied. Lack of popular support at the outset of a conflict does not mean that the terrorists' aims lack general appeal. Even though they cannot immediately mobilize widespread and active support, over the course of the conflict they may acquire the allegiance of the population. For example, the Algerian FLN used terrorism as a significant means of mobilizing mass support.[23]

On the other hand, it is wrong to assume that where there is terrorism there is oppression. Weakness may mean that an extremist organization deliberately rejects nonviolent methods of opposition open to them in a liberal state. Challengers then adopt terrorism because they are impatient with time-consuming legal methods of eliciting support or advertising their cause, because they distrust the regime, or because they are not capable of, or interested in, mobilizing majority support. Many terrorist groups operating in Western Europe and Japan in the 1970s illustrate this phenomenon. They lacked a readily identifiable constituency and espoused causes devoid of mass appeal. Similarly, the separatist movements represented at best only a minority of the total population of the state.

Thus, some groups are weak because weakness is imposed on them by the political system they operate in; others are weak because of unpopularity. In making this distinction we may be making value judgments about the potential legitimacy of terrorist organizations. In some cases resistance groups are genuinely desperate; in others they have alternatives to violence. It is also important not to forget that nonviolent resistance has been chosen in other circumstances, for example, by Gandhi and by Martin Luther King. Terrorists may argue that they had no choice, but their perceptions may be flawed.[24]

In addition to weakness, an important rationale in the decision to adopt a strategy of terrorism is impatience. Action becomes imperative. For a variety of reasons, the challenge to the state cannot be left to the future. Given a perception of limited means, the group often sees the choice as between action as survival and inaction as the death of resistance.

One reason for haste is external: the historical moment seems to present a unique chance. For example, the resistance group facing a colonial power recently weakened by a foreign war exploits a temporary vulnerability: the IRA against Britain after World War I, the Irgun against Britain after World War II, and the FLN against France after the Indochina war. Possibly the stalemate between the United States and North Vietnam stimulated the post-1968 wave of anti-imperialist terrorism, especially in Latin America. There may be other pressures or catalysts provided by the regime, such as the violent precipitants discussed earlier or the British decision to introduce conscription in Ireland during World War I.

A sense of urgency may also develop when similar resistance groups have apparently succeeded with terrorism and created a momentum. The contagion effect of terrorism is partially based on an image of success that recommends terrorism to groups who identify with the innovator. The Algerian FLN, for example, was pressured to keep up with nationalists in Tunisia and Morocco, whose violent agitation brought about independence in 1956. Terrorism spread rapidly through Latin America in the post-1968 period as revolutionary groups worked in terms of a continental solidarity.

Dramatic failure of alternative means of obtaining one's ends may also fuel a drive toward terrorism. The Arab defeat in the 1967 war with Israel led Palestinians to realize that they could no longer depend on the Arab states to further their goals. In retrospect, their extreme weakness and the historical tradition of violence in the Middle East made it likely that militant nationalists should turn to terrorism. Since international recognition of the Palestinian cause was a primary aim (given the influence of outside powers in the region) and since attacks on Israeli territory were difficult, terrorism developed into a transnational phenomenon.

These external pressures to act are often intensified by internal politics. Leaders of resistance groups act under constraints imposed by their followers. They are forced to justify the organization's existence, to quell restlessness among the cadres, to satisfy demands for revenge, to prevent splintering of the movement, and to maintain control. Pressures may also come from the terrorists' constituency.

In conclusion, we see that terrorism is an attractive strategy to groups of different ideological persuasions who challenge the state's authority. Groups who want to dramatize a cause, to demoralize the government, to gain popular support, to provoke regime violence, to inspire followers, or to dominate a wider resistance movement or are weak vis-à-vis the regime, and are impatient to act, often find terrorism a reasonable choice. This is especially so when conditions are favorable, providing opportunities and making terrorism a simple and rapid option, with immediate and visible payoff.

Individual motivation and participation

Terrorism is neither an automatic reaction to conditions nor a purely calculated strategy. What psychological factors motivate the terrorist and influence his or her perceptions and interpretations of reality? Terrorists are only a small minority of people with similar personal backgrounds, experiencing the same conditions, who might thus be expected to reach identical conclusions based on logical reasoning about the utility of terrorism as a technique of political influence.

The relationship between personality and politics is complex and imperfectly understood.[25] Why individuals engage in political violence is a complicated problem, and the question of why they engage in terrorism is still more difficult.[26] As most simply and frequently posed, the question of a psychological explanation of terrorism is whether or not there is a "terrorist personality," similar to the authoritarian personality, whose emotional traits we can specify with some exactitude.[27] An identifiable pattern of attitudes and behavior in the terrorism-prone individual would result from a combination of ego-defensive needs, cognitive processes, and socialization in interaction with a specific situation. In pursuing this line of inquiry, it is important to avoid stereotyping the terrorist or oversimplifying the sources of terrorist actions. No single motivation or personality can be valid for all circumstances.

What limited data we have on individual terrorists (and knowledge must be gleaned from disparate sources that usually neither focus on psychology nor use a comparative approach) suggest that the outstanding common characteristic of terrorists is their normality.[28] Terrorism often seems to be the connecting link among widely varying personalities. Franco Venturi, concentrating on the terrorists of a single small group, observed that "the policy of terrorism united many very different characters and mentalities" and that agreement on using terrorism was the cement that bound the members of Narodnaya Volya together.[29] A West German psychiatrist who conducted a pretrial examination of four members of the RAF concluded that they were "intelligent," even "humorous," and showed no symptoms of psychosis or neurosis and "no particular personality type."[30] Psychoanalysis might penetrate beneath superficial normality to expose some unifying or pathological trait, but this is scarcely a workable research method, even if the likelihood of the existence of such a characteristic could be demonstrated.

Peter Merkl, in his study of the pre-1933 Nazi movement – a study based on much more data than we have on terrorists – abandoned any attempt to classify personality types and instead focused on factors such as the level of political understanding.[31] An unbiased examination of conscious attitudes might be more revealing than a study of subconscious predispositions or personalities. For example, if terrorists perceive the state as unjust, morally corrupt, and violent, then terrorism may seem legitimate and justified. For example, Blumenthal and her coauthors found that "the stronger the perception of an act as violence, the more violence is thought to be an appropriate response."[32] The evidence also indicates that many terrorists are activists with prior political experience in nonviolent opposition to the state. How do these experiences in participation influence later attitudes? Furthermore, how do terrorists view their victims? Do we find extreme devaluation, depersonalization, or stereotyping? Is there "us vs. them" polarization or ethnic or religious prejudice that might sanction or prompt violence toward an out-group? How do terrorists justify and rationalize violence? Is remorse a theme?

The questions of attitudes toward victims and justifications for terrorism are especially important because different forms of terrorism involve various degrees of selectivity in the choice of victims. Some acts of terrorism are extremely discriminate, while others are broadly indiscriminate. Also, some terrorist acts require more intimate contact between terrorist and victim than others. Thus, the form of terrorism practiced – how selective it is and how much personal domination of the victim it involves – would determine the relevance of different questions.

Analyzing these issues involves serious methodological problems. As the Blumenthal study emphasizes, there are two ways of analyzing the relationship between attitudes and political behavior.[33] If our interest is in identifying potential terrorists by predicting behavior from the existence of certain consciously held attitudes and beliefs, then the best method would be to survey a young age group in a society determined to be susceptible. If terrorism subsequently occurred, we could then see which types of individuals became terrorists. (A problem is that the preconditions would change over time and that precipitants are unpredictable.) The more common and easier way of investigating the attitudes–behavior connection is to select people who have engaged in a particular behavior and ask them questions about their opinions. Yet attitudes may be adopted subsequent, rather than prior, to behavior, and they may serve as rationalizations for behavior engaged in for different reasons, not as genuine motivations. These problems would seem to be particularly acute when the individuals concerned have engaged in illegal forms of political behavior.

Another problem facing the researcher interested in predispositions or attitudes is that terrorists are recruited in different ways. Assuming that people who are in some way personally attracted to terrorism actually engage in such behavior supposes that potential terrorists are presented with an appropriate opportunity, which is a factor over which they have little control.[34] Moreover, terrorist groups often discourage or reject potential recruits who are openly seeking excitement or danger for personal motives. For instance, William Mackey Lomasney, a member of the Clan na Gael or American Fenians in the nineteenth century (who was killed in 1884 in an attempt to blow up London Bridge) condemned the "disgraceful" activities of the hotheaded and impulsive Jeremiah O'Donovan Rossa:

> Were it not that O'Donovan Rossa has openly and unblushingly boasted that he is responsible for those ridiculous and futile efforts . . . we might hesitate to even suspect that any sane man, least of all one professedly friendly to the cause, would for any consideration or desire for notoriety take upon himself such a fearful responsibility, and, that having done so, he could engage men so utterly incapable of carrying out his insane designs.[35]

Lomasney complained that the would-be terrorists were:

> such stupid blundering fools that they make our cause appear imbecile and farcical. When the fact becomes known that those half-idiotic attempts have been made by men professing to be patriotic Irishmen what will the world think but that Irish revolutionists are a lot of fools and ignoramuses, men who do not understand the first principles of the art of war, the elements of chemistry or even the amount of explosive material necessary to remove or destroy an ordinary brick or stone wall. Think of the utter madness of men who have no idea of accumulative and destructive forces undertaking with common blasting powder to scare and shatter the Empire.[36]

Not only do serious terrorists scorn the ineptitude of the more excitable, but they find them a serious security risk. Rossa, for example, could not be trusted not to give away the Clan na Gael's plans for terrorism in his New York newspaper articles. In a similar vein, Boris Savinkov, head of the Combat Organization of the Socialist-Revolutionary party in Russia, tried to discourage an aspirant whom he suspected of being drawn to the adventure of terrorism:

> I explained to him that terrorist activity did not consist only of throwing bombs; that it was much more minute, difficult and tedious than might be imagined; that a terrorist is called upon to live a rather dull existence for months at a time, eschewing meeting his own comrades and doing most difficult and unpleasant work – the work of systematic observation.[37]

Similar problems in analyzing the connection between attitudes and behavior are due to the fact that there are role differentiations between leaders and followers. The degree of formal organization varies from the paramilitary hierarchies of the Irgun or the IRA to the semiautonomous coexistence of small groups in contemporary West Germany or Italy or even to the rejection of central direction in the nineteenth-century anarchist movement in France. Yet even Narodnaya Volya, a self-consciously democratic group, observed distinctions based on authority. There are thus likely to be psychological or background differences between leaders and cadres. For example, a survey of terrorist movements found that leaders are usually older than their followers, which is not historically unusual.[38] In general, data are scant on individual terrorist leaders, their exercise of authority, the basis for it, and their interactions with their followers.[39] Furthermore, if there is a predisposition to terrorism, the terrorism-prone individual who obtains psychic gratification from the experience is likely to be a follower, not a leader who commands but does not perform the act.

An alternative approach to analyzing the psychology of terrorism is to use a deductive method based on what we know about terrorism as an activity, rather than an inductive method yielding general propositions from statements of the particular. What sort of characteristics would make an individual suited for terrorism? What are the role requirements of the terrorist?

One of the most salient attributes of terrorist activity is that it involves significant personal danger.[40] Furthermore, since terrorism involves premeditated, not impulsive, violence, the terrorist's awareness of the risks is maximized. Thus, although terrorists may simply be people who enjoy or disregard risk,[41] it is more likely that they are people who tolerate high risk because of intense commitment to a cause. Their commitment is strong enough to make the risk of personal harm acceptable and perhaps to outweigh the cost of society's rejection, although defiance of the majority may be a reward in itself. In either case, the violent activity is not gratifying per se.

It is perhaps even more significant that terrorism is a group activity, involving intimate relationships among a small number of people. Interactions among members of the group may be more important in determining behavior than the psychological predispositions of individual members. Terrorists live and make decisions under conditions of extreme stress. As a clandestine minority, the members of a terrorist group are isolated from society, even if they live in what Menachem Begin called the "open underground."[42]

Terrorists can confide in and trust only each other. The nature of their commitment cuts them off from society; they inhabit a closed community that is forsaken only at great cost. Isolation and the perception of a hostile environment intensify shared belief and commitment and make faith in the cause imperative. A pattern of mutual reassurance, solidarity, and comradeship develops, in which the members of the group reinforce each other's self-righteousness, image of a hostile world, and sense of mission. Because of the real danger terrorists confront, the strain they live under, and the moral conflicts they undergo, they value solidarity highly.[43] Terrorists are not necessarily people who seek "belonging" or personal integration through ideological commitment, but once embarked on the path of terrorism, they desperately need the group and the cause. Isolation and internal consensus explain how the beliefs and values of a terrorist group can be so drastically at odds with those of society at large. An example of such a divorce from social and political reality is the idea of the RAF that terrorism would lead to a resurgence of Nazism in West Germany that would in turn spark a workers' revolt.[44]

In their intense commitment, separation from the outside world, and intolerance of internal dissent, terrorist groups resemble religious sects or cults. Michael Barkun has explained the continued commitment of members of millenarian movements, a conviction frequently expressed in proselytizing in order to validate beliefs, in terms of the reinforcement and reassurance of rightness that the individual receives from other members of the organization. He also notes the frequent practice of initiation rites that involve violations of taboos, or "bridge-burning acts," that create guilt and prevent the convert's return to society. Thus the millenarian, like the terrorist group, constitutes "a community of common guilt."[45] J. Bowyer Bell has commented on the religious qualities of dedication and moral fervor characterizing the IRA: "In the Republican Movement, the two seemingly opposing traditions, one of the revolution and physical force, and the other of pious and puritanical service, combine into a secular vocation."[46]

If there is a single common emotion that drives the individual to become a terrorist, it is vengeance on behalf of comrades or even the constituency the terrorist aspires to represent. (At the same time, the demand for retribution serves as public justification or excuse.) A regime thus encourages terrorism when it creates martyrs to be avenged. Anger at what is perceived as unjust persecution inspires demands for revenge, and as the regime responds to terrorism with greater force, violence escalates out of control.

There are numerous historical demonstrations of the central role vengeance plays as motivation for terrorism. It is seen as one of the principal causes of anarchist terrorism in France in the 1890s. The infamous Ravachol acted to avenge the "martyrs of Clichy," two possibly innocent anarchists who were beaten by the police and sentenced to prison. Subsequent bombings and assassinations, for instance that of President Carnot, were intended to avenge Ravachol's execution.[47] The cruelty of the sentences imposed for minor offenses at the "Trial of the 193," the hanging of eleven southern revolutionaries after Soloviev's unsuccessful attack on the czar in 1879, and the "Trial of the 16" in 1880 deeply affected the members of Narodnaya Volya. Kravchinski (Stepniak) explained that personal resentment felt after the Trial of the 193 led to killing police spies; it then seemed unreasonable to spare their employers, who were actually responsible for the repression. Thus, intellectually the logic first inspired by resentment compelled them to escalate terrorism by degrees.[48] During the Algerian war, the French execution of FLN prisoners; in Northern Ireland, British troops firing on civil rights demonstrators; in West Germany, the death of a demonstrator at the hands of the police – all served to precipitate terrorism as militants sought to avenge their comrades.

The terrorists' willingness to accept high risks may also be related to the belief that one's death will be avenged. The prospect of retribution gives the act of terrorism and the death of the terrorist meaning and continuity, even fame and immortality. Vengeance may be not only a function of anger but of a desire for transcendence.

Shared guilt is surely a strong force in binding members of the terrorist group together. Almost all terrorists seem compelled to justify their behavior, and this anxiety cannot be explained solely by reference to their desire to create a public image of virtuous sincerity. Terrorists usually show acute concern for morality, especially for sexual purity, and believe that they act in terms of a higher good. Justifications usually focus on past suffering, on the glorious future to be created, and on the regime's illegitimacy and violence, to which terrorism is the only available response. Shared guilt and anxiety increase the group's interdependence and mutual commitment and may also make followers more dependent on leaders and on the common ideology as sources of moral authority.

Guilt may also lead terrorists to seek punishment and danger rather than avoid it. The motive of self-sacrifice notably influenced many Russian terrorists of the nineteenth century. Kaliayev, for example, felt that only his death could atone for the murder he committed. Even to Camus, the risk of death for the terrorist is a form of personal absolution.[49] In other cases of terrorism, individuals much more pragmatic than Kaliayev, admittedly a religious mystic, seemed to welcome capture because it brought release from the strains of underground existence and a sense of content and fulfillment. For example, Meridor, a member of the Irgun High Command, felt "high spirits" and "satisfaction" when arrested by the British because he now shared the suffering that all fighters had to experience. He almost welcomed the opportunity to prove that he was prepared to sacrifice himself for the cause. In fact, until his arrest he had felt "morally uncomfortable," whereas afterwards he felt "exalted."[50] Menachem Begin expressed similar feelings. Once, waiting as the British searched the hotel where he was staying, he admitted anxiety and fear, but when he knew there was "no way out," his "anxious thoughts evaporated." He "felt a peculiar serenity mixed with incomprehensible happiness" and waited "composedly," but the police passed him by.[51]

Vera Figner, a leader of the Narodnaya Volya, insisted on physically assisting in acts of terrorism, even though her comrades accused her of seeking personal satisfaction instead of allowing the organization to make the best use of her talents. She found it intolerable to bear a moral responsibility for acts that endangered her comrades. She could not encourage others to commit acts she would not herself commit; anything less than full acceptance of the consequences of her decisions would be cowardice.[52]

It is possible that the willingness to face risk is related to what Robert J. Lifton has termed "survivor-guilt" as well as to feelings of group solidarity or of guilt at harming victims.[53] Sometimes individuals who survive disaster or escape punishment when others have suffered feel guilty and may seek relief by courting a similar fate. This guilt may also explain why terrorists often take enormous risks to rescue imprisoned comrades, as well as why they accept danger or arrest with equanimity or even satisfaction.

It is clear that once a terrorist group embarks on a strategy of terrorism, whatever its purpose and whatever its successes or failures, psychological factors make it very difficult to halt. Terrorism as a process gathers its own momentum, independent of external events.

Conclusions

Terrorism per se is not usually a reflection of mass discontent or deep cleavages in society. More often it represents the disaffection of a fragment of the elite, who may take it upon themselves to act on the behalf of a majority unaware of its plight, unwilling to take action to remedy grievances, or unable to express dissent. This discontent, however subjective in origin or minor in scope, is blamed on the government and its supporters. Since the sources of terrorism are manifold, any society or polity that permits opportunities for terrorism is vulnerable. Government reactions that are inconsistent, wavering between tolerance and repression, seem most likely to encourage terrorism.

Given some source of disaffection – and in the centralized modern state with its faceless bureaucracies, lack of responsiveness to demands is ubiquitous – terrorism is an attractive strategy for small organizations of diverse ideological persuasions who want to attract attention for their cause, provoke the government, intimidate opponents, appeal for sympathy, impress an audience, or promote the adherence of the faithful. Terrorists perceive an absence of choice. Whether unable or unwilling to perceive a choice between terrorist and nonterrorist action, whether unpopular or prohibited by the government, the terrorist group reasons that there is no alternative. The ease, simplicity, and rapidity with which terrorism can be implemented and the prominence of models of terrorism strengthen its appeal, especially since terrorist groups are impatient to act. Long-standing social traditions that sanction terrorism against the state, as in Ireland, further enhance its attractiveness.

There are two fundamental questions about the psychological basis of terrorism. The first is why the individual takes the first step and chooses to engage in terrorism: Why join? Does the terrorist possess specific psychological predispositions, identifiable in advance, that suit him or her for terrorism? That terrorists are people capable of intense commitment tells us little, and the motivations for terrorism vary immensely. Many individuals are potential terrorists, but few actually make that commitment. To explain why terrorism happens, another question is more appropriate: Why does involvement continue? What are the psychological mechanisms of group interaction? We are not dealing with a situation in which certain types of personalities suddenly turn to terrorism in answer to some inner call. Terrorism is the result of a gradual growth of commitment and opposition, a group development that furthermore depends on government action. The psychological relationships within the terrorist group – the interplay of commitment, risk, solidarity, loyalty, guilt, revenge, and isolation – discourage terrorists from changing the direction they have taken. This may explain why – even if objective circumstances change when, for example, grievances are satisfied, or if the logic of the situation changes when, for example, the terrorists are offered other alternatives for the expression of opposition – terrorism may endure until the terrorist group is physically destroyed.

3 "Old" vs. "new" terrorism[1]

After the attacks of September 11, 2001, many policy makers, journalists, consultants, and scholars were convinced that the world was confronting a "new" terrorism unlike the terrorism of the past.[2] Thus the U.S. government and policy elites were blamed for not recognizing the danger of the new terrorism in the 1990s and therefore failing to prevent the disaster of September 11.[3] From this perspective, knowledge of the "old" or traditional terrorism is irrelevant at best, and obsolete and anachronistic, even harmful, at worst. Those who believe in a new terrorism think that the old paradigms should be discarded and replaced with a new understanding.[4]

For example, Bruce Hoffman concluded that

> The growth of religious terrorism and its emergence in recent years as a driving force behind the increasing lethality of international terrorism shatters some of our most basic assumptions about terrorists and the violence they commit. It also raises serious questions about the continued relevance of much of the conventional wisdom on terrorism particularly as it pertains to potential future terrorist use of WMD.[5]

He argued that assumptions that terrorism might be restrained might still apply to most secular terrorists, but that they appear to be dangerously anachronistic with respect to religious terrorists.

In 2000, however, in responding to Simon and Benjamin, Hoffman adjusted his views to suggest that the idea of a "profound and potentially catastrophic change in the nature of terrorism today," is "by no means as certain or even convincing as it is often portrayed . . ."[6] He warned against threat exaggeration, since however fanatical or irrational the new terrorists might seem, they remained operationally conservative, and that the era of new terrorism had not in fact materialized. Simon and Benjamin in turn responded that they were

> intrigued by Hoffman's heavy reliance on arguments based on historical inference at a time of dramatic change in the ideology of important terrorist groups and rapid technological advances. To be sure, history should be consulted, but it is by no means a foolproof predictor.[7]

Other analysts, primarily from the academic community, challenge this interpretation.[8] For example, Thomas Copeland argues that the old terrorism never really went away, that it is too soon to declare a new paradigm, and that the idea of a new terrorism is a particularly American way of framing the threat.[9] Duyvesteyn argues for continuity rather than rupture. She also notes the lack of historical research to substantiate the claim that current terrorism is new.[10]

If a new explanation of terrorism is necessary, what are the puzzles that the old paradigm cannot solve? The problem that stands out in the discussions is the increasing lethality of terrorism and the role of religion in motivating both terrorism and unusually deadly terrorism, extending to the deliberate pursuit of appropriately catastrophic weapons. The idea that the world confronted a new threat appears to have taken hold after the 1993 World Trade Center bombing, although Benjamin and Simon argue that the phenomenon began in 1990, with the assassination of Meir Kahane in New York.[11] The argument was well established, and had been criticized in turn, by the time of the September 11 attacks. The idea that there was a distinctively "religious" terrorism began to develop with the growth of radical Islamic movements after the Iranian revolution, particularly as a reaction to the use of suicide bombings in Lebanon, which began in the early 1980s. The 1993 World Trade Center bombing and the discovery of subsequent ambitious plots instigated by Ramzi Youcef (such as the so-called "bojinka" plot, which involved blowing up airliners over the Pacific) caused alarm because of the prospect of large numbers of civilian casualties, but also because of the apparent inchoate nature of the source of terrorism. The fear that terrorism could cause mass casualties was exacerbated by the prospect of terrorist groups acquiring nuclear, chemical, biological, or radiological weapons, especially considering the insecurity that followed the collapse of the Soviet Union.[12] The new terrorism idea gained momentum with the 1995 Aum Shinrikyo sarin gas attacks on the Tokyo subway and the bombing of the federal building in Oklahoma City by Timothy McVeigh. Growing awareness of the extent of the Al Qaeda conspiracy caused more alarm, especially after Osama Bin Laden moved from the Sudan to Afghanistan and called for jihad against the United States in 1996.[13] The 1998 bombings of American embassies in Kenya and Tanzania, the attack on the USS *Cole* in the port of Yemen in 2000, and the discovery of the millennium plots strengthened the perception of a new threat. After the September 11 attacks, the anthrax letters in the United States further heightened fears of the use of unconventional weapons. Since 2003, the global spread of suicide bombings against civilian targets has contributed to the feeling that terrorism has changed fundamentally.

It is critical to examine systematically the assumptions on which the appeal for the new paradigm is based and to question both their logic and empirical foundation before accepting them as self-evident. Accounts of a new terrorism have not always been grounded in sufficient knowledge of history or understanding of contemporary terrorism. The point is not that there has been no change in terrorism over the past century but that the changes that have occurred need to be precisely delineated. An assessment of change can be completed only by careful fact-based comparisons. What is needed in the argument for a new terrorism is careful specification of the concept of a new terrorism and of the distinction between new and old. First, what are the specific definitional attributes of the new terrorism? How are they different from those of the old? Second, a satisfactory theoretical framework needs to clarify which groups or practices belong in which category and explain how these cases satisfy the requirements of the definition.

My contention is that the departure from the past is not as pronounced as many accounts make it out to be. Today's terrorism is not a fundamentally or qualitatively new phenomenon but grounded in an evolving historical context.[14] Much of what we see now is familiar, and the differences are of degree rather than kind. Contemporary terrorism shares many of the characteristics of past terrorism, dating back at least to the late nineteenth century and the use of terrorism by groups of Russian revolutionaries, European anarchists, and Irish nationalists.

For example, accounts of new terrorism cite the common characteristic of religious doctrine as motivation.[15] However, although the new terrorists are all supposedly religious, not all religious groups are deemed to be new. The groups that are typically cited as examples of the genre are radical or jihadist Islamists in general (e.g., Al Qaeda, Al Qaeda in Mesopotamia, Jemaah al-Islamiya in Indonesia, the Abu Sayyaf Group in the Philippines, and the Salafist Group for Preaching and Combat in Algeria), the Christian Identity movement and its offshoots in the United States (including Timothy McVeigh, although it is not certain that he represented an organized group, and the attribution of a religious motivation to his violence is problematic), Ramzi Youcef and his cohort, Aum Shinrikyo, and the Jewish radical groups that plotted to blow up the Dome of the Rock and assassinated Israeli Prime Minister Itzhak Rabin. Hamas, however, is not included. The case of Hezbollah is treated with ambivalence; it is included by some (e.g., Hoffman) but not others (e.g., Simon and Benjamin). Laqueur includes Hezbollah, the LTTE, and the Taliban since he considers some nationalist groups to be in the "new terrorism" category.[16] Jessica Stern includes far-right groups and millenarian cults.[17]

Clarification of the distinction between categories is hard to find in the new terrorism literature. The National Memorial Institute for the Prevention of Terrorism's Terrorism Knowledge Base (TKB), which is based on event data collected by the Rand Corporation since 1968, lists 130 groups in the category of religious terrorism.[18] Of these 130 cases, 124 are linked to descriptive group profiles, which indicate that only fifty-four of the cases are labeled as exclusively religious. Almost all the others are simultaneously classified as national separatist groups, although reasons for classifications are not provided. Nevertheless, if it is the case, as Simon argues, that "the explicitly religious character of the 'new terrorism' poses a profound security challenge for the United States," are we to understand the statement to mean those groups that are only religious or those groups that are both religious and nationalist?[19] Which orientation will determine their actions? Why would Hamas be considered a nationalist group when it calls for the establishment of an Islamic state?

If old terrorism refers to secular groups or groups existing before 1990 and the end of the Cold War, we have over 400 examples, and more if we go back to the nineteenth century. Accounts of the new terrorism are not specific or comprehensive on this score. For example, Steven Simon lists only the Irish Republican Army, the Red Brigades in Italy, and the Palestine Liberation Organization as examples of "conventional" terrorist groups.[20] At another point, Simon and Benjamin associate the old terrorism with state sponsorship.[21]

There is a further problem. Even if a conceptual distinction between two types of terrorism can be established, it is not clear whether there is a chronological dimension. Should we assume that the new is replacing the old? When was the transition? If not, how do we explain the persistence of the old as well as the emergence of the new? David Rapoport dealt with these questions in analyzing the historical evolution of terrorism in terms of "waves," which in his terms are "cycles of activity in a given time period" characterized by a common international "energy" or ideology.[22] All waves feature nationalist movements that take on different forms according to the nature of the "wave," whether driven by anarchism, anti-colonialism, "New Left ideology," or now religion. Each wave ebbs as the new wave gathers strength. Although Rapoport does not espouse the idea that the religious wave is qualitatively different from preceding waves, he does see a process of replacement rather than coexistence. Although Simon and Benjamin are among the leading proponents of the new terrorism point of view, they have at times referred to the old paradigm being "joined by" rather than replaced by the new.[23] Laqueur also thinks that new and old coexist.[24]

In order to make the argument that old and new have more in common than proponents of a new terrorism seem to think, I analyze the propositions of the new terrorism school concerning the goals, methods, and organizational structure and resources of groups practicing terrorism.

Goals

First, the *ends* of the new terrorism are presumed to be both unlimited and nonnegotiable. These aims are also considered largely incomprehensible and amorphous. From the perspective of the new terrorism school of thought, the goals of new terrorists are derived exclusively from religious doctrines that emphasize transformational and apocalyptic beliefs, usually associated with Islam although they are assumed to be present in all monotheistic religions. Millenarianism is a key belief. Walter Laqueur, for example, characterizes the new terrorists as religious fanatics who suffer from delusion and persecution mania.[25] As his views indicate, some confusion exists over levels of analysis, since it is not clear whether it is individual motivation or group purpose that is being described.

In the world of politics, the new terrorists are presumed to hate Western and especially American values, culture, civilization, and existence. As Ambassador L. Paul Bremer expressed it, it is not that they do not understand us: "They hate America precisely because they *do* understand our society; they hate its freedoms, its commitment to equal rights and universal suffrage, its material successes and its appeals. . . ."[26] President Bush described the enemy thus:

> we face an enemy which cannot stand freedom. It's an enemy which has an ideology that does not believe in free speech, free religion, free dissent, does not believe in women's rights, and they have a desire to impose their ideology on much of the world.[27]

Further,

> we're not facing a set of grievances that can be soothed and addressed. We're facing a radical ideology with inalterable objectives: to enslave whole nations and intimidate the world. No act of ours invited the rage of the killers – and no concession, bribe, or act of appeasement would change or limit their plans for murder.[28]

The new terrorism threat is compared to the existential threat of Communism during the Cold War, not past terrorism.[29] In terms of this analogy, it is described as totalitarian and compared to the fascism that led to World War II.

The goals of terrorism are inextricably linked to the means, according to this point of view. The new terrorists are fanatics unconstrained by any respect for human life. Violence is at the heart of their beliefs. There is some ambiguity about whether violence is "strategic," since Simon and Benjamin argue that for the new actors terrorism is used strategically and not tactically, by which they mean killing is an end in itself.[30] If destruction is an end in itself rather than the means to an end, then it is not strategic but expressive. Nevertheless, the assumption of the new terrorism school of thought is that rather than choosing among alternative ways of achieving political ends, the new terrorists seek primarily to kill. Lethality is their aim rather than their means. As Benjamin and Simon explained in an editorial in the *New York Times* in early 2000,

> The terrorists allied with Mr. bin Laden do not want a place at the table: they want to shatter the table. They are not constrained by secular political concerns. Their objective is not to influence, but to kill, and in large numbers – hence their declared interest in acquiring chemical and even nuclear weapons. It is just this combination – religious motivation and a desire to inflict catastrophic damage – that is new to terrorism.[31]

The goals of the old terrorism, by contrast, are thought to have been negotiable and limited. Their ambitions were local, not global.[32] The aims of old terrorists were understandable and tangible, typically related to issues of nationalism and territorial autonomy. Deals could be struck. The state could bargain with the old terrorists. Conflicts could be resolved. In effect, these were presumably sensible terrorists whose objectives were realistic and pragmatic. As Laqueur describes the comparison, even the most indiscriminate of the old terrorists, which he locates in the second half of the twentieth century, hesitated at true mass murder because they feared a backlash and because such actions were alien to their traditions. He continues, "They hated their enemies, but they had not been totally blinded by their hate. For the radical religious practitioners of the new terrorism, however, murder and destruction on an unprecedented scale did not pose much of a problem."[33] Hoffman explains that

> Whereas secular terrorists regard violence either as a way of instigating the correction of a flaw in a system that is basically good or as a means to foment the creation of a new system, religious terrorists see themselves not as components of a system worth preserving but as "outsiders," seeking fundamental changes in the existing system.[34]

Is this an accurate depiction of the old terrorism? Unobtainable ends and flamboyantly bloodthirsty rhetoric are not unique to religion or to the contemporary political environment. The European anarchist movement of the late nineteenth century (of which the proponents of terrorism were a fringe) sought to abolish all government as well as capitalist society. Sendero Luminoso wished to establish a Maoist regime in Peru. Its leader, Abimael Guzman, launched the war in 1980 with a speech titled "We are the Initiators," which asserts that

> we begin the strategic offensive for world revolution, the next 50 years will see imperialism's dominion swept away along with all exploiters. . . . The people's war will grow every day until the old order is pulled down, the world is entering a new era.[35]

The speech continues,

> The people rear up, arm themselves, and rise in revolution to put the noose around the neck of imperialism and the reactionaries, seizing them by the throat and garroting them. They are strangled, necessarily. The flesh of the reactionaries will rot away, converted into ragged threads, and this black filth will sink into the mud; that which remains will be burned and the ashes scattered by the earth's winds so that only the sinister memory will remain of that which will never return, because it neither can nor should return.[36]

In the 1970s, revolutionary organizations in Germany (the Red Army faction) and Italy (the Red Brigades), with little to no popular support, thought that they could overthrow well-established liberal democracies, bring down NATO, and deal a death blow to imperialism.[37] Separatist organizations are not immune from overreaching. ETA sought to establish a Basque state that would include regions of both France and Spain. It was not particularly reasonable of Palestinian groups such as the Abu Nidal Organization or the Popular Front for the Liberation of Palestine, or Libya, to believe that they could destroy the state of Israel or bring about revolution in the Arab world. Patrick Seale, in a biography of Abu Nidal, describes his terrorism as "fitful and purposeless," "incoherent, incompetent, and invariably counterproductive to Palestinian interests." There was no "strategic vision":

> His claim that he wanted to prevent a compromise between the PLO and Israel so as to recover Palestine was not a credible objective. The vast imbalance of strength between Israel and its opponents made such pursuit suicidal. By degrading the Palestinian liberation struggle to mere criminal violence, Abu Nidal offered Israel the pretext for refusing to negotiate and to giving the Palestinians nothing but the sword.[38]

Do the new terrorism proponents' assumptions about objectives describe the new terrorism? Are such groups led by apocalyptic visionaries with no appreciation of reality? Groups claiming to act in the name of religious doctrine may be more extreme in their rhetoric than in their preferences (although analysis of their rhetoric is certainly worthwhile). They have often shown themselves to be astute political strategists, using terrorism successfully to compel the withdrawal of foreign military forces or to disrupt peace processes. Hezbollah is an excellent example, having transformed itself into a political party as well as a resistance organization. Some regional experts have interpreted Al Qaeda's activities in pragmatic terms.[39] Bin Laden's stated goal of expelling American military forces from Muslim territories is quite specific. He cites the encouraging historical precedents of Vietnam, Somalia, and Lebanon, as well as the Soviet withdrawal from Afghanistan.[40] His interpretations may not be completely accurate, but they are not illogical. Many other examples of pragmatism can be found in internal Al Qaeda documents captured by American forces.[41] Just as secular nationalist groups such as ETA and even the IRA took on a Marxist-Leninist veneer when it was ideologically fashionable to do so, nationalistic or revolutionary groups today may take on an Islamist cast. The Moro National Liberation Front became the Moro Islamic Liberation Front, and secular nationalist Fatah produced the Al Aqsa Martyrs Brigade as a rival to Hamas and Palestinian Islamic Jihad.

As noted above, whether these extreme motivations are individual or collective is not clear. For example, Walter Laqueur's account focuses more on the motivations or "mind-sets" of the individual than the objectives of the group. He says, for example, that the new terrorists, whose motivations include rage, aggression, sadism, and paranoia as well as fanaticism, can be found on the fringes of any extremist movement.[42] At other times he is contradictory; he seems to imply that the motive for terrorism, fanaticism, has not changed but that the availability of weapons has. At yet other times he suggests that religious fanaticism is different. The "new breed" of terrorist is said to enjoy killing.[43]

Marc Sageman, while asserting that the world faces a new type of terrorism driven by networks of fanatics, actually describes the jihadists about whom he was able to acquire biographical information in terms that are not dramatically different from descriptions of secular revolutionary terrorists.[44] He concludes that "Members of the global Salafi jihad were generally middle-class, educated young men from caring and religious families, who grew up with strong positive values of religion, spirituality, and concern for their communities."[45] Like the groups in the West in the 1970s and 1980s, they did not come from poor backgrounds. Their education was largely modern. They exhibited no signs of psychopathology. As is the case with the old terrorism, the group mattered more than the individual: "Social bonds are the critical element in this process [of joining the jihad] and precede ideological commitment."[46] They were not transformed into terrorists out of hatred for the United States.

A finding that remains constant over time is that while some members of radical organizations are motivated by sincere beliefs in the cause, others are less committed to doctrine. Individual militants may be manipulated by their leaders. Undoubtedly all members of the groups designated as new terrorists are not religious "fanatics."[47] Within Al Qaeda, the concerns of militants are often mundane and prosaic, such as salary disputes.

As Stephen Holmes observes with regard to the September 11 attacks,

> Many of the key actors in the 9/11 drama, admittedly, articulate their grievances using archaic religious language. But the very fact that the code involved is ancient while the behaviour we want to explain is recent suggests the inadequacy of causal theories that overemphasize the religious element.[48]

Holmes argues instead for a political explanation. He notes that Bin Laden's public statements stress secular rationales for the September 11 attacks and that historical circumstances rather than religion led Al Qaeda to target the United States. Because the governments of Egypt and Saudi Arabia could not be overthrown by force, Al Qaeda turned to the "far enemy." He concludes: "What hit the United States on 11 September was not religion, therefore. Instead, the September 11 terrorists represented the *pooled insurgencies* of the Arab Middle East."[49]

Journalist Terry McDermott also investigated the backgrounds of the September 11 hijackers.[50] He concluded that these men were ordinary. The Hamburg cell that provided the pilots was bound together by affiliation with the Al Quds mosque. The group had formed well before it was recruited to the Al Qaeda plot. All but one of the other hijackers were from Saudi Arabia. As McDermott points out, we know less about them because "Saudi Arabia has been parsimonious with the information in its hands, which is considerable, and has made the discovery of information by others difficult."[51] However, he notes that they were from an isolated province that was a stronghold of conservative religious belief. They were not poor and were relatively well educated. Jobs, however, were lacking, and the tradition of leaving home to participate in jihad abroad had been well established since the 1980s and the appeal to fight against the Soviet Union in Afghanistan. From a pragmatic point of view, it was easier for Saudi citizens to get American visas than it was for other nationalities from which hijackers might have been recruited.

Journalists Peter Bergen and Swati Pandey analyzed the seventy-nine individuals responsible for the 1993 World Trade Center bombing, the 1998 bombings of the

U.S. embassies in Kenya and Tanzania, the September 11 attacks, the 2002 Bali nightclub bombings, and the 2005 London bombings. They confirmed that

> History has taught that terrorism has been a largely bourgeois endeavor, from the Russian anarchists of the late nineteenth century to the German Marxists of the Bader-Meinhof gang of the 1970s to the apocalyptic Japanese terror cult Aum Shinrikyo of the 1990s. Islamist terrorists turn out to be no different.[52]

The terrorists were neither poor nor undereducated. More than half of those studied had some university education. None had attended a madrassa, Islamic schools that American officials have often considered the hotbeds of Islamic extremism.

Methods

Second, the *means* of the new terrorism are also assumed to be radically different from the past. The premise is that because the ends of the new terrorism are unlimited, so, too, are the means that groups espousing these goals are willing and able to use. The new terrorists are supposed to be dedicated to causing the largest possible number of casualties among their enemies. According to Walter Laqueur, "The new terrorism is different in character [from the old], aiming not at clearly defined political demands but at the destruction of society and the elimination of large sections of the population."[53] According to Steven Simon, "Religiously motivated terrorism, as Bruce Hoffman of the Rand Corporation first noted in 1997, is inextricably linked to pursuit of mass casualties."[54] Presumably for the new terrorists the means have become an end in themselves, not a way of reaching an audience other than a deity. They are not concerned with public support. The new terrorists seek only to destroy, and their deaths will result only in the reaching of the millennium and a place in paradise, not political change in the here and now.

Thus the new terrorists are also thought to be significantly more inclined than secular groups to use "weapons of mass destruction." Jessica Stern, for example, argues that the risk of terrorist use of nuclear, chemical, or biological weapons against civilians is growing not only because of the increased availability of such weapons but because of changes in terrorist motivation: "A new breed of terrorists – including ad hoc groups motivated by religious conviction or revenge, violent right-wing extremists, and apocalyptic and millenarian cults – appears more likely than the terrorists of the past to commit acts of extreme violence."[55]

The old terrorism is considered to be much more restrained and specific in targeting. The traditional terrorist wanted people watching, not people dead, according to Brian Jenkins' now famous aphorism. Hoffman describes the old terrorists as selective and discriminating.[56] Benjamin and Simon say past terrorists used "carefully calibrated violence" because "they knew that excessive brutality would deny them the place they sought at the bargaining table."[57] These terrorists imposed restraints on their actions because they aimed to change the attitudes of audiences who could help them achieve their goals. Although capable of being more destructive, they chose not to be. Their audiences and reference groups were tangible and present. They were limited by their dependence on constituencies and by their political interests. Their pursuit of legitimacy, in effect, restrained their behavior.

However, the old terrorists were not always discriminating in their choice of targets. Levels of selectivity and restraint vary across groups and across time, but not according to a religious-secular or past-present divide. A few examples show that killing large numbers is not restricted to groups espousing religious doctrines, although no single attack was near as deadly as September 11.[58] The French anarchists of the 1880s bombed restaurants frequented by the bourgeoisie in order to show the working class who the true enemy was. "No bourgeois is innocent" was their slogan. The history of anarchism in Spain was particularly violent. Martin Miller refers to a "will to destroy" in the European anarchist movement.[59]

Nationalist groups have also caused mass casualties. In 1946, the bombing of the King David Hotel in Jerusalem by Zionist extremists killed ninety-one and injured forty-five.[60] During the Algerian war, the FLN attacked Europeans indiscriminately, leaving bombs in cafes, on beaches, in soccer stadiums, and at bus stops in Algiers during the famous "Battle of Algiers." Their bombs often killed Algerians as well as Europeans. (The FLN also considered bombing the Eiffel Tower, in a campaign to bring the war home to France. They did bomb oil refineries near Marseille.)

Would-be revolutionaries could also be extremely lethal. The Japanese Red Army's attack on the Tel Aviv airport in 1972 killed twenty-four and wounded eighty people, most Puerto Rican pilgrims. The secular regime of Colonel Qaddafi was responsible for the midair bombing of Pan Am Flight 103 in 1988, which left 270 dead.

Far-right extremists have also been willing and able to cause mass casualties; for instance, eighty-five people were killed in the bombing of the Bologna railroad station in 1980.[61] As the Algerian war concluded, the Organisation de l'armée secrete (OAS) adopted a scorched earth policy of indiscriminate terrorism against Muslims. For example, on May 2, 1962 a car bomb on the Algiers docks killed sixty-two and wounded 110 among a crowd of Algerians waiting for day work.[62] It is also fair to say that Timothy McVeigh's actions should be placed in the category of rightwing extremism rather than religion.

The issue of possible resort to weapons of mass destruction is complicated. Aum Shinrikyo is the only group so far to have employed self-manufactured chemical weapons against a civilian population.[63] Terrorists have not used nuclear or radiological weapons to any serious destructive effect despite official concern over the prospect since at least 1976.[64] While both Aum Shinrikyo and Al Qaeda demonstrated a commitment to acquiring nuclear materials and devices, neither was successful despite their extensive resources, and, in Al Qaeda's case, state sanctuary.[65] However, Al Qaeda is known to have tested nerve gas in Afghanistan, and chlorine has been used opportunistically in Iraq, probably by Al Qaeda-linked groups. Al Qaeda also apparently planned to use chemical weapons in an attack on New York subways in 2003.[66]

While the September 11 hijackings caused the highest number of casualties of any single terrorist attack in history, other Al Qaeda or Al Qaeda-related terrorism has (fortunately) caused fewer casualties (overall and per incident) and has not involved such innovative methods or sophisticated planning. The bombings in Bali in 2002 (202 killed), Madrid in 2004 (191 killed), and London in 2005 (fifty-two killed) were tragically destructive, but not fundamentally dissimilar to past bombings by secular groups in crowded public venues.[67] Simultaneous explosions may be a hallmark of Al Qaeda, but such coordination was also characteristic of Palestinian nationalist groups in the 1970s. For example, the Popular Front for the Liberation of Palestine hijacked three airliners to Jordan simultaneously in 1970.

More evidence of strategic discrimination in targeting and practical concern for the future is found in the July 2005 letter from Ayman al-Zawahiri, former head of Egyptian Islamic Jihad and Bin Laden's second in command in Al Qaeda, to the late Abu Musab al-Zarqawi, leader of the Iraqi branch "Al Qaeda in Mesopotamia." The document is sharply critical of indiscriminate terrorism against ordinary Shia in Iraq, especially attacks on mosques. Zawahiri warns that sectarian terrorism will undermine the popular support that is essential to seizing power in the Sunni areas of Iraq following an anticipated American withdrawal. He cautions that any action that the masses do not understand or approve must be avoided, and he notes numerous questions about the wisdom and rightness of anti-Shia terrorism that were circulating among even Zarqawi's supporters.[68]

Looking further at the purported association between religion and lethality, it is instructive to evaluate the twenty most lethal of the groups classified as religious in the Memorial Institute for the Prevention of Terrorism (MIPT) Terrorism Knowledge Base. Each was responsible for over 100 total fatalities through December of 2005. However, only nine of the twenty are classified as *exclusively* religious. They include Al Qaeda and Al Qaeda affiliates in Europe, the Armed Islamic Group in Algeria, the Lord's Resistance Army in Uganda, Jemaah al-Islamiya in Indonesia, al-Gama'a al-Islamiya in Egypt, the Taliban in Afghanistan, and, curiously, Ansar Allah, which is regarded as an offshoot of Lebanese Hezbollah, an organization considered to have mixed motives. (Ansar Allah is thought to have used suicide bombings against Jewish and Israeli targets in Argentina in 1992 and 1994.) Ansar al-Sunnah in Iraq is considered purely religious, while other Iraqi groups are defined as national separatist as well. The other hybrid groups are (1) in Palestine, Hamas, and Palestinian Islamic Jihad; (2) three associated with the struggle in Chechnya; (3) three originating in the war in Iraq; (4) Lashkar-e-Taiba in Kashmir and Pakistan; (5) the Abu Sayyaf Group in the Philippines; (6) Hezbollah; and (7) the Moro Islamic Liberation Front in the Philippines. Thus purely religious groups killed a total of 6,120 people, and hybrid or mixed groups killed 4,657. Unfortunately the database does not explain the distinction between purely religious and hybrid groups. Most Africa specialists, for example, would not necessarily consider the Lord's Resistance Army in Uganda to be primarily a religious group.

There are other problems with the factual claim that religion is invariably associated with increased lethality.[69] The MIPT events database did not include domestic incidents until after 1998. Thus older groups that used extensive violence at home against local targets will be underweighted in the comparisons. For example, in 2003 the Peruvian Truth and Reconciliation Commission reported that between 1980 and 2000 Sendero Luminoso was responsible for fifty-four percent of the 69,280 total deaths in the conflict, thus over 37,000 people.[70] Although one might not define all of Sendero's violence as terrorism, the victims included in the tally were not from the security forces but from the civilian population. By contrast, the MIPT Terrorism Knowledge Base credits Sendero Luminoso with only 133 fatalities and 267 injuries from 1968 to the present. This discrepancy is significant. Furthermore, over time small group or individual access to destructive technologies as well as their knowledge of target vulnerabilities (i.e., capability rather than motivation) has increased. If most new groups are categorized as religious, the results will be biased because a number of factors come together to produce increased deadliness in the contemporary world. One cause of high numbers of civilian casualties, for example, is the adoption of suicide missions as a tactic of terrorism, which is practiced by both secular and religious groups.[71] The Liberation Tigers of Tamil Eelam in Sri Lanka are a prominent illustration.

Organization and resources

The *organization* of the new terrorism is also thought to be fundamentally different from earlier structures of terrorist actors. The new terrorists are said to be decentralized, with a "flat" networked apparatus rather than a hierarchical or cellular structure.[72] Subunits are supposed to have substantial autonomy, if not complete independence, and the scope is transnational (global reach). Much of the new terrorism is thought to be inspirational rather than directed from the top; it is diffuse rather than concentrated. The American government now says that the war on terrorism is against an ideology rather than an organized entity. Laqueur says that the new terrorism uses smaller groups that, in his view, are more radical.[73] Hoffman adds that the new groups are likely to be composed of amateurs rather than professional terrorists who devote their lives and careers to the cause; they are likely also to be less well trained and to rely on information they collect themselves, primarily from the internet.[74] Simon and Benjamin add that the absence of state support is a key feature.[75]

By contrast, the old terrorist structure was considered to be centralized and top-down. As Hoffman described it,

> In the past, terrorist groups were recognizable mostly as collections of individuals belonging to an organization with a well-defined command and control apparatus, who had been previously trained (in however rudimentary a fashion) in the techniques and tactics of terrorism, were engaged in conspiracy as a full-time avocation, living underground while constantly planning and

plotting terrorist attacks, and who at times were under the direct control, or operated at the express behest, of a foreign government . . .[76]

Hierarchies operated. The classic cellular structure was paramount.

Although Al Qaeda is a transnational actor, it is problematic to assume that it is entirely different from the past, that it is necessarily a model for the future, or that secular groups might not organize themselves similarly. First, among "religious" groups, Al Qaeda is the only example of such a network or franchise/venture capital operation. Other "religious" groups are more traditional in form (Hezbollah, Hamas, or Egyptian Islamic Jihad). Aum Shinrikyo was extremely hierarchical; like Sendero Luminoso, it was dominated by a charismatic leader. Second, before the war in Afghanistan in 2001, Al Qaeda was largely a centralized organization. Its functioning depended on extensive face-to-face communication. Apparently some actions were ordered by the top leadership, but there was also some local autonomy. The importance of the shared experience, socialization, and training in Afghanistan and subsequent access to recruits from diasporas and from other conflict zones cannot be underestimated in the organizational development of Al Qaeda. Its subsequent decentralization may not have been a choice but an adaptation to the loss of sanctuary in Afghanistan, pressure from security services around the world, and the war in Iraq.

Furthermore, the organization of the old or "canonical" terrorism was not always as tight and hierarchical as it might now appear. Peter Merkl, for example, has argued that the apparently monolithic quality of the Red Army Faction in West Germany was a myth.[77] The nineteenth-century anarchists formed a transnational conspiracy, linking activists in Russia, Germany, Switzerland, France, Spain, Italy, and the United States. The essence of anarchism was antipathy to central direction, and much terrorism was locally generated or inspirational. Well-publicized trials of anarchists would invariably spark retaliation by sympathizers who were not members of any organization. The secular Palestinian groups of the 1970s and 1980s split, merged, resplit, and remerged. The relationship of Black September to Arafat and Fatah was one of indirection and deniability. West German and Japanese groups cooperated with Palestinians; in fact, the Japanese Red Army relocated to Lebanon after being driven from Japan. In addition, some of the more hierarchical groups in the past actually allowed significant local autonomy. The Active Service Units of the IRA, for example, sometimes acted independently, without the approval of the Army Council. The Italian Red Brigades were organized in independent "columns" in different cities. The French Action Directe was actually two groups, one limited to France and the other operating internationally and linked to groups in Belgium.

The appeal of the new terrorism idea

Why is the idea of a fundamentally new terrorism attractive, if indeed it is as flawed as I claim? One reason may be that the conception of a new terrorism supports the case for major policy change – a justification for the global war on terrorism, the establishment of the category of "enemy combatant," brutal interrogation methods, reliance on a strategy of military preemption, and the use of tactics such as renditions, domestic surveillance activities, and other homeland security measures that restrict civil liberties. Defining jihadist terrorism as entirely new is a way of framing the threat so as to mobilize both public and elite support for costly responses that have long-term and uncertain pay-offs. The shock of the surprise attacks of September 11 was a turning point in the United States, especially for officials such as Richard Clarke (and including Simon and Benjamin as former staff members from the Clinton Administration National Security Council) who had long warned that terrorism could be a major danger and who felt that they had been ignored.[78] The effect of September 11 may resemble the impact of the North Korean invasion of the South on American policy makers, in cementing the ideas behind interpretations of the threat of Communism and the militarization of containment.[79] It seemed and may still seem impossible to consider terrorism a "first order threat" justifying military action unless it is defined as unprecedented. Linking the idea of a new terrorism to the threat of "weapons of mass destruction" magnifies the danger even more.

Furthermore, the new terrorism model permits top-down processing of information. If policy makers can rely on a set of simple assumptions about terrorism, they need not concern themselves with understanding a contradictory and confusing reality. In the presence of incomplete and ambiguous information, policy makers are prone to rely on prior cognitive assumptions. Doing so saves them time, energy, and stress. They rely on metaphors, narratives, and analogies that make sense of what might otherwise be difficult to comprehend. For example, defining groups such as Hezbollah and Hamas as "terrorist organizations" with whom the United States cannot negotiate saves policy makers from having to cope with the troublesome problem of how to deal successfully with hostile but democratically-elected nonstate actors.

For similar reasons, terrorism "experts," especially newcomers to the field, might find it convenient not to have to take the time to study the long and complicated history of the terrorist phenomenon.[80] If analysts and pundits can focus only on the new terrorism of the post-Cold War world, then they can safely disregard the record of terrorism that occurred from the late nineteenth century to the 1990s. The narrowed scope of their research streamlines the task of analysis. Furthermore, if analysts can safely assume that religion is the cause of terrorism, they need not look for other more complex explanations that necessitate linking religion to other political, social, and economic factors. The appeal of Islam in immigrant communities in the West, for example, is a political and social question involving issues of cultural assimilation and economic integration. Processes of radicalization cannot be understood without examining background conditions and individual propensities in particular societies. There is no generic new terrorist.

Conclusions

Rejecting our accumulated knowledge of terrorism by dismissing it as "obsolete" is dangerous. A misdiagnosis of what the new actually entails could lead to mistakes of prediction and of policy as grave as those attributed to lack of recognition of the threat. For example, the assumption that the sort of catastrophic terrorism that many defined as new would necessarily involve the use of "weapons of mass destruction" turned out to be mistaken. Similarly, before the September 11 attacks, many observers thought that hijackings were an outmoded tactic. They believed that terrorists had abandoned the method because governments had erected effective defense measures such as passenger screenings at airports. They did not imagine that the old terrorism tactic could be combined with suicide missions (which began in the 1980s in Lebanon) to produce such a cataclysmic effect.

Differences among groups and differences in patterns of terrorism over time do exist, but many of these shifts are due to a changing environment, largely processes associated with what is termed "globalization," in particular, such as advances in communications, access to weapons and explosives, and individual mobility. Differences can also be attributed to specific opportunity structures, such as Al Qaeda's emergence in protected spaces in Pakistan, the Sudan, and Afghanistan. The internet, for example, has proved an important resource for terrorists. It is a transnational means of communication, recruitment, indoctrination, instruction, propaganda, and fundraising that largely escapes government control.[81] Jihadist websites, for example, have proliferated. Political and military conflicts provide further opportunities. The American invasion of Iraq and the insurgency it provoked, for example, have provided both a stimulus and a training ground for jihadi militants. Furthermore, the development of terrorism exhibits evolutionary progression, as groups learn from their own experiences and those of others. They are not driven solely by doctrine, whether religious or secular, but react to what governments and publics do. They seek the support of constituencies and are sensitive to changing attitudes and values. Their behavior is highly contingent.

Thus, analysis of what is new about terrorism needs to be based on systematic empirical research that compares a wide range of cases over extended time periods. Without knowing the contours of the old terrorism, the shape of the new cannot be identified. Comparisons must also take into account the historical context within which terrorism occurs. Otherwise we cannot understand adaptation and innovation in terrorist behavior.

The new terrorism viewpoint is bound to overestimate the effect of religious beliefs as a cause of terrorism and as a cause of lethality. It underestimates the power of nationalism. The distinction between religious and nationalist or secular revolutionary motivations is not clearly established or substantiated in fact. Few groups are classified as exclusively religious; most have mixed motives. The statistical data on which the association between religion and mass casualties is based are incomplete, excluding as they do domestic terrorism prior to the late 1990s.

In particular, analysts need to recognize that secular ideologies can also be fundamentalist, exclusive, and totalitarian and that secular groups can promote excessive killing. Sendero Luminoso (the Shining Path) in Peru in the 1980s is a case in point, and it has inspired groups as distant as Maoist rebels in Nepal. According to Cynthia McClintock, Sendero Luminoso resembled the Khmer

Rouge in ideology, strategy, and social base. Both emphasized political violence in the revolutionary process and systematically terrorized civilians. Only seventeen percent of Sendero's victims were military or police:

> Between 1980 and 1992, Sendero murdered at least 8 ecclesiastics, 9 foreign development workers, 44 grassroots leaders, 203 businessmen, 244 teachers, 303 students, 424 workers, 502 political officials (primarily local officials such as mayors), 1,100 urban residents, and 2,196 peasants.[82]

Like contemporary jihadists, the attitudes of both the Khmer Rouge and Sendero Luminoso were characterized by emotional rage, complete confidence in the rightness of their cause, and hatred for the corruption they saw around them. Sendero Luminoso was politically uncompromising, ideologically rigid, and internally authoritarian. It wished to seize power and eliminate both the government and political rivals. It did not seek a place at the bargaining table or calibrate its violence judiciously, as the new terrorism proponents would predict of a secular old terrorist organization.

The "mechanisms of moral disengagement" that Albert Bandura described over fifteen years ago operate for all worldviews.[83] We should not assume that only groups claiming religious sanction will be capable of mass killing or that they are uniformly composed of irrational fanatics who seek only to destroy. Nor should we assume that all religiously motivated groups are dedicated to killing the largest possible numbers. We might note, for example, that the Egyptian Islamic Group, in contrast to Islamic Jihad, abandoned terrorism although the two groups shared many of the same religious beliefs.

In sum, then, a close look at the objectives, methods, and organizational structures of what is said to be new and what is said to be old terrorism reveals numerous similarities rather than firm differences. It cannot really be said that there are two fundamental types of terrorism. The question should be reframed in broader terms, to ask why some groups choose to cause or try to cause large numbers of civilian casualties and others do not, rather than assuming that religious beliefs are the explanation for lethality. If we settle on religion as the answer, we are likely to misunderstand both religion and terrorism.

Part II

Explaining terrorism

Organizations, strategies, and psychology

4 The organizational approach

Terrorism against the state is a specialized form of organized political violence. Terrorist acts result from decisions made by individuals who are members of identifiable organizations with distinctive characteristics.[1] As autonomous political organizations, terrorist groups share qualities with other organizations independent of the state. Yet other features – their reliance on violence, conspiratorial nature, and small size – are distinctive. Focusing on the organization as a determining factor in the process of terrorism can contribute to the development of theoretical analysis and comparison of different terrorist groups.

Political organizations that employ terrorism as a strategy are similar to other voluntary organizations: (1) the group has a defined structure and processes by which collective decisions are made; (2) members of the organization occupy roles that are functionally differentiated; (3) there are recognized leaders in positions of formal authority; and (4) the organization has collective goals that it pursues as a unit, with collective responsibility claimed for its actions. Specific groups tend to have identifiable modus operandi or standard operating procedures.

Other features distinguish terrorist organizations from different types of political association.[2] The goals of such organizations usually involve what Gamson in his study of social protest calls the "displacement of the antagonist."[3] Their aims are ambitious, calling for radical change in the distribution of power in society or challenging the legitimacy of existing political and social elites. Furthermore, these groups rely on violence to achieve radical change. Not all groups espousing fundamental change in the structure of society and politics wish to accomplish their aims through the forcible destruction of the existing order or the intimidation of its supporters. Moreover, the violence such organizations commonly employ is specialized, selectively directed against the institutions, officials, and symbols of the state, as well as against social classes or ethnic communities defined as the enemy. The techniques of "propaganda of the deed" and coercive intimidation are quite different from the organized collective violence that may accompany strikes, demonstrations, riots, or other expressions of mass discontent. This commitment to violence as a primary method of action (rather than incidental to other purposes) condemns terrorist organizations to illegality and dictates that they organize and operate clandestinely. Terrorist organizations are predominantly underground conspiracies, and their activities are governed by the strictest rules of secrecy.

The extremism of their goals, their dedication to a provocative and shocking form of violence, and their isolation from society are factors that contribute to another distinctive feature: the extremely small size of most terrorist organizations. Even in large organizations such as the Provisional Irish Republican Army or the Palestinian Fatah, actual operational decision making is conducted in small, primary groups for reasons of organizational security and maximum efficiency. The focus of analysis, therefore, must be the small primary group. Most decisions are made in face-to-face discussions in autonomous combat units, rather than handed down through an impersonalized hierarchy. Because of the organizational constraints imposed by clandestinity and the imperative of secrecy, decentralization and "compartmentalization" are essential. Thus, terrorist organizations are not as disciplined or as tightly controlled by the top leadership as legal organizations might be, and conflict between local units and central leaderships are frequent. Maintaining security involves some sacrifice of hierarchical authority and often of efficiency as well.[4]

Generalizing about the characteristics of terrorist organizations should not lead to the false assumption that all such organizations are identical. Significant variations emerge within their common structure. A major difference exists between groups that are largely isolated from society and those that are the extremist offshoots of broader social movements or political parties. Some organizations claim to represent a communal or ethnic constituency from which they derive support. In some cases, the terrorist organization may be, in effect, a subunit of a legal organization with a large public membership. The IRA, for example, or the Basque ETA were components of broader organizational structures and possess a reservoir of support in society because the grievances of the Catholic and Basque communities, respectively, remained unresolved. The Combat Organization of the Socialist-Revolutionary-Party (SR) in Russia in the period between 1901 and 1913 was essentially the fighting unit of a legal political party with seats in the Duma. The IRA was nominally the military wing of Sinn Fein, also a legally constituted political party. These broad-based organizations are usually multifunctional, with separate divisions for propaganda, fundraising, social work, intelligence, or training. Terrorism is one activity among many, although by its nature it is autonomous and self-contained.

Being part of a larger organization can be beneficial. As Gerhard Brunn comments on the ETA, which in 1974 reorganized itself from a largely decentralized system to "democratic centralism":

> This organizational structure indicates that ETA consists of more than just a small nucleus of terrorist cadres. It possesses a developed organizational network which permits it to safeguard its terrorist activities within a wider social context and to make political use of them far more effectively than would be the case if it commanded no more than a diffuse, unstructured circle of sympathisers.[5]

This organizational encadrement provided ETA the flexibility and stable sources of recruitment it needed to survive government repression and heavy attrition of membership ranks.

At the same time, the relationship between the center and the supposedly subordinate subunit can kindle intraorganizational conflict. As emphasized earlier, barriers between the terrorist wing of the organization and the nonviolent arms are essential to preserve the legal status of the parent organization and the security of the terrorist units. Yet, this confers an independence on the terrorist group that can be troublesome. As historian Manfred Hildermeier notes, although the SR was a mass party open to anyone who supported its goals, the terrorist activities of the Combat Organization were strictly separated from aboveground agitation and propaganda. The price for this new-found efficiency – Hildermeier claims that this was the first case of a mass political organization creating a wing exclusively devoted to terrorism – was a loss of control by the party leadership. In principle, the party leaders were to select targets and timing of attacks, but in practice the Combat Organization made its own decisions. This ambiguity was a constant source of tension.[6] The Popular Front for the Liberation of Palestine (PFLP) entrusted its hijackings to the "External Operations" branch. When Israeli security measures made the PFLP's leaders cautious about continuing this tactic, "Its notorious 'External Operations' branch . . . then took on a momentum of its own whose relevance to the Palestinian cause as such became, in the view of many other members of the guerrilla movement, increasingly attenuated."[7]

Groups lacking a social base usually possess a much simpler structure. The People's Will organization in Russia, for example, active roughly from 1878 to 1881, did not have the functional differentiation or range of the later SR. Groups such as the Red Army Faction (RAF), 2 June Movement, and Revolutionary Cells in West Germany, although they were originally the extremist factions of student movements, focused on terrorism to the exclusion of other mobilizing and organizing activities directed toward a mass constituency. The working class whose lot they aspired to improve rejected their efforts. A similar observation can be made about the Weathermen in the United States (also known as Weather or the Weather Underground), an offshoot of a wing of the Students for a Democratic Society. Such isolated groups lack the constraints and the resources conferred by membership in a larger organization.

There is also some indication that in the rare instance when a small terrorist organization gains a mass base, its organizational methods, developed during a conspiratorial period, are unsuited for mass mobilization. The Montoneros of Argentina, for example, active in the early 1970s as a Peronist organization, began terrorist activities with a membership of about a dozen people. With the return of Peron to power in 1973 (a result of events beyond their control but gratifying nonetheless) they suddenly found themselves the vanguard of a youth movement. The Montonero terrorist organization was elitist, authoritarian, and bureaucratic (despite its small size the organization was divided into functional units for logistics, documents, planning, and psychological action as well as into geographic sectors). This lack of internal democracy and "aparatismo" were serious organizational weaknesses as the conspiracy blossomed into a mass movement with Peron's accession to power.[8] The organization had trouble promoting the popular participation that would have made it politically effective aboveground. Nor was the Montonero organization efficient under the repressive military dictatorship that followed their brief heyday. Its leaders eventually fled the country.

It does not always follow, however, that a terrorist organization acting on the behalf of a minority community will automatically acquire a social base of support. The Front de Libération du Québec, for example, never achieved such a status, remaining isolated from society and from the political parties that supported similar political objectives. Black political activism in the United States remained nonviolent despite the emergence of the short-lived Black Panthers organization. Yet the Montoneros, in the context of an insurrection without roots in communal or ethnic divisions, was transformed, albeit briefly, into a large-scale organization with multiple functions and a mass base.

Two models of terrorist organizational design appear to prevail. The first form is a cellular structure in which decisions are made at the top of a pyramid and communicated downward to subordinate but compartmentalized units, with only the top echelon having any knowledge of the comprehensive structure or the identities of leaders. The second form resembles a wheel, with a central leadership at the hub in direct contact with the encircling units. J. K. Zawodny attributes the development of the centrifugal structure to the extremely small size of modern terrorist organizations.[9] He sees it as more flexible, interactive, and innovative than the cumbersome pyramidal structure. The centrifugal organization can react quickly to events and can exist independent of society, which is convenient for groups without even minimal popular support. Members have more intimate contacts with leaders, thereby facilitating control. The Revolutionary Cells (Rote Zellen or RZ) in West Germany are an example of such a diffuse organization, with loosely connected cells in different cities.[10] However, such decentralization is not new. The most extreme example of past decentralization is anarchist terrorism in nineteenth-century Europe and the United States. Like the Revolutionary Cells, each small subgroup acted independently, for the most part, in what they perceived as the common interest of the collectivity.

The degree of "underground" that characterizes terrorist organizations is also qualified. The members of some groups are professional terrorists, with no other employment or social role, who live in hiding from the authorities, under strict concealment. But other groups require only the part-time commitment of their members, who hold regular jobs or conduct their lives in society but who engage in terrorist activities in their spare time, so to speak. In West Germany, this difference was apparent in the RAF, professional terrorists, and the Revolutionary Cells, who were called "after-hours terrorists." This difference in membership requirements has consequences for organizational stability and cohesion as well as for choice of strategies. For example, part-time terrorists do not usually select actions that require extensive advance planning, such as kidnappings. On the other hand, supporting a professional terrorist organization is quite expensive and forces the organization to engage in fundraising activities such as bank robbery, kidnapping for ransom, and expropriation. The isolation of the professional terrorist group also increases group solidarity and can lead to conflicts with a central leadership in an extended organizational structure:

> Still more damaging was the fact that members of the combat organization often lived for years in complete isolation from the party. Under the strain of an illegal existence and exposed to constant persecution by the tsarist secret police, they developed their own values and their own elitist *esprit de corps*. With few exceptions, they adopted the arrogant view that it was they who accomplished the truly revolutionary deeds. Their inclination to take orders from a "civilian" party leadership was correspondingly slight.[11]

Most explanations of terrorist activity focus on the ideological goals of terrorists, and terrorist organizations are frequently classified along this dimension as, variously, revolutionary, anarchist, nationalist, separatist, or neo-Fascist.[12] Terrorism is interpreted as a useful means to these ends under certain conditions, such as a perceived vulnerability of the government or acquisition of resources by the terrorists. Yet the commitment of the terrorist organization to a given ideology is often weak or inconsistent. The Rand Corporation, for instance, notes that in France the group Action Directe, "in chameleon fashion, rapidly refocuses on the most attractive antigovernment issues."[13] From 1979 on, the organization opposed nuclear energy, imperialism, Israel, the Catholic Church, and French intervention in Chad. Ideological doctrines are rarely well formulated or elaborate. Ideas are frequently borrowed loosely from other theoretical sources, the most common today being varieties of Marxism-Leninism. Organizations may shift orientation, for example, from nationalism to social revolution as the IRA and ETA did. As Gerhard Brunn observed,

> ETA has not produced any notable ideologists or theoreticians of its own, nor a consistent ideology. Its ideological evolution tends to be marked by eclecticism, heterogeneity, leaps and internal conflicts which have led to numerous splits and the hiving-off of individual groupings.[14]

The same inconsistency characterized the Montonero organization but it may have been advantageous rather than costly: "The original group contained no outstanding theoretician, yet its very pragmatism was as often a source of strength as of weakness in the early years, facilitating tactical flexibility and the forging of political alliances."[15] A study of the West German terrorist organizations commissioned by the government of the Federal Republic reveals just how controversial the causal connection between ideology and terrorism is. While the authors disagree over whether the theoretical justifications of terrorism are meaningful as motivation, given their arbitrariness and impracticality, all agree that the terrorists did not have their own theories that guided strategy. Instead, they selected fragments of doctrine from other contexts; the concept of American imperialism in the Third World was applied to West Germany, for example. Their ideas lacked coherence and realism.[16] Thus, it is difficult to use ideology as the critical variable that explains the resort to or the continuation of terrorism. The group, as selector and interpreter of ideology, is central.

On the other hand, the psychological approach considers terrorism to be expressive rather than instrumental political behavior.[17] Terrorists are seen as people acting out their emotions, not rational calculators. Yet there is no single common motivation for terrorism; the group translates individual motivation into political action.

Other theories focus on the conditions that encourage or facilitate terrorism, often mentioning socioeconomic factors such as minority grievances, social cleavages, availability of weaponry, media access, or urbanization.[18] However, terrorist organizations are composed of a small social elite. From the 1960s through the 1980s, the average terrorist was a middle-class student or young professional, not a worker or peasant. Even in Peru, the significant and unusual peasant rebellion in the southern highlands was based on an alliance forged between the peasantry and the Shining Path terrorist organization of radical intellectuals, led by a philosophy professor from the local university. The terrorist organization grew out of the university and was composed mainly of students. It only subsequently sought and gained significant support from the rural populations.[19] When all members of a given group are affected by the same conditions, one is left to explain why only a small fraction reacts with calculated violence. It is through the decision making of organizations that social conditions are perceived, interpreted, and acted upon. Terrorism is not a spontaneous expression of widespread discontent.

Nevertheless, Waterman, in a study of collective political activity, rejects an organizational focus as too narrow and prefers instead to concentrate on the resources and opportunities available to the government's opponents.[20] Although at the time of this writing there were few studies of this dimension of terrorism,[21] focusing on organizational processes offers a way of integrating the variables of ideology, individual motivation, and social conditions into explanations of how terrorist campaigns get started and of why they continue despite the deployment of the government's superior powers of coercion against them. Organizational effectiveness also helps determine the outcomes of terrorist campaigns against governments. The critical question is how an organization's leaders view resources, opportunities, and threats, and how they decide to react.

The following analysis is a tentative, exploratory examination of how organizational considerations may affect terrorist behavior and outcomes. References to empirical events are illustrative. In general, the analysis suggests that acts of terrorism may be motivated by the imperative of organizational survival or the requirements of competition with rival terrorist groups. Terrorism is the outcome of the internal dynamics of the organization, a decision-making process that links collectively held values and goals to perceptions of the environment. An organizational approach assumes that members may be attracted to terrorist organizations as much for nonpolitical as for political ends. Incentives to join can include comradeship, social status, excitement, or material reward. The longer a terrorist organization exists, the more likely that group solidarity will replace political purpose as the dominant incentive for members. Leaders of terrorist organizations struggle to prevent the dissolution or destruction of the group through individual defections or destructive factionalism as much as to protect it from government persecution. Such discord is often the source of new groups, as dissident members splinter off from the main organization. Other terrorist organizations are formed as extremist factions of broader social movements that renounce violence but support the same political goals. These organizational factors are especially useful in explaining how terrorist behavior can become self-sustaining regardless of objective success or failure and of changing conditions.

Organizational maintenance and survival

The theories of James Q. Wilson, appropriately adapted, provide a useful point of departure for an analysis of terrorist organizations. Wilson argues that the fundamental purpose of any political organization is to maintain itself.[22] Survival is the minimal goal of any organization, but the goals of the people occupying roles in an organization go beyond the minimum. Leaders, in particular, wish to enhance the organization and ensure its viability. The fact that leaders' personal ambitions are tied to the organization's success seems particularly relevant to the setting of terrorism, where alternative opportunities are limited and outside power resources scarce. The skills required for organizing violence may not be easily transferable to the other fields of endeavor. Where the security of the organization depends on organizational cohesion, leaders must maintain a certain level of cooperative activity to keep the group together in order to preserve not only their positions of authority but their lives.

Wilson views the position of organizational leadership in terms of the nature of the incentives an organization provides for its members. The relationship between actual rewards for membership – what motivates individuals to join a terrorist group – and the organization's stated political objectives or ideology is not straightforward. The organization's followers may not actually have joined the organization for the purpose of fulfilling ideological goals. Collins and Guetzkow term these nonpolitical incentives "interpersonal" as opposed to "task-environmental" rewards.[23] The constraints and opportunities these nonpolitical attractions create for the leaders who must manipulate them to maintain a loyal following will affect the organization's political position. That is, the organization has to offer more than simply its claim to work toward a more just or egalitarian society or freedom from oppression in order to attract recruits. Interpersonal rewards strongly motivate group behavior because they are more immediate than vague prospects of radical change that can only be realized in the distant future, if at all. In sum, to gain security of tenure, leaders must be able to supply adequate levels of both tangible and intangible incentives to members, which do not necessarily involve the pursuit of the organization's collective public ends but which affect these goals as well as the means of their pursuit. The individual's primary incentive for joining an organization, especially one that is already established and of known character, may have only a tenuous connection with the organization's ideology, especially if that ideology is ambiguous. The person drawn to a terrorist organization may not distinguish among motivations, mixed as they are in a complex of conscious and unconscious attractions.

Are such nonpolitical incentives relevant to terrorist behavior? The popular image of the terrorist as an individual motivated exclusively by deep and intransigent political commitment obscures a more complex reality. At least four categories of motivation can be defined distinct from the organization's ideological purpose. If not strictly personal, these rewards are nevertheless unrelated to changing the group's environment or benefiting some external collectivity. Rewards for the individual rather than the group, they can consequently be apportioned by leaders. These incentives are (1) the opportunity for action, (2) the need to belong, (3) the desire for social status, and (4) the acquisition of material reward.

A major organizing principle of terrorist groups is the priority of action over talk. Terrorists are often individuals who are impatient for action. Carlos Marighela, the Brazilian leader whose famous "Minimanual of the Urban Guerrilla" profoundly influenced the 1960s and 1970s generation of European terrorist groups, asserted "action creates the vanguard." Further, "it is only through revolutionary action that an organization capable of carrying the revolution through to victory can be formed" and "What made us grow was action: solely and exclusively revolutionary action."[24] Nathan Leites, in a study of the publicized objectives of terrorist groups, notes the importance of the theme of "escaping the words."[25] Konrad Kellen observed that "The desire for effective – or at least noticeable – action appears to be one of the prime motivations of terrorists."[26] Regardless of the specific nature of the ideology to which the organization adheres, whether left or right, nationalistic or revolutionary, the organization offers a chance to act rather than to discuss action. Terrorists scorn passivity and view endless theorizing with contempt:

> Most of the "combatants" [of the SR Combat Organization] showed a marked scepticism towards any kind of theory and hardly bothered about the party's internal political debates. For them terror had become a "craft" . . . What counted in the combat organizations was organizing ability, daring, histrionic talent and skill in the forging of passports and construction of bombs – not socialist-revolutionary theory or ideological staying power.[27]

Thus, Azef, who was known for his "theoretical indifference," could rise to the leadership of the Combat Organization on the strength of his organizing abilities.

Opportunity for action and immediate pay-off distinguish the terrorist organization from other like-minded groups. Demand for action on the part of recruits may be due to diverse psychological needs, such as seeking risk, excitement, stress, or violence. For example, the establishment of the Black September Organization (BSO) as an offshoot of Palestinian nationalism was a reaction to the defeat of the resistance organizations in the Jordanian civil war in 1970:

> The BSO's sudden and immense popularity was due to its role as an expression of the emotions of a generation of young, highly politicized commandos. It functioned as a cathartic outlet for the feelings of utter helplessness which followed the sudden and unexpected defeat in Jordan.[28]

Its purpose was action, in order to restore the Palestinian identity and to displace the tensions of defeat onto the adversary.

Most voluntary organizations are cautious about undertaking commitments because they fear risking the organization's survival.[29] Terrorists, however, are denied the option of passivity. Because action is imperative, leaders must take risks in order to maintain the organization. They must cope with a constant tension between their desire to preserve the organization (since action risks destruction by government forces) and the membership's demand for action. Nor is it easy for terrorist leaders to find a substitute for violence, since many recruits rejected other similarly directed organizations precisely because of their nonviolence.

The action incentive also assumes some characteristics of what Wilson terms "individual solidarity" incentives.[30] That is, this reward is divisible: leaders can withhold it from some and offer it to others. Not everyone who joins a terrorist organization, even the smallest, can always participate directly in acts of terrorism; others must occupy supporting roles. The individuals who engage in special kinds of violence, for instance, sharpshooters, constitute an elite into which only the most skilled and trustworthy members are admitted. To be selected as a member of the terrorist hard core is a privilege reserved for a select few.

Belonging to the group or community in itself is also a powerful incentive. Verba found in his study of small groups and political behavior that small radical groups may satisfy a need for affective ties not otherwise satisfied in society, certainly not in the wider political system or in large organizations. Cohesion, solidarity, and pressure to conform tend to be strong in all primary groups, especially those in dangerous situations and isolated from society. Leaders must devote themselves to maintaining this affective satisfaction, which often conflicts with their desire to direct group activity toward the outside. There is constant tension between the responsibilities of leading and of nurturing members' sense of belonging.[31] Even in large and diversified organizations such as the IRA or ETA the terrorist subunits formed a closed community. Of the SR Combat Organization Hildermeier says,

> Solidarity amongst themselves ranked higher than their obligation of loyalty to the party. This alienation went so far that one terrorist, during the investigations against Azef, the police agent and leader of the combat organization, threatened to shoot the entire central committee, if it dared to prosecute him.[32]

The External Operations branch of the PFLP behaved in a similar fashion. It is probable that a significant number of individuals join a terrorist organization in order to belong to a group. They may be people who have an emotional need to find a family substitute or who seek personal identity in a collectivity.

There seem to be two patterns of group processes relating to the decision to resort to terrorism. In the first case, individuals join groups that are on the periphery of the actual terrorist organization, which is, in a sense, at the center of a concentric circle. People then move through the groups to the core, sometimes following close friends or relatives. The decision to resort to terrorism is gradual and indirect. Involvement in the terrorist organization may not, at the outset, have been a deliberate choice. In West Germany, the path to membership in the RAF or 2 June Movement was often through other nonpolitical organizations, student communes or residential cooperatives, or nonviolent but sympathetic organizations such as prisoners' aid committees.[33] Basque terrorists were often former members of youth mountain-climbing clubs who were recruited by their leaders. Recruitment is selective, as terrorist organizations are an exclusive elite: for example,

> The members of these [ETA] cadres are recruited after long observation of their work in legal organizations, such as students' associations or mountaineering clubs; in a process lasting several years they are gradually selected, via discussion circles, *charlas de formacion*, and trained by being tried out in auxiliary expeditions.[34]

The second pattern of group development occurs when the existence of the group precedes the decision to turn to terrorism. The adoption of the terrorist strategy is a collective decision by the group as a whole or by a faction within the group. Such decisions are usually hotly debated. The People's Will separated itself from the revolutionary movement over the question of terrorism, for example. The person who has become extremely dependent on the group will move with it to the new activity, without necessarily having made an independent choice. The dependence of members of underground groups on the group and on its leaders – a dependence that has its roots not only in the psychological bonds of solidarity that are formed in all primary groups but in the reality of the isolation and insecurity of a clandestine existence – means that leaders can threaten expulsion for noncompliance. This threat is probably rarely necessary, however, since peer pressure is intense, and members are reluctant to risk group disapproval or rejection. It is also known that risk-taking propensity increases when decisions are made by groups, and this increases the pressure the followers may place on the leaders. The risk-taking propensity of the group as a whole reinforces the demand for action and can lead to an escalation of violence.

Social status is a powerful third incentive for engaging in terrorist violence. The recruit may hope to win the respect and admiration of peers and family. Joining a terrorist organization in order to enhance one's appearance in the eyes of outsiders to the group is not uncharacteristic of nationalist and separatist groups, where a popular constituency exists that may deplore the method but applaud the goals of the organization. The ETA and the IRA, for example, clearly offered status incentives. Most terrorist recruits are adolescents, susceptible to fantasies of domination and heroism. Most terrorist organizations style themselves as "armies" engaged in a "war" or at least "armed struggle" with the government's forces. The terrorist, furthermore, may be acting in terms of a nonindigenous social reference group with whom he or she identifies. The terrorist may genuinely see his or her actions as the extension of a historic struggle led by distant heroes in the Third World, winning them the respect of other revolutionaries. Many West European groups compared themselves to the Tupamaros of Uruguay, who were regarded as popular heroes despite the failure of their movement. This incentive may be difficult for leaders to manipulate short of expulsion of unsatisfactory members. However, being in the inner activist circle may be more prestigious than ordinary participation for the action-oriented recruit. Leaders may not be able to deny this reward, but they can influence it by the strategies they or the group under their direction choose. The image of the terrorist is often important to the group's self-perception as well as to their popular reception. Loss of a "Robin Hood" image can result in a loss of respect and regard from the population. For the Tupamaros, for example, killing kidnapped hostages when the government refused to comply with demands resulted in popular disaffection.

The role of the news media is essential to communicating popular reactions (as well as in interpreting terrorist actions to the public). Media attention must be gratifying to the terrorist motivated by status considerations. Again, terrorist strategies are adapted to acquiring maximum publicity in terms of timing and choice of appropriate targets of violence. In groups where status is a salient incentive, one might expect a concentration on spectacular violence. Even the most isolated of undergrounds still has access to television.[35]

Last, terrorist organizations offer material incentives, although these are probably less important than the three described above, given the limitations life in the underground imposes on the enjoyment of wealth. Nevertheless, being a professional terrorist for a well-established organization in an area with high unemployment, such as Northern Ireland in the 1970s and 1980s, means at least some income. It may be preferable to the dole. Many terrorist organizations have acquired substantial financial resources through ransoms, bank robberies, and expropriations. Some are supported by foreign governments or publics. West German terrorists were frequently accused of enjoying an extravagant life style, preferring Porsches for their getaway cars. Kellen believes that terrorists are attracted to money and "increasing affluence" without work.[36]

Wilson finds nevertheless that purposive incentives, those related to achieving collective goals, changing the environment, and benefiting nonmembers, remain strong. Collective goals appeal to the terrorist's sense of satisfaction at contributing to what he or she considers a worthy political cause. Wilson suggests that the organization's political purpose affects its stability.[37] He distinguishes three categories of purpose: single-issue, ideological, and redemptive. Although most terrorist organizations are ideological, in the sense of being based on beliefs that comprise a systematic, comprehensive rejection of the present political world and the promise of a future replacement, some are single-issue groups. The Rand Corporation describes issue-oriented groups as common but short-lived.[38] The third incentive, redemption, is characteristic of organizations whose efforts concentrate primarily on changing the lives of their members or followers rather than changing the outside world. Groups like the nineteenth-century anarchists and the Weathermen of the 1960s, both cited by Wilson, focused on self-sacrifice, on living by stringent moral codes, or on conversion. The Russian People's Will, for example, based its actions on the concept of self-sacrifice as a moral justification for violence. In the Montonero organization, the Catholic element provided a millenarian theme, with an emphasis on self-sacrifice, life after death, and martyrdom. Fallen comrades were glorified as having joined "the people," in whose service the Montoneros imagined themselves, but whom they were barred from joining in life.[39]

In their redemptive aspects terrorist organizations resemble religious cults, which generally require the absolute commitment of members to a rigid system of belief that divides the world into the saved and the damned. Like terrorist organizations, cults totally reject society, offering instead the intimacy of a like-minded group. They generally practice severe sexual Puritanism and extreme authoritarianism.[40] Further, religious sects do not find persecution unwelcome, as it fulfills their expectations of the evil of the world. There is solidarity in adversity, and quite possibly some terrorist organizations also welcome government repression. Wilson suggests that redemptive organizations can never succeed; hence, their despair often leads to extreme destructiveness and willingness to take risks.

Religious orders sometimes practice terrorism. In a comparative analysis of three historical religious terrorist organizations – the Assassins of medieval Islam, the Hindu Thuggees of colonial India, and the Zealots or Sicarii of Hebrew origin – Rapoport emphasizes the consequences of violence meant to serve a deity rather than to change human affairs.[41] Seeing themselves as instruments of divine intervention, these terrorists usually chose ritualized or stylized forms of violence that frequently assured personal martyrdom. Their actions cannot be considered as rational or politically expedient. Extremely rigid and unable to adapt to changing circumstances, the organizations, rather than the destructiveness of despair, guaranteed their own eventual destruction.

Wilson concludes that all conspiratorial organizations tend over time to substitute group solidarity for political purpose as the dominant incentive.[42] This development is highly plausible for terrorist organizations, given the tendency toward cohesion present in all primary groups as well as the isolation and stress professional terrorists endure, thereby increasing their dependence on the group for emotional support. The group becomes simultaneously more introverted and unrealistic, as contacts with society are severed. Terrorism, thus, becomes self-sustaining, as the group acts to maintain itself rather than to instigate political change. Violence, necessary for group maintenance, cannot simply be abandoned for another purpose. This argument may explain why terrorism appears to persist despite its failure to achieve the organization's stated political objectives or despite changes in political circumstances that make its claims unrealistic. The IRA and ETA, for example, were both established as organizations at times when nonviolent alternatives appeared to be unsuccessful (the civil rights movement in Northern Ireland, for example, was met by Protestant violence), or when the regime was nondemocratic (Franco's dictatorship in Spain, and the Stormont regime under Protestant domination in Northern Ireland, respectively). Both organizations continued operating despite changes that satisfied many of the demands of the constituencies they claimed to represent. Catholic rights in Northern Ireland were better protected under British rule, and Franco's authoritarianism was replaced by democracy. Their persistence is explained by an intransigent refusal to compromise and by the strength of the organization itself.

Organizational analysis explains not only terrorism's staying power, but its origins. Wilson agrees that structural explanations of civil violence yield little, since the objective conditions likely to inspire grievances and, hence, incite violence are permanent, whereas violence is neither continuous nor universal.[43] Instead he finds entrepreneurship to be a critical ingredient. The founders of an organization must invent appropriate incentives to attract members, and must have an exceptional commitment to the group's purposes coupled with an exaggerated sense of its likely efficacy. Wilson further argues that there must be a demand for the organization from some actual or potential constituency and that the organization must possess a minimum threshold of readily mobilized resources. An essential condition appears to be the presence of skilled and determined leaders and some broader demand for action coinciding with "the salience of purposive incentives."[44] If potential recruits believe that matters of concern to them are being affected by a government whose behavior can be altered, a belief that is likely to emerge when a highly visible enemy appears to pose a serious threat to the values of the potential terrorists or their constituents, they are likely to organize and to act. Thus, terrorist organizations are much more responsive to the environment and to other actors during their inception than they are in their subsequent development.

The case of the Montoneros demonstrates the importance of the coincidence of ideas that legitimize violence, examples set by other terrorist organizations in similar circumstances, latent popular demand for political action, the encouragement of an outside actor, and a new threat posed by the government. The three founding leaders of the Montoneros had been students at the same school and members of a Catholic youth organization. Although two had participated in right-wing political activities, in 1967 all three, inspired by the liberation theology movement within the Catholic Church, joined the radical "Camilo Torres Command," named after the Brazilian worker-priest. Legitimizing social revolution, liberation theology was the single most important doctrinal element in the Montonero leaders' radicalization, although their desire for action seems to have been much stronger than their ideological motivation. Liberation theology was, after all, the inspiration for a large part of the Peronist youth movement in Argentina. Lending credence to revolutionary ideologies and to the anticipation of success from a terrorist strategy was the persuasiveness of the model of the Uruguayan Tupamaros, who were exceptionally active in the late 1960s. Peron's encouragement from exile was also a catalyst. Although "the launching of the urban guerrillas was an initiative 'from above,' the decision of small groups of militants rather than a response to widespread popular demand,"[45] in the late 1960s in Argentina a general alienation and rebelliousness particularly affected the middle class. This disaffection, more political and cultural than socioeconomic, was caused by the brutal but inefficient political repression of the military dictatorship. The universities were particularly threatened. The Montoneros, established in 1968, combined radical Catholicism, nationalism, Peronism, and socialism in an eclectic mixture that made them attractive to almost everybody, but the unifying focus of the organization was armed struggle. Beyond that the group did not plan for the future, as they naively believed that Peron would safeguard their interests.[46]

In general, this theoretical approach strongly suggests that the expectations of members of terrorist organizations may have only a slight connection with the organization's ideological objectives. The leaders of the organization play a critical role in balancing incentives to maintain the organization's viability. The two dominant incentives appear to be the opportunity for action and the chance to belong to a small group of sympathetic associates. From this perspective, terrorist organizations appear to be largely self-sustaining. Other theories must explain the decline from within.

Dissent and factionalism within organizations

Although the comparison between business firms and terrorist groups may have seemed bizarre when this chapter was written, the resemblance was noted by the Rand Corporation in 1984:

> Organizations are dedicated to survival. They do not voluntarily go out of business. Right now, the immediate objective of many of the world's hard-pressed terrorist groups is the same as the immediate objective of many of the world's hard-pressed corporations – that is, to continue operations.[47]

Albert O. Hirschman's theory of how economic firms cope with decline supports Wilson's idea that the vulnerability of an organization stems from inability to attract followers rather than to attain political purposes.[48] Yet, Hirschman's theory implies that organizations are fragile; they struggle to prevent decline through the loss of members or constituents or divisive quarrels.

He suggests that organizations behave differently in competitive than in noncompetitive environments. Unity is much more difficult to preserve when there are rivals. Often, terrorist organizations compete in the armed struggle: the Irish Republican Army vied with the Irish National Liberation Army, the Italian Red Brigades contended with Prima Linea, Fatah competed with the PFLP and a host of other groups, the Secret Army for the Liberation of Armenia shared the limelight with the Justice Commandos of the Armenian Genocide, ETA split into two branches, and the Montoneros faced the ERP and many smaller revolutionary organizations. Other organizations monopolize violence: the Shining Path of Peru, the Tupamaros of Uruguay, or the People's Will organization in czarist Russia are examples.

Hirschman maintains that dissatisfied followers of an organization have two options: "exit" or "voice." Each is exercised under different circumstances. Exit can indicate two courses of action: (1) joining an established rival organization that provides more satisfactory incentives or (2) leaving with enough similarly discontented associates to form a new organization. The incentives that operate for the members of an organization are assumed to remain constant, so that they still wish to pursue violent action against the government in a group context. The possibility of exit to legal organizations or simply to a normal life also exists, but these alternatives are rendered unattractive and costly by the threat of pursuit – by both the government and the terrorist organization. Exit often occurs after an attempt to exercise voice has failed. Arguments on group direction often occur when the most extremist members chafe under the restrictions imposed by the relatively moderate and demand an escalation of violence. In order for enough members to be sufficiently dissatisfied to establish a new organization, dissent must be serious. Where established competitors are available, exit is simpler.

Although terrorist organizations usually attempt to define exit as betrayal and threaten severe punishment for treason, factionalism is not uncommon. The Provisional IRA, for example, developed from the refusal of the parent or "Official" IRA to adopt a strategy of terrorism against Protestants and the British in the wake of the civil rights movement. To prevent the departure of a subgroup, especially if it endangers the survival of the organization, former moderates may consent to collective radicalization. The Official IRA subsequently followed the Provos into terrorism – both against the British and against each other. Only if there is no possibility of exit can the organization's leaders resist the demands of members for change without suffering a loss of membership. Although exit may often be difficult, it is rarely impossible.

Terrorist organizations tend, however, to view voice as a more serious threat than exit. Most are extremely intolerant of internal dissent, thereby promoting factionalism to resolve internal conflict. The authoritarianism of the Montoneros, despite its ideological ambiguity, provoked splintering. The existence, if fleeting, of breakaway groups

> at least illustrated a fundamental organizational, and basically political, weakness of the Montoneros: namely, their militaristic lack of any forms of internal democracy whereby differences could be resolved. Dissent was equated with treason, criticism with hostility; minority groups were regarded as threats to be exorcized by means of ostracism and expulsion, never through the strength of political argumentation.[49]

This rigidity has several sources. Cohesion and solidarity are important values, both to the organization (for which security is a paramount concern) and to the psychological well-being of members for whom belonging to the group is a dominant incentive. Furthermore, the organization is founded on the premise that action is preferable to discussion. The clandestine structure of a conspiracy and communications difficulties inhibit widespread participation in political debates over goals. Leaders appear to interpret any criticism as an accusation that their leadership is not representative of the organization. To enforce obedience and acceptance, leaders can rely basically on only two rational sources of authority (they also have a certain command over the group because of psychological dependencies). First, their skills at organization and strategy are known by their past record. Second, Verba suggests, generally with regard to small groups, that leaders rely on their position as an "agent of impersonal force" and as representative of group norms to legitimize their directives.[50] Any challenge to the leaders' interpretation of ideology, which is not their strong point in any case, is also a challenge to the foundations of their leadership.

The leaders of an organization with dissatisfied members try to avoid the extremes of exit and voice that will weaken the organization either through the loss of members or through internecine quarrels. They maneuver chiefly, according to Hirschman, by developing loyalty. Leaders stress commitment to group goals and try to strengthen group solidarity. Terrorist organizations often deliberately build loyalty through ideological indoctrination and through emphasizing the external threat. Loyalty is demonstrably strongest when the possibility of exit exists, but members choose to stay anyway. One can thus assume that in competitive situations it is imperative for leaders to inculcate loyalty. In a situation of monopoly, intense loyalty may be less necessary.

In addition, organizations establish what Hirschman terms "severe initiation costs" to prevent members' departures. If members have invested a lot to join an organization, they will be reluctant to leave. Terrorist organizations normally require the commission of an illegal act as the price of admission in order to eliminate the individual's option of abandoning the underground. This cost does not altogether preclude exit to a close competitor if one exists. However, by paying a high cost for entry, the terrorist has developed a stake in self-deception. Even if the terrorists believe the organization has failed to achieve its objectives, they will "fight hard to prove they were right after all in paying that high entrance fee" rather than admit defeat.[51] The higher the entrance fee paid to join the organization, the less likely that the terrorist will defect even in a competitive situation.

Terrorist organizations have also found alternative methods of dealing with the threat of exit. The Montoneros, for example, practiced what one might call an institutional merger. In moves styled as "unification of the resistance," the Montonero organization in effect absorbed smaller armed groups, whose identities were then submerged in a strengthened Montonero core. Another option was apparently selected by Fatah. In the aftermath of the Jordanian civil war and the defeat of the Palestinian forces, intense discontent among younger Fatah members resulted in the creation of the BSO, which was linked to Fatah in a shadowy fashion. While Fatah never openly claimed partnership with BSO, it seems likely that it did exercise some tutelage, perhaps in an attempt to prevent exit to Fatah's more radical competitors such as the Popular Front for the Liberation of Palestine. Eventually, however, when Fatah tried to gain a firmer hand over the BSO, its leaders did defect to form new rival groupings.[52]

Given high initiation costs and the corresponding constraints on exit they impose, discontent serious enough to surface is likely to be explosive, and it is not surprising that it often leads to bitter factionalism. Paradoxically, extreme discontent may sometimes motivate increased activity to achieve group goals rather than to dissolve the organization. The decline of the terrorist organization under government pressure may engender a psychological dynamic where initial complacency is succeeded by frenetic activism that goes beyond criticism of the leadership to desperate attempts to salvage the organization. Terrorist initiates, having paid a high price to enter the organization and facing an even greater penalty for exit, may react not by denying but by trying to change political reality. The response to decline, then, may be an escalation of violence.

Experimental psychological studies have in fact indicated that the person who has experienced a severe initiation will find even a low-cost exit (for example, to a similarly motivated group with its own terrorist strategy) unsatisfactory.[53] If there appears to be no alternative to exit when voice is prohibited or ineffective, then the disenchanted member will try to reduce the strain of exit by persuading others to join the defection. Once on the outside, these critics will be extremely hostile to the parent organization, fomenting bitter intergroup rivalry. Violence ostensibly directed at outside enemies may really be meant to demonstrate the superior ardor of the new organization and to provide attractive incentives to recruits in a formative period.

These psychological findings provide tentative support for the "fight harder" hypothesis. The dissatisfied but ultimately loyal terrorist who forsakes exit to change the organization's political direction may resort to "creative innovation" under pressure. The combination of high barriers to exit with discontent may thus increase the adaptability rather than hasten the destruction of the organization. When intensely loyal members of a terrorist group cannot exit, failure to achieve the organization's stated purpose may only make them work harder.[54] Especially when nonpurposive incentives are strong, as they are likely to be, terrorists may react to adversity by devoting themselves more fervently to the group. In the case of redemptive organizations, members may even feel that their commitment is being tested by fate or a deity.

The behavioral differences between terrorist groups in competitive versus noncompetitive situations may have significant implications for the intensity of violence in a terrorist campaign. Under competitive conditions, where exit is possible, there should be less internal dissent. Yet, the leaders of organizations threatened by factionalism may have to devote their efforts to distinguishing the group from its competitors, in order to prevent defection to more active rivals. Competition may inspire escalation, as each group tries to outdo the other in violence in order to not only keep their members but to attract recruits. Certainly much Palestinian terrorism against Israel in the 1970s and 1980s could be attributed to a dynamic of outbidding in extremism. On the other hand, where exit is easy but no competitors exist, small organizations are likely to proliferate. It may signify the weakness of solidary incentives, since exit is only likely to be painless where group cohesion is weak. In either case, the result may be competition by escalating extremism. Relationships within and between terrorist organizations may have an innate tendency to move from monopoly to competition.

High vs. low entrance fees may also affect the organization's viability. Groups such as the West German RAF, for example, require the total commitment of members who become professional terrorists, and such groups might find it harder to recover from decline than less structured groups like the Revolutionary Cells. Hirschman considers all terrorist organizations to be in this doomed category, as no organization can make itself completely immune to the possibilities of exit and voice. Where both outlets for dissatisfaction are blocked, the organization cannot survive long, because when discontent does surface openly it will be enormously strong.[55] Innovative responses to decline are the exception.

Conclusions

The organizational process approach to interpreting terrorist behavior assumes a complexity of motivation well beyond the strategy of challenging governments to effect radical change. It proposes that leaders of terrorist organizations struggle to maintain a viable organization. The incentives they offer members may require actions against the government regardless of the cost, *if* that cost is short of complete destruction of the organization. Factionalism and interorganizational rivalry may encourage escalation of the conflict with the government, intensifying violence even if the terrorist organizations are disintegrating through the exercise of exit or voice.

This perspective on terrorist behavior indicates that there may be a fundamental disparity between the outside world's perception of terrorists and their own self-perceptions. What the outside world perceives as "failure" may not appear as such to the terrorist organization. Most outside observers judged that the IRA continued to fail dismally in its effort to drive the British out of Northern Ireland. Its violence resulted only in direct rule from Westminster and increased determination on the part of both the British government in London and the Protestants in Ulster. Yet, the IRA persisted through the 1990s. In such conflicts both sides may suffer from illusory perspectives of the stakes of the opponent.

There are also instructive lessons for democratic governments in this approach to terrorism. Policy should aim to make the organization less destructive and less cohesive rather than to defeat it militarily. The government must try to reduce the likelihood of violence by altering the organization's structure of incentives. Offering new, nonviolent incentives, increasing opportunities for exit, or promoting the expression of internal dissent might hold promise. At the same time, the government should try to avoid a proliferation of new organizations or competition among rivals that involves escalating violence. Policy makers should be sensitive to the possibility of producing the sort of desperation that, in the absence of exit or voice or in the presence of intense loyalty and solidarity, leads terrorists to throw themselves into renewed and violent creativity.

The Italian experience is worth noting here. The apparent "repentance" of significant numbers of terrorists in response to offers of leniency from the Italian state enabled the police to act effectively against the Red Brigades. The offer of reduced prison sentences in exchange for information leading to the apprehension of other Red Brigades members seems to have coincided, perhaps fortuitously, with a period of disarray within the terrorist organization, when numerous members were questioning the group's purposes. The successful timing of this offer suggests that offering the possibility of exit to the aboveground world can work at a time of dissatisfaction and open expression of discontent.

Similarly, with regard to rewarding rather than punishing exit, governments might reconsider the wisdom behind the severe legal penalties for membership in terrorist organizations. The immediate reaction to this suggestion will surely be that increasing the costs of joining a terrorist organization deters prospective entrants. However, even if this is the case (and there is no proof that it is), the government may actually be helping the terrorist organization to establish the high entrance fees that make it difficult for terrorists to exit. Governments, after considering the situation of terrorist organizations, especially the existence of monopoly and the prospect of dissent and factionalism, should decide whether prohibiting exit is in the interest of reducing terrorism. It was to this end that governments in colonial wars often offered amnesty to rebels who surrendered.

Where incentives for many terrorists are nonpurposive, the government may be able to offer substitutes. Financial rewards may be influential, for example, where incentives are material. For example, legislation proposed by the Reagan Administration in 1984 contained the inducement of a $500,000 reward for information leading to the apprehension of terrorists, and this policy has been continued in other instances. Policy models developed for dealing with criminal organizations or youth gangs may also be applicable in circumstances where purposive incentives are weak. However, given the nature of terrorist goals, the government will find it difficult to find satisfactory substitutes for purposive incentives. Governments may also discover that redressing the terrorists' grievances will not undermine the organization's effectiveness in the short run. Organizations develop an independent momentum.

Nevertheless, a social base is useful to the terrorist organization, and there is no reason to adopt policies that create opponents of the regime. It would probably be easier to affect recruitment (remembering that not all terrorist organizations are equally dependent on steady supplies of new members – this depends on organizational structure and on rates of attrition) and support functions by influencing the attitudes of sympathizers than by directly undermining the loyalty of indoctrinated activists. The incentive structures for sympathizers are probably weaker than those for active members. Barriers to both entry and exit are lower, yet there is also little occasion to exercise voice. Sympathizers have little direct control over the organization's decisions. An increase in their frustration might cause the organization's support base to crumble. The problem is to identify incentives for sympathizers. Personal satisfaction or reward must be largely vicarious; there is no close-knit community of believers to belong to. It is possible that, in addition to purposive incentives, sympathizers are attracted by the status that accrues to a terrorist "connection."

The organizational approach suggests that terrorist groups are strengthened or weakened as much from their own internal dynamics as from government counteractions. "Winning" in a conventional sense may not be the actual goal of terrorists, despite the military terminology most employ. The reward is in playing the game. Simply being able to stay in may be sufficient for organizational maintenance.

5 Subjective realities

The actions of terrorist organizations are based on a subjective interpretation of the world.[1] Perceptions of the political and social environment are filtered through beliefs and attitudes that reflect experiences and memories. The psychological and ideological factors that constitute the terrorist's world-view are only part of a complex web of determinants of terrorist behavior, one of which is surely a strategic conception of means and ends. It is clearly mistaken, however, to assume that terrorists necessarily act in terms of a consistent rationality based on accurate representations of reality. In fact one of the aims of terrorist organizations is to convince skeptical audiences to see the world in their terms. An important aspect of the struggle between governments and terrorists concerns the definition of the conflict. Each side wishes to interpret the issues in terms of its own values.

Given this premise, that the way in which members of the terrorist organization see the world influences their behavior, it becomes essential to analyze the content and structure of the political beliefs of members of terrorist organizations. Commonly-held systems of beliefs may be derived from numerous environmental sources. The political and social context in which the terrorist organization operates and from which it developed constitutes one set of origins. General cultural influences (e.g., history, tradition, religion, and literature) imparted to individual members of society through socialization patterns as well as formally constructed ideologies or political philosophies are additional sources of terrorist beliefs.

Many people are exposed to the impact of culture or political ideas; however, only a few select terrorism. Explaining the receptivity of the small minority who turns to terrorism requires analysis of the psychological functions of beliefs. Psychological traits do not stand in isolation from social learning, but individual variations in susceptibility to social and political settings must be emphasized. Furthermore, the situation in which terrorists exist is stressful and uncertain, which contributes to extreme and unrealistic beliefs that are psychologically functional, durable, and resistant to change. Both cognitive processes and motivational factors encourage reliance on a set of unchanging beliefs that inhibit flexibility and openness. This combination of factors explains the tenaciousness of terrorist beliefs despite what may be a widening deviation from reality. It may also explain the bitterness and violence that control dissent within terrorist organizations. The dynamics of the group encourage cohesiveness and solidarity that stifle challenges to the dominant beliefs in the terrorist organization.

Any psychological analysis must proceed with caution. The data are scarce and imprecise, as terrorists do not readily submit to acting as experimental subjects. The "mindset" of the terrorist has yet to be systematically analyzed. As Jenkins claims, the perspective of the terrorist and the effect of context and circumstances on behavior remain areas of uncertainty.[2] It is also important to be sensitive to cultural differences and to avoid assuming that what is unusual by Western standards is also abnormal. The concepts of rationality and irrationality commonly employed in social-scientific analysis are culture-bound. Terrorists may hold convictions that the majority of society see as deluded. As Joseph Conrad explained, "perverse reason has its own logical processes."[3]

The policy implications of this preliminary analysis should be carefully drawn. In general, governments should avoid reinforcing the subjective reality of the terrorist. The aim of policy should be to loosen the hold of the group over its members and to make the individuals who have become committed to terrorism more responsive to reality. In hostage situations in particular, government decision-makers must use their knowledge of terrorist perceptions and beliefs to induce flexibility and compromise. Terrorists must be persuaded to look at a longer-run future and to develop a less abstract world-view.

The content and structure of beliefs

Members of terrorist organizations act in terms of organized belief systems that structure their interpretations of the world and filter the information they receive. As Holsti contends, the belief system "may be thought of as the set of lenses through which information concerning the physical and social environment is received. It orients the individual to his environment, defining it for him and identifying for him its salient characteristics."[4] What terrorists believe affects perception and action. The questions to be asked here concern whether or not sets of common beliefs can be identified. If not similar in terms of specific political positions, shared beliefs may be comparable in terms of general orientations or attitudes toward the world. Collective beliefs may also be like in structure if not content. That is, terrorists may not believe the same things, but their beliefs may resemble each other in degree of complexity, abstractness, or flexibility.

It is possible to view the beliefs of individual terrorists as extensions of the extremist mentality. Traditional "extremism" theory holds that radicals of both left and right will display less sophisticated reasoning than moderates because they are attempting to simplify an overly complex reality. Sidanius, however, argues the contrary.[5] Extremists, including political terrorists, exhibit greater cognitive complexity and flexibility.[6]

The proposition that the terrorist belief system may be cognitively complex is supported by the research of Hopple and Steiner.[7] Through content analysis of documents from the German Red Army Faction (RAF), the Italian Red Brigades, and the Basque Euzkadi ta Askatasuna (ETA) they found that terrorists view the world causally. That is, terrorists employ a variety of categories used to identify the causes of events: individual terrorists, the group, competitors or rivals, political parties, the public, the media, corporations, the situation, government policy and institutions, ideology, and foreign states.[8] In no case did terrorists consider a single cause as sufficient explanation. The beliefs held by members of these three groups fluctuated as the organization developed, although it is not clear whether these changes resulted from shifting attitudes or from shifting composition of the group. Given the high rate of attrition in terrorist organizations, membership is unlikely to remain stable. Although these three groups may not constitute a representative sample of all terrorist organizations, they include both revolutionaries and national-separatists. The differences between types appeared minimal.

Another question raised by the consideration of terrorism as a form of extremism is whether or not there are significant differences between left and right extremists. Sidanius found that links between the organization of the belief system and left-vs.-right ideology were difficult to demonstrate.[9] Horowitz argued that it does not make sense to distinguish between left and right terrorism. He asserted that "terrorism is a unitary phenomenon in practice and in theory."[10] Terrorist beliefs represent a fusion of jumbled symbols. Abstractions provide a blanket ideology for terrorists on the left and the right and permit multiple meanings and interpretations. Sheehan found right terrorists in Italy to have sophisticated metaphysical justifications for their actions.[11] Their beliefs seemed as complex as those of the revolutionaries and nationalists that Hopple and Steiner studied.

However, Hoffman distinguishes sharply between right and left terrorists.[12] The beliefs of right-wing extremists in Europe and the U.S. are nationalistic and racist. They oppose Communism and all forms of socialism, whereas to the left the opponent is the capitalist state. Furthermore, the beliefs of the right are more emotional, confused, and facile than those of the left. They tend toward hero-worship and obsession with power and strength. In Italy, rightist groups often derive their beliefs from fantastical conceptions in history and literature.

There are other differences among groups that should not be obscured. Not all terrorist belief structures are as complex as those of the RAF and the Red Brigades. The Weathermen, for example, exhibited a much greater naiveté. Jane Alpert demonstrates a combination of oversimplification and grandiosity when she explains why she never discussed the violent activities of two members of the Front de Libération du Québec whom she had sheltered: "The rationale behind the bombings was too obvious to require explanation. They wanted to topple the power structure as quickly and effectively as possible and ultimately install a revolutionary regime."[13] To Bernadine Dohrn, the social basis for revolution in the U.S. was equally simple and self-evident: "Freaks are revolutionaries and revolutionaries are freaks."[14]

The beliefs of terrorists of both left and right are characterized by the high level of abstraction Horowitz mentioned. For example, one of the most significant components of the belief system of an adversary in a conflict situation is the image of enemy.[15] To terrorists, the concept of the enemy is a depersonalized and monolithic entity. The Red Brigades defined the enemy as the "Multinational Imperialist State," abbreviated to "SIM."[16] Both the Red Brigades and the RAF regarded the state as merely the agent of distant external forces, not as an autonomous actor within the domestic context or as in any sense issuing from the people. The RAF considered German social democracy merely an arm of the oppressive system of American capitalism and militarism. They saw Germany as an occupied territory under the grip of "exterminators."[17] Palestinian nationalist organizations based their strategy of terrorism on the belief that Israel was an artificial state; not a reality but an outpost of Western imperialism that could be driven out of Arab territory. In the light of the general acceptance of the proposition that the relationship between the media and terrorists is symbiotic, each benefitting from the other,[18] it is interesting to note that the RAF viewed the mass media with great suspicion as a tool of the capitalist enemy.[19]

The Weathermen presented colorful if somewhat infantile images of the enemy. In the series of communiqués released from the underground in 1970 (announced as a declaration of war) the enemy was described variously as "American imperialism," "institutions of American injustice," the "killer-pig," or the "monster-state."[20] The threat posed by this enemy was nothing less than genocide.

To the Italian neofascists, the enemy was anyone who posed obstacles to their aspirations for an organic state. According to Ferracuti and Bruno "the enemy is non-human, not good enough. He is the enemy because he is not a hero and is not friendly to the hero."[21] Fascist terrorists often blame vague and faceless conspiracies of elites and despised classes, such as bankers and Jews, capitalists and Marxists.[22] To American rightists such as "The Order," the enemy was defined as the government, all nonwhites, and Jews. Anti-semitism is a predominant element in all these sets of rather disconnected conspiracy theories.

Most political belief systems are affective as well as cognitive. That is, they not only order information so as to make it meaningful but establish values by which behavior is judged. The beliefs of terrorists, in addition to being excessively abstract, also seem to be highly moralistic. The world is seen in black-and-white terms, and there is a strong concern with justification of violence. Two well-known traits of terrorist propaganda exhibit these tendencies. Terrorists usually employ elaborately legalistic terminology and practice. From the viewpoint of the Red Brigades, Aldo Moro was captured, held in prison, tried, convicted, and executed. They also view the conflict with the government as a war in which the terrorists are soldiers. Terrorist organizations are self-styled armies or brigades. To Ferracuti and Bruno, the "fantasy war" aspect of terrorism is extremely important to its practitioners.[23] The desire to appear as soldiers appears to be common to all types of terrorists. In their turn, terrorists of the right are concerned with cleansing communities of alien and immoral influences.

Both legalistic and military self-conceptions may be regarded as essential justificatory beliefs. As Menachem Begin explained, "in order to maintain an open underground you need more than the technique of pseudonyms. What is most necessary is the inner consciousness that makes what is 'legal' illegal and the 'illegal' legal and justified."[24]

The strength of the military self-image is shown in the Irish Republican Army's insistence on a military organizational structure long past its practical usefulness in Northern Ireland. Its power may also explain why the Provisional IRA did not resort to the hijackings and kidnappings that became popular techniques of terrorism in the 1970s and 1980s.[25]

For revolutionary terrorists, the concern with justifying violence is often accompanied by a strong emphasis on perceived injustice done by the state to a weak and helpless populace and the related necessity for revenge. Emma Goldman protested against the popular image of the nineteenth-century anarchist-terrorist as a lunatic or "wild beast," when

> those who have studied the character and personality of these men, or who have come in close contact with them, are agreed that it is their super sensitiveness to the wrong and injustice surrounding them which compels them to pay the toll of our social crimes.[26]

The Red Brigades

> participated at the outset in social questions like the Milanese campaign for free mass transportation, but, slipping further into the underground, they soon moved on to "justificational" violence: that is, retribution for what they considered injustices against the working class.[27]

A high level of abstraction was consistent with justification. Hopple and Steiner found that abstract or vague references to ideology tended to dominate the Red Brigades' thinking. Over time, their rhetoric became "strident, dense, and lacking in intellectual content. The targets are general and symbolic and the victims are not linked to specific wrongdoings."[28] Their goals became more ambitious and less feasible.

The beliefs of left terrorists generally appear to be interrelated and interdependent. That is, the components of their belief systems are not autonomous. They specify relationships among the enemy, the people, and the terrorists. The missing ingredient of the terrorist belief system, however, is the victim. How to sustain the conception of acting in the interest of the people in the light of the isolation of the small underground from the masses and the absence of popular support poses difficult theoretical problems. One way of explaining the distance between terrorist organization and domestic public opinion was, for the RAF, to conceive of its role as representative of the people of the Third World, not just the German proletariat. The ostensible goal of the RAF was not to overthrow the German state but to liberate the Third World from American imperialism. The destruction of the German regime was merely a means to that end. Ulrike Meinhof also insisted that the people could not recognize the RAF's representational role until the actions of the "urban guerrilla" had shown the way. According to the RAF, the objective fact of the alienation of the masses necessitated a war of liberation whether or not the people consciously sought it.[29]

As for national-separatist organizations, ETA also encountered problems in defining its role. In particular, nationalist and working-class interests in the revolutionary process appeared to diverge. The dominant "military" branch of ETA could only resolve this dilemma by advocating that the Basque people organize themselves independently from the terrorist underground and severing its ties with the popular masses.[30] Although Basque grievances against the Spanish regime run deep, the situation is not colonial and the working classes might not benefit by national autonomy.

Terrorists of both right and left seem to see themselves as a morally superior elite to whom conventional standards of behavior do not apply. They perceive their mission as an obligation, not a choice. In this aspect of terrorist belief systems, there may be a sharp divergence between revolutionaries and nationalists on the one hand and neo-fascists on the other. Terrorists of the left see themselves as avenging the victims of injustice and oppression, often extending the scope of their responsibility to the global level. Terrorists of the right do not share this concern with the people. Their justification seems to lie in their identification with transcendental forces of history rather than with the masses, whom terrorism is intended to mobilize. To right terrorists, the struggle between themselves and historical forces is two-sided. To revolutionaries and nationalists, the struggle is three-sided: state, people, and *avant-garde* resistance.

The distribution of beliefs among members of a terrorist organization is likely to be uneven. Given the extent of role differentiation within terrorist organizations, it is reasonable to expect that the leadership may possess more complex and differentiated belief structures than do followers. The basis for the authority of leaders may lie precisely in the ability to articulate beliefs held implicitly by followers. Or authority may derive from the relevance of the leader's background to the general belief system. Andreas Baader, for example, may have gained his position in the RAF not so much because of his theoretical ideas as his credentials as a member of the proletariat.[31] It may also be the case that the original founders of terrorist organizations are more ideologically inclined than are successor-generations. Their beliefs continue to dominate the organization even after they are removed from active positions. The imprisoned "historical nucleus" of the Red Brigades possessed strong influence over the subsequent development of violence. Appeals to their authority became a legitimating device within the outside organization. No subsequent leaders possessed their degree of control, and the organization was divided by rivalries between managerial and ideological leadership styles. Moretti, an important "second-generation" leader, based his authority on organizational expertise rather than doctrinal inventiveness. He was challenged by Senzani, a professor of criminology "who had risen quickly in the ranks because he was one of the few capable of writing theoretical documents."[32]

In conclusion, this overview suggests the following observations. The beliefs of terrorists are characterized by abstraction, impersonality, and impracticality. They may be complex to the point of abstruseness or naively simple. The provision of moral justifications for violence is an integral component. The world is divided between good, represented by the terrorist organization, and a much stronger and pervasive evil, usually embodied in governmental authority and the social classes identified as supporting the state. The terrorists see themselves as elites of superior consciousness and perceptiveness, acting alone through necessary and appropriate violence, with eventual victory guaranteed by the forces of history. Moral objectives are, for the left, the freedom of the people, and for the right, the restoration of traditional or mythical values of order and hierarchy. Their moral duty is to destroy a corrupt state and society, whether they see that corruption as materialism and inequality or as a racial impurity and social permissiveness. The categories in which terrorists think are rigid and undifferentiated. The enemy's hostility to the terrorists is implacable and unchangeable. Victims are by definition agents of the system – "genocidal robots," according to the Weathermen.[33]

Environmental sources of terrorist belief systems

Inquiry into terrorist belief systems is concerned not only with the content or nature of beliefs about world and self but also with how these conceptions are formed. On the one hand, beliefs are the product of social learning and thus reflect their context. On the other hand, beliefs are a product of the psychological characteristics of the individual. These two modes of understanding are not incompatible, but the first problem is to ascertain how the members of terrorist organizations – a minority of a given social group – are influenced by widely diffused environmental factors.

A possible method of selecting decisive influences from the universe of social surroundings is to search for those that provide the individual with a place in a historical process, that suggest a model for action appropriate to acquiring this status, and that furnish a vocabulary and a framework for articulating beliefs and justifying them to an audience. Both cultural and political environments can establish scripts or macronarratives that place present events in a historical continuity, linking the past to the future.[34] In addition to providing a universal explanation, these macronarratives must be directive, in the sense of answering the individual's problem of how to act in specific political situations and thus providing a role, or micronarrative. The macronarrative is an autonomous, comprehensive interpretation of reality, independent of current events, reaching far back into history and forward into the future to explain how events are related to each other. Within this essentially dramatic script is a role for the individual, a model for appropriate and justifiable action.[35] These narratives are activated only under the types of political circumstances that make them salient and relevant. At noncrisis times they lie dormant. These propitious situations may involve threats to strongly-held values, newly-opened opportunities, or puzzles – events significant to the individual and his or her community which are otherwise inexplicable.

The sources of these narratives or scripts may be cultural or political. The social, religious, literary, and linguistic traditions and myths ingrained in centuries of historical consciousness yield a pattern of socialization. Not only values but models of action are internalized and assimilated. In ethnic cultures (or subcultures), especially those in national communities struggling to preserve an autonomous existence in the face of majority pressure, such narratives are especially influential.

The second important source of narratives is political ideology. Ideas or philosophies are usually learned from adolescence on. They are explicitly elaborated and articulated as guides for political interpretation and action, which often specify the circumstances under which they are appropriate. It seems logical to assume that ideologies would be stronger in homogeneous, nondivided, modernized, secular societies. Yet examination of cases reveals that reality is more complex than this dichotomy might suggest.

That such myths, derived from centuries of experiences and embedded in oral and written sources, should motivate separatist terrorism is understandable. In a study of Armenian terrorism, Tololyan argues that terrorists are socially produced and can be understood only in terms of a specific cultural context.[36] He finds the "projective narratives" of the culture critical to this understanding: stories of the past that instruct individuals on how to live and die so as to symbolize collective values and identity. The times and places that are relevant and meaningful to the terrorist may be in the distant past or the promised future, not the temporal present. The past constitutes a mediating force between the individual and the reality which he or she experiences. Narratives convert historical facts into guides for political action, but the individual is not conscious of representing a symbolic model because these values have been thoroughly internalized.

Tololyan cites the importance of religion and literature, emphasizing that terrorist writings both alluded to and were continuous with mainstream social discourse. All Armenians shared a collective memory of injustice, experienced as families and as a nation. In confrontations with injustice specific patterns of action were both prescribed by narratives of resistance and understood as such by wider Armenian society. The particular cultural reality that nourished Armenian terrorism stemmed from the Middle Eastern diaspora, in countries such as Syria and Lebanon where assimilation is the exception. Two elements of the cultural experience dominated: the Genocide and the heroic legend of Vartan (fifth century AD). The model thus established of resistance and martyrdom was incorporated into an ethnonational identity. A willingness to accept risk and violent death was essential to faithfulness to properly Armenian values. Social approval and self-approval were thus inscribed on people's minds in these terms. Through terrorist actions, individuals could give their lives meaning by linking them symbolically with cultural myths. Terrorists could think of themselves as heirs to a noble tradition that others had forsaken. Failure in the present did not exist; the only failure was not to live up to the past. The individual terrorist's death might be necessary for the salvation of a political collectivity that had no other representation. Through this sacrifice traditions and narratives were reanimated, made continuous with the present, and given political relevance.

Tololyan contends that cultural narratives that dictate regulative autobiographies develop from centuries of accumulated tradition. Yet relatively recent events may raise behavioral models to the forefront of consciousness. Myths or scripts may also be deliberately created to serve political purposes, as many social traditions are. The case of Irish terrorism illustrates this proposition and demonstrates the often paradoxical effects of religion. Irish nationalism and Catholicism have become synonymous, but this coincidence is less than a century old. Early leaders of rebellion against British rule included Protestants, and their models of rebellion derived more from the French Revolution and continental republicanism than from Irish history. In the late nineteenth century this political and social rebellion was joined by a specifically cultural revival. While the IRA as a successor to the Irish Republican Brotherhood incorporated mysticism, idealism, and asceticism that had religious overtones, its violence was condemned by the institutionalized Church. The image of martyrdom stemmed as much from the Easter Rising of 1916 as from Catholicism.

The religious derivation of Protestant terrorism is as strong as that of Catholics. Ulster Protestants also have a merged religio-political identity, with roots dating from the seventeenth century and the victory of the Orange over the Green, a victory annually celebrated in symbol and ritual. That a modern war of religion could continue for so long in Northern Ireland cannot be explained by the specific attributes of either Catholic or Protestant faiths. Right-wing terrorists in the U.S. also claim allegiance to fundamentalist Christian principles.

Just as one would not hold Christianity accountable for the terrorism of the IRA, Protestant paramilitaries, or American right extremists and antiabortionists, one should not blame Islam for terrorism conducted in its name. The legends of the Assassins of medieval Islam and the history of Shi'ism as a source of revolt against dominant political elites notwithstanding, religion acquired its modern relevance to terrorism under specific political conditions. The defeats of 1967 and 1973 and the failure of the newly-oil-rich states to reap political benefits equivalent to their monetary wealth could not be explained by a secular nationalist or socialist ideology. Modernization and secularization did not lead to political power but to moral corruption. With the impetus given by Khomeini's ascent to power in Iran, the answer to these troubles seemed to lie in a return to a purity of faith. That religious fundamentalism has emerged among both Shi'ite and Sunni persuasions (and has taken form on both the left and the right, in conventional political terms) shows that terrorism is not an exclusive province of Shi'ism.[37]

Religious justifications for terrorism were analyzed by David Rapoport, who studied "sacred terrorism" in the cases of the Thugs of India, the Assassins of medieval Islam, and the Hebrew Zealots.[38] He found that although these groups took their transcendent justifications from the parent-religion, their beliefs were deviant and represented distortions of the doctrines on which they were based. Nevertheless, divine sanction was a prerequisite for terrorism and determined the forms it took. Religion established the boundaries of permissible violence.

Rapoport noted that both Islam and Judaism provided strong millenarian doctrines that can become sources of terrorism. In other research he argued that messianism, which is a component of all revealed religions, may lead to terrorism:[39] "once a messianic advent appears imminent, doctrine guides the expectations and the actions of believers, doctrines which, for the most part, are the creation of . . . such orthodox religious cultures as Judaism, Christianity, and Islam."[40] Terrorism may result when the millenium (conceived of as total liberation or historical transformation from a world of suffering to one of complete harmony) is thought to be imminent, when believers think that they can act so as to hasten its coming, and when violating the rules of the old order becomes imperative as a demonstration of faith. Millenarians may also believe in the necessity of withdrawing from secular or profane society to create a separate community of believers. These beliefs can contribute to the "politics of atrocity," or deliberate abandon of restraints, symbolic of the individual's depth of commitment to destroying the old and adhering to the new. All ties to the present must be severed so that there can be no return. Integrative world-views tend to divide the world into "good" and "evil" camps. No mercy can be shown evil; the righteousness of the good is absolute. Believers need not be convinced that their actions will actually bring about the millenium, because the righteous can be saved through personal actions regardless of political consequences. Setting a personal example of sacrifice of oneself or another may be sufficient. The full achievement of the organization's external goals is secondary. Any action in the service of the cause can be interpreted as a success. There can be no failure if all violence, whether its consequences are intended or unintended, brings the millenium nearer.

Secular ideologies that also embody traces of millenarianism are often identified as sources of terrorism.[41] Terrorists on the left in the 1960s, 1970s, and 1980s often presented themselves as followers of Marx, Lenin, Mao, Guevara, Fanon, Sartre, or Marcuse. Theories of revolution, anarchism, and fascism have been claimed as inspiration by practitioners of political violence in Western societies since the second half of the nineteenth century. It is difficult, however, to separate the influence of ideology from that of indigenous traditions and historical experiences, even in modern societies without ethnic cleavages. While the myth of resistance to an oppressive foe is strong in ethnic separatism, it was also influential in countries like West Germany and Italy. It cannot be pure coincidence that the Western societies most afflicted by terrorism in the 1970s were also those with a legacy of fascism in the 1930s and 1940s. The need to redeem the past and to act appropriately where the previous generation had not was a theme for both the RAF and the Red Brigades. Horst Mahler, a member of the RAF, explained their violence in terms of a need to redeem the past, to make up for their parents' failure to resist evil, and to break the bonds of identification with Hitler.[42] In Germany, the identification of existing elites with the Nazi leadership and the search for an external reference group, revolutionary movements in the Third World, reflect the influence of the past. In France, where actual resistance to the Nazis was more developed than in either West Germany or Italy, and where identification with the resistance is part of political culture, terrorism was later to develop.

The historian Gordon Craig found evidence of older cultural influences in terrorist activities.[43] He traced the historical roots of terrorism to the Romanticism of the early nineteenth century. Both terrorist and Romantic movements, their members drawn from the educated middle class, were based on a profound cultural pessimism. The modern rebels, terrorist and nonterrorist, shared with their predecessors of the nineteenth century and Weimar period three other characteristics: a flight from the real world into one of their own creation, a hostility toward theory and reason and a reliance instead on instinct, and a firmer grasp of what they disliked about the present than what they proposed for the future. The retreat of modern terrorists from the world was more drastic and their contempt for reason more pronounced. Craig adds:

> What is important to note is that the idealization of violence that was characteristic of the political Romantics of the 1920s was not only adopted by these middle-class rebels in the Federal Republic but made more consequential. For, if the terrorists had a guiding principle, it was that the use of the ultimately irrational weapon, violence, directed randomly at individual targets, would infect society with such unreasoning fear and anxiety that it would become paralyzed and inoperative and therefore ripe for a revolution that would destroy the false democracy and create a new society in the interest of the people and the working class.[44]

Further evidence for the claim that ideology is no stronger a motivation than cultural influences lies in the observation that although modern terrorists adopt ideological terminology, most are practitioners, not intellectuals or theorists. Emphasis is always on action rather than talking. Many terrorist groups break away from larger revolutionary or nationalist organizations precisely because their members think too much time is spent debating ideas rather than implementing them. To Ulrike Meinhof, discussion appeared vain and useless, a product of lethargy rather than intellectualism.[45] Carlos Marighela referred to the "profitless discussion" of other radicals in contrast to his organization's focus on "action: solely and exclusively revolutionary action."[46] Through debates in 1969 and 1970 ETA's development consolidated a trend exalting the strategy of armed conflict to the point of converting it into an end in itself rather than a means of obtaining political objectives. Anticolonialist ideology became only a device for legitimizing violence. All doctrinal and theoretical debate was paralyzed as the military faction enforced "the absolute priority of praxis and activism over theory and doctrine."[47]

The West German terrorist organizations are often considered the most ideological of left-wing terrorists. Yet a detailed study[48] concluded that ideology was part of their rhetoric but not a motivation. German terrorists were eclectic, selectively appropriating what suited them from contemporary leftist ideologies and excluding the more realistic components of ideology. In fact, ideology may have served the useful function of removing terrorists from an increasingly incongruent reality.

Rohrmoser, the coauthor of the German study, tried to find a hidden logic in fragmentary terrorist ideological pronouncements and to invent for them a synthetic and plausible ideology. He felt that terrorist beliefs could be linked implicitly to modern Marxist interpretations such as the Frankfurt School, Marcuse, Sartre, and Lukács. The terrorists, in Rohrmoser's view, were Utopians who regarded historical facts as deception. The future they sought was the source of their conception of their own rightness and popular legitimacy, as Craig says it was for their Romantic predecessors.[49] Their conception of "the people" was imaginary. To them, as for adherents to millenarian beliefs, present reality was irremediably evil; only in its destruction could there be personal fulfillment. Nothing existed between good and evil; compromise was betrayal.

Rohrmoser argued that terrorists sought out Marxism-Leninism and its revisionist modifications to buttress preexisting beliefs. Ideology accorded them automatic virtue as part of a preordained class struggle. They could not have persisted in their self-image of a revolutionary vanguard without the Marxist concept of true-vs.-false consciousness, which allowed them to think that the masses were deluded by capitalist ensnarements of consumerism and materialism. Their acts of terrorism represented an effort to compel reality to fit the image they had of it, for example, to shape the German government into a Nazi model. Terrorism also enabled them to think of themselves as saviors of the true Marxist inheritance that had been betrayed by the orthodox left. (A sense of betrayal by the left, particularly political parties, was also felt keenly by the Red Brigades.)

This analysis suggests that terrorism is not a product directly of particular patterns of political thought or ideas. Instead terrorists may first develop beliefs and then seek justification for them through the selection of fragments of compatible theories. The ideas that are most attractive include millenarian narrative structures that justify individual violence. Terrorists may seek in the ideas of others elements of confirmation for incompletely conceptualized beliefs and images. Ideology is used to articulate these beliefs to an outside audience who might otherwise dismiss the terrorist conception of the world as illusory. Perhaps for similar reasons of external justification, most separatist terrorist organizations also adopt Marxist terms of discourse. Furthermore, in the modern world it is difficult to distinguish ideology from culture. Marxism in particular has become part of twentieth-century political education. Its terms and concepts may be part of the internalized value-structures of both terrorists and publics.

In sum, the political and the nonpolitical environment shapes terrorist behavior, and many elements of this environment are nonpolitical. In specific conditions individuals deliberately or unconsciously assimilate models of appropriate action. These symbols, myths, or narratives have deep historical roots and are embodied in the institutions and cultural realities of a given society, but they may also be of recent creation. From family traditions, religious observances, art, and literature the individual learns how to live a life that will become meaningful in terms of the past and the future. The immediate political or personal consequences of terrorist actions may be less important than their transcendent and personal significance. Explicit political ideologies may play more of a role when strong cultural narratives are not present, but the two sources of belief interact. To terrorists, ideology may be secondary or even superficial but it represents an important reinforcement of extremist beliefs, making them easier to sustain in the face of an unpleasant reality. Rather than an uncritical borrowing of theories, terrorist beliefs may represent a selection of what is psychologically and politically useful.

Psychological functions of terrorist beliefs

Few of the people exposed to the same conditions – religion, literature, history, ideology, and current events – choose the path of terrorism. Receptivity to cultural and political influences is highly uneven. Although most psychological analyses of terrorism agree that there is no single terrorist personality or specific set of identifiable psychological traits,[50] the individuals attracted to terrorism may possess characteristics that make them comfortable with extremist belief systems and violence. Beliefs serve individual psychological needs. Particular belief systems may also be necessary to help to relieve the negative effects of the guilt and stress terrorists experience.

Emotional predispositions to terrorism, if there are such, are not in most cases pathological, although there is some evidence that terrorists of the right suffer more mental disorders than do those of the left.[51] Nor is the answer so simple as an attraction to violence or aggression *per se*. For one thing, the violence involved in terrorism is deliberate and premeditated and thus less likely to be emotionally satisfying to the impulsive personality. In addition, Knutson argued that many terrorists are actually ambivalent about the use of violence.[52] This internal conflict may explain why it is necessary for terrorists to believe that they have no choice and that the enemy bears ultimate responsibility for violence. If Knutson's argument is correct, then the avoidance of responsibility and shift of attribution common to terrorist belief systems (at least on the left) and the self-image of a victim rather than an aggressor may be important to personality integration. Belief systems that justify violence in terms of divine or secular necessity may reflect the terrorist's inability to accept his or her own violent tendencies. The act of violence is seen not as individual choice but historical determination.[53]

Role differentiation in terrorist organizations is relevant to the psychological functions of beliefs. The distinction between leaders and followers may be critical. It is important to remember that most followers are young. Leaders – particularly the imprisoned founders of a "first generation" – are older. The cognitive and emotional states of the adolescents or young adults who turn to terrorism may be in a state of transition. Their personalities may not yet be integrated or stable. Immaturity may heighten vulnerability to extremism. Knowing the age at which individual terrorists were recruited and how long they have been socialized into the organization is important to understanding their beliefs and convictions.

The structure of the terrorist belief system, portraying an all-powerful authority figure relentlessly hostile to a smaller, powerless victim, may possibly reflect early relationships with parents, particularly sons with fathers.[54] Some individuals may need to see the world as hostile, shaped as a confrontation between good and evil in which only the child and the father are important figures. Their beliefs may actually reflect feelings of inferiority, low self-esteem, and helplessness. The need to be engaged in a fantasy war may also be a delusional means of self-aggrandizement. Kaplan, for example, argues that the self-righteousness of terrorist beliefs reflects personal insecurity.[55]

The terrorist image of the enemy may also result from projection, reflecting a lack of integration of the different elements of the personality. The young child is unable to accept the fact that he or she may be both good *and* bad. All the bad characteristics of the self-aggressive impulses, for example, are projected onto an external figure.

Erikson's theories of developmental psychology,[56] centered on the concept of identity, may also help explain the individual's attraction to terrorist belief systems. Failure to establish basic trust, the first developmental hurdle the child confronts, might make the individual hostile and suspicious, prone to see the world as threatening and filled with enemies. Erikson also notes that for adolescents, ideologies serve a functional role as protectors of a still-precarious identity. Because adolescents need to believe in something unambiguous outside themselves, they are susceptible to ideologies that provide certainty. The emphasis on the future confers both hope for escaping an uncomfortable present and meaning for one's actions. Erikson also points out that the individual who has been deprived of something in which to have faith – disappointed by parents and the previous generation, for example – experiences an anger that is likely to gain outlet in ideologies that justify violence.

Böllinger, who studied eight West German terrorists, tentatively supports this view.[57] He found the terrorists who agreed to be interviewed to have suffered developmental setbacks because of lack of familial and social support at critical periods. In particular, the failure to acquire basic trust prevented them from integrating aggressive impulses. Later failure to develop personal autonomy created additional destructive tendencies. The child's world developed as a constant struggle for power with unresponsive parents. As young adults, these people were attracted to ideologies that posited inevitable hostility between a repressive government and a weak opponent. The child's rage at his or her helplessness was projected onto authority figures. Böllinger also claimed that belief systems based on violent resistance to an omnipotent enemy permit a process of collective identification both with victims and aggressors.

Erikson's concept of negative identity has also been used to explain terrorist behavior. In such cases, individuals who have been unable to find a positive, socially acceptable identity adopt roles that have been presented to them as most undesirable or "bad." Essentially the adoption of a negative identity is a rejection of family and society. Knutson's research[58] buttressed Erikson's further contention that members of minority ethnic groups are especially susceptible to the acquisition of a negative identity[59] because they are likely to internalize the prejudicial image of themselves held by the majority. They adopt a "bad" stereotype.

Explaining terrorist motivation through the concept of negative identity is problematic, however. Knutson notes that the assumption of a negative identity is a painful and difficult process, often a result of a severe disappointment in life that cuts off the route to a positive identity. She admits that the negative identity of national-separatists (such as Croatians in Yugoslavia) was not complete rejection of the social values of the relevant majority. In minority communities the majority holds traditional nationalistic values. Terrorists from these cultures perceive their role as guardians of a threatened national identity, rather than as the personification of traits rejected by family and society. In traditional cultures seeking to preserve old ways against the encroachments of modernity, the rebels against family and society are those people who assimilate, not those who resist absorption.

Perhaps the concept of negative identity is more applicable to radical groups in nondivided industrialized societies, such as West Germany or Italy in the 1970s. Post has argued that there is an important distinction between "anarchic-ideologues" and "nationalist-secessionists" in terms of their respective mindsets.[60] The difference is between terrorists who seek to destroy their own society, the "world of their fathers," and those whose intention is to uphold traditions. Terrorism may be "an act of retaliation" against parents for some, but for others it is an act of revenge against a society that harmed parents. Terrorism can represent dissent toward loyal parents or loyalty to parents who dissented from the regime.

However, rebellion against society may not symbolize rebellion against parents even in nondivided societies. In practice revolutionary terrorism in homogeneous societies may develop from obedience to the ideals of one's parents (which may not have been fulfilled) rather than rebellion. In Italy, West Germany, and the U.S. it was not uncommon for terrorists to be the children of social critics.[61] The motives for terrorism may be contradictory, reflecting the emotional conflict that the child feels. In Germany, terrorists may have felt a need to redeem the country's past because their parents were opponents who did not resist enough, rather than because they were Nazis. The sense of a mission left unaccomplished may have motivated their violence.

Another important function of the belief system for terrorists is the neutralization of guilt. People who become terrorists may experience guilt for the commission of violent acts, so the belief that someone else is responsible and that normal standards of moral behavior do not apply to them is comforting. The possibility that victims may be innocent must be excluded from consideration. The need to ward off guilt, the prompting of the conscience or super ego, may also necessitate the legalistic and military imagery inherent in terrorist beliefs. Terrorists conceive of their role as agents of higher authority – soldiers or administrators of justice – rather than as independent persons, acting out of free will.

There are sources of guilt other than the commission of violence. The child feels guilty and anxious for hostility felt against the parent or authority-figure, so that erecting an ideological structure that justifies a violent challenge against a wholly bad enemy is attractive. Terrorists may also experience survivor-guilt when their comrades are killed or imprisoned. Thinking of the deaths of fellow-terrorists in terms of sacrifices for a long-term transcendental goal may be an essential means of coping with guilt assumed by having lived when friends died. The need for a meaning beyond life also grows from the fear of death, a realistic prospect for the terrorist.

In conclusion, what terrorists believe is derived not only from their surroundings, through processes of socialization or deliberate adoption, but from inner emotional needs. For reasons having to do with the development of the personality, some people need to rebel against a hostile world. This resistance, however, might not take the form of terrorism if external justifications were not present. The individual is motivated to seek out certain types of beliefs or to feel comfortable with them if they are imposed on him. However, in arguing this premise, one should be realistic about how terrorists are recruited. Not all terrorists become so through choice. Accident, personal relationships, and growing commitment to a group identity are also reasons for participation in terrorist organizations.

Resistance to change in terrorist beliefs

The unrealistic abstraction of terrorist beliefs and the persistence with which believers cling to them encourage misperception. Terrorists seem to be able to maintain their commitment to a subjective reality in the face of overwhelming amounts of disconfirming information. Theories of cognitive consistency imply that terrorists confront serious challenges to their beliefs, inconsistences that require resolution if belief is to be upheld. The problem is why and how terrorist belief systems resist change.

This persistence may not be unusual. In general, psychological studies show that belief systems, once established, are resistant to change. One reason for the stability of beliefs involves cognitive processing. The way in which the human brain processes information tends to reinforce preexisting beliefs and attitudes.

Robert Jervis proposed a set of theories concerning the cognitive sources of misperception and the effects of misperception on foreign policy behavior.[62] His hypotheses about government decision making can be adapted to the processes by which terrorists make choices. Jervis argued that the principle of cognitive consistency implies that individuals resist information inconsistent with what they already believe to be true. Information is absorbed selectively, because people tend to recognize the familiar and thus isolate from the range of available facts only those that support their views. Selectivity prevails when the pattern demonstrated by the facts is ambiguous and difficult to interpret. Contradictory information will be ignored or reinterpreted as compatible with one's beliefs. When the facts are clear, the source of negative information may be discredited in order to permit disbelief.

Terrorists would thus in all honesty deny that there are innocent victims, despite objective evidence to the contrary. Claims of accidental victims would probably come from the government or the establishment press, so the source would be automatically devalued. Terrorists tend to believe only information from sources they trust, and the only trustworthy person would be someone who shared their beliefs. Leaders exercise a dominant influence. For example, a Tupamaro upon being asked if the movement had been destroyed by a government offensive that resulted in 2,000 captured revolutionaries, replied that these were "incorrect ideas" that clearly came from counter-revolutionaries, allies of the enemy, or defeatists who could think only in terms of quick solutions to historical problems.[63] The RAF contended that "terrorism" was what the German state practiced against the masses. "Urban guerrilla" activities, in contrast, were directly exclusively against the state apparatus, on behalf of, and never against, the masses. Therefore, any reports of RAF actions that harmed or endangered "the people" were part of a government campaign to discredit the resistance. If obliged to accept the fact that casualties among "the people" had occurred, RAF leaders dismissed these actions as provocations performed by government agents.[64]

Individuals avoid value conflicts in their choices. Leila Khaled, an early member of the Popular Front for the Liberation of Palestine (PFLP), for example, was able to deal with the presence of children on the plane she hijacked by turning her thoughts to Palestinian children and pushing the idea of the potential consequences of the hijacking out of her mind.[65] She admitted that she felt uncomfortable thinking of innocent victims and had to "rationalize" her distress. She was able to avoid coping with the conflict between two contradictory values because past injustice provided an alternative focus for her thoughts. Other means of ignoring the conflicts inherent in choices may lie in beliefs that one's actions are determined by historical forces or that the blame for violence lies with the enemy.

These ideas are based on assumptions about how people think and process information with the aim of reducing dissonance between beliefs and fact. Other studies emphasize the motivational factors that cause decision errors and misjudgments. They, too, can be adapted to explaining the inflexibility and persistence of terrorist beliefs. For example, Janis and Mann argue that making any consequential decision involves serious emotional conflict.[66] The need to reduce anxiety and to avoid fear and shame means that people often strive to avoid the acceptance of new information that might require innovation. Rather than adapting creatively to warnings that a present course of action should be changed, they engage in "defensive avoidance."

For example, ego-involvement in prior commitments is always strong: the deeper the commitment to a given course of action, the greater the anticipated cost of changing it. The individual fears peer- or reference-group disapproval or loss of self-respect if a commitment is abandoned. Violating a set of beliefs and expectations in which a person has invested time and ego is psychologically costly. In addition, when confronted with information that indicates that a decision must be made, people are strongly tempted to act immediately in order to relieve stress rather than to continue a search for more satisfactory alternatives. Little judgment will be exercised. Stress is especially acute when the individual must choose between two unpleasant alternatives – for example, surrendering to a government or dying with one's hostages. The perceived magnitude of the losses that a person anticipates from a choice also increases the intensity of emotional discomfort. The "unpleasantness" of these emotions impairs the ability to search for options and appraise the consequences of choices. In the face of serious threats, individuals who have insufficient time to find an alternative to a no longer feasible course of action are likely to fall into a condition of "hypervigilance," or panic. Isolation from social support systems and enforced inactivity (such as terrorists experience in barricade and seizure incidents particularly) also increase the likelihood of hypervigilance. People then make hasty judgments that they may later regret since the drawbacks or negative consequences of the alternative have been ignored in a frantic rush to escape disaster. On the other hand, when *no* escape route is perceived, the person may collapse into fatalism and indifference.

Holsti's work on decision making during World War I also notes the importance of time pressures in increasing psychological stress, which in turn impairs realistic and efficient decision making.[67] He also alludes to the tendencies of decision-makers in crisis situations to avoid assuming responsibility for unpleasant choices. As events led inexorably to war in 1914, each national leader felt that the responsibility for averting war lay with his enemy. Having lost control, he felt nevertheless that the adversary *could* change if he *would*. That he did not meant that he did not wish to, and thus that hostilities were inevitable and defensive action justified. The pressures under which terrorists act make it necessary to cast responsibility for violence onto the government, perceived as "in control" and capable of determining outcomes.

Terrorists, particularly in hostage seizures, are involved in making decisions that involve momentous consequences. Not only do they accept personal risk, but the fate of the organization and the beliefs to which they are passionately committed are at stake. Their lives and personal reputations as well as the status of the organization and the security of its members will be affected by the consequences of their choices. Surely the emotional conflict they experience is acute. They might reasonably be expected to fall back on the simple decision rules dictated by their beliefs rather than debate alternatives until the least costly is selected. Beliefs will bind them to the commitments they have already made, and decision errors resulting from misperceptions will be frequent. They will be emotionally pressured to act precipitously rather than to spend painful time calculating consequences. Isolated in a hostage-taking episode they are likely to lash out destructively if they perceive that time is running out. The premises of the popular "Stockholm syndrome" – that with the passage of time terrorists will feel an emotional affinity with their captives and become reluctant to harm them – are false if the decisional conflict theory is accepted. As stress intensifies, so may the irrationality of terrorist behavior. The cost of changing beliefs or courses of action promotes continuity to the point of counterproductiveness.

Michael, or "Bommi," Baumann, a recanted West German terrorist, explained that "the group becomes increasingly closed. The greater the pressure from the outside, the more you stick together, the more mistakes you make, the more pressure is turned inward – somewhere you have to even things out."[68] There is "total pressure" until someone collapses. Only in collapse is there failure. To avoid the humiliation of collapse, terrorists may bring about their own violent demise – and with it that of their hostages.

Objections have been made to the general theory that individuals must cope with cognitive dissonance or that consequential decisions cause emotional distress. There is evidence that unconventional beliefs are not fragile but extraordinarily persistent and that individuals do not experience difficulty in holding them.[69] Disconfirming facts may not challenge beliefs at all; people may not perceive the warnings or signals that indicate that their present course of action should be changed. The content of beliefs may make them resilient. The most resilient belief systems are both the least systematic and the least empirically relevant. Logical consistency and specificity are drawbacks. Ambiguity about expectations is an advantage. When beliefs are so abstract as to be unfalsifiable, discontinuing evidence is irrelevant. There is no need to acknowledge disparity and therefore no need to employ cognitive coping mechanisms or to suffer emotional distress. Social scientists expect their subjects to engage in the same reality-testing procedures as they do, when actually belief is more natural than disbelief. Beliefs that are remote from reality exempt their holders from testing them. The abstract quality of terrorist beliefs, as well as the inherent distrust of any information coming from outside the group, may make it easy for terrorists to sustain their subjective reality.

An example of incontrovertibility of belief comes from the Tupamaros.[70] Tactical defeats, according to the Tupamaro interviewed, were actually proof of "real advances" because they indicated a new level of struggle. Serious defeat at the hands of the Uruguayan army was actually evidence of the "state of war" necessary for a qualitatively new political position, which moved the confrontation from its previous state of equilibrium. That the popular struggle should be repressed was a sign of the historically irreversible nature of the revolution. Bloodshed only demonstrated the correctness of the road chosen.

Group psychology and belief systems

In addition to psychological dependence on beliefs, the dynamics of interaction within the terrorist organization prevent members from challenging collectively-held belief systems or for the group as a whole to change. In particular, the tendencies toward cohesion and solidarity present in all primary groups lead to the suppression of dissent and the internalization of group standards and norms. Individuals become extremely dependent on the group. Deliberate organizational strategies may be designed to enforce uniformity and to insulate the group from reality. Dissent is dangerous to underground conspiracies. Challenges to orthodoxy are threats to individual identity and group existence.

The importance of group explanations to terrorism is central. As in religious cults, the existence of a social infrastructure provides essential emotional support. The need to have other people agree with one's beliefs is also shown in the proselytizing drives in which many groups engage, an activity common to millenarian movements. In hostage seizures, terrorists often expend a great deal of effort in trying to convince their captives of the righteousness of their cause.

For the individuals who become active terrorists, the initial attraction is often to the group, or community of believers, rather than to an abstract political ideology or to violence. Baumann explained that his recruitment into a counterculture group came first, and that "things became political later."[71] In their search for identity and personality integration, terrorists may seek a substitute for a family they may never have had. A substantial number of West German terrorists seem to have come from incomplete or broken family structures. They seek to belong and to maintain a collective identity that is more comfortable for them than trying to maintain autonomy. Terrorist organizations in this sense form countercultures, or cults, with their own rules of behavior drawn from an unconventional belief system. They usually require the total obedience of members to group norms, which often dictate behavior in nonpolitical realms such as sexual practices. The Weathermen, for example, attempted to ban monogamy. Members of terrorist organizations are often required to accept not only a set of political beliefs but systems of social and psychological regulation. Political beliefs become part of a more comprehensive web of social and ethical rules.

Immensely strong forces promote cohesion and uniformity in such primary groups. Having entered a world of conspiracy and danger, the members are bound together before a common threat of exposure, imprisonment, or death. Theirs is truly a common fate. Each is responsible for the survival of the others and the group. Exposure to danger increases solidarity, as shown in Janis's studies of soldiers in combat.[72] Leaving the group or denying its doctrines not only risks provoking rejection by the only community the individual respects, but it endangers the lives of the remaining members.

Knutson found that perceptual distortions and lack of objectivity led to a form of "groupthink" that hampered the individual terrorist's ability to test reality.[73] Peer pressure was exerted on the individual to assume an ideological role and conform to group standards. She quotes a terrorist's statement that "We were increasingly losing our grip on reality" and that a "group personality" had emerged, isolated but with an internal drive of its own.[74] Individuality disappeared. Knutson explains:

> In such an atmosphere, group actions take on a predetermined, fatalistic quality in which *responsibility* for the occurrence of specific actions is progressively shifted onto the opposition players in government, general social forces, or an inactive populace, and terrorist players come to experience themselves as guided by an externally perceived necessity.[75]

Group leaders, who are the guardians and interpreters of doctrine, also work to maintain the loyalty and collective identification of the membership. Internal conflict is deflected to the outside, toward the enemy, the only acceptable target for aggressive drives. Deviations from the group's way of thinking are seen as signs of lack of faith and commitment. Betrayal of the organization is punishable by death.

Despite these pressures for cohesion, disagreements can exist within terrorist organizations. In the case of the Red Brigades, the divisive issues seemed to concern tactics and internal power struggles rather than doctrine, except for the question of whether or not the terrorist underground should maintain contacts with larger protest movements. Attempts by the central leadership to control the autonomous city "columns" and disputes between the "historical nucleus" in prison and the outside leadership seemed to animate endless and bitter discussions. All members of the Red Brigades agreed on the priority of the armed struggle and on a central core of beliefs; according to Enrico Fenzi, this coherence distinguished them from the rival organization, Prima Linea.[76] The question of dissent has not been systematically studied, but it seems plausible that when disagreements remain internal to the terrorist organization or even to the broader resistance movement, they are based on different conceptions of the best way to achieve ends with which all agree. Fundamental objectives remain unquestioned. When terrorists come to doubt these core beliefs, especially if they perceive that the armed struggle is doomed to failure and that its destructiveness is pointless, they abandon the struggle. One of the Italian *pentiti* explained that he decided to dissociate himself from terrorism both because he became aware of the harm done to his family and to innocent victims and because he realized that armed struggle would fail.[77] The kidnapping and murder of Aldo Moro and of Roberto Peci, the brother of the first "repentant," disillusioned many Red Brigadists.[78] The effect of this disillusionment for some was absolute. There can be no compromise in the terrorist belief system. Continuing to believe may be necessary to maintaining identity and commitment.

Policy implications

1980s American policy toward terrorism was generally consistent since 1972, when in the aftermath of the Palestinian attack on Israeli athletes at the Munich Olympics, President Nixon created the Cabinet Committee to Combat Terrorism. Its first principle was "no concession to terrorist demands." This insistence did not preclude negotiations in the event of a hostage seizure, but it did mean that no major political concessions were allowable under any circumstances.

The reason behind this operational goal was long term. The interest of the U.S. in preventing terrorism in the future could only be served by resisting it in the present. The assumption was widely accepted that submission to today's terrorist demands only encourages future terrorism. Yet in hostage situations, this goal often came into conflict with the humanitarian objective of saving the lives of innocent victims.

Because passive resistance, even coupled with extensive protective security, had neither halted terrorism nor enabled the U.S. to safeguard the lives of its citizens, the American government moved to an active stance. Policy measures included military rescue attempts when hostages were seized and efforts to strengthen deterrence against terrorism, a policy based not only on denying reward to terrorists (and encouraging other states to follow suit) but also on punishing aggression. In principle, threats of retaliation or preemptive attack increase the potential cost of terrorism to its perpetrators. The apprehension and punishment of terrorists also serves the purpose of making the cost prohibitive, as well as the goal of upholding international law and the norms of international society.

American policy was based on explicit standards of rationality. It presumed that denial of reward coupled with a credible threat of high cost would affect the terrorists' value calculus. The terrorist (or the government that supports the terrorist) would understand that terrorism does not pay. But terrorists then and now may not think in terms of this same framework of costs and benefits.

The typical circumstances of a terrorist group – isolated from society, constantly threatened, and deprived of reliable information sources and channels – and their extreme dependence on abstract and often fantastical beliefs about their relationship to the world suggest that the terrorist's ability to adapt to reality is limited. Terrorists are as likely to act in terms of internal drives and motivations as in response to government offers of reward or threats of punishment. They are not uniformly capable of evaluating a full range of alternatives or correctly anticipating the consequences of their choices. At the extreme, terrorists may exist in a state of collective delusion. The high cost of changing beliefs impairs creative adaptation to changing environmental circumstances. The terrorist organization, as a collectivity, is likely to be overconfident about successes and insensitive to failures, as well as impervious to evidence that contradicts central beliefs.

Conclusions

The lessons of this analysis of terrorist behavior are cautionary. Terrorism is difficult to understand, much less to predict. Governments must try to influence the decisions that terrorists make without fully comprehending the determinants of those choices. Misperception, miscommunication, and mistakes may unfortunately be the rule rather than the exception. The depth of distrust that terrorists feel for the state will distort any political message from authorities.

Yet it can only help government decision-makers to understand the view of the world that terrorists accept. Sensitivity to the particular subjective reality of the adversary is essential to appropriate policy responses. There are also two particular uses for this understanding. One lies in attempts to change terrorist beliefs, the other in the management of hostage-seizures or stand-offs.

The level at which the government can act to change terrorists' beliefs is that of the individual, not the group. There is little indication that the group as a collectivity will change. Yet governments should strive to avoid reinforcing the subjective reality of the terrorist. Their actions should not confirm the terrorists' stereotypes of the enemy or their self-image as heroes or as victims. Describing terrorism as a form of war fulfils the terrorists' most ambitious expectations. Contradictions between information about the world and terrorist belief systems should be stressed; it is thought that in order to affect beliefs, disconfirming information should be obvious and preferably come all at once, so that the impact of incongruence is overwhelming.[79] Belief systems are unlikely to change if the evidence of their lack of fit is not compelling. The least important components of images are likely to change first, while the most fundamental attributes of beliefs will be most resistant. If beliefs are logically inconsistent, however, then changing one component will not necessarily produce a comprehensive change of outlook in the terrorist. Government communications to terrorists should stress three things: that terrorism causes innocent victims, that it fails as a tactic, and that alternatives to violence can work in bringing about political change.

This prescription does not underestimate the difficulty of convincing terrorists that their strategies have failed. The more closed the belief system, the more unfalsifiable its predictions, and the less realistic its assessments, the more likely it is that terrorists can ignore disaster. If what matters to the individual is action that will win personal redemption rather than affect an outside audience, then evidence that external circumstances have not changed will not be significant. Yet a hopeful sign is that defections may result from the perception that the strategy of terrorism has failed.

The second application of this analysis is in dealing with hostage-seizures or possibly stand-offs. Governments should recognize the dangerous effects of time pressures. Perceptions of lack of decision-time are likely to force terrorists toward impulsive actions. They are also more likely to take rash steps when they see no acceptable way out of an intolerable situation. It is up to the government both to reduce time pressures – not to issue ultimatums, for example – and to offer an attractive alternative to killing hostages or themselves. The government must exercise great care in structuring and defining incentives to compromise. If there is to be successful bargaining, a common interest must be established. A settlement point must exist that is preferable to no settlement at all. In this respect, we should consider a question raised by game theory. Is a hostage-seizure basically modeled on the prisoner's dilemma, or on the game of chicken? In a prisoner's dilemma game, there are different outcomes, one of which will provide both sides with more gains than the worst possible outcome. The question is when parties to a conflict will choose it. In a game of chicken, the side most able to bluff – and perhaps the most irrational – wins. This preliminary analysis suggests that whatever the game, the players come to it with preconceived biases, derived from cultural, ideological, and psychological sources. Mutually comprehensible rules of the game may not exist.

Government leaders should also remember that forcing terrorists to accept the falseness of their beliefs (if this is possible) or denying them any way out of a threatening situation may lead to emotional breakdown. Panic may result in complete passivity and hopelessness, or in frantic unreasoning activity. As Baumann explained, at the point of desperation "there's no more sensibility in the group."[80] In either case, hopelessness or hyperactivity, extreme destructiveness may result. If terrorists cease to care about the outcome, restraint will disappear.

Government decision-makers in their turn should also avoid misperceptions and unrealistic expectations. Decision-makers often mistakenly think that an adversary will back down and are consequently surprised by the enemy's resolve.[81] There is a tendency to assume that a desired outcome is feasible because it is so badly wanted and that since one's own side cannot back down, the other side will have to do so. Because American policy makers know that political concessions to terrorism are not possible, they may think that terrorists also understand this determination and recognize the necessity of compromise. They may also react to crisis in terms of fixed preconceptions about terrorist behavior, when it is important to remain open to new information during a crisis, to learn as events proceed, to revise prior analyses in light of a changing situation, and, especially, to be alert to individual defection. It may be wishful thinking to suppose that terrorists will react to evidence of the government's determination to resist and to punish when they are actually driven by internal motivation, not external opportunity. Perhaps the most reasonable position is to start with the assumption of subjective rather than objective reality.

6 The logic of terrorism

This chapter explains terrorism as political strategy. It interprets the resort to violence as a willful choice made by a group for political and strategic reasons, rather than as the unintended outcome of psychological or organizational factors.[1]

Terrorism is assumed to display a collective rationality. The group possesses collective preferences or values and selects terrorism as a course of action from a range of perceived alternatives. Efficacy is the primary standard by which terrorism is compared with other methods of achieving political goals. Reasonably regularized decision-making procedures are employed to make an intentional choice, in conscious anticipation of the consequences of various courses of action or inaction. Organizations arrive at collective judgments about the relative effectiveness of different strategies of opposition on the basis of observation and experience, as much as on the basis of abstract strategic conceptions derived from ideological assumptions. This approach thus allows for the incorporation of theories of social learning.

Conventional rational-choice theories of individual participation in rebellion, extended to include terrorist activities, have usually been considered inappropriate because of the "free rider" problem. That is, the benefits of a successful terrorist campaign would presumably be shared by all individual supporters of the group's goals, regardless of the extent of their active participation and the risks they were willing to run. In this case, why should a rational person become a terrorist, given the high costs associated with violent resistance and the expectation that everyone who supports the cause will benefit, whether he or she participates or not?

One answer is that the benefits of participation are psychological. People enjoy belonging to the group, for example. A different answer, however, supports a strategic analysis. On the basis of surveys conducted in New York and West Germany, political scientists suggest that individuals can be *collectively* rational.[2] People realize that their participation is important because group size and cohesion matter. They are sensitive to the implications of free-riding and perceive their personal influence on the provision of public goods to be high. The authors argue that "average citizens may adopt a collectivist conception of rationality because they recognize that what is individually rational is collectively irrational."[3] Selective incentives are deemed largely irrelevant.

One of the advantages of approaching terrorism as a collectively rational strategic choice is that it permits the construction of a standard from which deviations can be measured. For example, the central question about the rationality of some terrorist organizations, such as the West German groups of the 1970s or the Weather Underground in the United States, is whether or not they had a sufficient grasp of reality – some approximation, to whatever degree imperfect – to calculate the likely consequences of the courses of action they chose. Perfect knowledge of available alternatives, and the consequences of each, is not possible, and miscalculations are inevitable. The Popular Front for the Liberation of Palestine (PFLP), for example, planned the hijacking of a TWA flight from Rome in August 1969 to coincide with a scheduled address by President Nixon to a meeting of the Zionist Organization of America, but he sent a letter instead.[4]

Yet not all errors of decision are miscalculations. There are varied degrees of limited rationality. Are some organizations so low on the scale of rationality as to be in a different category from more strategically minded groups? To what degree is strategic reasoning modified by psychological and other constraints? The strategic choice framework provides criteria on which to base these distinctions. It also leads one to ask what conditions promote or discourage rationality in violent underground organizations.

The use of this theoretical approach is also advantageous in that it suggests important questions about the preferences or goals of terrorist organizations. For example, is the decision to seize hostages in order to bargain with governments dictated by strategic considerations or by other, less instrumental motives?

The strategic choice approach is also a useful interpretation of reality. Since the French Revolution, a strategy of terrorism has gradually evolved as a means of bringing about political change opposed by established governments. Analysis of the historical development of terrorism reveals similarities in calculation of ends and means. The strategy has changed over time to adapt to new circumstances that offer different possibilities for dissident action – for example, hostage taking. Yet terrorist activity considered in its entirety shows a fundamental unity of purpose and conception. Although this analysis remains largely on an abstract level, the historical evolution of the strategy of terrorism can be sketched in its terms.[5]

A last argument in support of this approach takes the form of a warning. The wide range of terrorist activity cannot be dismissed as "irrational" and thus pathological, unreasonable, or inexplicable. The resort to terrorism need not be an aberration. It may be a reasonable and calculated response to circumstances. To say that the reasoning that leads to the choice of terrorism may be logical is not an argument about moral justifiability. It does suggest, however, that the belief that terrorism is expedient is one means by which moral inhibitions are overcome.[6]

The conditions for terrorism

The central problem is to determine when extremist organizations find terrorism useful. Extremists seek either a radical change in the status quo, which would confer a new advantage, or the defense of privileges they perceive to be threatened. Their dissatisfaction with the policies of the government is extreme, and their demands usually involve the displacement of existing political elites.[7] Terrorism is not the only method of working toward radical goals, and thus it must be compared to the alternative strategies available to dissidents. Why is terrorism attractive to some opponents of the state, but unattractive to others?

The practitioners of terrorism often claim that they had no choice but terrorism, and it is indeed true that terrorism often follows the failure of other methods. In nineteenth-century Russia, for example, the failure of nonviolent movements contributed to the rise of terrorism. In Ireland, terrorism followed the failure of Parnell's constitutionalism. In the Palestinian–Israeli struggle, terrorism followed the failure of Arab efforts at conventional warfare against Israel. In general, the "nonstate" or "substate" users of terrorism – that is, groups in opposition to the government, as opposed to government itself – are constrained in their options by the lack of active mass support and by the superior power arrayed against them (an imbalance that has grown with the development of the modern centralized and bureaucratic nation-state). But these constraints have not prevented oppositions from considering and rejecting methods other than terrorism. Perhaps because groups are slow to recognize the extent of the limits to action, terrorism is often the last in a sequence of choices. It represents the outcome of a learning process. Experience in opposition provides radicals with information about the potential consequences of their choices. Terrorism is likely to be a reasonably informed choice among available alternatives, some tried unsuccessfully. Terrorists also learn from the experiences of others, usually communicated to them via the news media. Hence the existence of patterns of contagion in terrorist incidents.[8]

Thus the existence of extremism or rebellious potential is necessary to the resort to terrorism but does not in itself explain it, because many revolutionary and nationalist organizations have explicitly disavowed terrorism. The Russian Marxists argued for years against the use of terrorism.[9] Generally, small organizations resort to violence to compensate for what they lack in numbers.[10] The imbalance between the resources terrorists are able to mobilize and the power of the incumbent regime is a decisive consideration in their decision making.

More important than the observation that terrorism is the weapon of the weak, who lack numbers or conventional military power, is the explanation for weakness. Particularly, why does an organization lack the potential to attract enough followers to change government policy or overthrow it?

One possibility is that the majority of the population does not share the ideological views of the resisters, who occupy a political position so extreme that their appeal is inherently limited. This incompatibility of preferences may be purely political, concerning, for example, whether or not one prefers socialism to capitalism. The majority of West Germans found the Red Army Faction's promises for the future not only excessively vague but distasteful. Nor did most Italians support aims of the neofascist groups that initiated the "strategy of tension" in 1969. Other extremist groups, such as the Euzkadi ta Akatasuna (ETA) in Spain or the Provisional Irish Republican Army (PIRA) in Northern Ireland, may appeal exclusively to ethnic, religious, or other minorities. In such cases, a potential constituency of like-minded and dedicated individuals exists, but its boundaries are fixed and limited. Despite the intensity of the preferences of a minority, its numbers will never be sufficient for success.

A second explanation for the weakness of the type of organization likely to turn to terrorism lies in a failure to mobilize support. Its members may be unwilling or unable to expend the time and effort required for mass organizational work. Activists may not possess the requisite skills or patience, or may not expect returns commensurate with their endeavors. No matter how acute or widespread popular dissatisfaction may be, the masses do not rise spontaneously; mobilization is required.[11] The organization's leaders, recognizing the advantages of numbers, may combine mass organization with conspiratorial activities. But resources are limited and organizational work is difficult and slow even under favorable circumstances. Moreover, rewards are not immediate. These difficulties are compounded in an authoritarian state, where the organization of independent opposition is sure to incur high costs. Combining violent provocation with nonviolent organizing efforts may only work to the detriment of the latter.

For example, the debate over whether to use an exclusively violent underground strategy that is isolated from the masses (as terrorism inevitably is) or to work with the people in propaganda and organizational efforts divided the Italian left-wing groups, with the Red Brigades choosing the clandestine path and Prima Linea preferring to maintain contact with the wider protest movement. In prerevolutionary Russia the Socialist-Revolutionary party combined the activities of a legal political party with the terrorist campaign of the secret Combat Organization. The IRA's legal counterpart was Sinn Fein.

A third reason for the weakness of dissident organizations is specific to repressive states. It is important to remember that terrorism is by no means restricted to liberal democracies, although some authors refuse to define resistance to authoritarianism as terrorism.[12] People may not support a resistance organization because they are afraid of negative sanctions from the regime or because censorship of the press prevents them from learning of the possibility of rebellion. In this situation a radical organization may believe that supporters exist but cannot reveal themselves. The depth of this latent support cannot be measured or activists mobilized until the state is overthrown.

Such conditions are frustrating, because the likelihood of popular dissatisfaction grows as the likelihood of its active expression is diminished. Frustration may also encourage unrealistic expectations among the regime's challengers, who are not able to test their popularity. Rational expectations may be undermined by fantastic assumptions about the role of the masses. Yet such fantasies can also prevail among radical undergrounds in Western democracies. The misperception of conditions can lead to unrealistic expectations.

In addition to small numbers, time constraints contribute to the decision to use terrorism. Terrorists are impatient for action. This impatience may, of course, be due to factors such as psychological or organizational pressures. The personalities of leaders, demands from followers, or competition from rivals often constitute impediments to strategic thinking. But it is not necessary to explain the felt urgency of some radical organizations by citing reasons external to an instrumental framework. Impatience and eagerness for action can be rooted in calculations of ends and means. For example, the organization may perceive an immediate opportunity to compensate for its inferiority vis-à-vis the government. A change in the structure of the situation may temporarily alter the balance of resources available to the two sides, thus changing the ratio of strength between government and challenger.

Such a change in the radical organization's outlook – the combination of optimism and urgency – may occur when the regime suddenly appears vulnerable to challenge. This vulnerability may be of two sorts. First, the regime's ability to respond effectively, its capacity for efficient repression of dissent, or its ability to protect its citizens and property may weaken. Its armed forces may be committed elsewhere, for example, as British forces were during World War I when the IRA first rose to challenge British rule, or its coercive resources may be otherwise overextended. Inadequate security at embassies, airports, or military installations may become obvious. The poorly protected U.S. Marine barracks in Beirut was, for example, a tempting target. Government strategy may be ill adapted to responding to terrorism.

Second, the regime may make itself morally or politically vulnerable by increasing the likelihood that the terrorists will attract popular support. Government repressiveness is thought to have contradictory effects: it both deters dissent and provokes a moral backlash.[13] Perceptions of the regime as unjust motivate opposition. If government actions make average citizens willing to suffer punishment for supporting antigovernment causes, or lend credence to the claims of radical opponents, the extremist organization may be tempted to exploit this temporary upsurge of popular indignation. A groundswell of popular disapproval may make liberal governments less willing (as opposed to less able) to use coercion against violent dissent.

Political discomfort may also be internationally generated. If the climate of international opinion changes so as to reduce the legitimacy of a targeted regime, rebels may feel encouraged to risk a repression that they hope will be limited by outside disapproval. In such circumstances the regime's brutality may be expected to win supporters to the cause of its challengers. The situation in apartheid South Africa furnishes an example. Thus a heightened sensitivity to injustice may be produced either by government actions or by changing public attitudes.

The other fundamental way in which the situation changes to the advantage of challengers is through acquiring new resources. New means of financial support are an obvious asset, which may accrue through a foreign alliance with a sympathetic government or another, richer revolutionary group, or through criminal means such as bank robberies or kidnapping for ransom. Although terrorism is an extremely economical method of violence, funds are essential for the support of full-time activists, weapons purchases, transportation, and logistics.

Technological advances in weapons, explosives, transportation, and communications also may enhance the disruptive potential of terrorism. The invention of dynamite was thought by nineteenth-century revolutionaries and anarchists to equalize the relationship between government and challenger, for example. In 1885, Johann Most published a pamphlet titled *Revolutionary War Science,* which explicitly advocated terrorism. According to Paul Avrich, the anarchists saw dynamite "as a great equalizing force, enabling ordinary workmen to stand up against armies, militias, and police, to say nothing of the hired gunmen of the employers."[14] In providing such a powerful but easily concealed weapon, science was thought to have given a decisive advantage to revolutionary forces.

Strategic innovation is another important way in which a challenging organization acquires new resources. The organization may borrow or adapt a technique in order to exploit a vulnerability ignored by the government. In August 1972, for example, the PIRA introduced the effective tactic of the one-shot sniper. IRA Chief of Staff Seán MacStiofáin claimed to have originated the idea: "It seemed to me that prolonged sniping from a static position had no more in common with guerrilla theory than mass confrontations."[15] The best marksmen were trained to fire a single shot and escape before their position could be located. The creation of surprise is naturally one of the key advantages of an offensive strategy. So, too, is the willingness to violate social norms pertaining to restraints on violence. The history of terrorism reveals a series of innovations, as terrorists deliberately selected targets considered taboo and locales where violence was unexpected. These innovations were then rapidly diffused, especially in the modern era of instantaneous and global communications.

It is especially interesting that, in 1968, two of the most important terrorist tactics of the modern era appeared: diplomatic kidnappings in Latin America and hijackings in the Middle East. Both were significant innovations because they involved the use of extortion or blackmail. Although the nineteenth-century Fenians had talked about kidnapping the prince of Wales, the People's Will (Narodnaya Volya) in nineteenth-century Russia had offered to halt its terrorist campaign if a constitution were granted, and American marines were kidnapped by Castro forces in 1959, hostage taking as a systematic and lethal form of coercive bargaining was essentially new.

Terrorism has so far been presented as the response by an opposition movement to an opportunity. This approach is compatible with the findings of Harvey Waterman, who sees collective political action as determined by the calculations of resources and opportunities.[16] Yet other theorists – James Q. Wilson, for example – argue that political organizations originate in response to a threat to a group's values.[17] Terrorism can certainly be defensive as well as opportunistic. It may be a response to a sudden downturn in a dissident organization's fortunes. Fear of appearing weak may provoke an underground organization into acting in order to show its strength. The PIRA used terrorism to offset an impression of weakness, even at the cost of alienating public opinion: in the 1970s periods of negotiations with the British were punctuated by outbursts of terrorism because the PIRA wanted people to think that they were negotiating from strength.[18] Right-wing organizations frequently resort to violence in response to what they see as a threat to the status quo from the left. Beginning in 1969, for example, the right in Italy promoted a "strategy of tension," which involved urban bombings with high numbers of civilian casualties, in order to keep the Italian government and electorate from moving to the left.

Calculation of cost and benefit

An organization or a faction of an organization may choose terrorism because other methods are not expected to work or are considered too time consuming, given the urgency of the situation and the government's superior resources. Why would an extremist organization expect that terrorism would be effective? What are the costs and benefits of such a choice, compared with other alternatives? What is the nature of the debate over terrorism? Whether or not to use terrorism is one of the most divisive issues resistance groups confront, and numerous revolutionary movements have split on the question of means even after agreeing on common political ends.[19]

The costs of terrorism

The costs of terrorism are high. As a domestic strategy, it invariably invites a punitive government reaction, although the organization may believe that the government reaction will not be efficient enough to pose a serious threat. This cost can be offset by the advance preparation of building a secure underground. Sendero Luminoso (Shining Path) in Peru, for example, spent ten years creating a clandestine organizational structure before launching a campaign of violence in 1980. Furthermore, radicals may look to the future and calculate that present sacrifice will not be in vain if it inspires future resistance. Conceptions of interest are thus long term.

Another potential cost of terrorism is loss of popular support. Unless terrorism is carefully controlled and discriminating, it claims innocent victims among bystanders. In a liberal state, indiscriminate violence may appear excessive and unjustified and alienate a citizenry predisposed to loyalty to the government. If it provokes generalized government repression, fear may diminish enthusiasm for resistance. This potential cost of popular alienation is probably least in ethnically divided societies, where victims can be clearly identified as the enemy and where the government of the majority appears illegal to the minority. Terrorists try to compensate by justifying their actions as the result of the absence of choice or the need to respond to government violence. In addition, they may make their strategy highly precise, attacking only unpopular targets.

Terrorism may be unattractive because it is elitist. Although relying only on terrorism may spare the general population from costly involvement in the struggle, such isolation may violate the ideological beliefs of revolutionaries who insist that the people must participate in their liberation. The few who choose terrorism are willing to forgo or postpone the participation of the many, but revolutionaries who oppose terrorism insist that it prevents the people from taking responsibility for their own destiny. The possibility of vicarious popular identification with symbolic acts of terrorism may satisfy some revolutionaries, but others will find terrorism a harmful substitute for mass participation.

The advantages of terrorism

Terrorism has an extremely useful agenda-setting function. If the reasons behind violence are skillfully articulated, terrorism can put the issue of political change on the public agenda. By attracting attention it makes the claims of the resistance a salient issue in the public mind. The government can reject but not ignore an opposition's demands. In 1974 the Palestinian Black September Organization, for example, was willing to sacrifice a base in Khartoum, alienate the Sudanese government, and create ambivalence in the Arab world by seizing the Saudi Arabian embassy and killing American and Belgian diplomats. These costs were apparently weighed against the message to the world "to take us seriously." Mainstream Fatah leader Salah Khalef (Abu Iyad) explained:

> We are planting the seed. Others will harvest it. . . . It is enough for us now to learn, for example, in reading the Jerusalem Post, that Mrs. Meir had to make her will before visiting Paris, or that Mr. Abba Eban had to travel with a false passport.[20]

George Habash of the PFLP noted in 1970 that "we force people to ask what is going on."[21] In these statements, contemporary extremists echo the nineteenth-century anarchists, who coined the idea of "propaganda of the deed," a term used as early as 1877 to refer to an act of insurrection as "a powerful means of arousing popular conscience" and the materialization of an idea through actions.[22]

Terrorism may be intended to create revolutionary conditions. It can prepare the ground for active mass revolt by undermining the government's authority and demoralizing its administrative cadres: its courts, police, and military. By spreading insecurity – at the extreme, making the country ungovernable – the organization hopes to pressure the regime into concessions or relaxation of coercive controls. With the rule of law disrupted, the people will be free to join the opposition. Spectacular humiliation of the government demonstrates strength and will and maintains the morale and enthusiasm of adherents and sympathizers. The first wave of Russian revolutionaries claimed that the aims of terrorism were to exhaust the enemy, render the government's position untenable, and wound the government's prestige by delivering a moral, not a physical, blow. Terrorists hoped to paralyze the government by their presence merely by showing signs of life from time to time. The hesitation, irresolution, and tension they would produce would undermine the processes of government and make the Czar a prisoner in his own palace.[23] As Brazilian revolutionary Carlos Marighela explained:

> Revolutionary terrorism's great weapon is initiative, which guarantees its survival and continued activity. The more committed terrorists and revolutionaries devoted to anti-dictatorship terrorism and sabotage there are, the more military power will be worn down, the more time it will lose following false trails, and the more fear and tension it will suffer through not knowing where the next attack will be launched and what the next target will be.[24]

These statements illustrate a corollary advantage to terrorism in what might be called its excitational function: it inspires resistance by example. As propaganda of the deed, terrorism demonstrates that the regime can be challenged and that illegal opposition is possible. It acts as a catalyst, not a substitute, for mass revolt. All the tedious and time-consuming organizational work of mobilizing the people can be avoided. Terrorism is a shortcut to revolution. As the Russian revolutionary Vera Figner described its purpose, terrorism was "a means of agitation to draw people from their torpor," not a sign of loss of belief in the people.[25]

A more problematic benefit lies in provoking government repression. Terrorists often think that by provoking indiscriminate repression against the population, terrorism will heighten popular disaffection, demonstrate the justice of terrorist claims, and enhance the attractiveness of the political alternative the terrorists represent. Thus, the West German Red Army Faction sought (in vain) to make fascism "visible" in West Germany.[26] In Brazil, Marighela unsuccessfully aimed to "transform the country's political situation into a military one. Then discontent will spread to all social groups and the military will be held exclusively responsible for failures."[27]

But profiting from government repression depends on the lengths to which the government is willing to go in order to contain disorder, and on the population's tolerance for both insecurity and repression. A liberal state may be limited in its capacity for quelling violence, but at the same time it may be difficult to provoke to excess. However, the government's reaction to terrorism may reinforce the symbolic value of violence even if it avoids repression. Extensive security precautions, for example, may only make the terrorists appear powerful.

Summary

To summarize, the choice of terrorism involves considerations of timing and of the popular contribution to revolt, as well as of the relationship between government and opponents. Radicals choose terrorism when they want immediate action, think that only violence can build organizations and mobilize supporters, and accept the risks of challenging the government in a particularly provocative way. Challengers who think that organizational infrastructure must precede action, that rebellion without the masses is misguided, and that premature conflict with the regime can only lead to disaster favor gradualist strategies. They prefer methods such as rural guerrilla warfare, because terrorism can jeopardize painfully achieved gains or preclude eventual compromise with the government.

The resistance organization has before it a set of alternatives defined by the situation and by the objectives and resources of the group. The reasoning behind terrorism takes into account the balance of power between challengers and authorities, a balance that depends on the amount of popular support the resistance can mobilize. The proponents of terrorism understand this constraint and possess reasonable expectations about the likely results of action or inaction. They may be wrong about the alternatives that are open to them, or miscalculate the consequences of their actions, but their decisions are based on logical processes.

Furthermore, organizations learn from their mistakes and from those of others, resulting in strategic continuity and progress toward the development of more efficient and sophisticated tactics. Future choices are modified by the consequences of present actions.

Hostage taking as bargaining

Hostage taking can be analyzed as a form of coercive bargaining. More than twenty years ago, Thomas Schelling wrote that "hostages represent the power to hurt in its purest form."[28] From this perspective, terrorists choose to take hostages because in bargaining situations the government's greater strength and resources are not an advantage. The extensive resort to this form of terrorism after 1968, a year that marks the major advent of diplomatic kidnappings and airline hijackings, was a predictable response to the growth of state power. Kidnappings, hijackings, and barricade-type seizures of embassies or public buildings are attempts to manipulate a government's political decisions.

Strategic analysis of bargaining terrorism is based on the assumption that hostage takers genuinely seek the concessions they demand. It assumes that they prefer government compliance to resistance. This analysis does not allow for deception or for the possibility that seizing hostages may be an end in itself because it yields the benefit of publicity. Because these limiting assumptions may reduce the utility of the theory, it is important to recognize them.

Terrorist bargaining is essentially a form of blackmail or extortion.[29] Terrorists seize hostages in order to affect a government's choices, which are controlled both by expectations of outcome (what the terrorists are likely to do, given the government reaction) and preferences (such as humanitarian values). The outcome threatened by the terrorist – the death of the hostages – must be worse for the government than compliance with terrorist demands. The terrorist has two options, neither of which necessarily excludes the other: to make the threat both more horrible and more credible or to reward compliance, a factor that strategic theorists often ignore.[30] That is, the cost to the government of complying with the terrorists' demands may be lowered or the cost of resisting may be raised.

The threat to kill the hostages must be believable and painful to the government. Here hostage takers are faced with a paradox. How can the credibility of this threat be assured when hostage takers recognize that governments know that the terrorists' control over the situation depends on live hostages? One way of establishing credibility is to divide the threat, making it sequential by killing one hostage at a time. Such tactics also aid terrorists in the process of incurring and demonstrating a commitment to carrying out their threat. Once the terrorists have murdered, though, their incentive to surrender voluntarily is substantially reduced. The terrorists have increased their own costs of yielding in order to persuade the government that their intention to kill all the hostages is real.

Another important way of binding oneself in a terrorist strategy is to undertake a barricade rather than a kidnapping operation. Terrorists who are trapped with the hostages find it more difficult to back down (because the government controls the escape routes) and, by virtue of this commitment, influence the government's choices. When terrorists join the hostages in a barricade situation, they create the visible and irrevocable commitment that Schelling sees as a necessary bond in bargaining. The government must expect desperate behavior, because the terrorists have increased their potential loss in order to demonstrate the firmness of their intentions. Furthermore, barricades are technically easier than kidnappings.

The terrorists also attempt to force the "last clear chance" of avoiding disaster onto the government, which must accept the responsibility for noncompliance that leads to the deaths of hostages. The seizure of hostages is the first move in the game, leaving the next move – which determines the fate of the hostages – completely up to the government. Uncertain communications may facilitate this strategy.[31] The terrorists can pretend not to receive government messages that might affect their demonstrated commitment. Hostage takers can also bind themselves by insisting that they are merely agents, empowered to ask only for the most extreme demands. Terrorists may deliberately appear irrational, either through inconsistent and erratic behavior or unrealistic expectations and preferences, in order to convince the government that they will carry out a threat that entails self-destruction.

Hostage seizures are a type of iterated game, which explains some aspects of terrorist behavior that otherwise seem to violate strategic principles. In terms of a single episode, terrorists can be expected to find killing hostages painful, because they will not achieve their demands and the government's desire to punish will be intensified. However, from a long-range perspective, killing hostages reinforces the credibility of the threat in the next terrorist incident, even if the killers then cannot escape. Each terrorist episode is actually a round in a series of games between government and terrorists.

Hostage takers may influence the government's decision by promising rewards for compliance. Recalling that terrorism represents an iterative game, the release of hostages unharmed when ransom is paid underwrites a promise in the future. Sequential release of selected hostages makes promises credible. Maintaining secrecy about a government's concessions is an additional reward for compliance.

Terrorists may try to make their demands appear legitimate so that governments may seem to satisfy popular grievances rather than the whims of terrorists. Thus, terrorists may ask that food be distributed to the poor. Such demands were a favored tactic of the Ejercito Revolucionario del Pueblo (ERP) in Argentina in the 1970s.

A problem for hostage takers is that rewarding compliance is not easy to reconcile with making threats credible. For example, if terrorists use publicity to emphasize their threat to kill hostages (which they frequently do), they may also increase the costs of compliance for the government because of the attention drawn to the incident.

In any calculation of the payoffs for each side, the costs associated with the bargaining process must be taken into account.[32] Prolonging the hostage crisis increases the costs to both sides. The question is who loses most and thus is more likely to concede. Each party presumably wishes to make the delay more costly to the other. Seizing multiple hostages appears to be advantageous to terrorists, who are thus in a position to make threats credible by killing hostages individually. Conversely, the greater the number of hostages, the greater the cost of holding them. In hijacking or barricade situations, stress and fatigue for the captors increase waiting costs for them as well. Kidnapping poses fewer such costs. Yet the terrorists can reasonably expect that the costs to governments in terms of public or international pressures may be higher when developments are visible. Furthermore, kidnappers can maintain suspense and interest by publishing communications from their victims.

Identifying the obstacles to effective bargaining in hostage seizures is critical. Most important, bargaining depends on the existence of a common interest between two parties. It is unclear whether the lives of hostages are a sufficient common interest to ensure a compromise outcome that is preferable to no agreement for both sides. Furthermore, most theories of bargaining assume that the preferences of each side remain stable during negotiations. In reality, the nature and intensity of preferences may change during a hostage-taking episode. For example, embarrassment over the Iran-Contra scandal may have reduced the American interest in securing the release of hostages in Lebanon.

Bargaining theory is also predicated on the assumption that the game is two-party. When terrorists seize the nationals of one government in order to influence the choices of a third, the situation is seriously complicated. The hostages themselves may sometimes become intermediaries and participants. In Lebanon, Terry Waite, formerly an intermediary and negotiator, became a hostage. Such developments are not anticipated by bargaining theories based on normal political relationships. Furthermore, bargaining is not possible if a government is willing to accept the maximum cost the terrorists can bring to bear rather than concede. And the government's options are not restricted to resistance or compliance; armed rescue attempts represent an attempt to break the bargaining stalemate. In attempting to make their threats credible – for example, by sequential killing of hostages – terrorists may provoke military intervention. There may be limits, then, to the pain terrorists can inflict and still remain in the game.

Conclusions

This essay has attempted to demonstrate that even the most extreme and unusual forms of political behavior can follow an internal, strategic logic. If there are consistent patterns in terrorist behavior, rather than random idiosyncrasies, a strategic analysis may reveal them. Prediction of future terrorism can only be based on theories that explain past patterns.

Terrorism can be considered a reasonable way of pursuing extreme interests in the political arena. It is one among the many alternatives open to radical organizations. Strategic conceptions, based on ideas of how best to take advantage of the possibilities of a given situation, are an important determinant of oppositional terrorism, as they are of the government response. However, no single explanation for terrorist behavior is satisfactory. Strategic calculation is only one factor in the decision-making process leading to terrorism. But it is critical to include strategic reasoning as a possible motivation, at a minimum as an antidote to stereotypes of "terrorists" as irrational fanatics. Such stereotypes are a dangerous underestimation of the capabilities of extremist groups. Nor does stereotyping serve to educate the public – or, indeed, specialists – about the complexities of terrorist motivations and behaviors.

7 Psychological constraints on instrumental reasoning

As noted in Chapter 6, terrorism can be considered the result of a strategic choice based on instrumental reasoning.[1] In this perspective, terrorism is analyzed as a form of political violence designed to affect the attitudes of specific audiences whose reactions determine political outcomes. Terrorism is interpreted as a calculated course of action, chosen from a range of alternatives according to a ranked set of values. The efficacy of terrorism as a means of political influence is assumed to be the primary criterion of choice. Decision makers in the organizations that use terrorism are supposed to rely on explicit strategic conceptions to guide group behavior. These conceptions then become the focus of analysis. To explain a particular terrorist action, one asks what strategic purpose it was meant to accomplish.

Like all rational choice explanations of political action, this one is incomplete. There are psychological barriers to purely strategic calculation in underground organizations. Psychological factors influence both the initiation and the conduct of terrorism and may be the source of actions that are incomprehensible if interpreted strictly as external goal-oriented behavior. Psychological interactions within underground organizations can provoke groups to action that is counterproductive in terms of long-term goals. Although psychological factors may occasionally reinforce the grounds for decisions that are instrumentally based, they may also interfere with strategic calculation of ends and means. I ask how group dynamics and collective belief systems influence the use of terrorism by making it possible, motivating it, determining its forms, and instigating its escalation or decline.

Any such analysis must be sensitive to variations in context. Terrorism is the resort of numerous groups acting in terms of different social and political situations, ideological backgrounds, and prospects of ultimate success. Yet there is a psychology of small, radical, illegal conspiracies that distinguishes them from other political and social actors. The hypotheses I suggest may be applicable primarily to underground organizations without substantial ethnic or other ascriptive constituencies and that are consequently isolated from society. Groups that are closed rather than open to contacts outside the group may be less likely to be strategic in their reasoning.

Group dynamics

The appropriate focus for a psychological explanation is the interaction of individuals within the group, not individual personality. The idea of terrorism as the product of mental disorder or psychopathology has been discredited. In 1988 Maxwell Taylor concluded that it was inappropriate to think of the terrorist as mentally ill in conventional terms and that the individual psychology of the terrorist cannot be characterized in general.[2] Such groups recruit selectively and exclude aspirants who are undisciplined or untrustworthy. Furthermore, the group takes on an independent collective identity that transcends individual characteristics. Radical organizations typically unite people of different backgrounds and temperaments. Participation in the extremist group and commitment to a collective belief system, rather than any shared propensity for violence or inclination toward aggression, bind members together. As Albert Bandura noted, "it requires conducive social conditions rather than monstrous people to produce heinous deeds."[3] Jerrold Post also emphasized that "once individuals join a terrorist group individual differences disappear in the face of the powerful unifying forces of group and organizational psychology" and that "group psychology provides a powerful explanation for this uniformity of behavior within the diverse population of terrorist groups."[4] Thus the topics of most interest to the researcher are group recruitment and socialization processes, not individual personality characteristics prior to joining the group.

For political oppositions, the initial decision to use terrorism against the state usually requires a transition to clandestine life in the underground, a decision that in many contexts is irreversible. "The roads of retreat are all closed; one blows up all the bridges behind one in the truest sense of the word," explains Michael "Bommi" Baumann, a member of a West German terrorist group.[5] The move to the underground may even be precipitated by acts of nonterrorist violence. For example, the West German Red Army Faction's attempt to rescue Andreas Baader from prison resulted in the accidental killing of a guard and thus criminality and illegality: "From this point on there was no going back but only the 'forward escape.'"[6]

The transition to clandestinity requires total commitment from an inner core of militants. Some undergrounds form a kind of counterculture, resembling that of religious cults or youth gangs. Illegality isolates the members of the group from society and encourages the development of distinctive values, norms, and standards of behavior. The collectivity usually demands the complete obedience of members. For reasons of security as well as discipline, the organization usually prohibits personal relationships outside the group. Contacts with the outside world are mediated through the institutions of the group. Insiders are trusted; outsiders are distrusted.

Relationships of leaders to followers in the group may contribute to the isolation of the group from society and to the growth of interdependence among members. A leader of the Uruguayan Tupamaros, in a prison interview with a journalist, explained that rather than trying to select recruits who possessed specific traits, the "Movement" tried to "proletarize" the new member: "the most important thing is to create in him a feeling of dependence on the group. He has to be aware of the fact that he cannot be self-sufficient – that the others are essential to him."[7] In addition to explicit indoctrination procedures, the structure of an underground organization creates dependence on a central leadership, because, for security reasons, it is essential to restrict knowledge of the overall organizational structure. Leaders usually control contacts with the outside world as well as the dissemination of information within the group. The authority of leaders within extremist undergrounds may be based on command of ideology (intellectual authority), operational expertise (military authority), or charisma (personal authority). Leaders also base their authority on the ability to manipulate incentives for followers. These incentives are both political – the ability to move the group toward accomplishment of collective goals – and psychological. For example, threatening expulsion from the group or from the inner circle is a powerful way of inhibiting dissent. In addition, leaders are under pressure to conform to group norms and to preserve ideological purity. Their freedom of action is thus limited.

In general, the recruits are not suddenly converted to terrorism but acquire their commitment gradually, often through belonging to a group, set of friends, or family unit that collectively turns to terrorism. That is, people are recruited into terrorism through personal associations that precede or accompany political commitment. With regard to the West German left-wing groups, Klaus Wasmund noted that "Most terrorists, in fact, have ultimately become members of terrorist organizations through personal connections with people or relatives associated with appropriate political initiatives, communes, self-supporting organizations, or committees – the number of couples, and brothers and sisters is astonishingly high."[8] Leonard Weinberg and William Lee Eubank found in Italy that

> it seems reasonable to suspect that the decision to become a terrorist was often not that of individual choice. Likely it involved a decision, and a gradual one at that, by a primary group whose members reached consensus over the desirability of violent political engagement.[9]

Ties to other members of the group are independent of commitment to collective goals. As a consequence, the importance of the group to the individual is heightened. Loyalty is primarily to the group or entity, not to abstract objectives or ideology. At the least, the individual is unable to separate these two emotional and cognitive commitments: the one to friends, the other to ideals.

Therefore the pressures toward cohesion and uniformity that exist in all primary groups are likely to be intensified under the circumstances of underground life. Solidarity is all the more critical because the group usually lives under conditions of acute threat and high stress. Exposure to danger increases cohesion. The tension created by the underground situation may lead to high levels of anxiety, aggravated by fatigue. Such conditions decrease a group's ability to identify alternatives, estimate costs and benefits, assess outcomes, evaluate audience perspectives, and adjust to changes in the environment.[10]

Furthermore, underground organizations usually suffer high rates of attrition. The death or imprisonment of group members may lead to the activation of the defense mechanism of identifying with the lost comrade. Through a process of introjection, the remaining members of the group take on the values of the dead or captured members.[11] As a result, adherence to group standards is strengthened because abandonment would be viewed as an act of disloyalty. In some ways, the behavior of members of such groups resembles that of soldiers under combat conditions. Disloyalty to one's comrades constitutes betrayal, the most serious violation of group norms.

Thus deviation from group standards is probably rare because of mutual interdependence, peer pressure, sensitivity to betrayal, and security risks. Ordinarily, members of these groups seek above all to avoid the disapproval of their peers. Dissent is emotionally painful. Both external danger and internal dissent may stimulate a need for reassurance, leading the faithful and loyal members to become more dependent on the group, its leaders, and collective beliefs. Thus where factionalism occurs – and it is common to many groups such as the Palestinian and Basque movements – solidarity within "survivor" groups may be intensified. Furthermore, the dissenters who form new factions are also likely to feel acutely dependent on the new group because they have sacrificed so much to join. The high entrance fee is likely to discourage exit.[12]

Whereas some groups such as the IRA permit their members to leave the group so long as they do not inform on it, others punish defection as "betrayal." There are then physical as well as psychological penalties associated with exit. One would expect dissent to be even more distressful under circumstances of high personal risk, which includes the prospect of punishment from the government as well as retribution from one's comrades.

Belief systems

A key role of the leadership is to develop or maintain a collective belief system that links overall ideological orientation to the environment in which the group operates. Ascertaining what terrorists believe is not a simple task.[13] Appropriate sources are difficult to acquire. It is difficult to distinguish motive from rationalization. The beliefs of violent extremists are often quite complex as well as hard to know. Nevertheless, understanding how underground groups view the world and themselves is essential to explaining terrorism. In particular, one must ask if their perceptions of the effects of their actions on audiences become distorted because of simplifying beliefs that guide action. For example, Alessandro Silj observed that the Italian Red Brigades "lost perspective on the situation" upon entering the underground; their misinterpretation of the likely reactions of relevant audiences resulted from isolation.[14] "In part, the very logic of clandestinity, the dynamic of a process which, once set in motion, was irreversible, contributed to such a misperception."[15] Mistakes – particularly the false expectation that the Italian government was on the verge of collapse in 1971 – were encouraged by the movement into the underground.

The sharpest and clearest aspect of the beliefs that may be conducive to terrorism is identification and characterization of the enemy. In a pattern that is typical of much social conflict, the enemy is portrayed as an undifferentiated and monolithic entity, usually an abstraction such as a system or a class. Wasmund observed that "a friend-enemy mentality exists which is typical of all totalitarian groupings" and that the enemy is a figure that symbolizes everything "bad."[16] The stereotypical enemy is both unrelentingly hostile and morally corrupt. Society as well as the state may be perceived as the enemy – the bourgeoisie, for example, or capitalism. The enemy may even be international; multinational imperialism is often a common enemy of the radical right and the radical left.

The self-image of the terrorist is ambivalent, even contradictory. Terrorists need to see themselves as doing good, to justify their actions, and to maintain morale. Consequently "auto-propaganda" may be more critical to group survival than are attempts to persuade external audiences, whether governments, constituencies, or like-minded groups.[17] The users of terrorism often see themselves as victims, but also as an avant-garde acting on behalf of victims of injustice. They act for "the people" who are unable to act for themselves. They are simultaneously victims and righteous avengers, targets of oppression and soldiers. This conviction may be strengthened by the belief that they do not stand to gain personally from their efforts. Altruism and self-sacrifice are dominant themes, yet the key metaphor in terrorist literature is struggle and combat. A strong trace of millenarianism, with its faith in personal redemption through violence, is evident.[18]

Beliefs about enemy and self overshadow references to the actual victims of terrorism, whose deaths or injuries are usually blamed on others (governments who refuse to heed warnings, for example). They do pay attention, however, to the audiences for terrorism and interpret the world in causal terms.[19] The image of the "people" in Western democracies, for example, is based on imperfect assumptions of benevolence and ignorance. The physical victims of terrorism, whatever their personal identity, are never seen as members of the social classes whom the terrorists claim to represent.

The sources of these beliefs, which justify terrorism, lie in political culture and in psychological needs. Beliefs are selectively derived from the group's political, social, and cultural environment and thus reflect prevailing ideologies as well as socialization patterns. The intellectuals who lead or participate in groups that use terrorism are rarely philosophical or ideological innovators. Beliefs also serve important psychological needs, such as compensation for an inability to deal with aggressive feelings. They may aid in the external attribution of blame and the projection of hostility onto the enemy. Ideological rationalizations may mask a form of generational rebellion against authority displaced onto political figures. The low self-esteem exhibited by some individuals in these groups and their view of the enemy as omnipotent may be signs of developmental immaturity. The fact that most terrorists are young provides some support for this hypothesis. People who commit acts of violence may also need to neutralize guilt – guilt over their victims, survivor guilt when comrades are lost, or guilt over aggressive impulses toward parents or surrogate authority figures.

Psychological research in different theoretical traditions suggests that individual beliefs are likely to be stable rather than volatile. Even greater stability should characterize collective attitudes that are constantly reinforced by group interaction. Theories of cognitive consistency indicate that individuals absorb only information that supports their beliefs, ignore disconfirming evidence, fail to recognize value conflicts, and neglect to reconsider decisions once they are reached. Other approaches emphasize the emotional conflict that lies behind decision making. The more costly the consequences of a decision, the more painful the reassessment. Members of the groups who use terrorism may engage in what Irving Janis and Leon Mann call "defensive avoidance."[20] Ego involvement in prior commitments is bound to be strong, and the cost of abandoning them unacceptably high. Furthermore, the nature of a belief system itself may preclude change. The least systematic beliefs are the most resilient, and the least empirically relevant are the most incontrovertible because they cannot be tested or falsified. Vague and distant long-term goals can be an advantage. "True believers" are not by nature skeptical.[21]

It is also possible that the resort to terrorism precedes and consequently determines beliefs. That is, rather than acting as a result of preconceptions, people may act impulsively or unthinkingly and then rationalize their actions. "Self-perception theory" is based on the assumption that individuals use their own actions as a guide to the formation of attitudes and beliefs, through a process of self-inference.[22] Engaging in terrorism, perhaps because of coincidence or group pressures, leads the individual to adopt beliefs and images that explain the moral necessity and practical efficacy of terrorism. Once convinced that terrorism is intellectually justified, an individual is persuaded in retrospect that the initial use of terrorism was based on prior ideological beliefs. Because terrorism is extreme behavior, usually condemned by society, it is important for the individual to generate an explanation for it. When terrorists are students, the need to intellectualize terrorist activity may be particularly strong.

Jeanne Knutson effectively described the relationship between group pressures and rigid but subjective belief systems: "Doubts are muted and are continuously attacked by the group, which employs great psychological pressure toward conformity. Basic concepts are challenged with great difficulty. . . . There is no real debate over primary assumptions."[23] The group seeks a "homogeneous level of . . . thought which stifles self-doubt and a consideration of alternatives."[24] She quoted one of her interviewees as admitting that "we were increasingly losing our grip on reality" and that cutting off contacts with the outside world led to a "group personality" with its own deadly internal momentum.[25] She concluded,

> In such an atmosphere, group actions take on a predetermined, fatalistic quality in which *responsibility* for the occurrence of specific actions is progressively shifted onto the opposition players in the government, general social forces, or an inactive populace, and terrorist players come to experience themselves as guided by an externally perceived necessity.[26]

The cohesiveness of the group strengthens adherence to beliefs, and in turn beliefs reinforce solidarity.

Implications for the practice of terrorism

These psychological factors have important implications for terrorist behavior. On a general level, members of groups may act simply to maintain a collective identity and thus seek to keep the group alive whatever its political accomplishments. Baumann explains, "I saw that it was going to go a hundred percent wrong. . . . I only participated out of solidarity."[27] Dependence on the group is likely to lead members to value the approval of other members of the group more than the achievement of long-term political goals. Thus an objective definition of success, predicated on the achievement of political ends, may not be appropriate.

One consequence of the centrality of the group is that motives that unite its members, such as vengeance, may take precedence over instrumental calculations, which can be deeply divisive. Newman and Lynch argue that terrorism may be a "cycle of violence" fueled by vengeance, leading to its self-perpetuation.[28] They argue that the only possible common ideology associated with terrorism is one of vengeance, a code of conduct that shapes behavior. The code of vengeance embodies its own justification, giving the terrorist not only a moral claim but an obligation. Terrorism thus becomes a sophisticated modern form of feuding. Vengeance, which is motivated by a sense of injustice and of powerlessness, is based on the principle of reciprocity. Escalation occurs because the act of retribution is never an exact match for the original offense. Those who administer it cannot resist adding an element of coercion, trying to make the response to perceived injustice sufficiently strong to deter counterretribution. The avenger develops identity through violence, thus generating a process without limits. Only vengeance can defend one's honor, which is an essential component of identity.

The intense loyalty that members of the underground group feel for each other, a loyalty strengthened by bonds of kinship or personal affection, makes revenge imperative when government security forces kill or imprison comrades. Such an outcome is highly likely once a group resorts to terrorism, which is bound to provoke a repressive government reaction. Because revenge motivates both sides, terrorism and the response to terrorism create an independent and self-contained logic. Eventually repression from the authorities provokes actions intended only to avenge comrades, not to change the positions of government or society.[29] Revenge is part of a process of using violence in order to strengthen group cohesiveness, confirm beliefs about self and world, and maintain group morale and individual self-esteem. These needs are frequently characterized in terms of upholding "honor."

Jerrold Post notes, moreover, that government "retaliation may actually strengthen the group and promote increased terrorist activity" because the terrorists' worldviews are confirmed and their cohesiveness is enhanced by threat and shared danger.[30] Coercive government responses thus make terrorism self-sustaining because the terrorists' expectations of hostility are proved right. Terrorism can then be justified as defensive. But, as noted earlier, governments may not be able to control their own response or prevent the development of a cycle of vengeance and retribution. Once terrorism begins, both sides are likely to lose control.

Terrorist and counterterrorist forces are often mirror images of each other. Each consciously imitates the other – terrorists act as "armies," while national armies develop specialized elite intervention forces that operate covertly. Each side's reputation is caught up in the struggle. The purpose of terrorism and of repression becomes to outdo the other. Each small, self-contained, and specialized unit tends to become autonomous from central authority. Examples include the Combat Organization of the Socialist Revolutionary Party in Russia, combatting the czarist secret police or Okhrana, and the Algiers terrorist units of the FLN against the French paratroopers. In these situations, the phenomenon of the double agent or agent-provocateur takes on special importance as the communication link between the two sides. The role of the informant or double agent remains a "neglected category" for analysis, as Gary T. Marx claimed.[31]

Because internal conflict threatens group cohesion and identity, leaders may try to deflect aggression onto external targets. For example, one reason for the creation of the Black September Organization was apparently to absorb the intense frustration of younger militants over the Palestinian expulsion from Jordan in 1970. Arafat apparently decided to permit, if not direct, terrorism outside the Middle East in order to prevent internal dissent within Fatah.

Furthermore, adherence to the group and to its standards helps to overcome guilt. Even if group values are internalized, some individuals will experience anxiety and self-doubt. Peer pressure encourages members of the group to commit actions they would normally find morally reprehensible, such as killing children. Distress engendered by guilt leads to greater dependence on the group and increased group influence over the individual, and consequently more terrorism. The unpleasant prospect of accepting responsibility and suffering remorse may then prevent the individual from leaving the group.

The collective belief system can aid in assuaging guilt. Albert Bandura explains that

> People do not ordinarily engage in reprehensible conduct until they have justified to themselves the morality of their actions. What is culpable can be made honorable through cognitive restructuring. In this process, reprehensible conduct is made personally and socially acceptable by portraying it in the service of moral ends.[32]

He refers to mechanisms such as contrasting one's behavior with the more inhumane practices of one's enemy (palliative comparison), using euphemistic language to disguise violence and make it respectable, obscuring the consequences of one's actions, dehumanizing the enemy, blaming the victim, or displacing responsibility onto others or in fact onto a collective instrumentality. All collective arrangements, he notes, obscure individual responsibility. He further explains that "people frequently engage in violent activities not because of reduced self-control but because their cognitive skills and self-control are enlisted all too well through moral justifications and self-exonerative devices in the service of destructive causes."[33] In effect, the beliefs of terrorist actors serve as a mechanism of "moral disengagement."[34] Upon entering an underground organization, the individual does not undergo a psychological conversion but comes to see violence as morally sanctioned.

Legal and military terms of discourse reinforce the image of the terrorist as the impersonal agent of larger forces. In the euphemistic language of terrorism, victims are "executed" after "trials." Terrorism becomes "urban guerilla warfare." Seeing oneself as a victim makes it hard to conceive of others as victims or oneself as an aggressor. The idea of acting on behalf of an oppressed but faceless constituency (the proletariat, the Third World, or prisoners) justifies practices that would be abhorrent if performed out of pure self-interest. William Ascher, in interviewing Armenian and Irish supporters of terrorism (admittedly not the terrorists themselves) identifies moral indignation as a critical attitude and links it to "disinterestedness" or "distance":[35] the less one has to gain personally from the outcome of violence, the more sincere and righteous one feels.

Psychological considerations may also explain the particular form terrorism takes. Hostage taking, for example, can be interpreted rationally as a form of coercive bargaining, a means of compensating for the greater power of governments, since weakness is not a disadvantage in situations of blackmail.[36] Yet, it is also possible that a desperate need to free imprisoned comrades genuinely motivates hostage taking. "Second generation" successor groups in West Germany and Italy devoted themselves to freeing imprisoned "historic" or "founding" leaders. The demand for the release of prisoners may thus be sincere rather than a disguise for publicity-seeking behavior. Dependence on the group and its leaders, fear of a hostile government, or survivor guilt, may combine to make hostage takers feel desperate. Hostage taking may also be a search for recognition by the government, a result of the terrorists' collective self-image as powerless victims.[37]

The desire to avoid responsibility for violent outcomes may also affect the form of terrorism. Terrorists wish to blame casualties on the government. The attribution of blame begins with an assignment of responsibility and a judgment about causality.[38] Terrorists may not see themselves as morally accountable because they believe that they did not originally intend or foresee a negative outcome. Their initial expectations upon seizing hostages, for example, are optimistic because they believe that the government will comply. Terrorists may be likely to think that governments know the outcome if concessions are refused. Furthermore, one way of reducing cognitive dissonance, induced by having to choose between the two negative options of killing hostages or giving up, is to believe that the only escape from the dilemma rests with the opponent.[39] The terrorists are also likely to see themselves as having been coerced, rather than seeing the government as having been blackmailed. They do not perceive the killing of hostages as a voluntary action but as something the government compelled them to do. Terrorists can thus not only exonerate themselves but feel self-righteous and confirm their image of the evil state.

Similarly, in leaving bombs a group may accept responsibility but not blame, which perhaps reveals an interesting ability to separate these two processes. Maria McGuire, an early member of the Provisional IRA, describes a car-bomb in Belfast in 1972 that killed six and injured 146 people. In this case, the Provisionals falsely accused the security forces of deliberately muddling the telephoned warning in order to discredit the IRA. McGuire continues,

> Despite blaming the security forces, the movement 'accepted responsibility' for the explosion, and it was a curious thing that the Provisionals felt that by doing so they somehow atoned for the casualties. . . . I admit that at times I did not connect with the people who were killed or injured in such explosions. I always judged such deaths in terms of the effect they would have on our support, and I felt that this in turn depended on how many people accepted our explanation.[40]

In barricade and hostage situations, where stress and tension are high, hostage takers may be prone to panic. Their behavior, Janis and Mann would suggest, is likely to be erratic.[41] They are tempted to precipitous action. If all choices appear unpleasant and time pressures are severe, their judgment will be poor. The responsibility for averting disaster will be seen to rest with the government. For example, during incidents such as the takeover of the Achille Lauro or the attempted hijacking of a Pan Am jet in Karachi, the aggressive behavior of the hijackers might have been the result of loss of emotional control, not deliberate calculation. What an instrumental approach would interpret as sequential killing of hostages in order to reinforce the credibility of a threat, a psychological approach would interpret as a panic reaction. The so-called "Stockholm Syndrome," a shorthand term for the hypothesis that with time hostages and their captors will become attached to each other because of the phenomenon of identification with the aggressor, is thus unlikely to operate. Hostage takers or kidnappers are acting as agents of a group on which they are emotionally dependent in the extreme; letting the group down is probably a worse alternative than killing hostages of whom one has grown reasonably fond or even confronting death. The relationship with the group also enables the hostage takers to think of themselves as impersonal agents of the collective entity and thus avoid assuming individual responsibility.

The escalation of terrorism to greater levels of destructiveness may also result from psychological processes. For example, it is possible that the "risky shift" that research in experimental social psychology finds characteristic of small groups applies to political undergrounds.[42] Participation in group discussions leads to a heightened propensity to take risks. The individual's reluctance to let the group "down" or lose face in the eyes of peers may encourage this process. Yet, we also know that most groups are risk-averse in the sense of selecting soft, unprotected targets. The expansion of targets toward increasingly innocent victims is a form of escalation. A group setting facilitates brutalization. Participation in terrorism conditions and desensitizes the individual. Discomfort with violence is overcome by performing it. Routine sets in. Thus the absence of conditioning may impede the adaptation of "second-generation" recruits who enter the group after its values have been formed. They may be the most likely defectors. On the other hand, candidates for membership in established organizations may be attracted to violence, while the founding members were attracted to the group.

To note the phenomenon of brutalization, however, is not to claim that all members of such groups actually participate in or are capable of participating in physical violence. Only a few elite members of the underground organizations are sharpshooters or bombers; most are support personnel. Role differentiation enables many members of the group to dissociate themselves from violence. Responsibility is diffused through the division of labor.[43]

Moreover, a common method of dealing with stress is to focus narrowly on the task at hand, rather than to reflect on the implication of one's actions.[44] This psychological defense or coping mechanism becomes less necessary as the task becomes habitual. Both compartmentalization and routinization reduce the discomfort an individual might initially feel upon committing an act of terrorism. When terrorists claim that they are only "soldiers," they are trying to achieve detachment and impersonality as well as to legitimize their actions.

Conclusions

This analysis suggests that a radical group's decision to enter the underground and isolate itself from society may be a decisive event in the development of terrorism. In circumstances where this decision entails extreme isolation from social support networks, clandestinity strengthens solidarity and dependence on group beliefs that justify violence. The more terrorism is used, the more it needs to be justified by moralistic attitudes. It may develop into a cycle of vengeance and retribution that is self-defeating.

Furthermore, this analysis suggests that justifications for terrorism and emotional support, both provided by the group, are critical. From this point of view, terrorism is likely to end when the bonds that link members of the group to each other are dissolved or when beliefs that justify violence break down or are discredited. But, as Franco Ferracuti has observed, "What happens in the mind of the terrorist who decides to abandon terrorism is not known."[45]

Part III

Responding to terrorism

8 Coercive diplomacy

Terrorism is a difficult test for the theory and practice of coercive diplomacy, which combines the judicious and limited use of force with positive inducements to change the behavior of an adversary. U.S. counterterrorism policy cannot routinely meet the basic requirements of the strategy. When coercive diplomacy is applied, the conditions that would make it successful are rarely met. While the United States has sometimes been effective in changing the policies of states that instigate or assist terrorism, it has not found an appropriate mix of threat and reward that could constrain the behavior of nonstate adversaries.

This chapter focuses on the U.S. response to terrorism from 1993 to the "war on terrorism" launched in 2001. It first outlines the general contours of the threat as it developed after the Cold War. This overview is followed by analysis of the general concept of coercive diplomacy in relation to terrorist strategies. The propositions thus generated are then tested against the instances of post-Cold War counterterrorism policy that most closely fit the definition of the concept of coercive diplomacy. These cases, when military force was used or threatened, provide the best basis for evaluating the success or failure of the strategy. They include the retaliatory strike against Iraq in 1993, threats against Iran following the bombing of U.S. military facilities in Saudi Arabia in 1996, cruise missile attacks against Sudan and Afghanistan in 1998, and efforts to compel the Taliban to yield Osama Bin Laden after September 11, 2001. This chapter concludes by assessing the strengths and weaknesses of coercive diplomacy as a response to terrorism.

The context

When the Clinton Administration took office in 1993, the threat of terrorism appeared to be receding. The incidence of international terrorism was diminishing. Iraq had been defeated in the Gulf War. The last remaining hostages in Lebanon had been released. The ideological hostility of the Cold War had evaporated. The Israeli–Palestinian conflict appeared to be on the brink of transformation. A multilateral consensus against terrorism seemed feasible, with the United Nations assuming a more active role. Under U.N. auspices, for example, sanctions were implemented against Libya in order to bring to trial the Libyan agents accused of the bombing of Pan Am 103 in 1988.

The Clinton Administration inherited a counterterrorism policy that had been applied reasonably consistently since 1972. It had four key principles: (1) no concessions to terrorist demands, (2) the imposition of diplomatic and economic sanctions against states that sponsored terrorism, (3) enforcement of the rule of law by bringing terrorists to trial, and (4) multilateral cooperation. It was accepted that the United States would take the lead in all these areas, yet frustration over lack of international cooperation often led to unilateral U.S. action. The Department of State officially designated six countries as sponsors of terrorism, which invoked automatic unilateral sanctions: Cuba, Iran, Iraq, Libya, North Korea, and Syria.

In addition, the 1986 attack on Libya had established a precedent for the use of retaliatory air power, although its effectiveness was questioned.[1] Earlier that year a task force led by Vice President George Bush had concluded that the "judicious employment of military force" might be necessary to a deterrent strategy. The report noted that a military show of force would be less risky than the use of force and might successfully intimidate terrorists and their sponsors. However, the task force also warned that a show of force could be considered gunboat diplomacy, that it might be perceived as a challenge rather than a credible threat, and, most important, that failure could require escalation to an active military response.[2]

The Clinton Administration initially assumed a moderate stance toward terrorism. In contrast to the strong rhetoric of the Reagan years, the President's public speeches treated terrorism not as a major national security issue but as one of a series of modern transnational, or "border-crossing," threats, along with drug trafficking, global organized crime, epidemics of disease, and environmental disasters.

Immediately, however, three developments made terrorism a priority: highly destructive attacks on U.S. territory from both domestic and foreign sources, the terrorist use of chemical weapons, and the emergence of new terrorist actors hostile to U.S. interests. The close sequencing of terrorist attacks in different locations, the diversity of terrorist sources, and the geographical scope of terrorism heightened the salience of the threat.

The first shock came in February 1993, with the first bombing of the World Trade Center. Subsequent judicial investigations revealed that the perpetrators were transnational actors, independent of state sponsorship, not a familiar organization from the past. As information was gathered over the next two years, the United States identified an amorphous group composed of Egyptian religious dissidents, veterans of the war against the Soviet Union in Afghanistan, and freelancers. Arrests in 1995 revealed that the conspirators, led by Ramzi Youcef, had plans to bomb the Lincoln and Holland Tunnels and other buildings in New York as well as U.S. airliners over the Pacific. At the same time, state-sponsored terrorism continued to challenge U.S. interests. In April 1993 Kuwaiti authorities uncovered a plot to assassinate former President Bush during a visit to Kuwait. In June the United States retaliated against Baghdad for its complicity in the thwarted attack.

Less than two years later, in March 1995, the Aum Shinrikyo religious cult disseminated sarin gas in the Tokyo subways, killing eleven people and injuring as many as 5,000. U.S. policy makers feared that this first terrorist use of chemical weapons would establish a dangerous precedent for a "catastrophic" terrorism that the United States was ill equipped to combat.

Within the month a truck-bomb exploded in front of the federal building in Oklahoma City, leaving 168 people dead. The bombing exposed the country's domestic vulnerability to mass-casualty terrorism and reinforced the apprehensions inspired by the World Trade Center bombing two years earlier. Combined with the Tokyo subway attack, these incidents raised the specter of an even more deadly terrorist attack against the U.S. homeland in the future.

Although concern, especially in Congress, mounted over inadequate "domestic preparedness," U.S. interests abroad continued to be at risk, particularly military forces stationed in Saudi Arabia. Two bombings in 1995 and 1996 were the most serious attacks on U.S. targets outside the country since the 1983 bombing of the U.S. Marine barracks in Lebanon and the 1988 midair bombing of Pan Am 103. In November 1995 an attack on a Saudi National Guard office in Riyadh used by U.S. military trainers killed five U.S. citizens.[3] In June 1996 a truck-bomb at the Khobar Towers military housing complex in Dhahran killed nineteen U.S. airmen and wounded more than 200 U.S. citizens. The Saudi government charged that Iran was responsible, and the United States considered but rejected military retaliation.

In July 1996 attention was again drawn to internal dangers. A small bomb at the Olympic Games in Atlanta led the secretary of defense to cut short a trip to Australia out of fear that it was part of a large-scale conspiracy, possibly connected to the Khobar Towers attack.[4] Fortunately, the initial reports turned out to be exaggerated.

Nevertheless, domestic worries about terrorism increased, focused especially on the prospective use of weapons of mass destruction (WMD). In May 1998 the president signed two presidential decision directives designed to upgrade the country's counterterrorism capability. These measures dealt primarily with the organization of the government to combat terrorism and with domestic defenses against threats to the nation's infrastructure, such as attacks on telecommunications or banking systems. The president appointed a national coordinator for security, infrastructure protection, and counterterrorism on the staff of the National Security Council (NSC).

In August 1998 the nation was shocked again when bombs exploded simultaneously at U.S. embassies in Kenya and Tanzania, resulting in 301 deaths and more than 5,000 wounded. The bombings were charged to Osama Bin Laden, whom U.S. authorities had recognized as a threat since at least 1996. The United States struck back with cruise missile attacks against Bin Laden's training camps in Afghanistan and against a pharmaceuticals plant in Sudan, which was purportedly developing chemical weapons for Bin Laden. Sudan's general support for Islamic extremist terrorism had long been an irritant to the United States, and the country had been added to the State Department's list of state sponsors of terrorism in 1993.

In early December 1999 the United States received intelligence information that Bin Laden planned a series of attacks on U.S. citizens around the world to coincide with the new year. Jordanian authorities had disrupted a plot to attack tourist sites in Jordan and Israel. A few days later, U.S. customs agents arrested an Algerian crossing the Canadian border into Seattle. Bomb-making materials were found in his car, and he had been trained in camps operated by Bin Laden in Afghanistan. His target was Los Angeles International Airport.

In October 2000 the U.S. military suffered another serious blow when the destroyer USS *Cole* was bombed in Yemen during a refueling stop. U.S. and Yemeni authorities suspected that Bin Laden was responsible for the attack, which killed seventeen U.S. sailors and crippled the ship, although in the immediate definitive proof was lacking.

Terrorism was not an issue in the 2000 presidential campaign. On assuming office, the Bush Administration did not consider it a top priority of the administration. The President's attention focused on domestic policy.

Over the spring and summer of 2001, U.S. intelligence agencies noticed an increased volume of communications among affiliates of the Bin Laden network and warned the government that a major attack was imminent. They could not predict, however, where or when or how an attack might occur. On the morning of September 11, the United States was the victim of a terrorist attack of unprecedented destructiveness. The inventiveness of the plot and the complexity of the planning also pointed to a new level of terrorism. The loss of the World Trade Center and a wing of the Pentagon, as well as recognition that the White House or the Capitol might also have been destroyed, thrust terrorism to the top of the national security agenda. Eliminating the threat from Al Qaeda suddenly became the nation's top priority.

Terrorism and coercive diplomacy

Coercive diplomacy is designed to persuade an opponent to stop an action already undertaken or actively threatened. It is not uncommon for coercive diplomacy to confront an adversary who is also engaged in a form of compellence, as in the case of international terrorist adversaries seeking the government's withdrawal from a political commitment.[5] Each party, the government and the terrorist, wants to erode the other's motivation to continue and tries to understand what the other values most. Each wants to create the expectation of costs of sufficient magnitude that the other will back down. Each attempts to calibrate the amount of force necessary to overcome the other's disinclination to comply with its demands. Subjective perceptions or estimates of the credibility and strength of threats are critical to each party's decision making. Positive inducements are difficult for both sides since the conflict typically has a zero-sum quality. Certain asymmetries are also inherent in this relationship of reciprocal compellence. Each side threatens to punish the other for noncompliance, but the coercing state's power to escalate beyond the exemplary use of force far exceeds the terrorist's capabilities. On the other hand, the terrorist is likely to be more risk acceptant.

Terrorism, however, imposes unusual constraints on coercive diplomacy.[6] Consider first the targets of coercive diplomacy. They are nonstate groups or states that are already isolated. Thus, governments are typically dealing with opponents lacking reliable internal control or valuable assets. Furthermore, the defending state is often trying to change the behavior of a loose alliance of states, nonstates, and autonomous individuals with ambiguous and complex interrelationships. Any strategy of coercive diplomacy must thus be directed toward multiple targets simultaneously, and each target's susceptibility to pressure and willingness to transgress vary. What is wanted of them will also vary. Thus, the defender has a complicated task involving critical trade-offs among different interests.

In addition, assessing the nature and intensity of the adversary's motivation is problematic. It is difficult for decision makers to put themselves in the frame of reference of the adversary. Because the essence of terrorism is concealment and deception, information about terrorist intentions is inherently difficult to obtain. When information is lacking, decision makers are tempted to rely on prior assumptions about motivation rather than on analysis of specific circumstances. Furthermore, a tendency to assume intention from behavior as well as poor understanding can lead states to focus on opportunities and vulnerabilities rather than on motivation. The propensity of policy makers to develop stereotypes and preconceptions that stress the fanaticism and irrationality of the adversary is reinforced when acts of terrorism are notably destructive and provocative. For example, policy makers may be tempted to ascribe terrorism to blind rage rather than instrumental reasoning, to personalize the adversary, and to see the enemy as monolithic. Terrorists' aspirations may be seen as unlimited and their demands nonnegotiable from the outset (especially if the "new terrorism" framework described in Chapter 3 is accepted). Lack of knowledge makes it hard to assess the accuracy of these assumptions.

However, asymmetrical motivation is probably always in favor of the nonstate terrorist, and in favor of some state actors as well. Neither survival nor material power is at stake for the United States, however painful terrorist attacks are. In contrast, for the terrorist, everything may be at stake. Terrorism is the only reason for the existence of some nonstate actors.[7] Moreover, precisely because of their superior motivation, and because terrorism is so unacceptable a method, the defending state is likely to want to destroy the terrorist organization, not just change its behavior. Reassurances that one's aims are limited may not be credible even at the early stages of a coercive strategy. Under these circumstances the nonstate will have little incentive to abandon terrorism. States sponsoring terrorism have more to lose by resisting demands for compliance, but their isolation may also limit their interests beyond terrorism. If the coercer explicitly or implicitly seeks the displacement of the offending government, then compliance is unlikely unless some faction of the regime defects.

While identifying the terrorist opponent and understanding his motivations are difficult, gaining sufficiently precise and timely warning of his intention to attack in order to communicate a counterthreat and a sense of urgency is almost impossible. Terrorism depends on surprise. Furthermore, if a government learns of and exposes a terrorist plot, it may simply deflect the terrorists onto alternative targets or alter the timing of their attack. Identifying concrete assets to threaten or damage is also difficult. First, terrorism requires few material resources. Second, the assets a nonstate actor possesses, such as physical bases or financial resources, are necessarily within the domain of a state, so that considerations of sovereignty and other foreign policy interests are involved. A government cannot track, locate, or punish nonstates without the cooperation or acquiescence of states. Terrorism may be considered private rather than public violence, but there is no private space within which terrorists can operate.

Another difficulty is that coercing states cannot judge the effect of a threat or an initial use of demonstrative force since typically there can only be evidence of noncompliance.[8] Even if an adversary should renounce terrorism and disarm, it requires significant trust to accept such promises since terrorism is an economical and thus easily resumed strategy. Verification is tricky. The coercer must usually infer compliance from the absence of overt noncompliance, which is inconclusive and even dangerous. This constraint also makes it difficult to use an ultimatum to create a sense of urgency.

Another problem with the use of threats or demonstrative force is that terrorist adversaries may not perceive the use of force as punishment. In fact, the purpose of terrorism may be to provoke overreaction. A limited punitive response may reward them by providing recognition and even legitimacy among their constituents. The resort to military force may erode the coercer's status as the victim, causing a loss of moral high ground. It can alienate allies who prefer persuasion to coercion. And it can lead to an endless cycle of revenge and retaliation.

A strategy of coercive diplomacy is further complicated because the coercing state seeks not only to curb present terrorism but also to dissuade future terrorists. The goal is to compel existing terrorist actors to stop and to deter successors from starting. Using more destructive force than coercive diplomacy strictly requires may be essential to the long-term purpose of deterrence, but extreme punitiveness may exacerbate the existing conflict. Escalation can jeopardize the post-crisis relationship that the coercing government seeks, which may be based on interaction with a different set of actors than those currently posing a threat.

The government's secrecy requirements also weaken coercive diplomacy. Any meaningful threat to the terrorist in advance of an anticipated attack publicizes what the government knows and permits the terrorist to design around the government's threats. Concealing plans to threaten or use force may be an operational necessity. However, maintaining strict secrecy is an impediment to building the necessary domestic or international political consensus to ensure policy legitimacy. Lack of consultation before the response almost guarantees public criticism afterward. In the aftermath, security considerations also restrict the government's ability to justify its actions, since persuasive explanations would reveal sensitive intelligence information. Furthermore, covert preemption of an attack cannot usually be revealed to the public. Thus, failures are visible, while successes mostly are not.

Liberal democracies are restricted to a proportional and discriminating use of force. They are reluctant to incur casualties among their own forces or among noncombatants on the opponent's side. They are sensitive to reputation and to international norms governing the use of force. For these reasons, threatening escalation should an initial exemplary use of force fail can be difficult. On the other hand, public demand for action after a terrorist outrage may lead the government to respond rashly. It is the public, after all, that is targeted in the most spectacular acts of terrorism. The government's response to terrorism may come to depend more on public expectations – or decision makers' perceptions of those expectations – than on calculations of the adversary's reaction. Moreover, the defending state that offers positive inducements for stopping terrorism is vulnerable to charges of being "soft on terrorism."

Because terrorism is a form of surprise attack outside the context of war, it usually takes time to identify and locate the perpetrators. By the time the government acquires convincing evidence of responsibility, the public's outrage may have dissipated and justifying a punitive response will be difficult. However, responding quickly without conclusive information will likely appear clumsy and vindictive.

In sum, the specific properties of terrorism complicate the case for coercive diplomacy. The strategic interaction between government and terrorist is a form of reciprocal compellence. The targets of coercive diplomacy are multiple, shifting, and diffuse. Their material assets are few and meager by conventional measures of state power. Not only are nonstate actors hard to identify and understand, but they deliberately conceal their intentions. Their tactics depend on surprise and deception. Governments lack tactical warning of attacks. The terrorist can also be expected to be more highly motivated and more risk acceptant than the coercing government. Moreover, the government must look to the future and practice deterrence, preemption, prevention, and coercive diplomacy simultaneously. The government must also be concerned with policy legitimacy, since both domestic support and international cooperation are essential to an effective counterterrorist strategy.

The U.S. response to terrorism before September 11

The cases analyzed here illustrate the applicability and effectiveness of coercive diplomacy in U.S. counterterrorist policy after the end of the Cold War and before the attacks of September 11, 2001. The analysis focuses on situations involving the use or threat of military force, which is an essential component of a strategy of coercive diplomacy. Selecting these cases as focal points for a detailed examination of U.S. decision making provides empirical evidence for the theoretical propositions sketched earlier, permits comparisons to be made among cases, and establishes a foundation for drawing conclusions about the effectiveness of coercive diplomacy against terrorism. This approach also distinguishes U.S. policy before the September attacks from policy after the attacks.

Retaliation against Iraq, 1993

The case of retaliation against Iraq is the most straightforward case of the application of coercive diplomacy.[9] The provocation was a plot to kill former President Bush in a car-bomb attack during his visit to Kuwait in April. FBI and CIA investigations produced convincing evidence that the Iraqi Intelligence Service was behind the attempt. The information included confessions by two of the sixteen suspects arrested by Kuwaiti authorities, physical evidence from the bomb, and threats by Saddam Hussein to seek revenge against Bush for his leadership of the anti-Iraq coalition during the 1991 Gulf War. President Clinton referred to incontrovertible evidence of Iraq's guilt as well as to Saddam Hussein's past behavior:

> We should not be surprised by such deeds, coming, as they do, from a regime like Saddam Hussein's, which has ruled by atrocity, slaughtered its own people, invaded two neighbors, attacked others and engaged in chemical and environmental warfare. Saddam has repeatedly violated the will and conscience of the international community, but this attempt at revenge by a tyrant against the leader of the world coalition that defeated him in war is particularly loathsome and cowardly.[10]

The decision to use force against Iraq was carefully considered, and the process was strictly secret. It was reached after two months of intensive investigation, the conclusion of final reports from the CIA and the FBI, and long meetings between Clinton and top aides in the final week.[11] Apparently, no more than five presidential aides knew of the discussions. The Pentagon had been drawing up a list of possible military responses for several weeks before the decision, including targeting Saddam Hussein's personal command post and military headquarters. The option that was chosen was, as the president explained, "firm and commensurate." The target was directly related to the offending behavior, and the method comported no risks for U.S. forces. Two U.S. Navy ships in the Persian Gulf and the Red Sea fired twenty-three Tomahawk cruise missiles directly at the headquarters of the Iraqi Intelligence Service in central Baghdad. The purpose, according to the president and to top military officials, was to send a message to the people responsible for planning the operation, not to target Saddam Hussein himself. They acknowledged that it was a show of force rather than an attempt to destroy the regime. As General Colin Powell put it, the intention was to "smack him whenever it's necessary." The president explained the attack's purpose as deterring further violence or "outlawed behavior." The United States chose to attack in the early hours of the morning in Baghdad, to avoid civilian casualties, and the attack was delayed a day in order to avoid the Muslim sabbath.

The United States also explicitly retained the option to escalate if necessary. Military officials stated publicly on several occasions that they did not rule out future military action. Clinton explained in his public address: "If Saddam and his regime contemplate further illegal provocative actions, they can be certain of our response."[12]

Although the attack was unilateral, the United States had apparently consulted Britain far in advance and informed some of its allies just before the attack. The United States also called for an emergency Security Council meeting and justified the attack in terms of Article 51 of the U.N. Charter. The operation was kept carefully separate from the U.N.-authorized military actions against Iraq in the no-fly zone.

The administration quickly declared the attack a success, although only sixteen of the twenty-three cruise missiles hit their intended targets. Three hit a residential housing area outside the intelligence headquarters complex, killing eight civilians, according to official Iraqi accounts that the United States did not dispute. U.S. officials claimed that major damage was done to the Iraqi facility, although they declined to be specific about the potential political impact of the raid on Iraq's future behavior. At home, Congress was generally favorable to the decision, and the president received high approval ratings in public opinion polls.[13] However, conservative columnist William Safire criticized Clinton for choosing the weakest military option, a "pitiful wristslap," in response to a provocation that was actually an act of war.[14] Among U.S. allies, the British government supported a limited, proportional response, although opposition parties denounced the raid as a calculated reprisal.[15] Critics also warned that the strike would only strengthen Islamic extremists. In the Middle East only the Kuwaiti government enthusiastically supported the U.S. attack. Other Arab states criticized the action on the grounds that an anti-U.S. backlash would strengthen Saddam Hussein.[16] They noted that the United States had not acted decisively to stop ethnic cleansing in Bosnia, indicating a lack of balance and objectivity in U.S. foreign policy.

As for the effect of the raid on Iraq's subsequent behavior, no concrete evidence linked Iraqi agents to further acts of anti-U.S. terrorism in the 1990s. It is possible, then, to infer compliance from the lack of evidence of noncompliance. However, Paul Pillar, former deputy chief of the Counterterrorist Center of the CIA, argued that the U.S. effort had only a minimal effect and was unlikely to have deterred Saddam Hussein from further action.[17] Although temporarily weakened by the need to rebuild its intelligence networks, Iraq retained its capability for action. Iraq's primary focus became the antiregime opposition in Iraq and abroad. The government also sheltered various rejectionist Palestinian terrorist groups such as the Abu Nidal organization and provided financial support for the families of "suicide" bombers in Palestine.

After September 11 the Bush Administration charged repeatedly that Iraq was linked to Al Qaeda. Iraqi support for terrorism was cited as one reason for the shift in U.S. strategy to a preemptive posture.

The reaction to the Khobar Towers bombing, June 1996

The truck-bomb attack was directed against a U.S. military complex that housed almost 3,000 personnel participating in Joint Task Force/Southwest Asia, charged with enforcing the no-fly zone in Iraq. The explosion killed nineteen U.S. airmen, wounded 372 other U.S. citizens, and injured more than 200 non-Americans. At least four classified CIA reports had warned of a terrorist threat to the housing complex since the November 1995 bombing that the Saudi government had traced to domestic Sunni opposition groups.[18] The perpetrators of that bombing had been executed just three weeks earlier, and retaliation was expected. The

Department of Defense concluded that although tactical intelligence was lacking, there was "considerable" information that terrorists had both the capability and the intention of attacking.[19]

The first routine step was to send an FBI team to assist in the investigations, but the United States had "woefully inadequate intelligence" about the opposition within Saudi Arabia.[20] This assessment was subsequently confirmed by the Defense Department's report on the bombing, issued in September. The reasons for this blind spot were both general and specific. Intelligence gathering in friendly countries cannot exceed the bounds of the host government's tolerance, and the Saudi government was unusually sensitive to U.S. intrusion. Apparently the United States relied primarily on the royal family for information, and only after the bombing was a special CIA task force organized to analyze security in Saudi Arabia. There were also reports of uneven cooperation between the FBI and the Saudi Ministry of the Interior in the investigation into the bombings. Saudi authorities were said to be deeply concerned about secrecy and the possibility of leaks on the U.S. side.

Nevertheless, in mid-October the Clinton Administration was said to be actively considering a more aggressive response, including preemptive strikes and covert operations.[21] An internal policy debate was sparked not only by the bombing but also by Republican criticism during the presidential election campaign, especially charges of being "soft on terrorism" from Republican candidate Robert Dole and House Speaker Newt Gingrich. In September CIA director John Deutch had reluctantly gone public to defend the CIA against criticism, announcing in a speech that the CIA was drawing up a list of military options as well as improving its intelligence capabilities.[22]

Decision makers disagreed, however, over whether to target states or nonstates, a recurrent theme in counterterrorism policy debates. They also argued over the potential effectiveness of military action and the risks it comported. They had to acknowledge, however, that the primary alternative to force – economic and diplomatic sanctions against Iran, including a comprehensive trade embargo imposed by Congress in 1995 – had not curbed Iranian support for terrorism. Shortly before the Khobar Towers bombing, Secretary of State Warren Christopher had publicly condemned Iran for its leadership in encouraging and financing terrorism designed to disrupt the Middle East peace process, specifically suicide bombings by Palestinian Islamic Jihad and Hamas in Israel.[23] He made no mention of a possible direct Iranian threat to the United States and recommended only increased economic pressure in order to deny Iran the resources to finance its support for terrorism. The question of responsibility was also disputed. Among the NSC staff, Richard Clarke apparently argued that Iran was guilty, but Anthony Lake believed that the case was circumstantial.[24] Similarly, Syria was known to allow Iranian agents to use Syrian territory to recruit Islamic militants for training in Iran. However, the U.S. need for Syrian support in the Middle East peace process limited its options.

By November Saudi authorities had arrested forty suspects in the bombing. Press reports claimed that the Saudi government was convinced that Iran had sponsored the attack.[25] The perpetrators were said to be members of a wing of Hezbollah, a Lebanese Islamic organization trained and equipped by Iran and known for the 1983 U.S. Marine barracks bombing. Other evidence was said to indicate a direct Iranian connection, possibly with Syrian assistance. However, U.S. officials appeared unconvinced; in public they were cautious and noncommittal. When Secretary of Defense William Perry suggested openly that Iran might be behind the bombing, other officials immediately replied that he lacked evidence. Some officials suggested privately that Saudi Arabia might find it convenient to blame foreign or Shi'ite sources rather than domestic Sunni extremists. Saudi Arabia still appeared reluctant to provide conclusive evidence to the United States, perhaps out of fear that the United States would respond precipitately. A show of force or limited punitive strike against Iran would put Saudi Arabia at risk, not the United States. FBI officials were said to be frustrated and dissatisfied over the progress of the "joint" investigation; they had not been allowed to see the specific evidence linking Iran to the attack. Even so, to allay Saudi fears of leaks, information about the investigation was tightly restricted within the U.S. official community.

After the elections in the United States, Saudi authorities gave FBI director Louis Freeh more detailed information linking Iran to the bombing.[26] The Saudi government remained divided, however, over what response to recommend. Some officials favored a strong policy that might include punitive military strikes or an international trade embargo, such as the one approved by the Security Council against Libya in order to compel the surrender of the agents accused of the Pan Am 103 bombing. Others urged restraint and moderation.

Although the timing was not opportune – some U.S. officials remained skeptical about Saudi claims, the administration was in a postelection transition period, and the FBI had not had time to evaluate the Saudi evidence – the discussion of policy options resumed in December.[27] Because the Saudi information was highly sensitive, only top officials were briefed fully, including National Security Adviser Anthony Lake, CIA director John Deutch, and Secretary of Defense William Perry. Alternatives included selective military strikes to shut down Iran's oil export terminal at Kharg Island or to destroy Iran's navy. The United States could also blockade Iranian ports or impose a selective embargo on shipping. Attacks on Hezbollah training camps in Lebanon would be a less confrontational and more proportional military option, but they would not directly damage Iran's interests. The fact that these discussions were leaked to the press could be interpreted as a veiled threat, and Iran apparently expected a strike at this time since its forces were placed on alert. It is not clear, however, whether the threats were meaningful to Iran.

By January 1998 the administration still hesitated, feeling that the evidence linking Iran to the bombing was not definitive enough to justify admittedly risky military action or even to expose Iran in order to mobilize support for sanctions.[28] Saudi Arabia still would not allow FBI access to the imprisoned suspects (all Saudi citizens) or provide comprehensive evidence. The previous December FBI director Freeh had told the families of victims that no indictments or charges were imminent. Nevertheless, by late 1998 or early 1999 U.S. officials had apparently acquired convincing evidence that Iran was behind the attack, even if it was insufficient for prosecution.[29]

Instead of publicizing the information, the administration decided to use it secretly in order to try to induce Iran to abandon terrorism. In May 1997 Mohammed Khatemi's election as president of Iran had led to rapprochement with Saudi Arabia, concluding in an agreement not to support further acts of terrorism. As its critics had urged, the administration decided to pursue an accommodationist strategy in the interest of shifting the regime toward a more moderate stance. In fact, administration officials appeared uncomfortable when reminded of the earlier threats of retaliation. Rather than threatening confrontation, in August 1999 Clinton sent a secret letter to Khatemi.[30] The letter, which had been drafted months earlier but not sent, apparently asked for Iranian cooperation in solving the problem of the bombing, which was cited as the most important barrier to a policy of engagement Congressional opposition, including charges that the administration was deliberately ignoring Iran's role in Khobar Towers, prevented the administration from changing policy without progress on the issue. But the administration had already begun to reduce unilateral sanctions against Iran and to issue public statements that communicated understanding of Iran's resentment of the United States. Iran, however, remained obstinate. At this point the United States again began to refer publicly to possible Iranian involvement, suggesting that Iranian officials were implicated but that it was unclear whether the government itself had directed the attack. Moderates dominated Iranian parliamentary elections in February 2000, further complicating the problem of combining coercion and diplomacy.

There were no further direct Iranian attacks on U.S. interests, but Iran remained on the State Department's list of state sponsors of terrorism.[31] In January 2002 President Bush singled out Iran as part of the "axis of evil." The government was also suspected of aiding Palestinian groups conducting bombings in Israel and of assisting Al Qaeda militants fleeing Afghanistan.

Military strikes against Sudan and Afghanistan, 1998

Cruise missile attacks on targets in Sudan and Afghanistan in response to the bombings of the U.S. embassies in Kenya and Tanzania were the most obvious use of military force against terrorism before September 11. However, the 1998 bombings must be interpreted in the context of increasing reliance on covert operations to apprehend or kill Bin Laden and disrupt Al Qaeda operations, beginning before 1998 and extending to September 2001.

Bin Laden was first identified as a serious threat during investigations into the 1993 World Trade Center bombing.[32] In 1991, after Saudi Arabia expelled him, he moved to Sudan. In 1994, at U.S. instigation, Saudi authorities stripped him of his citizenship and much of his property and assets. By May 1996 the United States and Saudi Arabia had convinced Sudan to expel him. Apparently, the United States urged Saudi Arabia and Egypt to accept him but they refused, and the president did not want to spend his political capital on the issue. Sudan was reportedly willing to turn him over to the United States, but the Justice Department lacked the evidence to mount a trial. In order to build regional support for efforts to induce Sudan to expel him, the United States circulated a dossier accusing Bin Laden of training the Somalis who attacked U.S. forces in 1993, a role he was pleased to acknowledge.[33]

Thus Bin Laden took refuge in Afghanistan on the eve of the Taliban's takeover. As the State Department's 1997 report on terrorism noted, from August 1996 on, Bin Laden became "very vocal in expressing his approval of and intent to use terrorism."[34] In March 1997, in an interview with CNN, for example, he declared a jihad against the United States, ostensibly as a response to U.S. support for Israel, its military presence in Saudi Arabia, and its "aggressive intervention against Muslims in the whole world."[35] This campaign culminated in 1998 with the establishment of an "International Front for Islamic Holy War against the Jews and Crusaders," which effectively merged the Egyptian Islamic Jihad and Al Qaeda.[36] The front issued an appeal for attacks on U.S. civil and military targets around the world in order to force a U.S. withdrawal from Saudi Arabia and an end to the Israeli occupation of Jerusalem. Although Bin Laden had no clerical authority, the appeal was presented as a *fatwa*, or religious edict, which all Muslims were called on to obey.[37]

In 1996 the United States had already launched a grand jury investigation into Bin Laden's activities, and the CIA had begun to "disrupt" his network, often with the assistance of foreign governments. By June 1997 the National Security Agency was monitoring telephone conversations in Nairobi. A sealed indictment in June 1998 provided a basis for the arrests of twenty-one Al Qaeda militants during the summer. It charged Bin Laden and his associates with attacks on U.S. and U.N. troops in Somalia and accused him of leading a terrorist conspiracy in concert with Sudan, Iraq, and Iran. Press reports later indicated the United States was simultaneously plotting a raid into Afghanistan to arrest Bin Laden, as a result of a 1998 finding by President Clinton authorizing specific covert operations that included blocking Bin Laden's financial assets and exercising close surveillance. A worldwide alert issued by the Department of State in March 1998 drew attention to threats against U.S. military and civilians following the February 23 *fatwa*.

Although Sudan had expelled Bin Laden, it continued to support terrorism, in the U.S. view. In 1993 the country had been added to the State Department's list of state sponsors because it provided a base of operations for several terrorist groups, including Hezbollah. In 1995 U.S. intelligence agencies found that Bin Laden and Sudan were cooperating to produce chemical weapons to use against the United States in Saudi Arabia.[38] However, owing to the risk of terrorism (reportedly including an assassination attempt against Anthony Lake), the CIA's Khartoum station was shut down in 1995, and the embassy staff was removed for security reasons in 1996. The U.N. Security Council imposed sanctions when Sudan refused to turn over three Egyptian dissidents linked to an assassination attempt against Egyptian president Hosni Mubarak. In the summer of 1997 U.S. suspicions that Sudan might be developing chemical weapons deepened. In November the United States imposed a wide range of economic sanctions.[39] The 1997 State Department annual report accused Sudan of harboring terrorist organizations and assisting Iran in its support of radical Islamic groups. At approximately the same time, the United States began investigating the Al Shifa pharmaceuticals plant, and in July and August 1998 the CIA issued intelligence reports detailing links between the plant and Bin Laden. In fact, an August 4 report referred to new intelligence indicating that Bin Laden had already acquired chemical weapons and might be ready to attack.

There were, however, divisions of opinion within the administration, as there would be throughout Clinton's term. Supporters of a less confrontational approach pointed to positive aspects of Sudan's behavior: assistance in apprehending the world-famous terrorist "Carlos" in 1994, reinstitution of visa requirements for Muslim visitors in 1995, expulsion of Bin Laden in 1996, and offers in February 1997 and June 1998 to assist in combating terrorism. Unimpressed, Assistant Secretary of State for African Affairs Susan Rice dismissed these offers as a "charm offensive."[40]

Before the embassy bombings, Afghanistan was not a primary area of U.S. interest. The United States did not recognize the Taliban government. Afghanistan had ceased to be of strategic importance after the Soviet withdrawal in 1989, and the country was isolated during the period of anarchy that followed the collapse of the government in 1992. When the Taliban seized power in 1996, the United States was not alarmed.[41] The Taliban's extremist creed was perceived as "antimodern" rather than "anti-Western," and its opposition to Iran was welcome. Pakistan and Saudi Arabia, both U.S. allies, were the regime's main outside contacts.

The August bombings of the embassies in Kenya and Tanzania surprised U.S. authorities. Added to the difficulties of obtaining credible and specific intelligence warnings, bureaucratic coordination was a problem, both between agencies and between Washington and the field. According to the reports of the Accountability Review Boards, in Dar es Salaam, a "low-threat" post, no information or intelligence warned of a possible attack. In Kenya, a "medium-threat" post, no intelligence reports were received immediately before the bombing, but earlier reports referred explicitly to threats of vehicle-bombs and assassinations. These reports, however, were discounted because the sources were discredited or the information was imprecise. It was also believed that actions taken by the CIA and the FBI to confront Bin Laden in Nairobi, including telephone intercepts, raids, and arrests, had effectively eliminated the threat by the latter part of 1997, although in May 1998 surveillance resumed. However, the FBI and the CIA may not have shared what they knew with the State Department.[42] For its part, the State Department found the threat of crime more immediate and specific, a critical "daily reality." The ambassador to Kenya was more sensitive to the threat of terrorism, but her requests for the construction of a less vulnerable building were not met.

On August 20, thirteen days after the embassy bombings, the United States launched six or seven Tomahawk cruise missiles against the Al Shifa pharmaceuticals plant in Khartoum. Probably sixty to seventy missiles, launched from navy ships in the Red Sea and the Persian Gulf, struck a complex of base, support, and training camps used by Bin Laden in Afghanistan, near the Pakistani border. The Defense Department released few details, but later accounts disclosed that Pakistan was not informed of the operation in advance and that two of the targeted camps were run by Pakistani intelligence services.[43]

Secrecy, controversy, and a growing sense of urgency had characterized the decision-making process.[44] President Clinton, Secretary of Defense William Cohen, Secretary of State Madeleine Albright, Under Secretary of State Thomas Pickering, CIA director George Tenet, National Security Adviser Samuel Berger, and Chairman of the Joint Chiefs of Staff General Henry Hugh Shelton were the key participants. On the NSC staff, Richard Clarke, now the national coordinator for counterterrorism, played a "pivotal role in planning the operation on behalf of the President," according to press reports.[45] An NSC staff member was quoted as saying, "For the first time, the White House is treating terrorism as a national-security problem, and not as a law-enforcement problem. America has joined the battle."[46]

On August 8, the day after the embassy bombings, presidential advisers asked the Pentagon Joint Staff and the CIA, including the Counterterrorist Center, to draw up a list of possible targets. Approximately twenty sites were selected in Sudan, Afghanistan, and an unidentified third nation. Four days later, the list was narrowed according to the evidence linking each target to terrorism and the risks involved, including the danger of hitting civilians. On August 13, however, the CIA received information that Bin Laden and his key associates planned to meet in Afghanistan on August 20, and this date was selected for the attack.[47] The intelligence report also indicated that he might be planning further attacks, possibly using chemical weapons. This development imparted a new sense of urgency to the deliberations.

On August 19, with one day left to select the targets, a meeting was held at the White House to decide on final recommendations for the president. The code name of the operation, Infinite Reach, was not coincidental; the administration was apparently determined to demonstrate that it could strike two targets simultaneously, to match the adversary. The choices were the camps in Afghanistan and two targets in Sudan: the Al Shifa pharmaceuticals plant and a tannery linked to Bin Laden. The attacks were to take place at night, in order to avoid civilian casualties.

The decision to target training camps in Afghanistan was not questioned, but the choice of the Al Shifa plant was contentious. The secrecy surrounding the decision and the haste with which it was made may have precluded a broader examination of the evidence linking Al Shifa to chemical weapons production, and some analysts in the CIA and the State Department remained unconvinced. The FBI and the Defense Intelligence Agency were apparently excluded from the decision, although the FBI was responsible for constructing the legal case to prosecute Bin Laden. Tenet apparently warned that the link between Bin Laden and the factory was indirect and inferential. Berger, however, later countered that the choice of target was not questioned and that the only objections concerned the wisdom of striking Sudan after Bin Laden had left. He concluded the meeting by warning of the consequences if the United States failed to act and Bin Laden then launched a chemical attack.[48]

Apparently, General Shelton also criticized the targeting plan. He felt that the tannery should be taken off the list because it was not involved in chemical weapons production and the attack might cause civilian casualties. He then explained the plans for a military strike to other officers among the Joint Chiefs, who shared his doubts. Later that day Berger informed the president of their objections, and the tannery was dropped from the list.

On the afternoon of August 19 Richard Clarke summoned other administration officials responsible for counterterrorism to his office at the NSC and told them to remain through the evening in order to prepare a public response to follow the bombing. These advisers had not been consulted about the targets and reacted with skepticism when told of the decision, according to reports that Clarke later denied. Similarly, as word of the prospective military strike leaked out, CIA and State Department analysts expressed doubts about the choice of targets. Pickering and Albright were shown a report by the State Department's Bureau of Intelligence and Research questioning the Al Shifa evidence, but they held firm.

The strike against Sudan provoked extensive debate and criticism, primarily in the domestic press and among the U.S. political elite. Top U.S. officials, especially Secretary Albright, vigorously defended the action in terms of a mix of objectives: self-defense, preemption, disruption, and deterrence. Albright appeared on all four major television networks to make the case. The U.S. refusal to provide the intelligence information on which the choice of targets was based, on grounds of the need for secrecy, exacerbated the controversy. Almost immediately critics charged that the U.S. government was wrong on several counts in its public explanations that the Al Shifa plant was set up to manufacture chemical weapons.[49] The Clinton Administration then revealed some of its information, insisting that soil samples the CIA had taken from the plant grounds had traces of Empta, a precursor chemical for the production of VX nerve gas.[50]

After the August strikes, the United States kept up the pressure on Bin Laden and Al Qaeda. A "Small Group" of the Cabinet met almost weekly, and a Counterterrorism Security Group led by Richard Clarke met two or three times a week. In early September 1998, for example, six bombers were sent to Guam on a training mission characterized as a show of force aimed at Bin Laden, and the secretary of defense was quoted more than once as not ruling out the possibility of further military strikes.[51] Apparently, the major constraint was time. Using air bases in the Middle East was considered too politically sensitive, but U.S. decision makers insisted on precise weapons. These restrictions meant that cruise missiles had to be launched from ships and required a minimum of six hours' notice. Moreover, U.S. policy was apparently not to strike just any Al Qaeda asset but to pinpoint Bin Laden and top Al Qaeda leaders, who were moving targets.[52] Clinton had reportedly authorized the CIA or its local recruits to use lethal military force against Bin Laden and his top associates, to the extent of shooting down civilian aircraft should he attempt to leave Afghanistan. In December 1998 CIA director Tenet had issued a written "declaration of war" against Bin Laden, but this move did not lead to budget shifts or reassignment of personnel, nor was his intent known widely through the intelligence community.[53]

The Joint Chiefs opposed using Special Forces in a limited military operation, rejecting such proposals from Clinton's advisers as too risky and "naive." Moreover, a raid by Delta Force, for example, would have taken twelve to fourteen hours of advance notice. On the other hand, the White House did not sense that there was sufficient popular support for a major combat commitment, which is what the military recommended. Clinton was also said to fear an embarrassing mistake.[54]

U.S. policy also stressed law enforcement and sanctions. On August 20 President Clinton had added Al Qaeda to the government's official list of terrorist organizations, which blocked their U.S. assets and prohibited all financial transactions. A $5 million reward was offered for Bin Laden's arrest. With the cooperation of the Kenyan and Tanzanian governments, as well as other allies, the U.S. criminal investigation produced a series of indictments. Within a week after the military strikes, the FBI had brought two suspects back to the United States for trial, and arrests continued at a regular pace. In November and December additional indictments were returned, including charges against Bin Laden.

Another critical part of U.S. policy was pressing Afghanistan to extradite Bin Laden. In October 1999, at U.S. urging, the U.N. Security Council imposed a deadline of thirty days for the turnover of Bin Laden to a country where he would be tried. The council threatened sanctions to freeze the country's economic assets abroad and curtail international flights by the national airline (the United States had already imposed a unilateral embargo). The Taliban's desire to assume the U.N. seat still held by representatives of the former regime suggested that a bargain might be possible. However, Taliban leaders replied that they had already restricted Bin Laden's movements and communications but that they could not turn him over. Accordingly, in November sanctions were imposed despite the Taliban's request for a delay. The Taliban's foreign minister, Wakil Ahmad Muttawakil, responded, "We will never hand over Osama bin Laden, and we will not force him out. He will remain free in defiance of America. . . . We will not hand him to an infidel nation."[55]

Still U.S. officials continued to meet with representatives of the Taliban, reiterating the message that the United States was always prepared to talk but that Bin Laden had to be surrendered.[56] The administration declined the Taliban's offer to convene a panel of Islamic scholars to decide the issue. According to later press reports, U.S. threats then were as "stark'" as those issued after September 11 by the Bush Administration.[57] If so, they were not implemented.

The United States also worked to persuade Saudi Arabia, Pakistan, and the United Arab Emirates, the only governments with diplomatic relations with Afghanistan, to secure compliance. The State Department coordinator for counterterrorism, Michael Sheehan, was said to have written a secret memorandum calling for more vigorous efforts to cut off financing, sanctuary, and other support from friendly states, Pakistan in particular.[58] Sheehan's memo was said to urge the administration to make terrorism the central issue in U.S. policy toward Pakistan, but it had only slight effect.

Pakistan had been an important conduit for aid to the rebels during the war against the Soviet Union, and a number of Islamic groups operating in Pakistan had well-known ties to the Taliban. The Pakistani Interservices Intelligence Division (ISI) was connected not only to the Taliban, and thus indirectly to Al Qaeda, but to the Harakat ul-Mujadeen, a Kashmiri organization added to the State Department's list of foreign terrorist groups in 1997. The 1998 cruise missile attack on the ISI-run training camps for Kashmiri militants had been a warning signal. Adding to these complications, General Pervez Musharraf seized power in a military coup in October 1999. The United States was thus restrained by Pakistan's status as an ally and by the worry that isolating the regime would interfere with other U.S. policy goals such as restoring democracy and controlling nuclear proliferation.[59] And Pakistan had been helpful in past instances, such as by arresting Ramzi Youcef in 1995.

Sudan also continued to be an irritant. The 1998 military strike had gained the regime some sympathy in the Arab world. Moreover, U.S. allies, such as Canada, began to show increased interest in investing in the country's oil industry, and Great Britain returned its ambassador. Within the Clinton Administration an intense dispute over policy toward Sudan broke into the headlines in late November 1999. Hard-liners argued for a tougher policy of isolation and pressure. Officials in the Africa bureaus of the State Department and the NSC backed legislation to permit the United States to give food assistance directly to Christian rebels in southern Sudan, who had been fighting the northern-dominated Islamic government since the early 1980s. (Previous legislation had prohibited such assistance.) Other officials, including the State Department's Bureau of Refugee Affairs and two former ambassadors, opposed intervention in the civil war as well as the use of food as a weapon of war. The U.S. embassy remained closed; Under Secretary of State Pickering sought to reopen it, but the Africa bureau countered his efforts. The State Department did appoint a special envoy to Sudan, but the United States still seemed determined to isolate the regime even though the FBI reported that any former terrorist camps in Sudan had been vacated.[60]

In early December 1999 the United States received intelligence information that Bin Laden planned a series of attacks on U.S. citizens around the world to coincide with the new year.[61] Jordanian authorities had broken up a plot to attack tourist sites in Jordan and Israel. At the White House, George Tenet and Richard Clarke worked for a month to produce a "Millennium Threats Plan" to disrupt terrorist planning through arrests of members of Bin Laden's network by allies around the world. After considerable argument, the White House also decided to issue a public alert on December 11.

Three days later, customs agents arrested an Algerian, Ahmed Ressam, crossing the Canadian border into Seattle. Some 130 pounds of explosives as well as detonators were in his car, and he was found to have trained in camps operated by Bin Laden in Afghanistan.[62] This surprise prompted the United States to issue a direct threat. Michael Sheehan telephoned the Taliban's foreign minister to warn him that the United States would not tolerate a refusal to turn over Bin Laden while disavowing responsibility for his actions. Apparently, Sheehan hinted that the

United States would use military force against Afghanistan should terrorist attacks occur. This message was reinforced in the State Department's 1999 annual report on terrorism, which declared that "[t]he United States repeatedly made clear to the Taliban that they will be held responsible for any terrorist acts undertaken by Bin Laden while he is in their territory."[63] Yet there were no specific public threats or an ultimatum.

In anticipation of the year's end, efforts to help European allies arrest suspected terrorists abroad were stepped up. After a further warning on December 21, which increased airport security and placed U.S. military bases on high alert, the president reassured the public that the holiday season would not be disturbed. On December 30 the FBI began questioning Arab Americans who appeared suspicious, and operational response teams were placed on the ready in Europe and the United States. Clarke's Counterterrorism Subgroup kept watch in a top-secret communications vault through New Year's Eve and concluded with relief that on this occasion the battle had been won. It seemed that the huge increase in the counterterrorism budget – over 90 percent since 1995 – had been worth it. However, Clarke was quoted as saying,

> It's not enough to be in a cat-and-mouse game, warning about his plots. . . . We need to seriously think about doing more. Our goal should be to so erode his network of organizations that they no longer pose a serious threat.[64]

In fact, by March 2000 U.S. officials were optimistic.[65] International cooperation had produced arrests in Britain, Germany, Canada, the United States, Jordan, and Pakistan. Experts agreed that Bin Laden had been significantly weakened, although his reputation among Islamic militants remained high. The United States also continued covert operations in Afghanistan. The Predator drone had recently been deployed, and the administration was pursuing the idea of equipping it with a Hellfire missile.

However, efforts to persuade Pakistan to change its policies proved unproductive. In a brief visit in March, Clinton asked Musharraf to halt incursions across the Line of Control in Kashmir and to crack down on militant groups operating in Pakistan, as well as to help pressure the Taliban to turn over Bin Laden. Musharraf was apparently reassuring on the last point but made no concrete promises. He denied that Pakistan was supporting violence against India in Kashmir. The United States had to be content with having made its position clear.[66]

As general policy, the State Department stressed "political and diplomatic efforts that reduce the space in which terrorists operate," criminal punishment for the perpetrators of terrorist acts, "depoliticizing the message of terrorism," and international cooperation. The instruments of counterterrorism policy were listed as U.S. leadership, zero tolerance for terrorism, and "draining the swamp" to deny terrorists safe refuge.[67] The 1999 annual report, an unusually detailed statement of policy, called for efforts to drain the "swamps" where governments were too sympathetic or weak to control terrorists. The aim of U.S. policy was to "compel" these states to end their support for terrorism through the use of political and economic pressures and "other means as necessary."[68] The report explained that the United States sought to remove states from the terrorism business entirely by persuading them to rejoin the community of nations committed to ending the threat. A "zero-tolerance" policy would delineate the steps state sponsors must take to be removed from the official list. Other policy differences would not be allowed to stand in the way. The report mentioned positive signs shown in North Korea and Syria, although no similarly veiled overtures were extended to Iran, Sudan, or Afghanistan. In fact, both Afghanistan and Pakistan were criticized, as well as Iran, although neither state was added to the list of state sponsors.[69] The report did recognize that Afghanistan was not otherwise hostile to U.S. interests, which could be interpreted as a positive signal.[70]

The policy of offering cautious inducements to state sponsors was further accentuated in June, when Secretary of State Albright explained that the Clinton Administration had officially replaced the label "rogue states" with the more innocuous term "states of concern."[71] The change reflected a belief that more "gentle" terms and a more "nuanced" American vocabulary would advance internal reforms more effectively. Specific mention was made of North Korea, Iran, and Libya. In October the Secretary of State paid an official visit to North Korea.

The United States also opened a counterterrorist "dialogue" with Sudan, although unilateral sanctions remained in force. By the summer of 2000 Sudan was eager to see U.N. sanctions lifted (even though they had not been strictly enforced) and, more ambitiously, lobbied for a regional seat on the Security Council.[72] The Sudanese argued that their behavior had changed and reminded Washington that the previous December Sudan's president had dismissed his radical Islamic mentor. Sudan had also improved its relationships with Ethiopia and Egypt.

U.S. policy toward nonstates also appeared to shift slightly by the spring of 2000. The 1999 State Department report announced that the goal of U.S. policy was to "eliminate the use of terrorism as a policy instrument," not destroy the organization in question. Should nonstates cease using terrorism, they would be removed from the State Department's list of terrorist organizations. Otherwise, they were reminded of the severe sanctions mandated by legislation enacted in 1996: members and representatives of foreign terrorist organizations (FTOs) are ineligible for U.S. visas and subject to exclusion from the country, their funds are blocked, and no U.S. citizen or person within U.S. jurisdiction can provide any material support or resources. This message was probably intended for organizations other than Al Qaeda, however.

The National Commission on Terrorism took a more hard-line approach, reflecting differences of opinion between Congress and the administration.[73] Its June 2000 report recommended that Afghanistan be added to the list of state sponsors and that Pakistan be considered for classification as a state "not cooperating fully," which requires the imposition of limited sanctions. It also recommended strengthening sanctions and legal penalties across the board as well as expanded FBI and CIA efforts to disrupt and prosecute nonstate actors.

In September the State Department added the Islamic Movement of Uzbekistan (IMU) to the list of foreign terrorist organizations. Administration officials explained that the IMU and other Islamic militants in the former Soviet republics in Central Asia were receiving financial support and training from Bin Laden's network.[74]

On October 12, 2000, in Yemen, a small boat armed with explosives rammed the naval destroyer *Cole* in the Aden harbor. Circumstantial evidence pointed to Bin Laden's involvement, although U.S. officials could not make a definitive case that would justify military retaliation. Yemeni authorities were reluctant to cooperate beyond a modest extent, which slowed and frustrated FBI investigations. In turn, the U.S. ambassador to Yemen, Barbara Bodine, was irritated by the FBI. Yemeni security police did discover, however, that an attack on another U.S. ship had failed the previous January and that planning for the bombing may have started as early as 1997.

In spite of official U.S. caution, a retaliatory missile attack was widely expected. Within the ranks of the NSC, Richard Clarke was said to have favored bombing Al Qaeda training camps in Afghanistan.[75] In December Yemeni president Ali Abdullah Saleh warned against a repetition of the 1998 attack against Afghanistan. It would be a mistake, he said, for a great power to use disproportionate force against a weaker enemy. Instead, if the case against Bin Laden could be proved, the United States should apprehend and prosecute him.[76]

In fact, in public the secretary of state and the president stressed accountability and did not threaten force. The president, at the end of his term, was absorbed with negotiating a peaceful settlement to the Israeli–Palestinian conflict. A retaliatory strike would have undermined that process. Thus, in addition to ongoing covert operations, the United States urged stiffer sanctions against Afghanistan, including an arms embargo, to force the Taliban to hand over Bin Laden and close all training camps for Islamic militants.[77] Russia supported the U.S. resolution submitted to the U.N. Security Council, but Pakistan rejected new sanctions, substantially reducing their potential effectiveness.

Terrorism was not an issue in the 2000 presidential campaign. The Bush Administration entered office without a great sense of urgency.[78] In January Richard Clarke briefed Condoleezza Rice on the terrorist threat.[79] He apparently described a strategy paper that the Clinton NSC had declined to take up in December. In it he had recommended a number of actions to break up or "roll back" Al Qaeda, including the introduction of Special Forces into Afghanistan, air strikes on the training camps, and increased support for the Northern Alliance. However, the proposals were not considered until April, and the policy review process did not conclude until September 4.

Beginning in late March, and continuing into the summer, intelligence agencies noted an unprecedented increase in threat reporting. However, tactical warning, or "actionable detail," was lacking.[80] The Fourth of July, for example, was considered a likely target date, and the State Department issued a worldwide caution on June 22. On June 26 the State Department presented a demarche to Taliban representatives in Pakistan. The Defense Department issued four threat warnings in June and July. There were indications of a planned attack on the president at the Genoa summit meeting in mid-July. The CIA briefed the president on August 6, apparently at his request.

Coercive diplomacy and the war on terrorism

After the September 11 attacks, coercive diplomacy was no longer an option for responding directly to the threat from Al Qaeda, if it had ever been. The "war on terrorism" assumed a strategy of destruction leading to defeat. However, the Bush Administration did attempt, unsuccessfully, to coerce the Taliban into giving up Bin Laden. Pakistan was also forced to reverse its policy of support for the Taliban, although it is hard to know what mixture of threat and reward the United States employed in this case.

The Bush Administration decided immediately that both the Taliban and Pakistan, as well as the rest of the world, should be told "you're for us or against us."[81] In the days following the attacks, the president and the secretary of state both telephoned General Musharraf to demand Pakistani assistance. In his conversation on September 13, Powell was said to have been set to throw a "brushback pitch." The ambassador to Pakistan then visited Musharraf to specify the details. On September 19 Musharraf delivered a televised speech to the nation in which he dramatically announced his support for the United States. He contended that Pakistan's survival was at stake and alluded to the danger that India, having quickly proposed allowing the United States to use its air and naval bases, would exploit Pakistan's isolation and even have it declared a state sponsor of terrorism.[82] He was rewarded with the lifting of sanctions, massive debt relief, and substantial economic assistance. Pakistan became the third-largest beneficiary of U.S. aid, after Israel and Egypt. The alternative was bleak. Pakistan would become a pariah state relegated to crushing poverty and internal instability. It would be vulnerable to Indian pressure. The U.S. war on terrorism could extend to military strikes against local militant groups operating in Afghanistan and Kashmir from Pakistani territory or to the seizure of Pakistan's nuclear facilities should they appear likely to fall into the hands of Islamic extremists.

Thus the U.S. government first communicated its demand to the Taliban to turn Bin Laden over for trial via a Pakistani military delegation led by General Mahmood Ahmed, the head of the ISI, within days after September 11.[83] The demand was accompanied by threats of military action, and heavy bombers and other military forces were moved to bases within striking range of Afghanistan.

The Taliban's response was equivocal. It rejected the demand, but Mullah Omar asked the United States for patience and for more information linking Bin Laden to the attacks. Apparently, Mullah Omar suggested that were he to surrender Bin Laden, he would need the endorsement of the Organization of the Islamic Conference, an organization of fifty Muslim nations dominated by Saudi Arabia.[84]

More contradictory signals followed. On September 20 a clerical grand council, or *shura*, issued a *fatwa* declaring that Bin Laden should be persuaded to leave the country immediately. The *shura* asked Mullah Omar to implement the decision. The United States, however, rejected the move as inadequate. Statements from officials at the Afghan embassy in Islamabad were confusing; some said that there would be no surrender, while others said that Bin Laden might surrender voluntarily.

During this time Bush decided to issue a public ultimatum, to be communicated in his speech to Congress on the evening of September 20. The idea apparently came from Prime Minister Tony Blair. The speech demanded that the Taliban deliver to the United States all Al Qaeda leaders, release all foreign nationals, close all terrorist training camps, and hand over all terrorists to "appropriate authorities." The president concluded: "These demands are not open to negotiation or discussion. The Taliban must act, and act immediately. They will hand over the terrorists, or they will share in their fate."[85] No deadline was imposed nor was a reward offered, at least not in public. Within hours, a Taliban emissary announced defiantly that its "final decision" was to reject the ultimatum: "So the only master of the world wants to threaten us. But make no mistake: Afghanistan . . . is a swamp. People enter here laughing, are exiting injured."[86] The Taliban official implied that Mullah Omar had overruled the *shura*'s decree that Bin Laden be asked to leave Afghanistan. It was not certain, however, that Taliban officials had the power to hand over Bin Laden should they wish to.

As the United States kept up a steady pace of military preparations, Mullah Omar issued his own demand and counterthreat that the United States withdraw its military forces from the Persian Gulf and end its "partisanship" in Palestine or risk involvement in a "vain and bloody war." Yet Taliban officials at the embassy in Pakistan read a statement from the Foreign Affairs Ministry asking "the American people to urge their authorities to save the people of Afghanistan and America from the impacts and consequences and untoward problems of a war."[87] The Taliban faced a growing refugee crisis – more than a million people were said to have fled the cities in anticipation of war – as well as diplomatic isolation. The United Arab Emirates and Saudi Arabia severed diplomatic ties and Pakistan withdrew its diplomats.

Possibly hoping to exploit divisions within the Taliban ranks, the United States asked the Pakistani ISI officials who had remained in Afghanistan after their first unsuccessful mission to go back to the Taliban and repeat the U.S. demand. This request apparently preceded a public Pakistani warning that it did not want to see a new government in Afghanistan, particularly one constructed as a result of U.S. support for the Northern Alliance.[88] The Pakistani overture appeared to bear fruit when the Taliban issued another statement announcing that Bin Laden had been asked to leave, interpreting this development as a hopeful sign, or at least as a reprieve, and desperate to avoid war, Musharraf again sent General Mahmood Ahmed, the head of the ISI. This time he was accompanied by a group of militant Islamic clerics who had taught many of the Taliban, including Mullah Omar, at madrassahs in Pakistan. The mission went to Kandahar to meet with Mullah Omar himself.[89] Pakistani authorities hoped that the group of clerics could serve as a substitute for the Islamic Conference that Mullah Omar had initially called for and that they could persuade him that resistance only harmed the cause of Islam. Information about political conditions in Afghanistan had become scarce since

Western reporters had been expelled, but there were indications that the Taliban's authority was eroding.

However, within almost a day the Pakistani mission was rebuffed.[90] One of the Pakistani clerics reported that Mullah Omar was not afraid of war. Some of the military officers in the delegation suggested that the Taliban's leaders had no grasp of U.S. military power or of the outrage that the September 11 attacks had provoked. One Pakistani official reportedly said, "You tell them they may die, and the Taliban with them, and they are unmoved." Furthermore, while the Pakistani clerics had the advantage of being credible intermediaries, they were also fundamentally unsympathetic to the U.S. demands.

This failure as well as contradictory statements from the Afghani ambassador to Pakistan may have convinced the U.S. government to apply more coercion. Bush secretly approved aid for the Northern Alliance as well as psychological operations (e.g., radio broadcasts and air drops of leaflets) as a "nonmilitary" way of pressuring the Taliban. The presence of Special Forces in Afghanistan was reported in the press. Defense Secretary Donald Rumsfeld set out on a tour of the region to build a supporting coalition, including Uzbekistan. It also became evident to the Taliban that the ISI and the CIA were trying to persuade Pashtun warlords in the border areas to defect.[91]

The Taliban's response was to hedge and try to buy time. The ambassador to Pakistan said that although the request to leave had been delivered to Bin Laden, he had not answered. Both Rumsfeld and Musharraf expressed public doubt that the Taliban would give him up.[92] Nevertheless, Pakistan resolved to send a third delegation to Kandahar, this time of clerics only, on October 2. Simultaneously, a blunt public threat came from Tony Blair on October 2. In a speech to the Labour Party annual conference he asserted: "I say to the Taliban: surrender the terrorists, or surrender power."[93] Within the day the Taliban's ambassador to Pakistan appealed to the United States not to initiate military action, saying that while Taliban leaders still required proof of Bin Laden's complicity, they were ready to negotiate with Washington.[94] He suggested that Bin Laden might be turned over to some third country, but he also replied to Tony Blair's threat earlier that day: only Allah, he said, could overthrow the Taliban. At the same time Mullah Omar continued to issue belligerent statements, in particular condemning U.S. moves to build a coalition to support the return of the former king, Zahir Shah. In tacit recognition of Pakistani complaints that they, too, lacked evidence, the U.S. ambassador to Pakistan visited Musharraf to brief him on Bin Laden's role.

In Washington, on October 6 Bush again publicly threatened Taliban leaders that they had been warned and that time was running out.[95] Winter would be closing in by mid-November, which also marked the start of Ramadan. Military mobilization was proceeding rapidly, with a thousand troops from the Tenth Mountain Division deployed in Uzbekistan and allied assistance lined up. It was clear that the United States intended to use force to disable the Taliban's air defenses in order to facilitate ground operations.

The Taliban responded by (1) preparing for military action, especially by trying to ensure the loyalty of regional commanders, (2) issuing rhetorical threats of a "holy war," and (3) offering to release eight imprisoned Christian aid workers *if* the United States stopped its threats, in effect making them hostages.[96] A spokesman reiterated the well-established Taliban position that it lacked evidence of Bin Laden's guilt, and he denied that there were terrorist training camps in Afghanistan in which the September 11 hijackers could have trained. Press reports now referred to splits within the Taliban ranks, with a more "realist" faction favoring compromise.

On October 7 the U.S. and British military campaign opened with cruise missile and long-range bomber attacks. Bush announced that the actions were designed not only to disrupt terrorism but also to damage the Taliban's military capabilities. Taliban leaders had been warned, he said, and now they would pay a price for resisting U.S. demands.[97] Secretary of Defense Rumsfeld added that the goal was to punish the Taliban and weaken it so severely that it would not be able to withstand an assault from the Northern Alliance or other opposition groups. The targets were military airfields, air defense sites, and command centers, including Mullah Omar's residence in Kandahar.[98] On the second day of bombing, the United States attacked Afghan ground forces north of Kabul who were fighting Northern Alliance units. Rumsfeld announced that a U.S. goal was to help Afghan forces interested in overthrowing and expelling the Taliban. After three days, the United States effectively controlled Afghan air space and began bombing troop facilities and other ground force targets using cluster bombs and other "area munitions." The next stage would involve helicopter gunships and special operations forces.

On October 11, in a White House news conference, Bush offered to reconsider the military offensive if the Taliban surrendered Bin Laden.[99] You have a second chance, he said, to cough up him and his people. Then the United States would reconsider its actions in Afghanistan. He also spoke for the first time of the prospect of nation building in Afghanistan, looking forward to a post-Taliban era.

The Taliban quickly rejected the invitation but said that it would begin discussions *if* the bombing stopped. A top Taliban leader, the second in command to Mullah Omar, responded:

> We would be ready to hand him over to a third country. It can be negotiated provided the U.S gives us evidence and the Taliban are assured that the country is neutral and will not be influenced by the United States.[100]

Bush countered by telling reporters emphatically and repeatedly: "When I said no negotiations, I meant no negotiations," "this is non-negotiable," "there's nothing to negotiate about," and "there is no negotiation, period."[101] He refused to discuss the question of providing evidence since "we know he's guilty." He reiterated the demands set out in his September 20 speech to Congress: the Taliban must turn over Bin Laden and the Al Qaeda organization; destroy the terrorist camps and give the United States access to them; protect all foreign journalists, diplomats, and aid workers; and release all foreign nationals in custody.

In the meantime Powell left Washington for a visit to Pakistan, India, and China. He arrived in Islamabad on the evening of October 15. There he learned that meetings between the Taliban's foreign minister and Pakistani officials, including the head of the military intelligence directorate, had resulted in a request for a bombing pause while Taliban moderates tried to persuade Mullah Omar to agree to hand over Bin Laden.[102] At least two or three days would be required for officials in Kabul to travel to Kandahar, since the bombing campaign had cut off all communications and made travel by road or helicopter too dangerous. Most observers interpreted the move as a sign of a split in Taliban ranks. Otherwise, the intentions behind the request were not clear: was it a sign of a genuine difference of opinion or an attempt to confuse and buy time? If the plea was sincere, was it likely that Mullah Omar could be convinced to change his mind, or that he could be displaced? Observers commented that the Taliban foreign minister was not a close associate of Mullah Omar. And, as was the case with earlier offers, it was not certain that the Taliban could implement a promise to turn over Bin Laden, given the strength of Al Qaeda forces as well as the disruption caused by the bombing campaign.

Probably as both an attempt to encourage defections within Taliban ranks by offering a reward for compromise and a concession to Pakistan's interests, Powell agreed with Musharraf that moderate elements of the Taliban could participate in a new Afghani government.[103] Powell's message was ambiguous, however. He referred to "listening to" the Taliban movement and "taking them into account," since the Taliban could not be "exported," but he also insisted that this "particular regime" had to go. It was also unclear whether Bin Laden had to be surrendered as a condition for "moderate" participation. In the previous twenty-four hours, bombing of Taliban positions near Kabul had escalated, although the United States generally refrained from attacking the Taliban front lines that prevented the Northern Alliance from moving against Kabul or Mazar-i-Sharif. The prospects for bargaining were further diminished when a spokesman for the Northern Alliance refused adamantly to accept any Taliban members in a future coalition government.

The day after the Powell-Musharraf news conference in Islamabad, Mullah Omar sent a radio message encouraging Taliban troops to continue to fight the infidel. He promised that they would triumph as they had over the Soviet Union in the 1980s. He added, "We will succeed whether we live or die. Death will definitely come one day. We are not worried about death. We should die as Muslims. It does not matter whether we die today or tomorrow. The goal is martyrdom."[104] The regime's last remaining ambassador, Mullah Abdul Salam Zaeef, just having returned to Pakistan from a week in Afghanistan, echoed his resolve. He denied that there was a "moderate" Taliban:

> All the Taliban are the same, and they follow the views of the leadership. . . . On the issue of Osama, there is no change in that Osama is a faith issue, and we are not going to change our faith for anyone.[105]

On October 19 the United States launched a helicopter commando raid against Mullah Omar's compound, the first large-scale commando attack since the intervention in Somalia in 1993. Two days later, bombing of Taliban front-line defenses around Kabul began, and Powell indicated that the Northern Alliance would be encouraged to move on Kabul. The United States had lost patience. The military campaign could no longer wait for Taliban compliance or a defection by "moderates."[106] The aim was now decisive military victory and the replacement of the regime.

Conclusion

The record

The record of coercive diplomacy is not encouraging. The outcomes of even the simplest cases of state-sponsored terrorism are not clear-cut.[107] The response to Iraq in 1993 can be considered an example of appropriately implemented coercive diplomacy, but its success or failure is hard to judge. That assessment depends on whether the United States was attempting to halt direct attacks on U.S. targets or force Iraq out of the business of supporting terrorism altogether. If the judgment is based on the first assumption, then compliance can only be inferred from lack of evidence of noncompliance. This is a weak standard, since Iraq never admitted to having organized the plot against President Bush, much less to having complied with U.S. demands not to continue. If the judgment is based on the second assumption, then coercive diplomacy failed.

The case of Iran in 1996 is even more problematic. A conclusion about whether or not coercive diplomacy was employed depends on estimating the seriousness of U.S. threats of military retaliation for the 1996 Khobar Towers bombing. Although the United States decided not to use force, Iran, like Iraq, did not directly attack U.S. targets again. However, like Iraq, Iran also stayed in the terrorism business and refused to cooperate in resolving the dispute over responsibility for the Khobar Towers bombing. The United States was initially constrained from using force by lack of information that linked Iran conclusively to the bombing. When the evidence was finally acquired, internal changes in Iran had made the use of force too costly in terms of its effect on other policy interests, especially reforming Iran. Saudi Arabia's reluctance to share data, in part a consequence of the fear of unilateral U.S. retaliation, contributed to the U.S. dilemma. Thus, paradoxically, a willingness to use force made it less feasible. Furthermore, unlike with the case of Iraq, the administration was divided over how to respond to Iran.

Dealing with the more lethal and ambiguous threat of Al Qaeda was even more complicated. This conflict was a zero-sum game. One cannot conclude either that the United States employed coercive diplomacy or that coercive diplomacy would have been an appropriate response to such an adversary, however expertly applied. From the beginning, the U.S. strategy was not to induce Bin Laden and Al Qaeda to stop terrorism but to disrupt and destroy so as to make continued terrorism impossible. It was not the group's collective intentions but its capabilities that mattered.[108] The cruise missile attacks in 1998 were not so much exemplary uses of coercive force as symbolic statements of political commitment to combating terrorism. They inflicted little pain on Al Qaeda. Covert operations in Afghanistan were meant to arrest or kill Bin Laden.[109] After 1998 Bin Laden's indictment by a U.S. court could not be ignored in the interest of striking a bargain. Coercive diplomacy and a strategy of law enforcement, or "bringing to justice," may not be complementary.

Furthermore, even if coercive diplomacy had been the intent, and Al Qaeda not been impervious to coercion, its use would not necessarily have prevented specific attacks, notably those of September 11. Although the United States received streams of warnings, none were specific or timely enough to issue a threat or use demonstrative force to compel Al Qaeda to desist. This limitation on coercive diplomacy was exacerbated by the organizational structure of Al Qaeda. Cells such as the one organized by Mohammed Atta operated with considerable autonomy. Changing the calculations of the top leadership at the last minute would probably not have defeated a plot already in the last planning stages.

Coercive diplomacy was more relevant when it came to altering the behavior of the states that directly or indirectly assisted Al Qaeda, but significant constraints existed. First, consider Sudan. The 1998 attack on the Al Shifa pharmaceuticals plant might be interpreted as a demonstration of force, but it was modest. Perhaps the strike communicated to Sudan that any further assistance to Bin Laden would be similarly punished, but the likelihood of escalation was low. Sudan's behavior improved, but probably not as the result of threats of military force. The United States also resisted opportunities to offer rewards. Perhaps Sudan's behavior was not threatening enough. Sudan, after all, had expelled Bin Laden. It took measures to reduce its ties to radical Islamic groups and offered other positive signals. The links to terrorism that remained were hard to prove. As a consequence of these ambiguities, U.S. officials disagreed on the subject of how to treat Sudan. None of these factors are favorable for successful coercive diplomacy.

Pakistan was also a difficult case. Pakistan's support for the Taliban was not disguised, and the United States tried unsuccessfully to exploit Pakistan's leverage over the Taliban to cut its ties with Al Qaeda. However, before September 11 the United States hesitated to put pressure on Pakistan, placing other foreign policy interests ahead of preventing terrorism. The United States objected to Pakistan's support for militant groups operating in Kashmir and distrusted Pakistan because of the ISI's connections with the Taliban, but the Clinton Administration took almost no visible action beyond the cruise missile attack on the ISI-run training camps in Afghanistan in 1998.

Policy shifted after September 11. The Bush Administration both promised rewards and threatened punishment, but it is hard to know whether these threats included military force. The threats, which were kept private, probably centered on economic and political costs. However, Pakistan's conflict with India and the risk of domestic unrest created at least an implicit sense of threat. This case shows that it is difficult to coerce allies whose assistance is needed even when they are uncooperative.

The least ambiguous case is the unsuccessful use of coercive diplomacy to induce the Taliban to turn over Bin Laden. Under both administrations, the objective of coercive diplomacy was precise. It was communicated clearly. After 1998 the Clinton Administration combined threats and rewards, although in principle officials rejected the idea of "rewarding terrorism." The 1998 cruise missile attacks were balanced against normalization of relations, which presumably meant the removal of sanctions and official recognition of the regime. The public record does not show any specific threats or the insistence on an ultimatum. Various options for coercion were apparently considered – aid to the Northern Alliance, for example – but rejected. Rhetorical threats were not implemented, even after the discovery of Al Qaeda plots in December 1999 and the USS *Cole* bombing in October 2000.

After September 11 the Bush Administration continued coercive diplomacy. Bush gave the Taliban several "second chances" after issuing a public ultimatum for compliance and even after launching military operations. However, the Taliban leadership may not have believed U.S. promises. In October the offer to "moderates" of a place in a future government was a threat to the leaders who were clearly not moderates. As coercive military pressure mounted, the Taliban's ability to comply decreased correspondingly. This relationship suggests another potential paradox: as the defending state escalates the use of force, the ability of the adversary to comply decreases. The adversary may become more willing but less able. At this point, the United States had superior motivation, but Taliban leaders may not have recognized it, despite Pakistan's efforts to convince them. The Taliban may have mistaken not just the new U.S. willingness to conduct a ground war but the prospect that a war could be fought at so little cost. Pakistani intermediaries reported that the Taliban had no conception of U.S. capabilities or motivation after September 11. One could argue that the Bush Administration should have been more patient in waiting for a response to its demands, and the public use of an ultimatum by both Bush and Blair may have set back efforts to reach a compromise. However, the United States had made the same demand consistently since 1998. The Taliban had taken three years to consider its options. Situational factors (the advent of winter and of Ramadan) also constrained the Bush Administration's choices.

Implications

It is important for a government to know which adversaries can be coerced and which cannot. This determination is harder to make in the case of states than of nonstates, probably because policy makers assume that states possess tangible assets that their leaders and citizens value enough not to want to risk losing them. A regime may be willing to sacrifice its hold on power rather than comply with the coercer's demands. Furthermore, the government may be mistaken in believing that the regime that is assisting terrorism can comply with its demands. Possibly the Taliban leaders believed that turning over Bin Laden would cost them their tenure anyway, because the surrender would remove what legitimacy they had. As they said, it was an issue of faith. Possibly the Taliban was also so dependent on or intermingled with Al Qaeda forces that it had no control over Bin Laden from the outset.

Before September 11 the United States found it difficult to threaten escalation or to communicate a sense of urgency. Terrorism was not the top national security priority. One could blame lack of domestic public support, owing to failure to recognize the threat or aversion to U.S. military casualties.[110] However, the Clinton Administration did not advocate or try to justify a stronger coercive policy against the Taliban or against Pakistan. The anticipation of international disapproval of the use of force might also have restricted policy choices. Furthermore, the hiatus between the last months of the Clinton Administration and the Bush Administration's conclusion of the policy review process the next fall created a policy vacuum.

Many questions remain. One is whether the Taliban's compliance with the demand to turn over Bin Laden and his associates and to shut down Al Qaeda's training camps would actually have halted terrorism or prevented the September 11 attacks. The hijacking plot, like most other spectacular terrorist attacks, was initiated years in advance. Al Qaeda might have survived without sanctuary in Afghanistan. The leadership of Bin Laden may not be critical to the organization's existence.

Another question concerns the alternatives to coercive diplomacy. Was there a strategy with a better conceptual fit, leaving aside the issue of whether it would be politically acceptable? Even the "war on terrorism" has not guaranteed long-term success. Terrorism is extraordinarily hard to control, much less defeat, especially in the short term. The outcomes of policies are highly uncertain and contingent. Neither scholars nor practitioners know precisely how and why campaigns of terrorism end.[111] Expectations of what coercive diplomacy can achieve may be too high.

Policy makers need a mix of strategies. They also need to be consistent and clear about the strategies they are using, to ensure that they are compatible with each other, and to tailor them to a range of different actors, not all of whom are adversaries. Policy makers must resign themselves to dealing with high levels of ambiguity, complexity, and uncertainty. Success and failure will be hard to judge.

9 Strategies and grand strategies

After September 11, 2001, terrorism took center stage in the debate among security studies, international relations, and foreign policy specialists over a grand strategy for the United States in the post-Cold War era. Stephen Walt, for example, asserted that the September 11 attack had triggered the most rapid and dramatic change ever in the history of U.S. foreign policy.[1] The transition commonly was termed a "watershed."

The threat of terrorism was not prefigured, however, by the debate over grand strategy. Prevailing theories of international relations did not predict the outcome of developments that had begun much earlier, much as they failed to foresee the end of the Cold War. Terrorism was not generally considered an important national security threat unless it combined two dangers: a threat to the U.S. homeland *and* the use of "weapons of mass destruction" (WMD) – defined as nuclear, chemical, biological, or radiological weapons. An underlying if unspoken assumption was that only the use of WMD could cause mass casualties. Even so, the idea that terrorism was critically important to national security was not widely accepted by foreign policy specialists inside and outside of government.

Nor did analysts in the "terrorism studies" community – a group distinct from national security specialists – offer much substantive input to the debate over grand strategy. They tended to focus on explaining terrorism rather than prescribing solutions, and they rarely considered terrorism in the context of other foreign policy issues. In fact, most of these specialists often doubted that a consistent approach to terrorism was possible.

Since the September 11 attacks, policy makers and academic specialists have been engaged in a rethinking of terrorism and the response to it. Whether the response to terrorism is a set of individual counterterrorist operations, designed for particular cases and circumstances, or a general strategy applied universally, it must be shaped in terms of a larger conception of American security and interests. Such an integrated conception should be based on new ideas of both power and security as well as tolerance for risk. Strategic thinking in the post-Cold War world must account for the unconventional power of nonstate actors: risk-takers who are willing to violate norms and who may be immune to military threats. A new conception of security also should consider the harmful consequences of the lack of power, as well as the damage that can be inflicted by power.

In this chapter I first establish the requirements for the development of a coherent response that would link means and ends. Next I analyze the period before the shock of September 11 in terms of the debate over grand strategy, the arguments of the "terrorism studies" specialists about responding to terrorism, and the government's actions. I then evaluate the impact of September 11 on grand strategy proposals and on the government's response to terrorism. Last, I ask whether the "war on terror" as originally conceived met the requirements for effective strategy, grand strategy, and policy.

Defining strategy, grand strategy, and policy

A necessary preliminary to analyzing the response to terrorism is a definition of the respective conceptual requirements for strategies, grand strategies, and policy. I distinguish among these concepts, but it is worth noting that in practice many accounts use the terms interchangeably.

A strategy – which typically refers to military operations – requires a precisely specified political objective. Strategy is a scheme for making the means produce the desired ends.[2] It is concerned with designing actions to produce outcomes that are desired and specified. The means must be sufficient to accomplish the ends, but a good design does not have goals that are so ambitious that resources cannot support them or so ambiguous that purposive actions cannot be crafted to reach them. The costs of any strategy must be acceptable in terms of the expected benefits, and the risks must be sensible. Yet however necessary strategy may be, it is not always possible. The constraints may be prohibitive. In other words, there may be threats against which a state cannot construct a coherent and workable strategy.

Grand strategy represents a more inclusive conception that should explain how a state's full range of resources can be coordinated to achieve national security. A grand strategy determines what the state's vital security interests are, identifies critical threats to them, and specifies the means of dealing with them. Thus, a grand strategy is complex, multifaceted, and directed toward a distant time horizon. It establishes a comprehensive framework that integrates the objectives of individual strategies. It would explain how defending the nation against terrorism can and should relate to other security objectives – such as, for example, maintaining alliances, preventing the emergence of great power challengers, spreading democracy, and controlling the proliferation of WMD.

Policy should define the goals of strategy as well as grand or higher strategy. It is a statement of purpose. Policy must determine priorities among competing values. The central aim of counterterrorist strategy is to prevent attacks on U.S. territory that cause large numbers of civilian casualties. Terrorism does not pose the threat of annihilation that the Soviet Union's nuclear capabilities did during the Cold War. What was and is at stake is not national survival, material power, or the integrity of our armed forces and national defense system but the individual security of American civilians at home. This objective, however, must be coordinated with other goals.

The grand strategy debate before September 11

Scholars engaged in the debate over the future of American foreign policy in the 1990s agreed about the purpose of grand strategy – it should define and rank American interests, identify the major threats to them, and establish policy guidelines for protecting those interests – while they disagreed profoundly with regard to its content. They shared, however, a lack of concern about terrorism. The policy recommendations of scholars in the security studies and international relations fields typically did not cite terrorism as a major threat to American security.[3]

Different schools of thought were alike in neglecting terrorism. Advocates of American primacy or preponderance focused on potential great power challengers, not clandestine undergrounds. Advocates of "selective engagement" urged the United States to concentrate its efforts only on the most powerful states. Proponents of "offshore balancing," who thought that the United States should play the role of balancer in the international system and avoid foreign commitments, were more likely than others to cite the risk of terrorism as a reason for decreased international involvement, but only as a peripheral argument. For instance, Layne supported the case for disengagement with the general claim that "the risk of conflict, and the possible exposure of the American homeland to attack, derive directly from the overseas commitments mandated by preponderance's expansive definition of U.S. interests."[4] A similar argument for "restraint" mentioned terrorism in a footnote as an exception to "the great news is that America faces almost no discernible security threats."[5] One paragraph subsequently was devoted to explaining that the United States should continue to try to prevent and respond to terrorism but that restraint in world affairs would reduce the incentives to attack U.S. targets.[6]

One reason for glossing over terrorism might be that studies of grand strategy usually proceeded from realist assumptions,[7] despite some attempts to include domestic variables.[8] In such a framework, threats emanate from the interests and power of states, not nonstates, and the strongest states are the most important for American interests. Weak or failed states and shadowy conspiracies could not constitute challenges to the American position in the world. From this perspective, threats are simple to interpret. They stem from rival states that can challenge one's power now or in the future.

Furthermore, the security studies and international relations fields were not especially hospitable to scholars interested in terrorism precisely because it was considered peripheral both to the discipline and to the development of grand strategy. As an intellectual approach, it did not easily lend itself to abstract theory or modeling.[9] The study of terrorism was too policy oriented to be of serious academic significance.

There were some exceptions to this general rule. Robert J. Art, defending a grand strategy of selective engagement, argued that a key American interest was preventing a WMD attack on the American homeland and that such an attack might come from "fanatical terrorists" using nuclear, biological, or chemical weapons.[10] In this framework, however, terrorism became a danger only when combined with WMD proliferation, and states continued to pose a greater threat than transnational actors. The most prescient analysts were Ashton B. Carter and William J. Perry, who defined "catastrophic" terrorism as a key threat and called for the response to terrorism to be incorporated into a general strategy of "preventive defense."[11] Their contribution had little impact on the overall grand strategy debate, however, perhaps because both authors were former high government officials rather than scholars.

"Terrorism studies" before September 11

In their turn, terrorism specialists tended to neglect the strategic dimensions of the issue. The study of terrorism was typically divorced from the study of foreign policy and national security, as well as from theories of international relations. As Ian Lesser, an analyst for the Rand Corporation, concluded,

> Most contemporary analyses of terrorism focus on terrorist political violence as a stand-alone phenomenon, without reference to its geopolitical and strategic context. Similarly, counterterrorism policy is rarely discussed in terms of its place in broader national security planning.[12]

Lesser implied that this oversight was due to the perception that terrorism was not an existential threat unless it used WMD.

In contrast, Richard Falkenrath argued that scholars focusing on terrorism were skeptical of the WMD threat.[13] In his view, the specialists were critical of the Clinton Administration's domestic preparedness program because they regarded the threat of WMD terrorism as highly unlikely and distracting – a judgment they based on observations of the past. Falkenrath suggested that the study of terrorism was useful for a variety of things, such as understanding motivation, but that it could not provide tactical warning, assess threats, or set priorities. Its predictions tended to be linear: a straight projection of the future from the past.

A possible explanation for the neglect of international relations was that specialists on terrorism usually represented interdisciplinary interests. Contributors came from backgrounds in sociology, psychology, anthropology, history, law, criminal justice or crimonology, and communications, as well as political science. Within political science, scholars focusing on terrorism did not often work in the field of international relations. They were equally or more likely to be specialists in civil conflict. Multidisciplinarity made it hard to build a unifying set of theoretical assumptions that could coordinate different approaches to understanding the threat of terrorism or analyzing responses.

Nevertheless, before September 11 most specialists on terrorism, inside and outside of government, had concluded that an undifferentiated response to terrorism was either inappropriate or politically impossible. The reasons for this conclusion were based on the variability of the threat and on the constraints of domestic policies.

Character of the threat

In 2000, Paul Pillar warned against inflexibility: "The terrorist threat is not really 'a threat' but rather a method used by an assortment of actors who threaten U.S. interests in varying ways and degrees."[14] Critical differences among contexts should "form the basis for tailoring what is, in effect, a different counterterrorist policy for each group or state."[15] Because the response should be shaped to individual circumstances, it is complicated and difficult and does not lend itself to generalization or rhetorical flourish. In Pillar's view, "Much attention has been paid to making counterterrorist measures stronger, broader, or more numerous. . . . More needs to be paid to gauging how effective or applicable such measures are to individual cases."[16]

Earlier analyses had made similar points. In 1986 Livingstone and Arnold observed that

> the task of designing and implementing effective national policies to deal with terrorism is overwhelming in its scope and permutations and argues less for a general all-embracing strategy to address the problem than a multitude of less-ambitious component strategies, which in sum provide an overall framework for controlling and suppressing terrorism on a global scale.[17]

Likewise, Marc Celmer – also analyzing the response of the Reagan Administration – agreed that the issue did not lend itself to strategy.[18] Grant Wardlaw, an Australian defense specialist and terrorism analyst, also cautioned that "the idea of a general policy against terrorism is inherently faulty – terrorism has to be countered in a discriminating, case-by-case way."[19] Wardlaw warned that policy should remain at a general level to retain flexibility and imagination in dealing with what he regarded as a "literally infinite range of possible terrorist scenarios." Similar observations continued in the 1990s. Jeffrey D. Simon, for example, concluded bluntly that one of the key lessons learned from the experience of countering terrorism was "do not declare any official 'policy' on terrorism."[20]

In fact, critics considered public statements of general policy not only ineffectual but also counterproductive in that they undermined domestic political support. Wardlaw argued that strident policy rhetoric was likely to embarrass the government when principles had to be compromised, as they inevitably would. He also noted that when the government announced to the public that it had a strategy for managing terrorism, each subsequent terrorist incident made that policy look ineffective. Similarly, as Simon pointed out, the no-concessions principle – an ostensible cornerstone of U.S. policy since 1974 – often was violated.[21] The Iran-Contra affair was only the most conspicuous of such public contradictions. Consistency in policy is necessary only if the government has promised it.

An additional aspect of the conceptual difficulty of dealing with terrorism was the tension between criminal justice and national security approaches to the issue, which was reflected in institutional rivalries within the government. Since the early 1980s specialists had debated whether terrorism should be defined as crime or as warfare. Each type of problem calls for a different set of policy responses. If it is a crime, a law enforcement strategy is appropriate. If it is warfare, a military response is warranted.

Domestic politics

An alternative position within the "terrorism studies" school aspired to the development of a more systematic and overarching policy structure but considered it unlikely for reasons of domestic politics rather than the inherent intractability of the problem. Yehezkel Dror, an Israeli scholar specializing in policy analysis, argued that "terrorism is an unusual, though not extraordinary, phenomenon with some features of an extreme case" – which makes it difficult to understand and almost impossible to predict.[22] He concluded, however, that "grand policies" or "grand strategies" were unlikely because democratic governments were not disposed to construct them, not because the phenomenon was indeterminate. He observed that as long as "disjointed incrementalism" and normal decision making seemed to work, governments had no incentive for more ambitious strategies. Thus, "when a problem is handled in what is perceived to be a satisfying way, there will be little propensity to engage in policy innovation."[23] Because governments confront so many pressing problems, they are tempted to keep an issue in the "realm of the ordinary" as long as possible. At the same time, democracies lack the requirements for preparing grand policies. They learn poorly and handle complexity badly. Furthermore, Dror suspected that democracies, characterized by dispersed authority and ad hoc reactions, would not implement grand policies even if they were available. He predicted that a catastrophic shock might jolt a democratic government into action, if the shock revealed decisively that incremental policies had failed.

Over the years analysts emphasized the same domestic obstacles to effective strategy.[24] One barrier was the ever-expanding number of government agencies tasked with a counterterrorism mission. In many ways bureaucratic proliferation was the result of the complexity of the threat, but the expansion of responsibilities also was the result of inertia and incrementalism, as new functions were layered on old ones. The policy-making process also required coordinating the activities of agencies with both domestic and foreign policy jurisdictions. In this context, critics noted the absence of strong leadership from the top. The process was highly decentralized, permitting and encouraging rivalries among different executive branch agencies. The result of intermittent attention from the White House and the president was uncoordinated policy. With each terrorist crisis, terrorism rose to the top of the presidential agenda. In between crises, it sank to the bottom, as other critical issues competed for attention. Presidential advisers tended to regard terrorism as a no-win issue. Sequential attention was also encouraged by the news media, especially television. During the 1980s more interest groups became involved in the policy process, including victims' families (for example, the families of the victims of Pan Am 103). Largely as a result of public awareness, Congress also came to play a stronger role in pressing the executive to be more proactive and forward looking. With such widely dispersed and autonomous centers of authority, all sensitive to public constituencies, any American government would find planning and implementing a consistent strategy a formidable task.

U.S. government response before September 11

The Clinton and first Bush Administrations tended to interpret terrorism in light of their preconceptions about American policy in a post-Cold War world. As scholars did, policy makers defined the threat of terrorism and formulated counterterrorist strategies in a way that supported worldviews that were established in other contexts. Terrorism was fitted into a preexisting framework.

Although terrorism became an increasingly serious threat in the post-Cold War world, the Clinton Administration was not initially inclined to regard terrorism as a major national security issue. David Tucker, a former Foreign Service officer writing a history of American policy toward terrorism, concluded that a "strategic vacuum" followed the Reagan Administration's strategy, which linked terrorism to the Soviet Union and the Cold War.[25] Terrorism was not part of general foreign policy planning, as Paul Pillar confirmed.[26]

The Clinton Administration entered office holding to the principle that terrorism best fit into a category of "modern" problems such as global organized crime, epidemics of disease, and environmental disasters. These dangers were not represented as threats directed specifically against American interests but common perils all states face in an era of globalization. This framing of the issue was consistent with the administration's preferences for a multilateral approach to international issues and its rejection of a "clash of civilizations" world view. Thus the Clinton Administration was inclined at the outset to take a modest position that minimized the threat.

Events quickly commanded the government's attention, as noted in the previous chapter on coercive diplomacy. The 1993 bombing of the World Trade Center, the 1995 Aum Shinrikyo sarin gas attack on the Tokyo subway system, and the Oklahoma City bombing brought terrorism firmly onto the domestic policy agenda. Pressure from Congress and from local law enforcement agencies and "first responders" created a sense of urgency about the prospect of terrorist use of WMD – particularly chemical and biological weapons. "Homeland defense" against chemical and biological threats preoccupied policy makers, even though terrorism specialists still remained dubious about the likelihood of WMD terrorism.[27] Even the simultaneous bombings of American embassies in Kenya and Tanzania in 1998, the "millennium" plots of 1999, and the October 2000 attack on the USS *Cole* in Yemen did not make terrorism a national security priority or an essential element of foreign policy planning. If it had been, the U.S. might not have decided to use Yemen as a refueling port. A series of congressionally mandated reports and studies warned that terrorism should rank higher on the national agenda, but other international issues competed for attention: for example, crises in Somalia, Haiti, Bosnia, Kosovo, and South Asia and managing relations with Russia, North Korea, and China. The president was also focused on mediating a settlement of the Israeli–Palestinian conflict.

The Clinton Administration was not passive. The government responded to the East Africa bombings with cruise missile attacks on a pharmaceuticals plant in the Sudan suspected of links to Al Qaeda and on training camps in Afghanistan, some run by Pakistani intelligence services. Covert operations by the Central Intelligence Agency (CIA) to disrupt Bin Laden's operations expanded steadily from 1996 to 2001. These operations focused on apprehending Bin Laden and bringing him to trial – or possibly killing him, should these efforts fail. Arrests of suspected Al Qaeda militants led to more than thirty successful prosecutions in U.S. courts. These convictions included the persons responsible for the first World Trade Center bombing as well as some of the perpetrators of the 1998 East Africa bombings. Economic and diplomatic sanctions against the Taliban regime in Afghanistan were gradually tightened, with the support of the United Nations. The administration believed, however, that the public would not support an escalation of military counterterrorist efforts – especially not the use of ground troops. The government also declined to put strong pressure on Pakistan to cease its support for the Taliban. Other foreign policy interests dominated the threat of terrorism.

In the period between the resolution of the drawn-out contest over the 2000 presidential election and September 2001, the Bush Administration also had other concerns, most domestic. In the foreign policy arena the administration appeared more comfortable in seeing the world as a system of states. There appears to have been no great sense of urgency about dealing with terrorism.[28] In the last months of the Clinton Administration, the National Security Council (NSC) staff had developed a plan for a more active counterterrorist strategy, including arming the Northern Alliance against the Taliban. The new NSC decided to put the proposal through a policy review process that did not conclude until the following September.

Impact of September 11 on the grand strategy debate

The attacks of September 11 propelled terrorism from obscurity to prominence in the wider field of international relations and foreign and security policy. Terrorism now dominated the grand strategy debate. Scholars who had previously ignored or dismissed terrorism now acknowledged it as a major national security concern; in fact, some saw the threat of terrorism as occasion for a complete reorientation of post-Cold War foreign policy. Barry Posen, for example, called for an end to treating terrorism as "administered policy" and the inauguration of a genuine strategy – the prior absence of which he blamed on domestic politics, bureaucratic inertia, and a weak intelligence effort.[29] Similarly, Stephen Walt cited faults associated with the domestic political process: the lack of serious public interest in foreign policy, the failure of leaders to see the risks inherent in foreign engagements, their partisanship, the influence of special interests, and congressional irresponsibility. He proposed that the United States take the role of being a great power more seriously.[30]

As Barry Posen observed, however, after September 11 the advocates of alternative grand strategies generally superimposed them on their interpretation of terrorism rather than using the case to reexamine their prior assumptions.[31] Each proponent of a foreign policy vision saw the "new" threat of terrorism as confirmation of the opinions or theories he proposed before September 11.[32] Several analysts thought that American policy was unlikely to change course. Walt, for example, did not think that the United States needed a new grand strategy, merely a reordering of priorities to include managing the antiterrorism coalition, controlling weapons of mass destruction, reconstructing Afghanistan, and improving relations with the Arab and Muslim worlds. Although not necessarily favoring the status quo, Steven Miller agreed that the September 11 attacks did not alter the basic policy of unilateralism that the Bush Administration had originally pursued.[33] Although in the short run the issue captured the public and presidential agendas, grand strategy was not likely to change. Miller predicted that the impact of the attacks would be transitory. As it turned out, the attacks bolstered the case for unilateralism.

On the other hand, Ashton Carter regarded the events of September 11 as confirmation of his prior view that the United States was pursuing the wrong grand strategy and urgently needed a new one, along the lines of the one he proposed before September 11.[34] In his view, catastrophic terrorism, not great-power rivalry, was likely to be the centerpiece of international security studies for the foreseeable future.

Proponents of a restrained American foreign policy predictably cited the U.S. pursuit of preponderance as a partial cause of the September 11 attacks, which they interpreted as a wake-up call for a new and radically different grand strategy of reduced international involvement.[35] After all, Bin Laden was ostensibly reacting to the American military presence in Saudi Arabia. In their view, American hegemony was the cause; reorientation of American foreign policy toward a less prominent world role would be the solution. Responsibility for maintaining order and stability should be devolved onto other states, so as to encourage multipolarity rather than primacy. The United States should become a fatalistic bystander in international affairs.

American response after September 11

The history of American foreign policy exhibits a pattern of reaction to shock, and it may have been inevitable that only a devastating blow from terrorism, causing thousands of civilian casualties on American soil, could bring about fundamental policy change.[36] The United States was slow in responding to emerging threats in the past, and comparisons to the galvanizing effects of the 1941 attack on Pearl Harbor and the 1950 North Korean invasion of South Korea became commonplace after September 11.

After the shock of the multiple attacks, the Bush Administration decisively rejected a policy of restraint and declared a war on terror. The war metaphor was both diagnostic and prescriptive, since it defined the problem and identified a solution. Using the metaphor of war made terrorism a threat to national security, prescribed the answer as military engagement, and predicted eventual victory over the adversary, although officials cautioned the public that the war would be long.[37] In this framework, the alternative to an offensive strategy could only be defeat, which was unacceptable. The war metaphor also was compatible with American political culture and discourse, which also endorsed wars on drugs, poverty, crime, and other social problems.

The generic war metaphor was further reinforced by concrete historical analogies, linking the war on terror to World War II and to the Cold War. Comparisons to the surprise attack at Pearl Harbor and the miscalculations at Munich were rife. The president used language such as "axis of evil" and "Islamic fascists" to describe the enemy. The U.S. was said to be combating a form of totalitarianism. Thus "appeasement" was an unacceptable policy option. In 2002, President Bush observed that

> we're not facing a set of grievances that can be soothed and addressed. We're facing a radical ideology with inalterable objectives: to enslave whole nations and intimidate the world. No act of ours invited the rage of the killers – and no concession, bribe, or act of appeasement would change or limit their plans for murder.[38]

The extraordinarily high number of casualties caused by the September 11 surprise attacks, as well as the nature of the targets (actual and intended), raised the stakes considerably. The United States was now immediately willing to use means previously considered politically unacceptable: intervention with ground forces to overthrow a regime that actively supported a terrorist organization and destruction of that organization's territorial base. Both the Clinton and Bush Administrations previously had considered and employed alternative options to end the Taliban's support for Bin Laden and bring him to the U.S. for prosecution. The military campaign in Afghanistan in October 2001 followed a series of unsuccessful demands that the Taliban surrender Bin Laden, accompanied by the imposition of multilateral sanctions endorsed by the U.N.[39]

Regional and international alliances were cemented to support the campaign. Pakistan – formerly an ally of the Taliban – was induced to support the American war effort, as were Uzbekistan and Tajikistan. The war effort went beyond direct military operations to defeat the Taliban regime in Afghanistan and destroy the infrastructure of the Al Qaeda organization; it also incorporated military assistance, including training, to regimes confronting local insurgencies with links to Al Qaeda – principally Yemen, the Philippines, and Georgia. The United States also organized an international coalition to legitimize the war on terrorism, provide operational assistance in Afghanistan, and disrupt Al Qaeda operations. National police and intelligence services from Europe to Asia were mobilized to apprehend Al Qaeda suspects and cut off their financial resources. The CIA's covert operations against terrorism were intensified. Hundreds of suspects were seized – some kept as "unlawful combatants" at Guantanamo Bay in Cuba, others left in or transferred to the hands of governments willing to hold and interrogate them. The American government also emphasized public diplomacy to reduce the popular support bases of Islamic militancy in Muslim countries, especially in the Middle East.

The State Department's annual report for 2001 described American policy as (1) make no concessions to terrorists and no "deals" if hostages are seized, (2) bring terrorists to justice (i.e., to trial in the United States), (3) isolate and apply pressure to states that support terrorism to induce them to change their behavior, and (4) bolster the counterterrorist efforts of countries that help the United States.[40] The statement summarized efforts in the fields of diplomacy, intelligence, law enforcement, and finance. Military instruments, principally Operation Enduring Freedom in Afghanistan, were mentioned last. The document emphasized international cooperation on all fronts.

After the Taliban regime was overthrown and Al Qaeda's territorial base in Afghanistan eliminated, perhaps buoyed by what appeared to be success despite the escape of the terrorist leadership, the Bush Administration began to expand its foreign policy conceptions. The formal statement of a new set of principles came in September 2002 with the release of *The National Security Strategy of the United States of America*.[41] Many elements of this plan predated the war on terrorism.[42] According to National Security Adviser Condoleeza Rice, however, September 11 was an "earthquake" or tectonic plate shift, analogous to the events that precipitated the Cold War in 1945–7. This jolt clarified and sharpened the American conception of its role in the world.[43] The aims of opposing terrorism and preventing irresponsible states from acquiring WMD, in her view, now defined the national interest. This combination still preoccupies the Obama Administration.

The 2002 national security strategy was innovative in recognizing that nonstates are independent and important enemies and that weak states can be just as dangerous as powerful states. It was ambitious in calling for a response to threats before they are fully formed and justifying preemption as anticipatory self-defense. To this end, the United States would seek international support but would act alone if American interests and "unique" responsibilities required. The strategy required a more global and interventionist military presence. At the same time, it included public diplomacy or a "war of ideas" to delegitimize terrorism and alter the conditions and ideologies that permit it to flourish. The Bush Administration explained this strong response as a moral necessity in dealing with "evil." The designated "rogue state" enemies – Iran, Iraq, and North Korea – were states that demonstrated generally hostile intent, oppressed their own citizens, threatened their neighbors, and possessed or were in the process of acquiring WMD as well as the means of delivery.[44]

A first requirement of the new national security strategy was regime replacement in Iraq.[45] Replacing Saddam Hussein was considered to be a solution not only to the threat of a rogue state with the potential to use highly lethal weapons but also to a range of problems in the Middle East, including the Palestinian–Israeli conflict and lack of democracy. The expectation was that a new, democratic Iraq could serve as a model for other Arab states and a new source of regional stability. The administration also claimed that Iraq was linked to Al Qaeda and was likely to supply the organization with WMD. Thus, Saddam Hussein's removal also would serve the purposes of the war on terrorism.

In February 2003 the administration published a complementary *National Strategy for Combating Terrorism*. The strategy was based on the assumption that the September 11 attacks were acts of war, that terrorism, rather than a named adversary, was the enemy, and that defeating terrorism was the primary and immediate priority of the U.S. government. The strategy's purpose was to identify and defuse threats before they materialized into attacks on U.S. territory and interests. It stipulated that the U.S. would act unilaterally if need be and that it would act preemptively in self-defense. The U.S. would not wait for terrorists to act; instead it would employ an aggressive offensive strategy based on law enforcement and intelligence, military power, and international cooperation to block terrorist financing. Preventing terrorists from acquiring and using WMD was a central goal of the strategy; this threat was regarded as real and immediate. The "4D" strategy was summarized as "defeat, deny, diminish, and defend": the United States intended to destroy terrorist organizations; deny them the support of states; address the underlying conditions that permit and encourage terrorism (including finding a solution to the Israeli–Palestinian conflict); and defend the country, its citizens, and its interests abroad against attack. Victory was defined as the achievement of a world in which terrorism did not define the daily lives of Americans and their friends and allies. The goal, attainable only after long and sustained effort, was to eliminate terrorism as a threat to the American way of life.

Shortly thereafter, the Bush Administration demonstrated the ambitious reality of its preemptive and unilateralist strategy by launching the war against Iraq. The military campaign was justified as necessary to remove a regime that did and was likely to continue to support terrorism and had acquired and intended to keep acquiring WMD. The United States was successful in quickly ending Saddam Hussein's reign in Iraq and in doing so with a minimum of U.S. and allied casualties. The cost, however, was the alienation of many of the United States' closest allies. The false premises on which the war was based undermined U.S. credibility. The postwar occupation proved arduous, vexed, and costly in human and material terms. The administration was forced to revise its initial military strategy for Iraq and to alter its conception of the war on terror as well. In the meantime, the eroding situation in Afghanistan also required strategic rethinking.

Critical evaluation

How well did the American response fulfill the requirements of strategy? Can the response to terrorism – whether a comprehensive general approach or a set of case-by-case reactions tailored to circumstances – be fitted into a grand strategy for the United States?

Consider first counterterrorist strategy. The September 11 attacks broke what appeared to be a pattern of incrementalism in the American response to terrorism. The ambitiousness of the war on terrorism was not in doubt, although there was more continuity between the Clinton and Bush Administrations' responses than the latter preferred to recognize. The definition of the objective and the logic of the relationship between ends and means in the war on terrorism, however, were not clear from the beginning. My assessment suggests that American goals for the global war on terrorism were too ambitious and too ambiguous. The aims of the United States were based on an inappropriate characterization of the adversary, inadequate understanding of the causes of terrorism, and faulty appreciation of the nature of the struggle. Value trade-offs were minimized. The means employed were not well suited to the ends and were not always compatible with each other. Policy makers did not appear to realize that some prescriptive measures, however desirable, are not feasible, despite vast American economic and military power. Official statements of strategy showed limited ability and willingness to recognize problems in the conceptualization of the strategy and in its implementation.

The war in Afghanistan had two objectives. As a war against the Taliban regime, the strategy apparently succeeded in the short run because the Taliban regime was overthrown. Mullah Omar, however, remained unaccounted for. The outcome of the military campaign against Al Qaeda was problematic. Elements of the organization remained in areas of Afghanistan and Pakistan and continued to use terrorism against Western interests. Significant attacks occurred in Tunisia, Morocco, Saudi Arabia, Kenya, and Indonesia. Furthermore, such an adversary – a nonstate actor structured as a global network or conglomeration of franchise operations, with considerable local autonomy and flexibility – seemed to be able to reconstitute itself even after a physical defeat in a specific location. Al Qaeda appeared to be independent of state support; conceivably, the organization could exist without a fixed territorial base, relying on multiple decentralized operational centers. Thus, preemptive strikes against states might have little effect.

The United States initiated the war not just against the Taliban and Al Qaeda but in principle against "terrorism of global reach." This war was waged not against Al Qaeda as a distinct nonstate entity but against the means the organization – or, for that matter, any other organization – chose to employ. This goal was so open-ended that accomplishing it might never be possible.

Moreover, an unintended and potentially costly consequence of counterterrorist strategy specifically as well as the new national security strategies could be the encouragement of future incarnations of the threat, as a reaction to extended U.S. military involvement around the world, outside Iraq. Encouraging states to crush terrorism could lead to the suppression of all opposition, provoking the establishment of new underground conspiracies with radical objectives and hatred for the United States. The strategy did not define limits to American assistance to regimes battling various violent challenges linked to terrorism "with global reach" – a phrase also left undefined. For example, how strong should the link be between a local conflict and Al Qaeda for the United States to intervene?

The strategy of preemption announced in 2002 applied to all threats, not just terrorism. It aimed to destroy the enemy's capacity to attack in advance, not influence its "will" or calculus of decision. The strategy's advocates perceived it as an attempt to alter a threatening status quo to defend American interests. Reliance on preemption also is a way of escaping the dilemma created by lack of tactical warning of terrorist attack or absence of a "smoking gun" of proven state complicity.[46] At the same time, fear of a preemptive attack can lead adversaries to strike first. North Korea, Syria, and Iran could be cases in point.

Thus, the war on terrorism became the centerpiece of a grand strategy of preponderance and unilateralism that the administration favored well before the September 11 attacks.[47] However, the use of military force to preempt state adversaries, particularly Iraq, could be costly in terms of defeating terrorism. If the new national security strategy was a grand strategy, it was not necessarily compatible with an effective counterterrorist strategy. For example, the war against Iraq alienated members of the antiterrorist coalition, allies that are essential to American law enforcement and intelligence efforts. Even governments that supported the U.S. confronted deep public opposition to their involvement.

American strategic planners seemed not to have thought deeply about what happens after a preemptive war is fought and won. The United States was unprepared to cope with the level of insecurity and disorder that followed the collapse of the Iraqi regime. The consequences for the war on terrorism itself were negative. The occupation of Iraq inspired further terrorism from Al Qaeda and its allies and affiliates. Afghanistan remained unstable and volatile after a military victory was declared, and terrorism spread to Pakistan. Neither Osama Bin Laden nor Zawahiri was killed or taken into custody.

If in the long term the removal of Saddam Hussein's regime results not in the democratization of Iraq and neighboring regimes but in heightened instability and repressiveness, the prospect of continued terrorism is further heightened.[48] If one conceives of terrorism directed against U.S. interests as a form of internationalized civil conflict – a spillover of local grievances onto the international scene, facilitated by the processes of globalization[49] – then violence that initially is limited and localized could be transformed into "terrorism of global reach" in areas beyond Iraq. It is worth noting that past demonstrations of U.S. power did not dissuade terrorists. The raid on Libya in 1986 was followed by the bombing of Pan Am 103 in 1988. The 1998 strikes against the Sudan and Afghanistan did not halt Al Qaeda.

American efforts to "diminish" the conditions that are presumed to give rise to terrorism included resolving the Israeli–Palestinian conflict as well as establishing democratic stability in Iraq. After the war in Iraq, the Bush Administration took on a much more active role than it had initially anticipated. The risks of failure remained high, however. The consequences could extend far beyond the scope of the conflict itself. If the United States – by virtue of its involvement, its power, and its alliance with Israel – is held responsible for continued Israeli violence against Palestinians, its attractiveness as a target of terrorism will grow.

Conclusions

This review of the American response to terrorism raises several critical questions. What sort of American foreign policy or grand strategy would be compatible with controlling terrorism? How might the material and the ideological or normative environment be shaped to discourage and prevent resort to such means? How can all the resources of the United States be coordinated? In particular, how should military means relate to economic and political instruments?

A first conclusion is that policy makers should avoid decontextualizing terrorism. For this reason, counterterrorist strategy must be linked to grand strategy, and grand strategy to policy goals. These distinctions are not always clear in the American response to terrorism. It is tempting to attach the response to terrorism to an overarching conceptual structure that dictates top-down reasoning. However, the local political context within which terrorism emerges shapes its trajectory and threat assessments should not overgeneralize or assume that terrorism is a monolithic force. Strategy must be flexible. Policy makers must learn to deal with complexity and ambiguity.

For example, Al Qaeda evolved under specific and perhaps unique historical circumstances. The Soviet invasion of Afghanistan, the American support for the moudjahidin, and the allied victory in the 1991 Gulf War were key precipitating events that will not be duplicated. Thus, the assumption that Al Qaeda will be a model for future terrorism may be incorrect. A successful strategy for defeating Al Qaeda might not be effective against other threats. In fact, responding uniformly can be dangerous if adversaries thereby are enabled to design around the threats they know.

Moreover, wars are waged against adversaries, not methods. Whether or not one can outlaw a practice by waging war against those who use it is an open question. Eradicating all "terrorism of global reach" establishes an open-ended policy goal. It may be too ambitious for any strategy. Measuring success may not be possible, especially if one considers the number and variety of actors that could practice terrorism.[50]

Although in the past states may have been the only adversaries who counted, the United States can no longer afford to act under this assumption. Yet efforts to justify a strategy of preemption toward Iraq in terms of a war on terrorism demonstrated just such a reliance on old thinking. The threat was no longer the autonomous nonstate actor Al Qaeda but a familiar adversary: Iraq. Reference to the possibility that Iraq might provide chemical, biological, nuclear, or radiological weapons to Al Qaeda was a way of shifting the focus of policy back to a state-centric world and its power balances. In this framework, nonstate actors acquire significance only if they are proxies of states; they are not regarded as independent actors.

Encouraging the liberalization of regimes that are intolerant of dissent, opening space for the expression of moderate opposition, and promoting democracy also form part of a grand strategy that shapes the international environment to make it less conducive to terrorism. The United States must work toward providing an attractive alternative future to persons dissatisfied with the status quo.[51] Otherwise many of the aggrieved are likely to be attracted to radical and anti-American causes. It is not clear that a grand strategy of preemption of threats could further this purpose, and in fact the Bush Administration moved away from this posture by 2006.

It is equally critical that U.S. counterterrorist efforts be legitimate in the eyes of the international community. The support of other nations is indispensable to the disruption of terrorist operations and controlling the spread of weapons of mass destruction. U.S. grand strategy should not ignore interdependence in the domain of international security.

10 Counterterrorism policy and the political process

American counterterrorism policy is not just a response to the threat of terrorism, whether at home or abroad, but a reflection of the domestic political process. Perceptions of the threat of terrorism and determination and implementation of policy occur in the context of a policy debate involving government institutions, the media, interest groups, and the elite and mass publics. The issue of terrorism tends to appear prominently on the national policy agenda as a result of highly visible and symbolic attacks on Americans or American property. However, the threat is interpreted through a political lens created by the diffused structure of power within the American government.[1]

In general, focusing events, such as crises or disasters, trigger attention to a problem by attracting the attention of the news media and the public.[2] Such sudden and harmful events, rare by definition, come to the notice of the mass public and policy elites simultaneously. In the case of terrorism, focusing events frequently come in clusters, so that it is often difficult to trace a specific policy response to a single event. The reaction to the Oklahoma City bombing, for example, is linked to perceptions of the 1993 World Trade Center bombing and the 1995 Aum Shinrikyo sarin gas attack on the Tokyo subways. Under the Reagan Administration, the 1986 military strike against Libya was a response not just to the La Belle disco bombing in Berlin but to earlier attacks such as the TWA and Achille Lauro hijackings and the shooting attacks at the Rome and Vienna airports in 1985. Thus, sequences of events rather than single disasters typically serve as policy catalysts.[3]

As Robert Johnson has emphasized, in the United States threatening events are filtered through a political process that is characterized by lack of consensus among political elites.[4] The decision-making process is disaggregated and pluralistic, and power is diffused. Because not all issues can be dealt with simultaneously, political elites – the president, different agencies within the executive branch, Congress, the media, interest groups, and "experts" in academia and the consulting world – compete to set the national policy agenda. They compete to select certain problems for attention, interpret their meaning and significance, conceive of solutions, put them into practice, and evaluate their outcomes. Despite the secrecy inherent in formulating and implementing policy toward terrorism, issues are developed, interests formed, and policies legitimized through public debates.[5] Decision makers with different identities and preferences define and represent problems, or frame issues, in order to gain public support for their positions. Furthermore, the selection and implementation of policy depend on the particularistic interests of the actors or coalitions that assume the initiative as much as consistent policy doctrine or strategy based on a broad national consensus about what can and ought to be done. Lack of coordination and fragmentation of effort are often the result.

The politics of the executive branch

The political process within the executive branch is characterized by progressive expansion of the number of agencies involved, overlapping lines of authority among them, expansion of jurisdictions to encompass new issues, parochialism, and competition. No agency in the executive branch of the government wants an issue on the agenda unless it has an efficient and acceptable solution for it. Thus, public policy problems such as terrorism are typically linked to proposed solutions that are in turn linked to specific institutions within the government. How an issue is defined will typically determine which government institution has jurisdiction over it and can thus take charge of policy solutions, often with corresponding budget increases. (Spending on antiterrorism programs jumped from $61.7 million to $205.3 million in the fiscal 1999 appropriations.[6] Overall spending on terrorism is generally estimated at $7 billion per year.)

As the definition of the threat of terrorism changes, so too does jurisdiction. If the image of an issue can be changed, then its institutional venue may change accordingly. Issues can be partitioned among agencies, or different institutions can have more or less authority at various stages or sequences of a decision. For example, if terrorism is defined as a crime, it is a problem for the Department of Justice and the nation's law enforcement agencies such as the Federal Bureau of Investigation (FBI). However, if it is defined as warfare or as a threat to national security, responsibility shifts accordingly. The Central Intelligence Agency (CIA) and the military become central to the process. Nevertheless, the FBI did not lose its role with the internationalization of the issue. In 1986, major legislation established extraterritorial jurisdiction for crimes committed against Americans abroad, which has led to prosecutions in the World Trade Center bombing and East Africa bombing cases, along with others. Definition of the threat of terrorism as "bioterrorism" in the 1990s brought a host of new agencies into the jurisdictional competition, including Health and Human Services (HHS) and its Center for Disease Control. Previously, when the threat of "super terrorism" was interpreted as the danger of the acquisition of nuclear materials, the Department of Energy assumed a key role. In the 1990s, as the threat of terrorism came to be seen as a threat to the "homeland," not only did local and state governments enter the picture but the military was called on to provide "homeland defense." The Defense Authorization Act for Fiscal Year 1997 called on the Defense Department (DOD) to train local "first responders" and to establish response teams to assist civilian authorities should there be a terrorist incident involving weapons of mass destruction (WMD).[7] The result was Joint Task Force Civil Support, established in 1999.[8]

Responsibility for dealing with terrorism is widely distributed, and lines of jurisdiction tend to be blurred and overlapping, with no clear institutional monopoly of the issue. The U.S. government first tried to deal with this problem by establishing the "lead agency" concept. The Department of State is the lead agency for responding to international terrorism, while the FBI is the lead agency for domestic terrorism.[9] Nevertheless, the White House National Security Council (NSC) and the Department of State have traditionally competed for institutional control of the issue of international terrorism, and the FBI and the State Department sometimes clash. For example, Secretary of State Cyrus Vance resigned after his advice against a hostage rescue mission in Iran was overruled by the president and the NSC under National Security Adviser Zbigniew Brzezinski. Former Director of Central Intelligence Stansfield Turner described the relationship between the NSC and executive branch agencies as it affected the rescue decision:

> The National Security Adviser and his staff often are frustrated because they have no direct authority to carry out the president's decisions. That's the task of the bureaucracy, which frequently resists outside direction, even from the President. Bureaucrats are even more likely to resist what they suspect are directives from the National Security Council staff. A result of these tensions is that the staff of the NSC often attempts to sidestep the bureaucracy and do as much as possible on its own.[10]

Turner and the CIA also resisted the NSC's proposals for covert operations against Iran, seeing the dispute as a case of "the professionalism of the experts keeping the political leadership from undertaking ventures that would be embarrassingly unsuccessful."[11]

Rivalries between the NSC and other executive branch agencies also emerged under the Clinton Administration. In April 1998, as a result of having read the Richard Preston novel, *The Cobra Event*, the president held a meeting with a group of scientists and Cabinet members to discuss the threat of bioterrorism. The briefing impressed Clinton so much that he asked the experts to brief senior officials in DOD and HHS. On May 6 they delivered a follow-up report, calling for the stockpiling of vaccines (an idea that was soon dropped). *The Washington Post* reported with regard to the stockpiling proposal that

> Some administration officials outside the White House expressed surprise at how fast the president and his National Security Council staff had moved on the initiative . . ., noting with some concern that it had not gone through the customary deliberative planning process.[12]

Critics noted that not all scientific experts were disinterested; some stood to gain financially if the government invested large sums in developing technology against bioterrorism.

In the investigation of the October 2000 bombing of the destroyer *U.S.S. Cole* the State Department was said to be less than enthusiastic about the FBI's hard-line approach to Yemeni authorities.[13] While the FBI appealed to the president to demand that Yemen accept a central FBI role, the State Department countered by warning that the pressure would likely backfire.

Clinton's move to establish the position of a national coordinator for counterterrorism policy on the NSC staff also provoked opposition from within the executive branch. *The New York Times* reported that Clinton's May 1998 initiative "had provoked a bitter fight within the Administration, with the Departments of Defense and Justice opposing a key provision that critics feared would have created a terrorism czar within the White House."[14] As a result, Clinton created a national coordinator with limited staff and no direct budget authority. *The Washington Post* reported,

> It is not clear how much real authority [Richard] Clarke will have. . . . The Defense Department successfully fought off proposals to give this coordinator a large staff and independent budget similar to those of the drug policy coordinator. . . . Clarke's appears to be essentially a staff job, reporting to National Security Adviser Samuel R. "Sandy" Berger.[15]

Moreover, agencies may reject jurisdiction and try to exclude issues from the agenda, especially if they think that they do not have a solution or that the new task is not appropriate to their mission or routine. The DOD, for example, appeared divided and ambivalent about its new role in homeland defense. As early as July 1995, some Pentagon officials were calling for an expanded military role in counterterrorism, but this view did not appear to reflect an internal consensus. In a speech to the Council on Foreign Relations in New York in September 1998, Secretary of Defense William Cohen prominently mentioned terrorism.[16] His description of the military mission, however, was vague; he said that the administration hoped to consolidate the task of coordination into one lead federal agency, and that DOD would provide "active support" for that agency's operation. Falkenrath et al. argued that the DOD is not "fully committed to this mission."[17] The military see "homeland defense" as law enforcement, which the military supports only if ordered and when possible. Essentially, in their view, it is a diversion and misuse of defense dollars, and they would prefer that the entire domestic preparedness program be shifted to the Federal Emergency Management Agency (FEMA). The military's reluctance is confirmed by John Hillen, who sees DOD as dominated by interservice rivalries rather than leadership from the president or the secretary of defense: "Today the services are interested in neither the White House's new wars (peacekeeping, terrorism, organized crime, and the like) nor the Joint Staff's futuristic technological blueprint. . . ."[18] The military really wants to fight wars that are like those of the past, only with upgraded equipment on all sides. In January 1999, press reports announcing Cohen's decision to seek presidential approval for a permanent DOD task force, with a senior officer, to plan for a chemical or biological attack on the U.S. quoted Deputy Defense Secretary John Hamre as saying "Frankly, we're not seeking this job."[19]

Similarly, FEMA did not want to take charge of the domestic preparedness program.[20] FEMA officials opted out on budgetary grounds, fearing that the program would be inadequately funded, and thus be a drain on already scarce resources, and that the agency would then be criticized for ineffective implementation of the program. Since they could not afford the solution, they did not want to take on the problem.

In 1998, the decision to retaliate against the Sudan and Afghanistan also revealed disarray within the executive branch, a state of confusion and contentiousness that threatened to eclipse terrorism as the issue at the forefront of public debate.[21] The FBI and the CIA were accused of failing to share complete information on threats in East Africa with the State Department.[22] Disagreement surfaced between Washington and bureaucracies in the field. The ambassador to Kenya in December 1997, and again in April and May 1998, asked unsuccessfully for support from the State Department Bureau of Diplomatic Security for the construction of a new and less vulnerable building. The decision to retaliate was controversial. Some analysts in the CIA and the State Department Bureau of Intelligence and Research remained unconvinced of the reliability of the evidence linking Osama Bin Laden's network to the pharmaceuticals plant in Khartoum and informed the news media of their doubts after the cruise missile strikes. The FBI and the Defense Intelligence Agency were excluded from the decision. Apparently Chairman of the Joint Chiefs of Staff General Shelton objected to the original targeting plan and succeeded in reducing the number of targets.

Congressional politics

Congress frequently plays a critical role in shaping the counterterrorism policy agenda, without the constraint of necessarily having to present an integrated solution to the problem. Although the president typically has the most power to set the agenda, he depends on Congress to appropriate funds for the measures he proposes, and Congress can block issues or push forward others that the president has not chosen. Furthermore, executive branch agencies usually have their own channels of communication and influence with congressional committees. Congressional staffers and career bureaucrats often have extensive back-channel contacts. Individuals move back and forth between positions in Congress and in the executive branch. Thus, even if the president wants to keep an issue off the agenda or to minimize a problem, he may have to confront it because congressional actions have captured media and public attention. Confrontation is especially likely when the government is divided along partisan lines. The president cannot afford to appear to ignore a potential threat of terrorism, even if restraint might be the most appropriate and effective response. In the 1990s, the president and Congress often seemed to be engaged in a highly partisan politics of anticipatory blame avoidance.

Examples of congressional influence on critical policy decisions include President Reagan's decision to withdraw American troops from Lebanon in the aftermath of the 1983 bombing of the Marine barracks. Reagan was apparently dissuaded by congressional and military opposition encountered in the context of an upcoming campaign for reelection.[23] Initially Reagan resisted the idea of withdrawal, although the House Committee on Armed Services urged him to reconsider his policy and issued its own report critical of security at the Marine barracks. Reagan withheld the release of the DOD's Long Commission report for several days in order to limit the damage he feared it would create as a rallying point for opposition in Congress. Congressional responses from both Republicans and Democrats to Reagan's press conferences and speeches were lukewarm at best. Although the movement to reassess policy was largely bipartisan, House Speaker O'Neill assumed a prominent role in the debate, organizing the passage of resolutions calling for an end to the military presence in Lebanon, and Democratic presidential candidate Walter Mondale seized on withdrawal as a campaign issue. The State Department and the National Security Adviser opposed withdrawal, but DOD and the Joint Chiefs favored it. In early January, Reagan sent his national security adviser, secretary of defense, and the chairman of the Joint Chiefs of Staff to speak with leading House Republicans. Nevertheless, Minority Whip Trent Lott stated publicly that the Republicans had told them that they wanted the Marines out by March 1985. Still, in his State of the Union address in January 1984, Reagan persisted: "We must have the courage to give peace a chance. And we must not be driven from our objectives for peace in Lebanon by state-sponsored terrorism."[24] Within two weeks of the State of the Union address, Reagan announced the withdrawal.

An earlier instance of congressional influence over policy occurred during the Ford administration. Secretary of State Kissinger ordered the recall of the ambassador to Tanzania, Beverly Carter, when he learned that Carter had played an active role in facilitating negotiations for the release of American students held hostage in Zaire. Kissinger took strong exception to this violation of the official policy of no concessions and reportedly intended to end Carter's State Department career, although Carter had expected to be appointed ambassador to Denmark. However, when the Congressional Black Caucus intervened on Carter's behalf, generating negative publicity for the State Department, Kissinger relented.[25] It was also helpful to Carter's defense that he was a former journalist.

In the 1990s, as Richard Falkenrath points out, one source of the difficulties of the domestic preparedness program was "its origin in a series of discrete, uncoordinated legislative appropriations and administrative actions," the result of ad hoc initiatives rather than strategic concept.[26] In 1996, for example, Congress began "earmarking" specific counterterrorism projects, such as providing $10 million for counterterrorism technologies for the National Institute of Justice in the Fiscal Year 1997 Department of Justice budget. The FBI counterterrorism budget was also dramatically increased, largely as a result of the Oklahoma City bombing. Congress also instructed the Departments of Justice and Defense to prepare long-term plans for counterterrorism, and established an independent National Commission on Terrorism to investigate government policy. Lawmakers are also concerned about lack of congressional oversight of administration efforts.

Outside the government

Actors outside the government also try to shape the public policy agenda. Interest groups and communities of "experts," sometimes associated with professional consulting firms, or think tanks, seek access to decision makers in order to promote favored issues. They often accumulate the scientific or technical information about the problem that then causes decision makers to recognize it. They can promote a specific conception of an issue, such as the idea of a new, more lethal and irresponsible terrorism in the 1990s.[27] They contribute the "talking heads" who appear regularly on television news programs such as CNN. They may also be influential in shaping policy solutions because of their expertise.

Among interest groups, in the area of terrorism, business interests may oppose economic sanctions against state sponsors. Interest groups devoted to protecting civil liberties are likely to oppose measures that restrict individual freedoms, such as expanding the power of the FBI or the use of passenger profiling at airports. The American Civil Liberties Union, for example, has frequently opposed legislative initiatives such as assigning responsibility for domestic preparedness to the military. Along with conservative Republicans, civil liberties interest groups blocked the wiretapping provisions of the 1996 bill.

The families of victims of terrorism, as well as victims themselves, such as the former hostages in Lebanon, have mobilized to influence policy. They have lobbied the State Department, as well as the White House and Congress, and gone to the courts to press their claims against Iran and Libya. For example, the Victims of Flight Pan Am 103 organization established a political action committee, a legal committee, an investigation committee, and a press committee. They lobbied the State Department, published a newsletter, picketed Pan Am offices, and met with the president and Congress.[28] They were instrumental in the creation of a presidential Commission on Aviation Security and Terrorism to investigate the bombing. They played an influential role in the 1996 Iran–Libya Sanctions Act of 1996.[29] Their intervention led to major changes in airline procedures for handling disasters.

During the Iran hostage crisis, the families of the victims formed the Family Liaison Action Group, which, according to Gary Sick, "played a crucial role in public and government perceptions throughout the crisis."[30] Sick adds that President Carter promised the families that he would take no action that would endanger the lives of the hostages, although Brzezinski was pressing for a decisive response that would protect national honor.

The early development of counterterrorism policy was influenced by interactions between individual government agencies and specific interest groups. The debate over the Airport Security Act of 1973 shows how insider-outsider coalitions form.[31] The government players included Congress, the Departments of Transportation, State, and Justice, and the Federal Aviation Administration (FAA). The outside actors were the Air Line Pilots Association (ALPA), the Air Transport Association of America (ATAA), and the Airport Operators Council International (AOCI). In the jurisdictional dispute between Justice and the FAA, the ATAA and AOCI preferred the FAA, while ALPA preferred Justice. In fact, Justice did not want jurisdiction. While the interest groups wanted the federal government to take responsibility for airport security measures, the Department of Transportation and the FAA wished to rely on local law enforcement.

All of these actors use the news media to articulate and disseminate their views not only to the public but to other elites. Government officials (or former officials) are the main source of information for reporters, as well as for Congress, sometimes openly and sometimes through strategic leaks. Leaks to the press can be a way of conducting internal battles as much as informing the public. The media's attraction to drama and spectacular events also makes it hard for the government to ignore an issue when policy makers assume that public opinion will track media attention. But the news media do not set the agenda, according to John Kingdon: "The media's tendency to give prominence to the most newsworthy or dramatic story actually diminishes their impact on governmental policy agendas because such stories tend to come toward the end of a policy-making process, rather than at the beginning."[32] The media tend to be responsive to issues already on the agenda, to accelerate or magnify them, rather than initiate attention. They report on what the government is doing or not doing.

Jeffrey D. Simon agrees.[33] He argues that the media image of crisis is due to the way presidents and their aides handle events; the press depends almost exclusively on authoritative official sources. Government officials set the tone through background briefings and off the record interviews as well as public speeches and press conferences. Presidents, not reporters, make hostage seizures into personal dramas. On the other hand, Brigitte Nacos argues that government policy is exceptionally sensitive to the news media and to public opinion, especially during hostage crises.[34] Yet the tone of general mass media coverage of U.S. counterterrorism policy is positive.[35]

Conclusions

It is unlikely that the politics of the domestic policy process will change. Thus, expectations for the future should be grounded in the assumption that the trends described in this article will continue. Terrorist attacks, especially spectacular incidents causing large numbers of casualties or targeting important national symbols, will contribute to putting the issue on the national policy agenda. They focus public attention on the threat of terrorism. However, policy will be developed within a general framework of diffusion of power. Multiple actors, inside and outside government, will compete to set the agenda and to determine policy through public debate, conducted largely in the news media. Each actor, whether an executive branch agency, Congress, or an interest group, wants to forge a national consensus behind its particular preference. Due to pressures from Congress, the president will not be able to set the agenda for counterterrorism policy with as much freedom as he can in other policy areas. Where the president dominates is in the rare use of military force, but these decisions may also be controversial within the executive branch. Implementation of policy decisions will also be affected by controversy, due to rivalries among agencies with operational responsibilities. Thus it will be difficult for any administration to develop a consistent policy based on an objective appraisal of the threat of terrorism to American national interests.

Part IV

How terrorism ends

11 How terrorism declines

How campaigns of terrorism come to an end is a critical question for public policy, but in the mid-1980s the problem had not attracted the attention of many scholars.[1] Schmid's classic review of the general literature contained no reference to explanations of the decline of terrorism.[2] Theories of conflict usually focused on causes rather than outcomes,[3] and research on terrorism followed this tradition. Furthermore, the persistent and often distracting obsession with definition impeded research, as did normative biases of the time. Adherents of the view that terrorism was an expression of the nefarious designs of the Soviet Union and its cohorts in a world communist conspiracy[4] confronted equally committed advocates of the opposite persuasion, who blamed the United States and its imperialistic ambitions for rising levels of global violence.[5] Fortunately a growing number of scholars remained aloof from these ideological preoccupations, but academic knowledge had not reached the level of general explanatory theories. The few relatively comprehensive studies of terrorism contained implicit suggestions about the government role in the decline of terrorism, but these inferences were abstract and inconsistent.

In order to move toward understanding how terrorism declines, I assessed the implications of the mainstream literature on terrorism. Finding them unsatisfactory, I surveyed the available data on the life cycles of post-war oppositions that were significant practitioners of terrorism. I then suggested that the decline of terrorism occurs for three reasons: physical defeat of the extremist organization by the government, the group's decision to abandon the terrorist strategy, and organizational disintegration.

Contradictory ideas about outcomes

Several competing hypotheses about the outcomes of terrorism can be inferred from conceptions of the origins of terrorism.[6] These interpretations focus either on the conditions that motivate terrorists or on the government response to terrorism.

For example, the growth of terrorism is often linked to the development of modern mass communications media. Terrorism is said to thrive on publicity, so presumably media attention, especially sensationalist television coverage, stimulates it.[7] The relationship is symbiotic. Terrorists want to communicate a message, and the commercial press wants to attract readers and watchers. This view implies that without publicity terrorism would disappear. Yet the causal link between media coverage and the diffusion of terrorism has rarely been investigated, much less established. It has not been shown that publicity serves to communicate the terrorists' message effectively or to change popular attitudes. Furthermore, democratic governments usually reject press censorship as a policy option. The remedy, even if it were effective, is not feasible for liberal democracies.

This perspective finds its opposite in the idea, advanced by Schmid and De Graaf, that lack of access to the news media is actually the source of terrorism.[8] Violence is an effective way of gaining access to publicity and social power in capitalist societies. Lowering the "threshold of communication" and creating a more egalitarian media should therefore remove the need for terrorism. The authors concede, however, the absence of empirical evidence for the benefits of establishing a "right to communicate." Their own analysis assumes the effectiveness of violence in getting attention. Peaceful persuasion is unlikely to be as newsworthy. Nor does it seem possible that governments would wish to guarantee the dissemination of information supporting the grievances or causes that motivate terrorism. In addition, countries with noncommercial media establishments (Great Britain and France, for example) as well are still troubled by terrorism.

Another interpretation assumes that terrorism would end if governments consistently adopted hard-line policies and coordinated their international implementation. Wilkinson argues that firmness and determination, avoiding the extremes of both appeasement and illegal repression, are central to ending terrorism.[9] Although he acknowledges the complexity of the causes of terrorism, Wilkinson assumes that concessions to terrorist demands will encourage terrorism. He recommends resistance and denial of opportunities, although resistance for Wilkinson excludes military retaliation.

Although Wilkinson argues that terrorism is not by and large a rational strategy, his prescription is based on the assumption that reducing the rewards for terrorism and increasing its costs affect the calculations of terrorists. However, the Rand Corporation observed that the evidence that a no-concessions policy is effective is "meager and unconvincing."[10] Certainly American adherence to tough standards under the Reagan Administration (even before the unfolding of the Iran-Contra scandal) did not appear to reduce American vulnerability. In 1985 and 1986, after over a decade of hard-line policy, roughly a quarter of international terrorist incidents were directed against American targets.[11] Nor did Israel's defiant response to Palestinian militancy end terrorism, but it is impossible to know what levels violence might have reached had Israel and the United States pursued different policies.

On the domestic level, Guelke suggests that the key to the decline of terrorism lies in changing perceptions of its legitimacy by the groups who use it.[12] Terrorism is likely to end when terrorism no longer seems justifiable in terms of the ends it serves, or efficacious in moving the organization toward them. Hard-line government policies, if consistently followed, would not end terrorism but lead to widened violence. Governments can become the victims of their own stereotype of terrorists as responsive only to force. Guelke concluded that in Northern Ireland the "prospects for peace, such as they are, are less likely to depend on the techniques employed by government to deal with terrorism than on the evolution of perceptions of those engaged in political violence."[13]

To other authors, terrorism can only be ended if the underlying social and economic conditions that motivate it are radically changed. Rubenstein, for example, implied that terrorism would decline if young intellectuals in society had the opportunity to participate in mass-based movements for change.[14] The absence of viable social movements leads to terrorism as a measure of desperation. Terrorism will not end when the perceptions of terrorists change but when fundamental structural transformation of society occurs. Genuinely revolutionary alternatives for political expression must exist. Terrorism decreases as the potential for radical collective action increases.

An earlier analysis by Targ is similar.[15] He sees terrorism as the product of historical conditions, namely settings that are not conducive to mass revolutionary action. Terrorism is characteristic of preindustrial or postindustrial capitalist societies, but not of the industrial state. It is thus a permanent feature of the postindustrial state as we know it.

Chesnais also argues that terrorism is linked to conditions, although his analysis is more politically focused.[16] He predicts that terrorism will not decline until the structural conditions that permit it – the immaturity of specific Western democracies – change. Terrorism is a remnant of feudalism, to which Mediterranean Europe is highly vulnerable.

A problem with these views is that revolutionary terrorism declined significantly in both the Federal Republic of Germany and in Italy during the 1980s even though fundamental social, political, and economic conditions did not appear to have changed and a new state of democratic maturity did not appear to have been reached. Such general concepts of propitious settings for terrorism are extremely difficult to operationalize.

Establishing the facts

The scope of this preliminary survey of cases was restricted to political oppositions that had mounted significant campaigns of terrorism against the state. The following overview questions the conventional wisdom on terrorism and establishes a basis for comparative research on decline.

The search for useful information on the life cycles of underground organizations is frustrating. Table 11.1 lists seventy-seven organizations, with their country of origin, and the approximate dates of their existence or activity. Simply compiling such a list presents a number of unavoidable conceptual and practical problems. It is important to recognize that treating information on terrorism as though it were unambiguous can lead to false conclusions. Claims of precision are misleading and even controversial.

A first research question is deciding which organizations to include. In order to ensure comparability among the cases considered, this list includes selected organizations active in the post-World War II period. It focuses on autonomous organizations, whether left, right, or separatist in orientation, that rely significantly on terrorism as a strategy of opposition to regimes in power. It excludes mass-based independence movements against foreign occupiers in colonial contexts. Terrorism is defined as unorthodox and unexpected violence designed to coerce and intimidate rather than to destroy an opponent. It is meant to influence the political behavior of adversaries by attacking and threatening targets that possess symbolic rather than material significance. Consequently its victims are often civilians. It is essential that incidents of terrorism are elements in systematic campaigns of violence and not isolated events.

The selection is further limited to groups of substance, measured in terms of coherent organizational structure, longevity, and level of activity. Making such determinations is not simple. Some groups responsible for extensive terrorism are unstructured. While they are perceived as collective entities, in reality they are small, uncoordinated groups linked by a common cause. South Moluccan terrorism in the Netherlands in the 1970s, for example, was the product of several small groups of youths, all motivated by the same goal and inspired by the same models. Islamic Jihad or Hezbollah in Lebanon in the early 1980s, the far right in Italy, the Front de Libération du Québec (FLQ) in Canada in the 1970s, and various Croatian groups also fall into this category. Yet their actions are sufficiently important that excluding them would distort the history of terrorism.

Similarly, it is often difficult to track right-wing groups. They tend to be more decentralized and unstructured than groups on the left. Consequently the right may be underrepresented in databases because its operations are deeply clandestine, loosely organized, and often unclaimed. Right extremism is likely to be represented by a succession of minor groups, rather than a single large organization that dominates a conflict over an extended period of time. Yet the cumulative impact of their violence is as consequential as that of a unified left. For example, in Italy, the New Order, banned in 1973, essentially became the Black Order, which in 1977 became the Armed Revolutionary Nuclei (NAR). This example also demonstrates that organizations can disband or abandon terrorism but individual members may remain active by joining rival groups or forming new ones. The strategy of terrorism may then be continued under different auspices.

Specifying the time period in which groups are active is equally problematic. Some groups turn to terrorism years after their founding. In Peru, the Shining Path (Sendero Luminoso) was created in 1970 but opened its campaign of terrorism in 1980. In general, this list uses the date when the strategy of terrorism was apparently adopted. Similarly, if an organization openly abandons the strategy of terrorism, terrorism is considered to have ended at that point. Accuracy in this matter is an elusive goal, considering the secrecy surrounding the decisions of violent undergrounds. Some organizations undoubtedly continue to exist despite apparent passivity. It is hard to predict when terrorism is likely to be reactivated.

These ambiguities prohibit definitive conclusions, but the survey suggests that some conventional assumptions about terrorism should be reassessed. For example, terrorism seems to end in democracies as often as in authoritarian states, although democracies are most likely to be affected. The opportunities provided by democratic societies are not necessarily conducive to the continuation of terrorism although they may facilitate its initiation. Almost half of the organizations listed no longer exist or no longer use terrorism. However, most currently active organizations have persisted for over ten years. Such stable and tenacious groups pose intractable and long-term public policy problems. At least ten groups have been in operation for twenty years. Possibly there is a threshold point, beyond which the extremist organization becomes self-sustaining. The younger the organization, the greater the likelihood of its ending.

Links between terrorism and conditions are hard to establish. For example, it is not evident that the persistence of terrorism is linked primarily to divided societies, where separatist or nationalist movements predominate. In general, revolutionary and nationalist goals appear equally well represented among groups that have lasted over ten years. Nor is it clear that the duration of terrorism is connected to the level of development of the host state, since there appears to be little difference in the duration of terrorist campaigns in the developed West and in the Third World. Nor is terrorism always absent in the presence of mass-based movements. The two forms of pressure for social change may not be mutually exclusive.

With regard to government policies, concessions to demands in specific cases are not always associated with the persistence of terrorism. Brazil, Uruguay, and Argentina, as well as the Federal Republic of Germany and Italy, have met demands, but in all of these nations terrorism has ended or declined significantly. There is no necessary correlation between the government's coerciveness toward terrorism and yielding to specific demands when hostages are seized.

The "success" of modern terrorism is often deplored. Yet terrorism is rarely associated with political instability or with radical political change. In three exceptional cases revolutionary terrorism preceded military intervention in politics – Uruguay, Argentina, and Turkey – but if organizational survival is considered to be a goal of terrorism (as argued in Chapter 4), then the strategy failed. The outcome in each case was provocation of a repressive government response. In Argentina, the struggle against terrorism took the severe form of a brutal war to suppress all opposition, leading to thousands of "disappearances." In Iran, terrorism was one form of violent opposition to the reign of the Shah, but after the revolution the secular left was soon alienated from Iran's religious regime and unsuccessfully revived its terrorist strategy. It does not seem reasonable to conclude that terrorism declines because it accomplishes its long-term ideological goals.

This brief overview indicates that there are no easy answers to questions about the decline of terrorism. A satisfactory explanation requires analysis that is sensitive to specific historical contexts.

Explaining individual processes of decline

Ross and Gurr presented a comparative political analysis of the declining incidence of domestic terrorism in Canada and the United States.[17] Their argument is based on an assessment of terrorist capabilities, which they distinguish as coercive or political. Preemption and deterrence are government measures that destroy the terrorists' coercive capabilities. Political capabilities, on the other hand, diminish through "burnout" (declining group commitment) and "backlash" (reduced popular support). These analytical distinctions are helpful in understanding the process of decline, particularly as they suggest further questions about the interrelationships among external and internal variables. For example, what effect does government coercion have on the underground's cohesion and legitimacy, and which are its key political resources? What conditions lead to loss of commitment among the group members or to popular disaffection? When do terrorist groups perceive "backlash"? Does the withdrawal of popular support that symbolizes decline precede or follow the government's mobilization for preemption or deterrence? Are disunity and "burnout" synonymous?

The conceptual formulation I proposed focused on a different set of variables and was designed to apply to a wider range of cases. It emphasized the strategy of extremist organizations. The decline of terrorism appeared to be related to the interplay of three factors: the government response to terrorism (which is not restricted to preemption or deterrence), the strategic choices of the terrorist organization, and its organizational resources. The government role can be decisive, but often in nonobvious ways. Attempts to defeat a terrorist underground by destroying its organizational structure, removing leaders, causing large-scale attrition, or blocking recruitment do not always have the same effect. Reforms that decrease the utility of terrorism or positive inducements that encourage individual defections can be as important as the deployment of coercive resources. Decisive defeats are rare in the absence of other contributing factors, such as organizational disintegration. Yet disunity does not necessarily signal the end of terrorism or reflect declining commitment. Disagreements over strategy are common. Members can defect to rival groups or establish a new, more militant organization. Splits and mergers are a form of propagation of terrorism. Power struggles among generations of leaders (especially if the original leadership is imprisoned) and prior patterns of cleavage among supporters, whether states or ethnic groups, also reduce cohesiveness. Strategic reversals may result from dependence on states whose support is withdrawn or sanctuaries that are lost, the appearance of more attractive or justifiable alternatives, or a collective perception of failure. Possibly cycles of terrorism exist. An escalation in destructiveness may precipitate decline, as extreme terrorist activity provokes government intervention, alienates or frightens sympathizers, and generates internal disagreement.

A few examples illustrate these complex interactions. Relevant cases include domestic terrorism in Western and Third World democracies, including both police and military responses (an important difference between the United States and Canada). International terrorist campaigns are also discussed.

Domestic terrorism did not pose a significant threat in the United States, but in the late 1960s it seemed plausible that offshoots of the civil rights protest movement might be capable of serious violence. In 1969 the FBI decided that the Black Panthers were the most dangerous internal threat in the country. By the next year all senior leaders were in prison, in court, dead, or out of the country. Local police forces also reacted vigorously, in large part because they were the chosen targets. In 1972, Huey Newton, the Panthers' Minister of Defense, announced that the program of "militant self defense" was over. With the original leadership gone, the remaining cadres, mostly young and inexperienced, were unable to hold the organization together. Organizing on a national basis posed problems of coordination and continuity. Internal quarrels (frequently bloody) led to significant defections, such as that of Eldridge Cleaver. In retrospect, the FBI's estimation of the threat seems highly exaggerated and police and FBI enforcement of the law overzealous. The apparent success of these policies should not be allowed to obscure the fact that the decline was also the result of organizational overextension, inexperienced cadres, loss of leadership through defections as well as arrests, unrestrained factionalism, and poor strategic choices (attacks on police).

In contrast to the United States, left extremist groups in Italy enjoyed measurable popular support, and the state appeared weak in terms of both legitimacy and coercive capabilities. Yet terrorism receded because an innovative government policy apparently coincided with the emergence of discontent within the terrorist underground. The government's offer of leniency for "repented" terrorists was effective because the Red Brigades were in disarray. Gian Carlo Caselli, a judge in Turin, claimed that the Italian "victory" over terrorism was due to applied sociology, psychology, and political science, not police and judicial repression.[18] "We lost a lot of time before understanding that military measures – I mean the use of the army (in the Moro affair, notably) – accomplished nothing except to create 'repressive illusions'."[19] Once the Italian government recognized the need to attack terrorism at its source and to coordinate the police response, especially in terms of acquiring intelligence, terrorism was quickly suppressed. He points to two laws as decisive: one requiring people renting or selling apartments to inform the authorities of the names of new tenants or purchasers, and the other the "repentants" law, which offered accused terrorists freedom or reduced sentences in exchange for informing.[20] He also observed that public opinion switched to the side of the government when it became clear that the terrorists were not romantic figures. Open demonstrations of public hostility to terrorism were important to its delegitimization.

An analysis by Tarrow and della Porta suggested that Italian terrorism was transitory, a sign of the decline of mass protest.[21] It represented the end of a cycle of the rise and fall of social movements. Terrorism only emerged as the momentum of mass protest drew in new political actors with new issues. Small extremist groups were inspired to join the action but were unable to influence events due to receding popular support (the public was often repelled by their violence) and increasing government coercion. Terrorism declined as the Italian government responded with sanctions that would not have been tolerated against peaceful protest but were justified by terrorism.

Legault argues that terrorism ended because of a poor strategic choice on the part of the Red Brigades, a decision that was criticized at the time by competing groups in the far left.[22] The decision to kidnap and to murder Aldo Moro forced the Italian population to choose sides and compelled a divided government to mobilize. The result was the reaffirmation of the legitimacy of the Italian state, which terrorism was meant to undermine.

Legault also sees left-wing Italian terrorism as cyclical.[23] First in the "pre-revolutionary" or "pre-discourse" period, opposition movements begin to question the established order in a context of decentralizing authority, especially in the universities, and growing discontent among students and workers. Second, "the terrorist discourse" involves the elaboration and refinement of ideological themes that legitimize violence. Extremists come to believe that violence is both morally justified and likely to succeed. The third stage, "implementation of discourse through action," is marked by steadily escalating terrorism. The range of targets expands as the terrorist group abandons "armed propaganda" for "revolutionary civil war," culminating in the 1978 attack on Moro, which was deliberately intended to strike at the heart of the state and to provoke destabilization at the top levels of government. In the fourth stage of "counter-discourse or repression," state and society react by uniting against terrorism as much as by the destruction of the terrorists' coercive capabilities. By 1979–80, Italy had entered the final stage of "counter counter-discourse." The clear public preference for security and order accentuated divisions within the terrorist organizations, who became "schizophrenic."[24] Violence had become an end in itself, almost a religion based on myths of arms and death. The terrorists vainly sought new constituencies in the sub-proletariat and among prisoners, but their violence appeared increasingly meaningless to society. The kidnapping of General Dozier – an attempt to renew links with a broader base in the anti-imperialist left – ended in failure. Terrorism lost support when the ambitiousness and overconfidence of the Red Brigades precipitated a direct confrontation between government and terrorists.

In the French case, government policy followed a sequence of coercion, accommodation, and then renewed coercion. Action Directe emerged in the 1980s, a decade later than similar groups in West Germany and Italy. When Francois Mitterrand was elected president in 1981, he amnestied the members of violent left-wing groups who had not been convicted of common crimes. This partial amnesty provoked two responses: a hunger strike by the remaining prisoners, and terrorist pressure from their comrades outside. After 35 days, the hunger-strikers were released on medical grounds.[25] Some members of Action Directe, particularly the two "historic leaders," returned to the underground and initiated a strategy of political assassinations, whereas before the group had restricted itself to relatively harmless bombings. Although 80 per cent of the amnestied prisoners did not return to violence, the resurgence of a more murderous Action Directe made the government appear naive and weak. Nevertheless, the much smaller organization, even if more committed and cohesive, was also more vulnerable to police penetration. When key leaders were arrested in 1987, the organization was effectively destroyed. The demonstrated failure of conciliatory alternatives as well as the escalation of terrorism, both from Action Directe and from Middle Eastern groups, served to justify government action.

In the United States, Italy, and France terrorism was inspired by revolutionary ideologies. In Canada, the FLQ mixed national-separatism with self-conscious imitation of Third World national liberation struggles. In 1970 the government responded to the FLQ's seizure of hostages, one British and one Canadian official, with a declaration of martial law and the dispatch of 8,000 federal troops to the province. This extremely coercive response, which was implemented with precision and efficiency, apparently halted separatist terrorism. However, Fournier argues that terrorism subsided not because of the numerous arrests made under martial law (which lasted for three months) but because of internal developments in the FLQ (the decision to form a Marxist-Leninist movement based on mass mobilization, not terrorism) and the growth in power of the legal independence movement, which won elections in Quebec in 1976.[26] Ross and Gurr also stress the development of feasible alternatives to violence.[27] However, the FLQ clearly made a strategic mistake in kidnapping Cross and Laporte and murdering Pierre Laporte. This miscalculation or accident was due in part to the unstructured nature of the FLQ, since two independent cells were actually behind the kidnappings. Their actions were not centrally coordinated.

Military responses to terrorism are more common in the Third World, where terrorism is usually linked to rural insurgency and popular grievances. The example of India shows that an attempt to deprive terrorists of coercive capabilities can backfire. In 1984 India responded to Sikh terrorism with a declaration of martial law in the Punjab, in conjunction with a military attack on the Golden Temple shrine in Amritsar, where Sikh terrorist leader Bhindranwale was headquartered. The central government sent in 2,000 troops to seize the temple, with an additional 70,000 troops to seal off the state. Leaf argues that this inappropriate reaction "far from ending Bhindranwale's influence and activities . . . actually served as evidence of what he was trying to prove."[28] The terrorists did not represent or speak for even a large minority of the Sikh population, urban or rural, but the government response was self-destructive in misrepresenting the real issues in the Punjab (popular discontent actually focused on economic issues, not political autonomy) and confirming Sikh expectations that the government was not responsive to their demands and that Indira Gandhi was motivated primarily by the desire to establish autocratic rule. Consequently Indira Gandhi was assassinated by two of her Sikh bodyguards. In the rioting after the assassination, more than 1,500 Sikhs were killed. The government response appears only to have widened social divisions, and violence continues.

Uruguay is another case of military reaction to domestic terrorism. The Tupamaros were defeated in 1972, after the declaration of a state of siege and the deployment of the armed forces in a sustained military offensive.[29] The civilian government had already suspended constitutional rights and imposed media censorship. The military (and its allies in the ruling government coalition) may have overestimated the revolutionary threat, due in part to the Tupamaros' own overconfidence as well as a vested interest in increasing the power and resources of the security forces. The Tupamaro threat created a consensus among the armed forces that made intervention into politics possible. Yet the defeat of the Tupamaros was also related to internal disintegration, caused by disagreement over the appropriate response to the military crackdown. The Tupamaros tried unsuccessfully to move back into rural areas they thought would be harder for the military to control. But the movement could not challenge a mobilized army in urban or rural areas.

It is much more difficult for governments to defeat international terrorist organizations, most of which at the time were centered in the Middle East. Decision making in the Popular Front for the Liberation of Palestine (PFLP) is instructive with regard to the constraints affecting such groups. Abu Khalil argues that the PFLP decision to halt hijackings in 1971 (after having initiated the tactic in 1968) was possible only because of the iron discipline and charismatic authority exercised by George Habash, who decreed that international operations were manifestations of petit bourgeois spirit and adventurism.[30] The PFLP's ideology seemed to be as flexible as the organization was autocratic. Every change that Habash approved was presented as "tactical" rather than "strategic." In the 1970s with increasing bureaucratization, resulting from an increase in financial resources, the organization grew more conservative. In 1981 the leadership dismissed guerrilla warfare as inappropriate and instead stressed "quasi-conventional" war. The 1982 Israeli invasion of Lebanon discredited this strategy, and apparently a new clique, allied with Syria and Libya rather than Iraq, gained power. In 1984, the "comrades and cadres of the PFLP" split off from the moderate faction. In February 1987, Habash declared extremism to be detrimental to the Palestinian national interest. "Strikes at imperialist interests" (attacks on foreign targets) in the Middle East were condemned. The PFLP then appeared to wish to abandon its terrorist image in order to gain official recognition, perhaps following the lead of its patron, Syria, a government embarrassed by Britain's severing of diplomatic relations in 1986 and eager to regain respectability. However, after the Iraqi invasion of Kuwait in 1990, the PFLP seemed prepared to return to terrorism.

The Armenian Secret Army for the Liberation of Armenia (ASALA) and the Justice Commandos of the Armenian Genocide, both active internationally, suffered a serious decline. Tololyan argued that diminished terrorism was not due to instrumental success or failure.[31] Changing attitudes of populations in the Armenian Diaspora and, secondarily, loss of secure bases outside Turkey were the critical factors. Internal quarrels over strategy and over the relevance of the Palestinian model split the movement from the beginning. The collapse of Lebanon, a result of the 1982 Israeli invasion, and subsequent Shi'ite hostility to Armenians deprived them of a base of operations. The British crackdown on Iranians, a response to Iranian-sponsored terrorism, restricted the activities of ethnic Armenians in Britain. Greek Cyprus may also have ceased to provide support for ASALA. The Orly bombing in 1983 resulted not only in repression from the French police (largely ineffective in apprehending actual ASALA members) but also a mixture of alienation, outrage, and fear among French Armenians. Expressions of popular disaffection reinforced existing splits in the terrorist groups, and in turn, bloody internecine quarrels diminished the movement's legitimacy vis-à-vis its Diaspora constituency. Terrorism generated strains and pressures that the movement did not anticipate and from which it could not recover. Tololyan concludes:

> The Armenian terrorist movement deeply miscalculated the kinds and amounts of violence and dissension which the Diaspora consensus could tolerate; it miscalculated equally badly the degree to which its own success depended on at least the silent acquiescence, if not the support, that such consensus enables – in part because the terrorists' initial successes led them to overconfidence concerning their ability to manipulate events and opinion.[32]

Tololyan concludes that the beliefs and perceptions of the political community out of which terrorism springs are more important than the physical defeat of the terrorist organization. His analysis suggests that specific acts of terrorism can violate the legitimizing beliefs that support violence.

Conclusions

It is difficult for democratic governments to anticipate and forestall the emergence of underground organizations dedicated to the use of terrorism. Before extremist groups turn to action, the most expert intelligence agencies cannot distinguish reliably between legitimate dissent and disloyalty or between potentially violent and nonviolent oppositions. The first indication of the path a group has chosen to follow is not its rhetoric but the commission of an act of terrorism. Governments then need time to organize a response: collecting and analyzing intelligence information, establishing special units in the security forces, coordinating bureaucratic resources, and securing legal changes to facilitate the apprehension and conviction of terrorists. All of these measures would be rejected by public opinion if terrorism were not obviously threatening. By the time the government is equipped to combat terrorism, the task is no longer prevention but bringing an active terrorist campaign to an end. At this point dealing with the causes of terrorism, even if feasible or desirable in the long term, must take second place to restoring order.

The assumption that the decline of terrorism is due simply to the physical defeat of extremist organizations is far too simple a conception of the process. Government policies and actions, whether coercive or conciliatory, are only one among several factors contributing to the evolution of terrorist campaigns. These determinants include the organization's cohesiveness and its decisions. Analyzing terrorists' perceptions not only of government policies but of popular attitudes is essential to understanding the miscalculations that discredit terrorism before its supporters, provoke internal dissension, and justify government repression. In liberal democracies where violent oppositions rely exclusively on terrorism, there may be a pattern in which terrorist actions, brought about by overconfidence and misperceptions of consequences, divide the radical opposition and undermine the legitimacy of all violent extremism. It is possible that misjudgments such as the kidnapping and murder of Aldo Moro, Pierre Laporte, or Dan Mitrione occurred because the Red Brigades, FLQ, or Tupamaros, respectively, were isolated from reality (a condition of underground conspiracies, noted in Chapter 5) and arrogant in their expectations of success. Terrorists may not recognize failure, but when terrorism becomes an end in itself, it loses its justifiability in the eyes of the public it was meant to convince. In these cases, terrorism is self-defeating.

Table 11.1 Organizations with terrorist strategies[a]

I. In existence 1–5 years:

Organization	*Country*	*Dates*
Revolutionary Popular Vanguard (VPR)	Brazil	1968–71
National Liberating Action (ALN)	Brazil	1968–71
Armed Proletarian Nuclei	Italy	1974–77
Argentine Anti-Communist Alliance (AAA)	Argentina	1973–76
People's Revolutionary Armed Forces (FRAP)	Mexico	1973–77
Cellules Communistes Combattantes	Belgium	1984–85
Jewish Underground	Israel	1980–84
Hoffman Military Sports Group	W. Germany	1979–81
The Order	U.S.	1983–84
United Freedom Front	U.S.	1982–85
Secret Army Organization	France	1961–62

II. In existence 5–10 years

Organization	*Country*	*Dates*
People's Revolutionary Army (ERP)	Argentina	1969–77
Montoneros	Argentina	1970–77
Japanese Red Army	Japan	1969–77
Weatherman	U.S.	1969–75
Black Panthers	U.S.	1966–72
EOKA	Cyprus	1955–60
EOKA-B	Cyprus	1971–78
Prima Linea	Italy	1976–82
South Moluccan Independence Movement	Netherlands	1975–80
Quebec Liberation Front (FLQ)	Canada	1963–72
23rd of September Communist League	Mexico	1974–81
First of October Anti-Fascist Resistance Group (GRAPO)	Spain	1975–82
Popular Front for the Liberation of Palestine – International Operations	Mideast	1972–78
2nd of June Movement	W. Germany	1971–80
Armed Forces of National Liberation (FALN)	U.S.	1974–82
Omega-7	U.S.	1974–82
Armenian Secret Army for the Liberation of Armenia (ASALA)	Turkey	1975–84
Action Directe	France	1979–87
Islamic Jihad/Hezbollah	Lebanon	1983–

III. In existence over 10 years:

Organization	*Country*	*Dates*
Dal Khalsa (Sikh separatists)	India	1978–
Tupamaros	Uruguay	1968–80
Grey Wolves	Turkey	1968–80
Turkish People's Liberation Army (TPLA)	Turkey	1969–80
Red Hand Commandos	N. Ireland	1972–82
Armed Forces of National Liberation (FALN)	Venezuela	1961–72

Movement of the Revolutionary Left (MIR)	Venezuela	1960–73
Red Flag	Venezuela	1969–79 1981–82
Communist Party of India – Marxist-Leninist (Naxalites)	India	1969–72
Breton Liberation Front (FLB)	France	1969–78
Armed Revolutionary Nuclei (and former Black Order)	Italy	1973–82
Red Brigades (BR)	Italy	1968–82
Moujahidin-e-Khalq	Iran	1971–
Fedayeen-e-Khalq	Iran	1971–
Jewish Defense League (JDL)	U.S.	1968–
Croatian National Resistance (or Revolutionary Brotherhood)	Yugoslavia	1950–
Justice Commandos of the Armenian Genocide/Armenian Revolutionary Army	Turkey	1975–
Corsican National Liberation Front	France	1976–
Irish National Liberation Army (INLA)	N. Ireland	1974–87
Ulster Defence Association (UDA)	N. Ireland	1974–
Ulster Freedom Fighters	N. Ireland	1973–
Ulster Volunteer Force (UVF)	N. Ireland	1966–
Red Army Faction (RAF)	W. Germany	1968–
Revolutionary Cells (RZ)	W. Germany	1973–
Armed Revolutionary Forces of Colombia (FARC)	Colombia	1966–
April 19 Movement (M-19)	Colombia	1974–89
National Liberation Army (ELN)	Colombia	1964–
Popular Liberation Army (EPL)	Colombia	1967–89
Movement of the Revolutionary Left (MIR)	Chile	1967–
Farabundo Marti National Liberation Front	El Salvador	1972–
Liberation Tigers of Tamil Eelam	Sri Lanka	1977–
Moro National Liberation Front	Philippines	1972–
New People's Army	Philippines	1969–
Provisional Irish Republican Army	N. Ireland	1970–
Basque Homeland and Freedom (ETA)	Spain	1959–
Popular Front for the Liberation of Palestine (PFLP)	Mideast	1967–
Democratic Front for the Liberation of Palestine (DFLP, formerly PDFLP)	Mideast	1969–
Fatah Revolutionary Council/Black June (Abu Nidal group)	Mideast	1978–
Palestine Liberation Front	Mideast	1977–
Popular Front for the Liberation of Palestine – General Command (PFLP-GC)	Mideast	1968–
Fatah	Mideast	1967–88
Guerrilla Army of the Poor (EGP)	Guatemala	1975–
Rebel Armed Forces (FAR)	Guatemala	1962–
White Hand (MANO)	Guatemala	1966–
Shining Path	Peru	1980–
Popular Forces of 25 April (FP-25)	Portugal	1980–

Note

a Note that this list dates from 1991. I generally used English translations of names but provided the acronyms by which some groups are commonly known, for example, ETA, Euzkadi ta Akatasuna. An important source for the data is Peter Janke, *Guerrilla and Terrorist Organizations: A World Directory and Bibliography*, London: Macmillan, 1983, supplemented by the Jaffee Center for Strategic Studies, "Inter 85: A Review of International Terrorism in 1985," Jerusalem: The Jerusalem Post, 1986, and Jaffee Center for Strategic Studies, "Inter 86: A Review of International Terrorism in 1986," Jerusalem: The Jerusalem Post, 1987. See also Schmid, *Political Terrorism: A Research Guide*, and the U.S. Department of State, 1986 and 1988.

12 Why terrorism is rejected or renounced

Scholars usually ask why violence occurs rather than why it does not.[1] This study attempted to fill that gap by asking why political actors reject terrorism as a method of opposition to the state or to the international society of states when it appears to be an available option for resistance. It also asks why oppositions abandon or renounce terrorism after its initiation as a form of political action.

My argument applies to specific cases, not to patterns of general decline in the measurable incidence of terrorism over time. Its focus is on decision making in political organizations acting in the context of particular historical settings and cultures. The complexity of each case is emphasized, and no predictions are offered about the future of terrorism in aggregate terms. A further note of caution: this analysis of terrorism as a form of radical opposition to the status quo is not meant to deny that some governments use terrorism to control their citizens or to impose their values on other states. The rejection or repudiation of terrorism as a means of social and political control is an important subject, but it is beyond the scope of the present analysis.

It is also important to acknowledge that the concept of terrorism is both ambiguous and controversial. The term is often used in a careless or pejorative way for rhetorical reasons. My analysis is based on the premise that terrorism is simply one form of political violence. The method, not the identity or ideology of the user, determines whether or not an action can be defined as terrorism. Terrorism involves the use or threat of physical harm in order to achieve a disproportionately large psychological effect. It is demonstrative or propagandistic violence without significant military value, directed against symbolic rather than utilitarian targets. States as well as nonstates may use terrorism as a political weapon, although in this case I am concerned with oppositional rather than repressive violence.

This analysis considers the rejection or abandonment of terrorism from the point of view of the actors using it, in effect, as a problem of political decision making. My interpretation here differs from most other approaches to political violence. For example, a common assumption is that oppositional terrorism ends only when governments militarily defeat groups practicing terrorism or that terrorism fails to emerge because potentially violent actors in society are deterred by the prospect of punishment or retribution. Actually government policies intended to suppress terrorism (or the potential for terrorism) constitute only one of the many factors that influence the decisions of groups embracing terrorism. Groups can maintain their integrity and organizational continuity while abandoning terrorism. Nor does the answer lie simply in conditions. In the same context different organizations or different factions within movements make different choices. Furthermore, the possible reasons for the initiation of terrorism, such as lack of access by minorities to the political arena, need not be those that groups or individuals consider in their decisions to abandon it.

This argument about the autonomy of political actors and the importance of their choices is developed from the three theoretical frameworks presented in Part II of this volume. One is the view that terrorism is the result of strategic choice. A second approach focuses on terrorism as the outcome of internal organizational politics. A third view of the problem draws on theories of psychological motivation and group interaction. A combination of these theories is needed to explain why political organizations either reject terrorism at the outset of a conflict or abandon the strategy after having practiced it.

If terrorism is instrumental behavior, the answer to my questions is relatively simple. Decisions result from calculations of relative costs and benefits. Methods of resistance are chosen because of their utility compared to other alternatives. Behavior is thus primarily a reaction to external considerations. Likely effectiveness in achieving long-term interests is the chief criterion for choices. Terrorism is thus purposeful in terms of ultimate political objectives. However, explanations based on psychological and organizational considerations suggest that the choice of terrorism as a method is only indirectly related to the pursuit of ideological ends. From this perspective, it is critical to understand how organizations form, what binds their members together, and how leaders and followers interact. Organizational integration and disintegration may be the keys to behavior. Organizational cohesion depends on psychological incentives for participation, which in turn require justifications for the use of terrorism that go beyond political effectiveness. Decisions about using terrorism are based not only on the anticipation of government response and the likelihood of achieving a desired outcome but on disputes over strategy and divergent perceptions of conditions, particularly the likelihood of acquiring popular support and moving to mass action. Collective belief systems and values and loyalty to the group are as important as interests. Self-image and concepts of identity help determine beliefs about the appropriateness of violence. Thus organizational and psychological costs and benefits are part of a mixture of considerations that do not exclude strategic logic. Decisions to avoid terrorism may be based on misperception and misconception as much as on accurate appreciation of conditions and especially of the reactions of other actors – the government, the public, and rivals for leadership of the opposition.

The initial rejection of terrorism

What reasons do opposition groups offer for rejecting terrorism in situations where it was a realistic alternative? The following examples, which are illustrative but not exhaustive, are taken from conflicts where terrorism was largely avoided, but also from those where one group rejected terrorism while another embraced it. The arguments that political actors make against terrorism can be summarized in terms of the following general themes.

Terrorism is rejected as a matter of principle because it is elitist and does not involve the masses

This is a condition that violates an essential philosophical and moral principle stating that the masses must be engaged in the struggle for political change. This view is usually an offshoot of revolutionary socialism or nationalism. Collective action is seen as morally preferable and only secondarily as more efficient. The preference for mass action is sufficiently strong to overcome the recognition that collective action is not feasible, at least not in the foreseeable future. The group does not see itself as acting for the people, only as acting with them. This conception of the appropriate role of a revolutionary or nationalist party is often based on ideas of the future. Costs and benefits are perceived in long rather than short terms. That is, even if the opposition succeeds through terrorism in securing immediate goals (e.g., demoralization of the adversary), the long-term outcome will not be satisfactory because the people will not have taken part in their own liberation.

Gandhi, for example, argued that terrorism in the struggle for Indian independence was elitist. Reliance on terrorism would mean that British rule would only be replaced by that of another small minority. Although Parekh argues that Gandhi was wrong to assume that terrorism does not require community support or that nonviolence avoids elitism,[2] Gandhi clearly felt that noncooperation, civil disobedience, and fasting were preferable because they engaged the masses in the struggle. Interestingly, a British government assessment of the decline of terrorism in India in 1936 concluded that Gandhi's campaigns actually stimulated upsurges of terrorism, whereas "improvement" was due not only to tougher laws and prosecutions of the terrorists but to the conversion of the terrorists to communism and socialism, ideologies that stressed involvement.[3]

In the late nineteenth and early twentieth centuries, debates within communist or Marxist-Leninist movements in Russia and Germany over the use of terrorism were bitter. Arguments over terrorism split the Russian revolutionary movement, especially during the early twentieth century when Lenin vigorously attacked the Socialist-Revolutionary Party for its endorsement of terrorism.[4] Lenin's 1902 *What Is To Be Done?* criticized terrorism as a form of spontaneous release of indignation for intellectuals who were unable or unwilling to take on the task of organizing the masses. He demanded to know why terrorism should be expected to incite mass resistance if all the cruelties associated with the tyranny of the czarist regime had not. Opponents of terrorism insisted that mass organization had to precede a violent confrontation with the regime and that terrorism would only reinforce the passivity of the population.

Leaders of the German Communist Party under the Weimar Republic insisted that terrorism would weaken and divide the proletariat and that it would distract the party from organizing the masses.[5] The opponents of terrorism thought that genuine revolution was impossible without mass involvement, a belief they adhered to with surprising tenacity despite the growing realization that a socialist revolution was unlikely in Germany in the 1930s. That is, the likelihood of the success of alternatives to terrorism was not a decisive factor in the decision to reject it.

A question that has often puzzled researchers is why terrorism did not emerge in France in the early 1970s when it did under comparable circumstances in Germany and Italy. A leader of the Gauche Prolétarienne (GP), which was the major radical organization of the post-1968 period, explained French "exceptionalism" in terms of group beliefs.[6] Members of the GP did not regard themselves as heroes or professional revolutionary elites. Their faith in the masses kept them from approving individual actions. Although in retrospect it became clear that the group had misperceived the nature of "people's war" in Vietnam, a key source of inspiration, at the time they were convinced that only popular uprisings could start a revolution.[7] Furthermore, they overestimated the likelihood of collective action, thinking that the radical left had some influence over the workers and that spontaneous revolution might eventually erupt. To them the apparent linking of worker and student protest in May 1968 was an encouraging precedent.[8] Thus the rejection of terrorism was based on miscalculation and misperception.

Terrorism is rejected because its costs will be excessive

This judgment may be based on considerations of timing or calculations about the appropriate stage for violence; for example, the organization is still too weak and should wait to challenge the regime until it is able to defend itself against government retaliation. Terrorism is thought likely to provoke repression that the organization cannot survive. This is a particularly interesting argument because terrorism is often characterized as the "weapon of the weak." Also paradoxical is the fact that government repressiveness that increases the cost of popular mobilization is often thought to motivate terrorism, which requires only small numbers. Yet some revolutionaries perceive government strength as an obstacle to using terrorism (at least early in the life of an organization).

The costs of terrorism may also be perceived in terms of its impact on the achievement of political goals. Oppositions always have to juggle short- and long-term interests. For example, resorting to terrorism may likely preclude eventual compromise, necessitated by the power of the government or by the strength of popular opposition to what revolutionaries or nationalists want. De Nardo argues that in a revolutionary movement both terrorists (who together with the proponents of mass mobilization are absolutists or "purists") and advocates of compromise are similarly impatient; they want to see immediate results.[9] But compromisers may actually be realists, while the terrorists see no need to form a coalition with other groups in society. Compromisers or "reformist pragmatists" understand that they need support from constituencies who will be alienated by terrorism. Their conceptions of strategy differ accordingly.

These arguments against terrorism also reveal that radicals need not see mass mobilization and terrorism as mutually exclusive, as De Nardo suggests. Terrorism is often thought to be appropriate only when the organization is ready to mobilize mass violence. It is seen as the catalyst for revolution.

In South Africa the African National Congress (ANC) formed its military wing, the "Spear of the Nation," in 1961. But terrorism was deliberately rejected as a form of armed struggle because the ANC sought a negotiated political settlement, not the destruction of the government.[10] The founding ANC leaders believed that terrorism would only cause bitterness and alienate South Africa's powerful white minority, whose reactions to terrorism were expected to be excessive. Terrorism might also cause the frontline states to deny sanctuary to the ANC.[11] Furthermore, terrorism was not considered likely to bring about a revolution, only turmoil. "A radical ANC pursuing terrorism would short-circuit attempts to achieve other prerequisites for a successful uprising."[12] Unlike the Pan African Congress, an antiapartheid organization willing to use terrorism against civilians, ANC leaders seemed quite sensitive to the costs of terrorism.

In the 1930s, leaders of the German Communist Party also feared that terrorism would only provoke repression.[13] They also hoped to attract some of the Nazi rank-and-file and feared that the use of terrorism would make this impossible.[14]

Most of Lenin's objections to terrorism were based on considerations of expediency. He thought terrorism likely to provoke repression before the revolutionary organization was prepared to meet it. Since terrorism had not worked in the past, in the days of the People's Will revolutionaries who assassinated the Czar in 1881, there was no reason to think it would work in the future. Despite Lenin's objections, however, when terrorism appeared to be successful in Russia, Marxists were reluctant to condemn it.

Many Irish nationalists were distressed when a small faction, the "Irish National Invincibles," assassinated the British chief secretary for Ireland and his under secretary in Phoenix Park in Dublin in 1882. They were aware of the political damage terrorism could do to the nationalist movement (primarily by discrediting moderates such as Charles Stewart Parnell) and to the likelihood of a repressive British reaction. Interestingly, radicals in Ireland were more likely to reject terrorism than were Irish-American nationalists in the United States. Opponents of terrorism argued that it was only appropriate in a genuinely insurrectionary situation; otherwise it would result in the destruction of all nationalist opposition. It was premature, in fact "mad, criminal, and suicidal," before the masses were organized and armed.[15] Various opponents labeled it as "imprudent," "foolish," and "immoral."[16] Some feared a British reaction that would drive Irish public opinion away from the nationalists.

Terrorism may also be costly as a strategy if its implementation is botched. Incompetence by inexperienced and ill-trained aspirant terrorists damages an organization's credibility. Terrorism may be the weapon of the weak, but it is not suitable for amateurs. As William Mackey Lomasney said apprehensively of the Irish nationalist "Skirmishers" who wanted to bomb targets in London in the 1880s, "The amount of folly and bungling in connection with these attempts is simply disgraceful."[17] Similar problems of incompetent implementation of a terrorist strategy plagued the right-wing Secret Army Organization during the last years of the Algerian war (1961–2).

Terrorism is undesirable because it cannot be controlled by the leaders of the organization

Escalation will lead to adverse effects on audiences, but more importantly on the group itself. Militarization of the movement is a likely outcome of a terrorist strategy. Terrorism has a tendency to escalate, so that it no longer serves its original strategic purpose, and it corrupts the organization using it, thus altering its character. Such militarization in turn would affect the nature of a future government should the opposition come to power. This view also reinforces the argument that terrorism is potentially too costly in the long term, since uncontrolled terrorism can only divide society and prevent compromise with the government.

Gandhi advanced this argument in the 1920s.[18] So, too, did ANC leaders in the 1960s and 1970s.[19] With regard to the left in France, Alain Geismar refers to the "repulsive image" of the Japanese Red Army, whose violence was turned inward and resulted in self-destruction through torture and killing of group members.[20] These expectations represent a form of social learning. The experiences of other radical groups made an impression on the French left, and not all these impressions were favorable.

In organizations that reject terrorism, the leadership often resists pressures from the rank and file. Successful rejection of terrorism may thus require a strong leadership that is both committed to its views and capable of imposing them on their followers. This argument is applicable to the ANC's experience as a resistance organization. Davis points to discipline breakdowns in the Spear of the Nation's underground units in South Africa in 1985–6, which led to unauthorized attacks on civilians.[21] In 1931 the German Communist Party issued a resolution condemning "individual" terrorism, which it continued to reaffirm as late as 1933. This "Leninist orthodoxy" was not popular with party members, who confronted the strong determination of the leadership. A member of the Central Committee was even expelled from the Politburo and publicly condemned for criticizing the party's antiterrorist line. While party theoreticians and publicists developed negative stereotypes of "terrorists," their constituencies continued to support terrorism as a defense against Nazi violence.[22]

Similarly, the GP in France in the 1970s was only able to enforce the decision to reject terrorism because the leadership could control the organization (an ironic factor, since the group itself was philosophically "anti-organization").[23] The leaders, the original "founders" who had been in power since May 1968, were able to resist pressures from below. This "oligarchy" deliberately decided to dissolve the organization in 1974, a measure that took them about a year to implement.

What effect does competition among groups have on decisions to reject terrorism? In terms of organizational theories of political action, the existence of rivals is often thought to make the problem of "exit" more severe, since radicals can always move to another organization with similar goals.[24] Leaders who are unable to retain the loyalty of their followers offer violence as an incentive to prevent dissolution of the organization and the flight of its members to other rival groups. Perhaps terrorism is easier to reject when there are no rivals. Liniers and Geismar explain that the GP "occupied the space" of the radical left in France.[25] The GP and its armed clandestine section had a monopoly on the violence of the extreme Left. Anyone attracted to terrorism in the 1969–73 period would have joined the GP, which played the role of a "pied piper."[26] Yet in South Africa, the fear that the government might choose to negotiate with Buthelezi's Inkatha movement apparently helped prevent the ANC from turning to terrorism. The existence of a rival led to moderation, not extremism. The violence that occurred during the transition to majority rule targeted rival groups rather than the government or the white minority. It is also well to remember that Gandhi rejected terrorism even though other factions of the independence movement were using it.

Terrorism, especially indiscriminate violence against civilians, is morally wrong, even if its benefits exceed its costs

This view is often related to the existence of moral reference groups, such as the European Resistance movements during World War II. Furthermore, terrorism is expected to alienate international public opinion because it is perceived as morally wrong. This view is also connected to self-conceptions of legitimacy. It is not strongly related to expectations of the likely success of potential alternatives; some people would rather be losers who played fair. That is, universal values inhibit the resort to terrorism. Not only does the group maintain these values, but it perceives the wider audience as reacting in the same terms. The group does not believe that audiences will agree that the ends justify the means.

This argument is not characteristic of early twentieth-century Marxism, perhaps because at that time terrorism referred primarily to selective assassinations of government leaders, not to violence against civilians in the mode of the nineteenth-century anarchists. The public reaction to terrorism may not have been as negative as it is today, as the nature of terrorism has changed to be less discriminating and more destructive. The meaning of the term has also changed, reflecting changes in the political context.

Gandhi saw the choice of means as a moral, not a pragmatic, choice. To him, terrorism was less courageous than nonviolent resistance. He did, however, distinguish between offensive and defensive violence. The People's Will in Russia considered terrorism noble because it spared ordinary people, the masses, the suffering of costly and futile rebellion. The terrorists regarded their actions as a form of self-sacrifice. Yet the ANC's sensitivity to public opinion is one reason for the rejection of terrorism in favor of sabotage. Davis notes that

> since the exile leadership sought to portray the ANC as a principled and responsible contender for power, it imposed restrictions against terrorist tactics that specifically target noncombatant whites. President Tambo even went to the extent of signing a protocol of the Geneva Convention which legally

> bound the ANC to avoid attacks on civilian targets and to 'humanitarian conduct of the war,' marking the first time a guerrilla group had ever done so. The hoped-for result would be a growing sense among whites that black resistance cannot be stopped, and that things might not be so bad if the ANC were to have a hand at governing.[27]

The leaders of the GP also note that the philosophical principles that led them to reject terrorism – an antiorganizational bias, a depreciation of the role of revolutionary intellectuals, confidence in the masses, and the subordination of military to political action – were based on a set of moral ideas that included a strong element of antifascism. Their chief reference group was the French Resistance. This sort of role modeling may have contributed to their refusal to cooperate with or emulate Palestinian terrorism.[28] West European groups were asked to perform "anti-Zionist" actions as payment for weapons from radical Palestinian factions. The GP refused and even went so far as to condemn the 1972 Munich Olympics attack, which cost them support since most of their "worker base" was Arab.[29]

In this respect the press may be an inhibiting factor. Although most analysts see publicity as encouraging terrorism, groups that are sensitive to international public opinion may avoid terrorism because it will be communicated to audiences whose approval and assistance they seek. Howe thinks that increased press attention reduces the temptation to use terrorism.[30] Paradoxically, however, Davis thinks that the South African government's monopoly over communications gave it the power to interpret ANC violence as inept or accidental.[31] Even if the ANC had been successful in attacking civilian targets, their message would not have gotten across because of Pretoria's "propagandist acumen." Thus there was no point in using terrorism. Press censorship reduced its benefits.

Decisions to abandon terrorism

The question of why oppositions abandon a strategy of terrorism is intriguing because such reversals seem to be unusual. They are certainly poorly documented. Insufficient data are available on individual motivations for forming and joining terrorist undergrounds,[32] but even less is known about decisions to abandon terrorism in radical organizations. Franco Ferracuti notes that "what happens in the minds of terrorists who decide to abandon terrorism is not known. The material available consists of a few interviews and autobiographies in which real motives lie hidden beneath rationalizations and self-serving reinterpretations of reality."[33]

Whereas an instrumental approach to violence suggests that decisions to abandon terrorism are based on calculations of its diminishing utility, organizational and psychological interpretations of terrorist behavior imply that terrorism is rarely abandoned as long as the organization using it continues to exist. After a campaign of terrorism starts, psychological pressures and organizational politics are likely to encourage the continuation of violence even if it becomes counterproductive in an instrumental sense. A group may not perceive mounting costs, decreasing benefits, or emerging alternatives. Decision makers may lack the cognitive capacity to judge the consequences of their actions. They fail to consider new information and new opportunities. In psychological terms it is painful to reverse a decision already taken, especially if that decision was costly.

In democracies, an internal dynamic that encourages the continuation of violence is likely to be established in the early period of an underground group's existence, when the government is still trying to come to grips with the challenge to its authority. The group is pushed into an isolated underground life by having adopted illegality, but government pressure is not yet so constrictive as to pose a serious threat to its survival. As external pressure mounts, the group becomes more isolated from society, and it becomes more cohesive and inner-directed. Terrorism may no longer possess a strategic utility, but it serves the critical function of maintaining the group. It may become justifiable as defense against government repression or revenge for persecution.

These organizational and psychological pressures may explain why changes in the political conditions that made terrorism seem appropriate or even necessary at the outset of a conflict may not reduce violence. The process of terrorism can become independent of original motivations. For example, in Spain, Basque terrorism intensified after the transition to democracy, which resulted in political reforms as well as the establishment of nonviolent alternatives for political participation. Terrorism also persisted in the Philippines after the fall of Ferdinand Marcos.

This analysis will consider three general sets of reasons for abandoning terrorism. First, groups may cease to practice terrorism because it has succeeded in fulfilling its original purposes. Second, organizations may abandon terrorism because its utility declines. Third, new alternatives that are preferable to terrorism may become available or more attractive. Explaining these decisions exclusively on the basis of calculations of objective costs and benefits, that is, as purposive in terms of external goals, is too simple. Among the costs and benefits of terrorism are organizational coherence and maintenance, depending on the psychological, social, and material benefits the organization can offer members. If resorting to terrorism produces internal disintegration that threatens the existence of the organization, then leaders may abandon it regardless of external results.

Terrorism may be abandoned because it has accomplished its purpose

In considering this possibility, the analyst must distinguish between short- and long-term interests of organizations.

Claims that terrorism succeeded in attaining ultimate objectives are often made in the cases of the Front de Libération Nationale (FLN) against the French in Algeria (1954–62) and the Irgun and Lehi against the British during the Palestine Mandate (1937–48). In both cases conflicts in which terrorism played a part resulted in fundamental political change. However, in neither instance can one say that terrorism alone would have been sufficient to assure the success of resistance to foreign rule, and it is difficult to demonstrate even that terrorism was necessary to the outcome. Urban terrorism in Algeria may have been counterproductive. The majority of Jewish opinion in Palestine disapproved of terrorism, and at times the Haganah (the armed defense force of the official Jewish Agency) openly fought the Irgun.

Although leaders of the Irgun and Lehi acquired positions of power in Israel some thirty years after independence, and the FLN instituted single-party rule in Algeria that has lasted for over forty years, practitioners of terrorism do not typically emerge on top, even when the revolutionary or nationalist movement wins the struggle. In Iran, for example, the secular mujahideen turned against Khomeini after the Shah was overthrown. That is, the revolution succeeded, but the new religious state was hostile to the faction most prone to use terrorism. The mujahideen then embarked on a campaign of terrorism against the Khomeini regime.

Organizational theory suggests that organizations exist primarily to maintain and enhance themselves and that over time organizational maintenance replaces political purpose as the group's aim. Clearly the success of terrorism must be measured in terms of the accomplishment not only, or even primarily, of long-term political interests involving fundamental political and social change but of proximate objectives. Winning public attention, arousing popular support, blocking paths to compromise, visibly intimidating public officials, and other signs of incremental progress may be sufficient to maintain an organization in the absence of ultimate success. Attaining proximate goals can provide critical emotional rewards for individual participation, such as satisfying demands for vengeance. This conception of success implies that terrorism may continue because it is effective, but also that it may be abandoned when a short-term objective, such as political recognition, has been reached.

It is worth noting that most theories of insurgency in the 1960s regarded terrorism as the first stage of revolution, to be followed by guerrilla warfare and then conventional warfare. Terrorism was meant to be abandoned after having worked to gain control of a population and draw attention to the cause.[34]

The case of the Palestine Liberation Organization (PLO) is instructive. By 1974 Arafat had abandoned what he defined as international terrorism. He renounced it more explicitly in 1988, at American insistence, although it is doubtful that the two parties had accepted a common definition of terrorism. Abu Iyad, for example, the late second in command to Arafat who was assassinated in 1990 by a rival Palestinian faction, expressed these definitional ambiguities in his 1978 autobiography.[35] He insisted that revolutionary violence and terrorism were distinct. The latter, in his view, consisted of individual attacks divorced from organizational interests and strategic conceptions. Terrorism is subjectively motivated and designed to substitute for mass action. Revolutionary violence, by contrast, occurs in the context of a large and structured movement. It is meant to give the movement new spirit during periods of defeat. It becomes superfluous when the movement scores political successes. Accordingly, the Black September Organization (BSO) was not a practitioner of terrorism, nor was their attack on Israeli athletes during the 1972 Munich Olympics an act of terrorism.

Nevertheless, excluding a brief return to terrorism in 1985, and a refusal to condemn the Palestine Liberation Front in 1990, Arafat's position against international terrorism was consistent. The PLO's emphasis was on political processes over armed struggle (of which terrorism was a key expression) after the 1973 war, despite the fact that every move toward compromise produced disunity within Palestinian ranks. The 1985 lapse was probably "merely an improvised and essentially local reply to specific and immediate problems" due to intra-Palestinian rivalry over the leadership of the PLO.[36] Arafat may have recognized the costs of terrorism in terms of damage to the PLO's profile in international public opinion, since he desperately wanted a respectable image and a political settlement with Israel. Yet one of the most important reasons for the abandonment of terrorism was the PLO's new acceptability in Western Europe. Terrorism may have transformed the PLO into a political entity with not only diplomatic recognition but significant legitimization. The decision to refrain from terrorism was "a brilliant political stroke"[37] because only renouncing terrorism could safeguard PLO gains.[38] Nevertheless the PLO did not succeed in translating these achievements into a satisfactory political outcome in the long run. Diplomacy was a viable alternative to terrorism, but it failed to turn recognition into legitimacy. Thus Arafat's initial calculations did not necessarily change. Furthermore, not all Palestinian factions agreed with Arafat. They continued to use terrorism, which undermined his diplomatic strategy. In 1990 the United States broke off its incipient "dialog" with the PLO because Arafat would not condemn a subordinate organization's thwarted attack that was suspected of having been directed against Israeli civilians. Thus the perception of terrorism as having attained its objectives was not uniform within the Palestinian movement.

Organizations may abandon terrorism because its costs increase and/or its benefits decline

Abandonment may occur even though the strategy has not secured either short- or long-term interests because perceptions of costs and benefits may change independently of objective measures.

A key determinant of the high cost of terrorism is the government response. An efficient coercive policy could make terrorism too dangerous and unproductive to continue. The American policy of "no concessions" to terrorist demands is based on this premise. If terrorism is always punished and never rewarded, its users will presumably be deterred. At the outset of a campaign of terrorism an opposition organization may underestimate the government's capabilities and strength of will. Governments usually take time to organize an effective response to terrorism, especially if they are taken by surprise and unprepared for violent dissent (a matter not just of intelligence capabilities but political culture). Security bureaucracies are reorganized and centralized, intelligence capabilities are improved, punitive legislation is enacted, and more resources are devoted to combating terrorism and defending the vulnerable points of society. However, as Gurr notes, in liberal democracies deterrence and punishment work best in combination with other processes;[39] abandonment is rarely the result solely of coercive government policies.

For example, consider the Canadian declaration of martial law in Quebec in order to counter the terrorism of the Front de Libération du Québec (FLQ). Hewitt notes in a comparison of Canada, Northern Ireland, and Spain that the greater the number of imprisoned terrorists, the lower the level of violence.[40] Yet Fournier argues that police repression did not prevent the FLQ from reemerging as a powerful political force in 1972.[41] Ross and Gurr concur.[42] In Britain, the enactment of the Prevention of Terrorism Acts "had no immediate discernible effect."[43] The moderation of terrorism that followed was due to a change in IRA strategy. In addition, as terrorism became increasingly internationalized, it became harder for governments to increase costs because it is easier for terrorists to evade capture. Merari and Elad conclude that "in the final analysis, it is difficult to evaluate the direct influence of Israel's measures on the conduct of Palestinian terrorism outside of Israel."[44]

Nevertheless, the government response may contribute to the internal costs of terrorism by provoking organizational disintegration, involving the breakdown of the incentives that the leadership of an organization can offer followers and the dissolution of the psychological bonds that promote solidarity and help provide moral justification for terrorism. Government arrests or assaults may deprive an organization of key leaders who are irreplaceable. In West Germany and Italy the first generation of imprisoned leaders tried to maintain control over the outside organization and came into conflict with the second generation leadership, whose sources of authority were less ideological than pragmatic. They were less adept at framing objectives or elaborating doctrine than at organizing operations. The suicides of the founding members of the Red Army Faction after the failure of the hijacking at Mogadishu in 1977 signaled the beginning of decline, although remnants of the organization persisted into the late 1990s. However, the imprisonment or death of colleagues can also bind militants to the group. Those left outside cannot surrender as long as their comrades are resisting from the inside. Government coercion may help maintain the organization by promoting cohesion and confirming their hostility toward the outside world. Paradoxically, what appears to be military "defeat" may be a source of organizational strength.

Other costs associated with terrorism may be more significant than the direct or indirect penalties that governments can exact, especially in democracies. One of the most important costs is the withdrawal of popular support. The attitudes of an initially sympathetic community on which any underground organization depends may change as a result of both terrorism (especially if it escalates and becomes more random) and the government response, which raises the cost of participating in violent opposition. In a comparison of terrorism in the United States and Canada, Ross and Gurr refer to this phenomenon as "backlash."[45] Although the public's fear of government repression may contribute to a negative reaction to terrorism, initially a disproportionate government response may make the public more sympathetic. The behavior of the challenging organization matters significantly to public attitudes. For example, the FLQ's abduction and murder of Pierre Laporte alienated nationalists. Ross and Gurr agree that the murder "helped swing public opinion among Québecois away from the FLQ and toward more conventional forms of political participation."[46] Similarly, in Italy, the Red Brigades lost public support after the kidnapping and murder of Aldo Moro in 1978. The downfall of the Tupamaros of Uruguay may have begun with the kidnapping and murder of Dan Mitrione. In India, the decline of terrorism in Bengal in 1934 was attributed not only to police pressure but to public rejection of the terrorists because they had tried to assassinate the Governor: "Certainly the unequivocal and unqualified condemnation of this outrage by the nationalist press was unparalleled in the history of terrorism in Bengal."[47] Tololyan argues that Armenian terrorism declined because the radical organizations lost legitimacy in the eyes of Armenian diaspora communities, on whose acquiescence they depended.[48] In his view, the Armenian terrorist organizations, the Armenian Secret Army for the Liberation of Armenia (ASALA), and the Justice Commandos of the Armenian Genocide miscalculated the tolerance of the diaspora for terrorism. Early successes led them to be overconfident about their ability to manipulate public opinion. As terrorism became more indiscriminate, public support diminished.

At the beginning, underground organizations may miscalculate the susceptibility of the public to the appeals of violent extremism. Left-wing extremist groups in Germany and Italy, for example, failed to comprehend that the working classes on whom they wished to base the revolution would not support their efforts. In Germany realization of the absence of support was slow, due in part to the social isolation and ideological rigidity of the underground groups. In Italy, the Red Brigades enjoyed a much higher level of support and operated in an atmosphere of generalized low-level violence, with more extensive connections to social movements.

Terrorism may also become too costly if it results in a withdrawal of support from foreign governments. Many undergrounds, especially those with international operations, depend on governments for funds, weapons, documents, technical assistance, and asylum. When Palestinian terrorism began to target moderate Arab governments, financial aid to the PLO decreased. Saudi unhappiness may have contributed to Arafat's renunciation of international terrorism in 1974. Arafat would surely have recalled that unauthorized terrorism from the PFLP provoked the Jordanian civil war in 1970, which led to the expulsion of Palestinians.

Another cost of terrorism is related to the need of the organization's leaders to maintain the loyalty of militants. Morale may suffer not only because of government pressure but through an onset of disillusionment and demoralization that Ross and Gurr describe as "burnout."[49] Group solidarity and cohesion break down and individual members begin to abandon both group and strategy. Abandoning terrorism may then be the only way for the leadership to prevent individual "exit." The tension caused by constant danger and recognition of waning popular support puts a strain on political conviction. Self-doubt may also be a result of the escalation of terrorism. For example, Hans-Joachim Klein, a former West German terrorist, claimed that the experience of participating in a terrorist action (the seizure of OPEC ministers in Vienna in 1975) convinced him to abandon the underground.[50] He was unable to adjust to a set of beliefs he regarded as callous and cynical with regard to human life. He felt that for the group violence became its own end.

The benefits of terrorism may also decrease regardless of the costs. The targets of terrorism may adapt. A population may become numbed, for example, and immune to psychological manipulation. They may not reject the terrorists but may no longer respond because terrorism has become routine. Governments that initially give in to ransom demands may cease doing so when the external costs (financial, diplomatic, political, etc.) become too high. Germany is a case in point. In terms of domestic politics, appearing "weak" on terrorism was a serious disadvantage for the Socialist Party in the 1970s. Media coverage may decrease as audiences tire of yet another terrorist spectacular. As terrorism becomes less unusual, it also has less publicity value. Multinational corporations improve security for their executives or move their operations to safer climates, and large monetary ransoms become harder to acquire.

The availability of new options is a third reason for abandoning terrorism

Alternatives to terrorism, whether violent or nonviolent, may emerge with or without government intervention.

Opportunities for collective action, such as mass protest or revolution, may occur independently of government actions. Alternatively, government repression may be a catalyst for the sort of mass mobilization that makes terrorism unnecessary, or a transition to democracy may permit effective legal opposition. The nineteenth-century anarchist movement turned from violence to anarchosyndicalism and to emphasis on the general strike rather than on individual terrorism, as the working classes became more active and also as governments and society became more tolerant of worker protest. It seems logical that larger and more diversified groups, for whom terrorism is only a subsidiary means, would be more likely to switch to alternative strategies for political change when they become available. They are likely to have more resources and more options than small groups that depend exclusively on terrorism. However, collective action and terrorism are not mutually exclusive alternatives. Sometimes the prospect of collective violence encourages the use of terrorism as a catalyst to mass mobilization, which happened in Russia after the near revolution of 1905. Similarly, FLN terrorism during the Battle of Algiers (1957) may have reflected optimism and the anticipation of victory over the French, not desperation over the failure of rural guerrilla warfare.

The nonviolent alternatives to terrorism usually involve cooperation with the government, on a collective or individual level. A government offer to negotiate, grant amnesty, or permit democratic participation may create new options for the organization as a collective entity, regardless of the costs associated with continuing terrorism. Terrorism may then become less attractive in comparison to other alternatives, although it is important to remember that the decision to cooperate with the government carries risks for radical oppositions in protracted conflicts. For example, if a formal offer to negotiate requires the prior demobilization of opposition forces, then it may be answered with violence to demonstrate that defeat is not eminent and to gain a better bargaining position. Moreover, the acceptance of compromise may provoke violence from more intransigent factions and split the organization. In Spain, for example, the issue of negotiation with the government split the Basque organization ETA. If the government cannot protect its interlocutors, they will be reluctant to enter into cooperative ventures.

There are a number of instances of government offers of participation in addition to amnesty (which affords the opportunity for the individual to return to society without penalty but not necessarily to pursue political activity). In Venezuela, the government legalized the Venezuelan Communist Party in 1968 and the Movement of the Revolutionary Left (MIR) in 1973 (the MIR had rejected a 1969 amnesty offer, and its own splinter group rejected the 1973 offer.) In 1982 in Colombia, the government offered a unilateral and unconditional amnesty to the four major revolutionary organizations and in 1984 signed a cease-fire with the major rural-based insurgent organization, the Armed Revolutionary Forces of Colombia (FARC). The other violent opposition organizations rejected the offer, while the FARC established a political party (the Union Patriotica) that contested elections. In 1988, another major organization, the M-19, accepted another peace plan and joined the government, participating in deliberations to draw up a new constitution. In the meantime, the FARC returned to the opposition. One reason for this change of course may have been that hundreds of Union Patriotica candidates were assassinated by shadowy right-wing groups, probably linked to drug cartels or the military. According to Americas Watch, M-19's acceptance of the peace plan was related to organizational weakness (M-19 was an urban organization and lacked the peasant support the FARC could muster) and to a "tarnishing of M-19's image" after the Palace of Justice episode, when the Chief Justice and ten members of the Supreme Court were killed during a hostage-taking.[51] It was also important to the M-19 that the government offered not just participation in the existing political system but a role in forming a new one through democratic means.

In contrast to such offers of accommodation, which permit maintenance of the organization, other policies provide alternatives to terrorism for the individual rather than the group. For example, the Italian government's policies of encouraging "repentance" as well as strengthened security measures are credited with reducing the terrorism of the Red Brigades in the 1980s. According to Weinberg and Eubank, coercive measures enacted by the government in 1978 and 1980 reinforced the state security apparatus and broadened the scope of the state's control.[52] Even membership in an association promoting violence became a crime. Yet "another section of the 1980 law stimulated less debate but proved to be more important than the above in bringing about the terrorist groups' elimination"; it was the "extension of leniency in return for disassociation that had the greatest impact."[53] The Italian policy essentially dealt with terrorism by encouraging individual exit from the group. Reduced prison sentences were offered in exchange for information that would enable the government to dismantle the underground structures of the Red Brigades. Militants who were already becoming disillusioned, bored, or remorseful were attracted to the offer. By 1989, 389 terrorists had repented.[54] Thus the costs of continuing terrorism mounted while "exit" became easier. Both developments hastened the process of internal disintegration.

Ferracuti suggests that in Italy terrorists who "repented" were less stable and well adjusted than those who refused to abandon terrorism.[55] The founders of organizations and originators of terrorist strategies are the least likely to give up. It may be the case that whereas the rank and file press for terrorism at the beginning of a conflict, they are the first to abandon it under pressure. Ferracuti points out that the decision to abandon terrorism may reflect a reappraisal of self-interest after recognizing the failure of terrorism rather than a change of attitude toward the use of violence. Yet somehow the incentives that have bound individuals to the group and followers to leaders break down. Commitment, affective ties, and identification with the group weaken. Perhaps militants are no longer able to continue violence because they can no longer dehumanize the enemy, see themselves as heroic, or otherwise justify their behavior in moral terms. The analogies that support violence no longer hold up, such as the fantasy that militants are engaged in a "war" with the government. Their isolation from society may somehow be lessened, thus forcing them to recognize the absence of mass support. On the other hand, decline may occur not so much when the general population rejects terrorism as when a supportive radical subculture either disappears or repudiates the extremist minority that is using terrorism. The social movement out of which the faction using terrorism originated may have disbanded, depriving the terrorists of a supportive milieu and a pool of potential recruits.[56]

Conclusions

In order to understand the rejection of violence as a strategy of political resistance, it is helpful to focus on the decisions made by organizations in opposition to the state. Groups as well as individuals make choices about the use of terrorism that contribute significantly to outcomes. This analysis distinguished the initial rejection of terrorism at the outset of a campaign of resistance from the abandonment of terrorism, whether or not the underlying conflict that originally led to terrorism has been resolved. A combination of instrumental, organizational, and psychological reasons explains both types of decision.

Initial decisions to reject terrorism depend on assessments of its likely consequences. One frequently expressed reason for rejection is that mass action is more highly valued. A second reason refers to considerations of expediency: based on expectations of likely consequences, the costs of terrorism will be too high. It will provoke repression from the government that will destroy all opposition and discourage popular involvement. The use of terrorism will preclude eventual compromise and foreclose other options more likely to succeed. The opportunity costs are excessive. A third set of reasons concerns the effects of terrorism on the internal dynamics of the organization; it is likely to lead to a loss of control that in turn results in militarization and political corruption. Last, terrorism may be unacceptable because it is thought to be morally wrong, even if it should be likely to involve the masses, defeat the government, or invigorate resistance.

Decisions to abandon terrorism depend on the lessons learned from experience. One reason for early abandonment of terrorism is the perception that it has worked to produce a satisfactory outcome, primarily in the short run. Conversely, a second reason is that terrorism has failed; the group recognizes that it has insufficient utility. The government may have made participation in terrorism too dangerous for the individual, so that recruitment is impossible. Militants may perceive that terrorism, especially if it has escalated to random attacks on civilian targets, alienates the public rather than precipitating mass revolt. Foreign governments may have withdrawn their assistance. Governments and businesses may have begun to resist demands in hostage seizures. Militants may have become disillusioned and demoralized.

A last set of possibilities for the abandonment of terrorism involves a change in conditions rather than attitudes. On the one hand, collective action in another form may have become a possibility. Collective action may involve the use of violence, but it may also be peaceful if the government offers opposition organizations the opportunity to participate in the political process. The government may also open up alternatives for the individual to exit from the group, through amnesty and reintegration programs.

These reasons are not mutually exclusive in each case. Government offers of cooperation, for example, may coincide with policies that make the resort to terrorism more costly. Coercive policies may be most effective when they occur in a context of public loss of sympathy with terrorist methods, more the result of terrorist miscalculation than government efforts. A government's offer of negotiations may provide the recognition that persuades oppositions to abandon terrorism because it has succeeded. The perception that terrorism has worked in the short run may coincide with the opening of alternatives for long-term change.

From the government's point of view, these developments are characterized by high levels of uncertainty. It is clear that many of the consequences of terrorism, those anticipated at the outset or realized later by experienced opposition leaders, are independent of government control. Violence may be rejected or abandoned because of misperceptions or miscalculations. The processes by which outcomes are realized are complex and involve interactions among many different political actors under changing circumstances. The use of terrorism automatically involves the public, always as audience and often as victim, and the sensitivity of the public is greatest in democracies.

Unfortunately, the rejection or abandonment of terrorism does not necessarily lead to peaceful compromise. Political actors may reject or abandon terrorism because they prefer other forms of political violence or because they fear that any resistance to authority will meet violent repression. A shift to peaceful opposition may still provoke violence from the state. The government that adopts a conciliatory policy may inadvertently signal that terrorism works. Thus the alternative to terrorism is not always nonviolence, and the choice of a nonviolent strategy is not always reciprocated by one's opponent. The choice of peaceful methods does not guarantee a peaceful result.

Notes

Preface

1 Princeton Studies in World Politics #1, New York: Praeger, revised ed., 1962, pp. 76–8.
2 Lisa Stampnitzky, *Disciplining an Unruly Field: Terrorism Studies and the State, 1972–2001*, Ph.D. dissertation, Department of Sociology, University of California at Berkeley, 2008.

Introduction

1 See my earlier articles, "Current Research on Terrorism: The Academic Perspective," *Studies in Conflict and Terrorism*, 15, 1, 1992, pp. 1–11, and "The Psychology of Terrorism: An Agenda for the 21st Century," *Political Psychology*, 21, 2, June 2000, pp. 405–20.
2 For a useful overview of the literature see *Social Science for Counterterrorism* ed. Paul K. Davis and Kim Cragin, Santa Monica, CA: The Rand Corporation, 2009.
3 U.S. Department of Defense, Nuclear Posture Review Report, April 2010, available at http://www.defense.gov/npr/docs/2010%20Nuclear%20Posture%20Review%20Report.pdf, p. 25.
4 United Nations, *Report of the Secretary-General's High-level Panel on Threats, Challenges and Change: A more secure world: Our shared responsibility*, 2004, p. 52.
5 I also refer to definitional issues in "Organized Disorder: Terrorism, Politics and Society," in Ray C. Rist, ed., *The Democratic Imagination and the Social Science Persuasion*, New Brunswick, NJ: Transaction Press, 1994.
6 See Martha Crenshaw with Arie W. Kruglanski, Jerrold M. Post, and Jeff Victoroff, "What Should This Fight Be Called? Metaphors of Counterterrorism and Their Implications," *Psychological Science in the Public Interest*, 8, 3, December 2007, pp. 97–133.
7 Among academics, sociologist Jeff Goodwin also follows this convention: "A Theory of Categorical Terrorism," *Social Forces*, 84, 4, 2006, pp. 2027–46.
8 Charles Mohr, "Data on Terrorism under U.S. Revision," *The New York Times*, April 24, 1981, p. 17.
9 The database is available at http://www.start.umd.edu/gtd/. It covers 1970 through 2007 and includes domestic as well as international incidents.
10 Chantal de Jonge Oudraat and Jean-Luc Marret, "The Uses and Abuses of Terrorist Designation Lists," in Martha Crenshaw, ed., *The Consequences of Counterterrorism*, New York: The Russell Sage Foundation, 2010.
11 Philip Shenon, "U.S. Says it Might Consider Attacking Serbs," *The New York Times*, March 13, 1998, p. 10.
12 Indications that the question of causation is not closed: Tore Bjorgo, ed., *Root Causes of*

Terrorism, London and New York: Routledge, 2005, and Louise Richardson, ed., *The Roots of Terrorism*, London and New York: Routledge, 2006.

13 Kenneth Waltz, *Man, the State and War*, New York: Columbia University Press, 1959.

14 For example, John Horgan, "From Profiles to Pathways and Roots to Routes: Perspectives from Psychology on Radicalization into Terrorism," *The Annals of the American Academy of Political and Social Science*, Vol. 618, 2008, pp. 80–93, and Magnus Ranstorp, ed., *Understanding Violent Radicalisation: Terrorist and Jihadist Movements in Europe*, London and New York: Routledge, 2010.

15 Thomas Kuhn, *The Structure of Scientific Revolutions*, Chicago: University of Chicago Press, 1962.

16 On Al Qaeda's interest, see Rolf Mowatt-Larssen, "The Armageddon Test," Belfer Center Discussion Paper #2009-09, Harvard Kennedy School, 2009.

17 Victor Asal and R. Karl Rethemeyer, "The Nature of the Beast: Terrorist Organizational Characteristics and Organizational Lethality," *Journal of Politics*, 70, 2, 2008, pp. 437–49.

18 For example, Eli Berman, *Radical, Religious, and Violent: The New Economics of Terrorism*, Cambridge: MIT Press, 2009.

19 Michael Kenney, *From Pablo to Osama: Trafficking and Terrorist Networks, Government Bureaucracies, and Competitive Adaptation*, University Park, PA: Pennsylvania State University Press, 2007.

20 Gordon H. McCormick, "Terrorist Decision Making," *Annual Review of Political Science* 6, 2003, pp. 473–508.

21 A prominent example is Marc Sageman, *Understanding Terror Networks*, Philadelphia: University of Pennsylvania Press, 2004. For a critical view of social network theory, see Aiden Kirby, "The London Bombers as 'Self Starters': A Case Study in Indigenous Radicalization and the Emergence of Autonomous Cliques," *Studies in Conflict and Terrorism*, 30, 5, 2007, pp. 415–28.

22 Max Abrahms, "What Terrorists Really Want: Terrorist Motives and Counterterrorism Strategy," *International Security*, 32, 4, Spring 2008, pp. 78–105.

23 As argued by Andrew Kydd and Barbara F. Walter in "Sabotaging the Peace: The Politics of Extremist Violence," *International Organization*, 56, 2, Spring 2002, pp. 263–96.

24 See Chapter 4. Mia Bloom developed a comprehensive argument along these lines in "Palestinian Suicide Bombing: Public Support, Market Share, and Outbidding," *Political Science Quarterly*, 119, Spring 2004, pp. 61–88.

25 See my article, "Explaining Suicide Terrorism: A Review Essay," *Security Studies*, 6, 1, Spring 2007, pp. 133–62. Pape not only argues that suicide terrorism is unusually effective, but he also claims that suicide terrorism is only used in circumstances of foreign occupation.

26 "The Effectiveness of Terrorism in the Algerian War" in *Terrorism in Context*, ed. Martha Crenshaw, University Park, PA: Pennsylvania State University Press, 1995.

27 See my chapter "Have Motivations for Terrorism Changed?" in *Tangled Roots: Social and Psychological Factors in the Genesis of Terrorism*, ed. Jeff Victoroff, NATO Security through Science Series, Human and Societal Dynamics, Vol. 11. Amsterdam: IOS Press, 2006.

28 *My Life with the Taliban*, edited by Alex Strick van Linschoten and Felix Kuehn. New York: Columbia University Press, 2010, especially Chapters 14 and 15.

29 Ibid., p. 147.

30 See Martha Crenshaw, ed., *The Consequences of Counterterrorism*, New York: The Russell Sage Foundation, 2010.

31 Joshua Partlow, "Karzai's Taliban reconciliation strategy raises ethnic, rights concerns at home," *Washington Post Foreign Service*, Thursday, February 4, 2010, p. A08.

32 *Toward Integrating Complex National Missions: Lessons from the National Counterterrorism Center's Directorate of Strategic Operational Planning*, available at http://www.pnsr.org/data/files/

pnsr_nctc_dsop_report.pdf. See also Eric Schmitt and Thom Shanker, "Hurdles Hinder Counterterrorism Center," *The New York Times*, February 22, 2010, available at http://www.nytimes.com/2010/02/23/us/politics/23center.html.

33 Frank Foley, "Reforming Counterterrorism: Institutions and Organizational Routines in Britain and France," *Security Studies*, 18, 3, 2009, pp. 435–78.

34 Gary LaFree, Sue-Ming Yang and Martha Crenshaw, "Trajectories of Terrorism: Attack patterns of foreign groups that have targeted the United States, 1970–2004," *Criminology & Public Policy*, 8, 3, August 2009, pp. 445–73.

35 Fareed Zakaria, "Obama's foreign-policy success in Pakistan," *Washington Post*, March 15, 2010, available at http://www.washingtonpost.com/wp-dyn/content/article/2010/03/14/AR2010031401387.html?wpisrc=nl_politics, March 15, 2010.

36 Text of the letter available on the website of the Countering Terrorism Center at West Point at http://www.ctc.usma.edu/harmony/harmony_docs.asp.

37 "How al-Qaida Ends: The Decline and Demise of Terrorist Groups," *International Security*, 31, 1, 2006, pp. 7–48; *Ending Terrorism: Lessons for Defeating Al-Qaeda*, International Institute for Strategic Studies, Adelphi Paper No. 394, Abingdon, Oxon: Routledge, 2008; and Audrey Kurth Cronin, *How Terrorism Ends: Understanding the Decline and Demise of Terrorist Campaigns*, Princeton: Princeton University Press, 2009.

38 In *How Terrorism Ends* Audrey Kurth Cronin lists decapitation of the leadership and loss of public support as two of six patterns of decline or demise, but I define them as contributing factors to outcomes rather than outcomes in themselves. Organizations such as Hamas, for example, have survived sequential leadership decapitations.

39 Ibid., 2009, pp. 210 and 220. She acknowledges measurement difficulties in ascertaining dates of founding and termination of the group.

1 The concept of terrorism

1 Giovanni Sartori, "Concept Misformation in Comparative Politics," *American Political Science Review*, 64, 1970, p. 1040.

2 Ibid., p. 1052.

3 Jerzy Waciorski, *Le terrorisme politique*. Paris: A. Pedone, 1939, pp. 24–7.

4 Ibid., pp. 27–31.

5 Ibid., p. 71.

6 Ibid., p. 98.

7 J.B.S. Hardman, "Terrorism", *Encyclopedia of the Social Sciences*, 14, 1948, p. 575.

8 Charles W. Thayer, *Guerrilla*, New York: Signet Books, 1965, p. 116.

9 Brian Crozier, *The Rebels*, Boston: Beacon Press, 1960, p. 159.

10 Lucien Pye, *Guerrilla Communism in Malaya*, Princeton, NJ: Princeton University Press, 1956, p. 102.

11 Klaus Knorr, "Unconventional Warfare: Strategy and Tactics in Internal Strife," in J. K. Zawodny, ed., "Unconventional Warfare," *Annals of the American Academy of Political and Social Science*, 1962, p. 56.

12 Thomas P. Thornton, "Terror as a Weapon of Political Agitation," in Harry Eckstein ed., *Internal War*, New York: Free Press, 1964, p. 73.

13 Eugene Victor Walter, *Terror and Resistance*, New York: Oxford University Press, 1969. "The study of Communist regimes' use of 'terror,'" in Alexander Dallin, and George W. Breslauer, *Political Terror in Communist Systems*, Stanford: Stanford University Press, 1970, is too restricted in scope to be useful for this paper, although it is an excellent work on the functions of governmental terrorism.

14 Thornton, "Terror as a Weapon," pp. 72–3.

15 Walter, *Terror and Resistance*, pp. 6–7.

16 Sartori, "Concept misinformation," pp. 1039–40.

17 This concept of revolution would include for example "mass revolution" and "revolutionary coup" seen in Raymond Tanter and Manus Midlarsky, "A theory

of revolution, *Journal of Conflict Resolution*, 11, 1967, p. 265; "authority wars" and "structural wars" seen in James N Rosenau, "Internal war as an international event," in J. N. Rosenau, ed., *International Aspects of Civil Strife*, Princeton, NJ: Princeton University Press, 1964, pp. 63–4; "political" and "social" revolutions and "wars of independence" seen in Harry Eckstein, "On the Etiology of Internal Wars," *History and Theory*, 4, 1965, p. 136; and the theories in Chalmers, Johnson, *Revolutionary Change*, Boston: Little, Brown, 1966, and Hannah Arendt, *On Revolution*, New York: Viking, 1965.

18 Walter, *Terror and Resistance*, p. 8.

19 Thornton, "Terror as a Weapon," p. 76.

20 Ibid., pp. 2–3.

21 The discussion of the symbolic nature of terrorism, which distinguishes it from sabotage and assassination, is found in Thornton, "Terror as a Weapon," pp. 77–8.

22 A "direct target group" is the same as the "identification group" in Thornton, "Terror as a Weapon," p. 79. The significant distinction between direct and indirect targets is the reason for the different terminology here.

23 See Omar Chair, "Des Musulmans si tranquilles," *Historia Magazine*, 195, 1971, p. 59.

24 See Pierre Bourdieu, "The sentiment of honour in Kabyle society," in J. G. Peristiany, ed., *Honour and Shame: The Values of Mediterranean Society*, London: Weidenfeld and Nicolson, 1965, pp. 201–3.

25 One might think that any violence employed after warning would be punishment, not terrorism, but whereas punishment is a relatively certain sanction performed by an authority, terrorism even after warning is unpredictable. One increased his vulnerability by disobeying FLN directions, but did not make an attack inevitable.

26 See "Le FIDAI: Sentinelle avancée de la revolution," *El Moudjahid*, 9, 1957, p. 3. It is interesting to note that, faithful to its origins, terrorism was still a term of opprobrium. The FLN insisted that they were not "terrorists" but *fidayine*, militants engaged in liberating combat, "enlightened heroes"; "The 'terrorist' when he accepts a mission lets death enter his soul. . . . The *fidai* has a rendezvous with the life of the Revolution and with his own life." Moreover "it is because he is not a terrorist that the *fidai* cannot be terrorized by . . . General Massu," p. 3, who headed French antiterrorist efforts in Algiers.

27 "Second Front," *El Moudjahid*, 29, 1958, p. 9.

28 Yves Courrière, *La guerre d'Algérie*, Vol. 1: *Les fils de la Toussaint*. Paris: Fayard, 1968; Vol. 2: *Le temps des léopards*, 1969; Vol. 3: *L'heure des colonels*, 1970; Vol. 4: *Les feux du désespoir*, 1971.

29 Amar Ouzegane, *Le meilleur combat*, Paris: Juliaard, 1962, p. 257. Also, Thornton, "Terror as a Weapon," p. 76, states that "the insurgent must attempt to communicate effectively to his audience the idea that terror is the only weapon appropriate to the situation," but he fails to explain why this is true. This statement does not hold for all FLN terrorism.

30 Jacque Massu, *La vraie bataille d'Alger*, Paris: Plon, 1971, p. 120.

31 See Crozier, *The Rebels*, 159 pp. 127–9; Peter Paret, *French Revolutionary Warfare from Indochina to Algeria*, London: Pall Mall Press, 1964, pp. 12–15; and John J. McCuen, *The Art of Counter-Revolutionary War*, Harrisburg, PA: Stackpole Books, 1966, pp. 30–40.

32 Thornton, "Terror as a Weapon," pp. 92–3.

33 See Freida Fromm-Reichmann, "Psychiatric Aspects of Anxiety," in Maurice R. Stein, ed., *Identity and Anxiety*, New York: Free Press, 1960, p. 130; Kurt Riezler, *Man: Mutable and Immutable*, Chicago: Regnery, 1950, pp. 131–2; and Irving Janis, "Psychological Effects of Warnings", in George W. Baker and Dwight W. Chapman, eds, *Man and Society in Disaster*, New York: Basic Books, 1962, p. 59.

34 See Irving Janis, *Air War and Emotional Stress*, New York: McGraw-Hill, 1951, pp. 23–4, 173–4.

35 See Bruno Bettelheim, *The Informed Heart*, New York: Free Press, 1960; Hilde O Bluhm, "How did they survive? Mechanisms of defense in Nazi concentration camps," in Bernard Rosenberg et al., *Mass Society in Crisis*, New York: Macmillan, 1964, p. 201; Eugene Kogon, *Daily Routine in Buchenwald*, in Bernard Rosenberg et al., *Mass Society in Crisis*, New York: Macmillan, 1964, p. 198; and Leo Lowenthal, "Crisis of the Individual: Terror's Atomization of Man," *Commentary*, 1, 1946, pp. 3–5.
36 Johnson, *Revolutionary Change*, p. 8.
37 Mouloud Feraoun, *Journal, 1955–62*, Paris: Seuil, 1962, p. 97.
38 Ibid., p. 109.
39 Ibid., p. 170.
40 Ibid., p. 160.
41 Jacques Soustelle, *Aimée et souffrante Algérie*, Paris: Plon, 1956, p. 121.
42 Ibid., pp. 123–4.
43 See "Document on Terror," *News from behind the Iron Curtain*, 1, 1952, pp. 44–57; Joost A. M. Meerloo, "Brainwashing and Menticide," in Maurice R. Stein, ed., *Identity and Anxiety*, New York: Free Press, 1960, pp. 512–13; and Janis, *Air War*, pp. 117–18.
44 Feraoun, *Journal*, p. 203.
45 Howard Leventhal, et al., "Effects of Fear and Specificity of Recommendation upon Attitudes and Behavior," *Journal of Personality and Social Psychology*, 1965, 2, pp. 20–9.
46 See Ted Gurr, "Psychological Factors in Civil Violence," *World Politics*, 1968, 20, pp. 247–51; Leonard Berkowitz, *Aggression: A Social Psychological Analysis*, New York: McGraw-Hill, 1962. Recall that "now" was 1972.
47 Berkowitz, *Aggression*, p. 118.
48 Ibid., p. 119.
49 Ibid., p. 130.
50 Ibid., pp. 42–3.
51 Ted Gurr, *Why Men Rebel*, Princeton, NJ: Princeton University Press, 1970, p. 213.
52 Nathan, Leites, and Charles Wolf, *Rebellion and Authority*, Chicago: Markham, 1970, p. 10.
53 Ibid., pp. 10–3.
54 Ibid., p. 149.
55 Feraoun, *Journal*, p. 47.
56 See de Sanche Gramont, "Muslim Terrorists in New Job", *New York Herald Tribune*, International Edition, July 9, 1962, p. 1; Germaine Tillion, *Les ennemis complémentaires*, Paris: Minuit, 1960, pp. 176–7.
57 Tillion, *Les ennemis complémentaires*, pp. 49–50.
58 See Mohamed Lebjaoui, *Vérités sur la révolution algérienne*, Paris: Gallimard, 1970, p. 242; Massu, *La vraie bataille*, p. 306.
59 Tillion, *Les ennemis complémentaires*, pp. 52–3.
60 Franz Fanon, *The Wretched of the Earth*, New York: Grove Press, 1968, p. 94.
61 Ouzegane, *Le meilleur combat*, p. 261.
62 Ibid., p. 85.
63 Ibid., pp. 85–6.
64 Philippe Ivernel, "Violence d'hier et d'aujourd'hui", *Esprit*, 1962, 30, pp. 392–3.
65 Ouzegane, *Le meilleur combat*, p. 257.
66 General Massu, *La vraie bataille*, pp. 30, 151–2, in fact complained that the government allowed too many such sensitive officials to remain in positions of responsibility in Algeria. He claimed that they seriously impaired the efficiency of the army and the police.
67 Irving Janis, and Daniel Katz, "The Reduction of Intergroup Hostility", *Journal of Conflict Resolution*, 3, 1959, pp. 91–3.
68 Franz Neumann, "Anxiety and Politics," in Maurice R. Stem, ed., *Identity and Anxiety*, New York: Free Press, 1960, pp. 288–9.

69 Tillion, *Les ennemis complémentaires*, p. 47.
70 Ibid., and personal communication with the author; Saadi Yacef, *Souvenirs de la bataille d'Alger*, Paris: Julliard, 1962.
71 Tillion, personal communication; Massu, *La vraie bataille*, pp. 183–90.
72 Massu, *La vraie bataille*, p. 182.
73 Zohra Drif, *La mort de mes frères*, Paris: Maspéro, 1960.

2 The causes of terrorism

1 For discussions of the meaning of the concept of terrorism, see Thomas P. Thornton, "Terror as a Weapon of Political Agitation," in Harry Eckstein, ed., *Internal War,* New York, 1964, pp. 71–99; Martha Crenshaw Hutchinson, "The Concept of Revolutionary Terrorism," *Revolutionary Terrorism: The FLN in Algeria, 1954–1962,* Stanford: The Hoover Institution Press, 1978, chap. 2; and E. Victor Walter, *Terror and Resistance,* New York: Oxford University Press, 1969.
2 Walter Laqueur, "Interpretations of Terrorism – Fact, Fiction and Political Science," *Journal of Contemporary History*, 12, January 1977, pp. 1–42. See also his major work *Terrorism*, London: Weidenfeld and Nicolson, 1977.
3 See, for example, Paul Wilkinson, *Terrorism and the Liberal State*, London: Macmillan, 1977, or J. Bowyer Bell, *A Time of Terror: How Democratic Societies Respond to Revolutionary Violence*, New York: Basic Books, 1978.
4 This is not to deny that some modern terrorist groups, such as those in West Germany, resemble premodern millenarian movements. See specifically Conor Cruise O'Brien, "Liberty and Terrorism," *International Security*, 2, 1977, pp. 56–67. In general, see Norman Cohn, *The Pursuit of the Millenium*, London: Seeker and Warburg, 1957, and E. J. Hobsbawm, *Primitive Rebels: Studies in Archaic Forms of Social Movement in the 19th and 20th Centuries*, Manchester: Manchester University Press, 1971.
5 A sampling would include Douglas Hibbs, Jr., *Mass Political Violence: A Cross-National Causal Analysis*, New York: John Wiley and Sons, 1973; William J. Crotty, ed., *Assassinations and the Political Order*, New York: Harper and Row, 1971; Ted Robert Gurr, *Why Men Rebel*, Princeton: Princeton University Press, 1971 and Peter Gurr, N. Grabosky, and Richard C. Hula, *The Politics of Crime and Conflict*, Beverly Hills: Sage Publications, 1977.
6 For a summary of these findings, see Gurr, "The Calculus of Civil Conflict," *Journal of Social Issues*, 28, 1972, pp. 27–47.
7 Gurr, "Some Characteristics of Political Terrorism in the 1960s," in Michael Stohl, ed., *The Politics of Terrorism*, New York: Marcel Dekker, 1979, pp. 23–50 and 46–7.
8 A distinction between preconditions and precipitants is found in Eckstein, "On the Etiology of Internal Wars," *History and Theory*, 4, 1965, pp. 133–62. Kenneth Waltz also differentiates between the framework for action as a permissive or underlying cause and special reasons as immediate or efficient causes. In some cases we can say of terrorism, as he says of war, that it occurs because there is nothing to prevent it. See *Man, the State and War*, New York: Columbia University Press, 1959, p. 232.
9 Boris Savinkov, *Memoirs of a Terrorist*, trans. Joseph Shaplen, New York: A. & C. Boni, 1931, pp. 286–7.
10 The major theoreticians of the transition from the rural to the urban guerrilla are Carlos Marighela, *For the Liberation of Brazil*, Harmondsworth: Penguin Books, 1971 and Abraham Guillen, *Philosophy of the Urban Guerrilla: The Revolutionary Writings of Abraham Guillen*, trans. and edited by Donald C. Hodges, New York: William Morrow, 1973.
11 Hobsbawm, *Revolutionaries: Contemporary Essays*, New York: Pantheon, 1973, pp. 226–7.
12 Grabosky, "The Urban Context of Political Terrorism," in Michael Stohl, ed., pp. 51–76.

13 See Amy Sands Redlick, "The Transnational Flow of Information as a Cause of Terrorism," in Yonah Alexander, David Carlton, and Paul Wilkinson, eds. *Terrorism: Theory and Practice*, Boulder: Westview, 1979, pp. 73–95. See also Manus I. Midlarsky, Martha Crenshaw, and Fumihiko Yoshida, "Why Violence Spreads: The Contagion of International Terrorism," *International Studies Quarterly*, 24, June 1980, pp. 262–98.

14 Monica D. Blumenthal et al., *More About Justifying Violence: Methodological Studies of Attitudes and Behavior*, Ann Arbor: Survey Research Center, Institute for Social Research, University of Michigan, 1975, p. 108. Similarly, Peter Lupsha, "Explanation of Political Violence: Some Psychological Theories Versus Indignation," *Politics and Society*, 2, 1971, pp. 89–104, contrasts the concept of "indignation" with Gurr's theory of relative deprivation, which holds that expectations exceed rewards, see *Why Men Rebel*, esp. pp. 24–30.

15 Hobsbawm, *Revolutionaries*, p. 143.

16 Luigi Bonanate, "Some Unanticipated Consequences of Terrorism," *Journal of Peace Research*, 16, 1979, pp. 197–211. If this theory is valid, we then need to identify such blocked societies.

17 See Barbara Salert's critique of the rational choice model of revolutionary participation in *Revolutions and Revolutionaries*, New York: Elsevier, 1976. In addition, Abraham Kaplan discusses the distinction between reasons and causes in "The Psychodynamics of Terrorism," *Terrorism – An International Journal*, 1, 3, and 4, 1978, pp. 237–54.

18 For a typology of terrorist organizations, see Paul Wilkinson, *Political Terrorism*, London: Macmillan, 1974. These classes are not mutually exclusive, and they depend on an outside assessment of goals. For example, the Basque ETA would consider itself revolutionary as well as separatist. The RAF considered itself a classic national liberation movement, and the Provisional IRA insists that it is combatting a foreign oppressor, not an indigenous regime.

19 Bell presents a succinct analysis of Irgun strategy in "The Palestinian Archetype: Irgun and the Strategy of Leverage," in *On Revolt: Strategies of National Liberation*, Cambridge, MA: Harvard University Press, 1976, chap. 3

20 See Thornton's analysis of proximate goals in "Terror as a Weapon of Political Agitation," in Eckstein, ed., pp. 82–8.

21 Walter's discussion of the concept of "forced choice" explains how direct audiences, from whom the victims are drawn, may accept terrorism as legitimate; see *Terror and Resistance*, pp. 285–9.

22 See Marighela, *For the Liberation of Brazil*, pp. 94–5. The West German RAF apparently adopted the idea of provocation as part of a general national liberation strategy borrowed from the Third World.

23 See Hutchinson, *Revolutionary Terrorism*, pp. 40–60.

24 See Michael Walzer's analysis of the morality of terrorism in *Just and Unjust Wars*, New York: Basic Books, 1977, pp. 197–206. See also Bernard Avishai, "In Cold Blood," *The New York Review of Books*, March 8, 1979, pp. 41–4, for a critical appraisal of the failure of recent works on terrorism to discuss moral issues. The question of the availability of alternatives to terrorism is related to the problem of discrimination in the selection of victims. Where victims are clearly responsible for a regime's denial of opportunity, terrorism is more justifiable than where they are not.

25 See Fred I. Greenstein, *Personality and Politics: Problems of Evidence, Inference, and Conceptualization*, Chicago: Markham, 1969.

26 See Jeffrey Goldstein, *Aggression and Crimes of Violence*, New York: Oxford University Press, 1975.

27 A study of the West German New Left, for example, concludes that social psychological models of authoritarianism do help explain the dynamics of radicalism and even the transformation from protest to terrorism. See S. Robert Lichter, "A Psychopolitical Study of West German Male Radical Students," *Comparative Politics*, 12, October 1979, pp. 27–48.

28 This conclusion from 1981 still holds.
29 Franco Venturi, *Roots of Revolution: A History of the Populist and Socialist Movements in Nineteenth Century Russia*, London: Weidenfeld and Nicolson, 1960, p. 647.
30 Quoted in *Science*, 203, 5 January 1979, p. 34, as part of an account of the proceedings of the International Scientific Conference on Terrorism held in Berlin, December, 1978. Advocates of the "terrorist personality" theory, however, argued that terrorists suffer from faulty vestibular functions in the middle ear or from inconsistent mothering resulting in dysphoria. For another description see John Wykert, "Psychiatry and Terrorism," *Psychiatric News*, 14, February 2, 1979, pp. 1 and 12–4. A psychologist's study of a single group, the Front de Libération du Québec, is Gustav Morf, *Terror in Quebec: Case Studies of the FLQ*, Toronto: Clarke, Irvin, and Co., 1970.
31 Peter Merkl, *Political Violence Under the Swastika: 581 Early Nazis*, Princeton: Princeton University Press, 1974, pp. 33–4.
32 Blumenthal et al., p. 182.
33 Ibid., p. 12. Lichter also recognizes this problem.
34 Ibid., pp. 12–3.
35 William O'Brien and Desmond Ryan, eds. *Devoy's Post Bag*, vol. II, Dublin: C.J. Fallon, Ltd., 1953, p. 51.
36 Ibid., p. 52.
37 Savinkov, *Memoirs*, p. 147.
38 Charles A. Russell and Bowman H. Miller, "Profile of a Terrorist," *Terrorism – An International Journal*, 1, 1977, reprinted in John D. Elliott and Leslie K. Gibson, eds. *Contemporary Terrorism: Selected Readings*, Gaithersburg, Md.: International Association of Chiefs of Police, 1978, pp. 81–95.
39 See Philip Pomper's analysis of the influence of Nechaev over his band of followers: "The People's Revenge," *Sergei Nechaev*, New Brunswick, NJ: Rutgers University Press, 1979, chap. 4. The absence of studies of leadership is still noticeable in 2010.
40 A Rand Corporation study of kidnappings and barricade-and-hostage incidents concluded that such tactics are not necessarily perilous, while admitting that drawing statistical inferences from a small number of cases in a limited time period, August 1968 to June 1975 is hazardous. See Brian Jenkins, Janera Johnson, and David Ronfeldt, *Numbered Lives: Some Statistical Observations from 77 International Hostage Episodes*, Rand Paper P-5905, Santa Monica: The Rand Corporation, 1977.
41 Psychiatrist Frederick Hacker, for example, argues that terrorists are by nature indifferent to risk; see *Crusaders, Criminals and Crazies*, New York: Norton, 1976, p. 13.
42 Menachem Begin, *The Revolt*, London: W.H. Allen, 1951.
43 J. Glenn Gray, "The Enduring Appeals of Battle," *The Warriors: Reflections on Men in Battle*, New York: Harcourt, 1970, chap. 2, describes similar experiences among soldiers in combat.
44 Statements of the beliefs of the leaders of the RAF can be found in *Textes des prisonniers de la Fraction armée rouge et dernières lettres d'Ulrike Meinhof*, Paris: Maspero, 1977.
45 Michael Barkun, *Disaster and the Millennium*, New Haven: Yale University Press, 1974, pp. 14–16. See also Leon Festinger et al., *When Prophecy Fails*, New York: Harper and Row, 1956.
46 Bell, *The Secret Army*, London: Anthony Blond, 1970, p. 379.
47 Jean Maitron, *Histoire du mouvement anarchiste en France, 1880–1914*, Paris: Societé universitaire d'éditions et de librairie, 1955, pp. 242–3.
48 S. Stepniak, pseudonym for Kravchinski, *Underground Russia: Revolutionary Profiles and Sketches from Life*, London: Smith, Elder, and Co., 1882, pp. 36–7; see also Venturi, pp. 639 and 707–8.
49 See "Les meurtriers délicats" in *L'Homme Révolté*, Paris: Gallimard, 1965, pp. 571–9.
50 Ya'acov Meridor, *Long is the Road to Freedom*, Tujunga, CA: Barak Publications, 1961, pp. 6 and 9.

51 Begin, p. 111.
52 Vera Figner, *Mémoires d'une révolutionnaire*, trans. Victor Serge, Paris: Gallimard, 1930, pp. 131 and 257–62.
53 Such an argument is applied to Japanese Red Army terrorist Kozo Okamoto by Patricia Steinhof in "Portrait of a Terrorist," *Asian Survey*, 16, 1976, pp. 830–45.

3 "Old" vs. "new" terrorism

1 I wish to thank Audrey Kurth Cronin and Bruce Hoffman for their comments, as well as participants in a seminar at the Center for International Security and Cooperation, Stanford University, at a conference at the University of Utah, at the 2005 annual meeting of the International Society of Political Psychology, and the 2007 annual meeting of the American Political Science Association.
2 Examples include Bruce Hoffman, *Inside Terrorism*, New York: Columbia University Press, 1998, although Hoffman is sometimes ambivalent; Daniel Benjamin and Steven Simon, *The Age of Sacred Terror: Radical Islam's War Against America*, New York: Random House, 2003; Walter Laqueur, *The New Terrorism: Fanaticism and the Arms of Mass Destruction*, New York: Oxford University Press, 1999; and Ian O. Lesser et al., *Countering the New Terrorism*, Santa Monica: The Rand Corporation, 1999. Ambassador L. Paul Bremer contributed "A New Strategy for the New Face of Terrorism" to a special issue of *The National Interest*, Thanksgiving 2001, pp. 23–30. A recent post September 11 overview is Matthew J. Morgan, "The Origins of the New Terrorism," *Parameters*, the Journal of the U.S. Army War College, 34, 1, Spring 2004, pp. 29–43. However, not all proponents of this point of view are American. See the text of a lecture by, Professor Lord Anthony Giddens, delivered at the London School of Economics November 10, 2004, "The Future of World Society: The New Terrorism" available at Columbia International Affairs Online (CIAO). Farhad Khosrokhavar also refers to "new" terrorism in *Les Nouveaux Martyrs d'Allah*, Paris: Flammarion, 2003.
3 See, for example, Simon and Benjamin, *The Age of Sacred Terror*, p. 381. See also the September 11 Commission report (Final Report of the National Commission on Terrorist Attacks upon the United States), ch. 2, "The Foundation of the New Terrorism."
4 See Hoffman, *Inside Terrorism*, pp. 196 and 205; Simon and Benjamin, *The Age of Sacred Terror*, pp. 221 and 384; Lesser, *Countering the New Terrorism*, p. 2; and Laqueur, *The New Terrorism*, p. 7.
5 *Inside Terrorism*, pp. 204–5.
6 Bruce Hoffman, "America and the New Terrorism: An Exchange," *Survival* 42, 2, Summer 2000, p. 162.
7 Hoffman, op cit. p. 171.
8 See, e.g., David Tucker, "What is New about the New Terrorism and How Dangerous is It?" *Terrorism and Political Violence* 14, 3, Fall 2001, pp. 1–14; Thomas Copeland, "Is the 'New Terrorism' Really New?: An Analysis of the New Paradigm for Terrorism," *The Journal of Conflict Studies* 21, 2, Winter 2001, pp. 7–27; Isabelle Duyvesteyn, "How New is the New Terrorism? *Studies in Conflict & Terrorism* 27, 5, 2004, pp. 439–54; Doron Zimmerman, *The Transformation Of Terrorism*, Zurich: Andreas Wenger, 2003; Rik Coolsaet, *Al-Qaeda: The Myth*, Gent: Academia Press, 2005; and Jonny Burnett and Dave Whyte, "Embedded Expertise and the New Terrorism," *Journal for Crime, Conflict and the Media* 1, 4, 2005, pp. 1–18. After the July 2005 bombings in London, Professor Richard Aldrich of the University of Nottingham criticized the idea in an editorial, "The new terrorism," in *The Independent*, July 10, 2005. Also see Olivier Roy, *Globalized Islam: The Search for a New Ummah*, New York: Columbia University Press, 2004, especially pp. 41–54; "Is Jihad closer to Marx than to the Koran?;" and Frederick W. Kagan, "The New Bolsheviks: Understanding Al Qaeda," a National Security Outlook report from

the American Enterprise Institute for Public Policy Research, November 2005. In addition, Audrey Kurth Cronin draws lessons from the past in "How al-Qaida Ends: The Decline and Demise of Terrorist Groups," *International Security* 31, 1, Summer 2006, pp. 7–48. Both John Mueller, *Overblown: How Politicians and the Terrorism Industry Inflate National Security Threats, and Why We Believe Them*, New York: Free Press, 2006 and Ian S. Lustick, *Trapped in the War on Terror*, Philadelphia: University of Pennsylvania Press, 2006 have argued that the United States has overreacted to the threat.

9 Copeland, "Is the New Terrorism Really New?"

10 Duyvesteyn, "How New is the New Terrorism?"

11 Simon and Benjamin, *The Age of Sacred Terror*, pp. 3–4. See Tom Morgenthau, "The New Terrorism," *Newsweek*, July 5, 1993, p. 18.

12 See Jessica Stern, *The Ultimate Terrorists*, Cambridge: Harvard University Press, 1999.

13 See the review essay by Gideon Rose, "It Could Happen Here: Facing the New Terrorism," *Foreign Affairs*, March–April 1999. Accessed online. Ashton B. Carter and William J. Perry in *Preventive Defense: A New Security Strategy for America*, Washington, D. C.: Brookings Institution Press, 1999 warned of "catastrophic terrorism," defined as acts of an order of magnitude more severe than "ordinary" terrorism and unprecedented outside of warfare, p. 150.

14 For an argument about civil war that helped inspire this analysis, see Stathis N. Kalyvas, "'New' and 'Old' Civil Wars: A Valid Distinction?" *World Politics* 54, October 2001, pp. 99–118.

15 The classic work on religion and terrorism is Mark Juergensmeyer's *Terror in the Mind of God: The Global Rise of Religious Violence*, Berkeley: University of California Press, 2000. Although he argues that religion adds a distinctive dimension to terrorism, he does not assume that the association between religion and violence is new. Instead he refers to its reappearance at a particular historical juncture, p. 7. See also *The New Cold War? Religious Nationalism Confronts the Secular State*, Berkeley: University of California Press, 1993. It should be noted that Juergensmeyer's analysis is based on a broad cross-cultural comparison of religious movements in difference societies.

16 See Laqueur, *The New Terrorism*, p. 82.

17 Stern, *The Ultimate Terrorists*, p. 8.

18 The Institute was established as a memorial to the victims of the 1995 Oklahoma City bombing, available at http://www.mipt.org/terrorism/MIPT-Mission-History.asp, last visited October 9, 2007. For the period before 1998 the database only contains international incidents, not domestic. The classification of groups was done by DFI International, a Washington consulting firm. See http://www.tkb.org/AboutTKB.jsp, last visited October 9, 2007.

19 Steven Simon, "The New Terrorism: Securing the Nation Against a Messianic Foe," *The Brookings Review* 21, 1, Winter 2003, p. 18. It is important to look closely at the Rand data, since it is the main source of the argument that religiously motivated terrorism is, (1) increasing and, (2) more lethal and indiscriminate than other forms. See Hoffman, *Inside Terrorism*, pp. 92–4.

20 Simon, "The New Terrorism."

21 Simon and Benjamin, "America and the New Terrorism," pp. 59–75.

22 "The Four Waves of Modern Terrorism," in Audrey Kurth Cronin and James M. Ludes, eds., *Attacking Terrorism: Elements of a Grand Strategy*, Washington: Georgetown University Press, 2004, p. 47.

23 See Simon and Benjamin, "America and the New Terrorism," pp. 59 and 66.

24 Laqueur, *The New Terrorism*, pp. 80–1.

25 "Left, Right, and Beyond: The Changing Face of Terror," in James F. Hoge, Jr. and Gideon Rose, eds., *How Did This Happen? Terrorism and the New War*, New York: Public Affairs Press, 2001, p. 80.

26 Bremer, "A New Strategy," p. 24.

27 White House, Office of the Press Secretary, January 11, 2006, "President Participates in Discussion on the Global War on Terror," Kentucky International Convention Center, Louisville, Kentucky.
28 Graduation Speech, United States Military Academy, West Point, New York, June 1, 2002.
29 October 6, 2005, address to the National Endowment for Democracy, "The Nature of the Enemy We Face and the Strategy for Victory."
30 See for example Simon and Benjamin, *The Age of Sacred Terror*, p. 419.
31 "The New Face of Terrorism," *The New York Times*, January 4, 2000. This indicates perhaps that the new terrorists must be more than religious.
32 Anthony Giddens, for example, explains that "old style terrorism is fundamentally local therefore because its ambitions are local" and that violence thus tends to be "relatively limited." Giddens, "The Future of World Society."
33 Laqueur, "Left, Right, and Beyond," p. 74.
34 Hoffman, *Inside Terrorism*, p. 95.
35 Quoted in Gustavo Gorriti, *The Shining Path: A History of the Millenarian War in Peru*, Chapel Hill: The University of North Carolina Press, 1999, pp. 34–5.
36 Ibid.
37 See the communiques reproduced in *Europe's Red Terrorists: The Fighting Communist Organizations* compiled and annotated by Yonah Alexander and Dennis Pluchinsky, London: Frank Cass, 1992.
38 *Abu Nidal: A Gun for Hire*, New York: Random House, 1992, p. 231.
39 See for example Michael Doran, "The Pragmatic Fanaticism of Al Qaeda: An Anatomy of Extremism in Middle Eastern Politics," *Political Science Quarterly*, 117, 2, Summer 2002, pp. 177–90. See also Quintan Wiktorowicz and John Kaltner, "Killing in the Name of Islam: Al-Qaeda's Justification for September 11," *Middle East Policy* X, 2, Summer 2003, pp. 76–92. They analyze debates over the use of violence within the Salafi movement.
40 See *Messages to the World: The Statements of Osama Bin Laden*, edited and introduced by Bruce Lawrence, London: Verso, 2005.
41 Translations of a number of these documents can be found on the website of the Combating Terrorism Center at West Point: http://www.ctc.usma.edu.
42 Laqueur, *The New Terrorism*, p. 281.
43 Ibid., p. 231.
44 *Understanding Terror Networks*, Philadelphia: University of Pennsylvania Press, 2004.
45 Sageman, *Understanding Terror Networks*, p. 96.
46 Ibid., p. 135. On the importance of the group in prejihadist terrorism, see Martha Crenshaw, "The Psychology of Political Terrorism," in Margaret G. Hermann, ed., *Political Psychology: Contemporary Problems and Issues*, San Francisco: Jossey-Bass, 1986, pp. 379–413 and "Decisions to Use Terrorism: Psychological Constraints on Instrumental Reasoning," in Donatella della Porta *Social Movements and Violence: Participation in Underground Organizations*, International Social Movement Research, Volume 4, pp. 29–42, Greenwich, CT: JAI Press Inc., 1992.
47 See Alan Cullison, "Inside Al-Qaeda's Hard Drive: A Fortuitous Discovery Reveals Budget Squabbles, Baby Pictures, Office Rivalries – and the Path to 9–11," *The Atlantic Monthly*, September 2004, pp. 55–70.
48 Stephen Holmes, "Al-Qaeda, September 11, 2001," in Diego Gambetta, ed., *Making Sense of Suicide Missions*, Oxford: Oxford University Press, 2005, pp. 134–5. He presents a plausible argument that nonreligious motivations were dominant. Steven Simon and Jonathan Stevenson admit this heterogeneity in "Thinking Outside the Tank," *The National Interest*, 78, Winter 2004–2005, pp. 90–8.
49 Holmes, "Al-Qaeda, September 11, 2001," p. 168.
50 Terry McDermott, *Perfect Soldiers*, New York: Harper Collins, 2005.
51 McDermott, *Perfect Soldiers*, p. 217.

52 Peter Bergen and Swati Pandey, "The Madrassa Scapegoat," *The Washington Quarterly*, 29, 2, Spring 2006, p. 122.
53 Laqueur, *The New Terrorism*, p. 81.
54 Simon and Benjamin, *The Age of Sacred Terror*, p. 18.
55 Stern, *The Ultimate Terrorists*, p. 8.
56 Hoffman, *Inside Terrorism*, p. 197.
57 In "The New Face of Terrorism," 2000.
58 Also see the similar conclusions of Chris Quillen, "A Historical Analysis of Mass Casualty Bombers," *Studies in Conflict and Terrorism*, 25, 5, September–October 2002, pp. 279–302. The article provides a chronology.
59 Martin A. Miller, "The Intellectual Origins of Modern Terrorism in Europe," in *Terrorism in Context*, ed. Martha Crenshaw, University Park, PA: Pennsylvania State University Press, 1995.
60 J. Bowyer Bell, *Terror Out of Zion*, New York: St. Martin's Press, 1977, p. 172.
61 Note, however, that some authors who think that there is a "new" terrorism, such as Stern, include the far right in that category.
62 Bernard Droz and Evelyne Lever, *Histoire de la guerre d'Algérie, 1954–1962*, Paris: Seuil, 1982, p. 337. See also Alexander Harrison, *Challenging De Gaulle: The O.A.S. and the Counterrevolution in Algeria, 1954–1962*, New York: Praeger, 1989.
63 Another possible example is the LTTE's use of chlorine gas in an attack on a Sri Lankan army base, but their use appears to have been circumstantial and opportunistic, not planned. See in general Jonathan B. Tucker, ed., *Toxic Terror: Assessing Terrorist Use of Chemical and Biological Weapons*, Cambridge: MIT Press, 2000. According to this study, there had so far been only nine instances of what might be defined as chemical or biological terrorism, which included deliberate food poisonings. The anthrax mailings of 2001 could be added to the list. See also Richard A. Falkenrath, Robert D. Newman, and Bradley A. Thayer, *America's Achilles' Heel: Nuclear, Biological, and Chemical Terrorism and Covert Attack*, Cambridge: MIT Press, 1998 and Stern, *The Ultimate Terrorists*.
64 See U.S. Central Intelligence Agency, "Research Study: International and Transnational Terrorism: Diagnosis and Prognosis", April, 1976.
65 Sara Daly, John Parachini, and William Rosenau, *Aum Shinrikyo, Al Qaeda, and the Kinshasha Reactor: Implications of Three Case Studies for Combating Nuclear Terrorism*, Santa Monica: The Rand Corporation, 2005.
66 See Sammy Salama in the Martin Center for Nonproliferation Studies report "Manual for Producing Chemical Weapon to be Used in [2003] New York Subway Plot available on Al-Qaeda Websites Since Late 2005," 2006. Ron Suskind describes the proposed use of the "mubtakkar device" in *The One Percent Doctrine*, New York: Simon and Schuster, 2006.
67 Figures are from Martin Asser, "Al-Qaeda shadow looms over London," July 7, 2005, BBC Online, available at http://news.bbc.co.uk/2/hi/uk_news/4661273.stm.
68 Text accessed on the Office of the Director of National Intelligence website, where it was posted on October 11, 2005: http://www.dni.gov/letter_in_english.pdf.
69 See, e.g., Hoffman, *Inside Terrorism*, p. 94: "The reasons why terrorist incidents perpetrated for religious motives result in so many more deaths may be found in the radically different value systems, mechanisms of legitimization and justification, concepts of morality, and world-view embraced by the religious terrorist, compared with his secular counterpart." Hoffman's calculations are based on Rand data, which is the basis of the MIPT database.
70 For the text of the report see: http://www.cverdad.org.pe/ingles/ifinal/conclusiones.php.
71 See Martha Crenshaw, "Explaining Suicide Terrorism: A Review Essay," *Security Studies*, 6, 1, Spring 2007, pp. 133–62.
72 According to Ian Lesser, "This new terrorism is increasingly networked. . . . As a result, much existing counterterrorism experience may be losing its relevance as network

forms of organization replace the canonical terrorist hierarchies. . . ." In Lesser, "Countering the New Terrorism: Implications for Strategy," p. 87.

73 Laqueur, *The New Terrorism*, p. 5.

74 Hoffman, *Inside Terrorism*, pp. 197 and 203.

75 See "America and the New Terrorism," pp. 59–75.

76 Hoffman, *Inside Terrorism*, p. 197.

77 See Peter Merkl, "West German Left-Wing Terrorism," in Martha Crenshaw, ed., *Terrorism in Context*, University Park, PA: Pennsylvania State University Press, 1995.

78 Richard Clarke, *Against All Enemies: Inside America's War on Terror*, New York: Free Press, 2004.

79 Indeed Simon, 2003 calls for a policy of containment, as the U.S. contained the Soviet Union during the Cold War. Simon and Benjamin, *The Age of Sacred Terror.*

80 Burnett and Whyte, 2005, go further to say that "It is certain that some elite groups will make a great deal of political and social capital out of this war on terror. It is equally certain that state interventions against the terrorists will continue to be supported by a manufactured conception of 'new terrorism' that is founded upon a highly questionable knowledge base," p. 15. They are particularly critical of the role of the Rand Corporation.

81 See Gabriel Weimann, *Terror on the Internet: The New Arena, the New Challenges*, Washington: United States Institute of Peace Press, 2006.

82 Cynthia McClintock, *Revolutionary Movements in Latin America: El Salvador's FMLN and Peru's Shining Path*, Washington: United States Institute of Peace Press, 1998, p. 68.

83 "Mechanisms of moral disengagement," in Walter Reich, ed., *Origins of Terrorism: Psychologies, Ideologies, Theologies, States of Mind*, Cambridge: Woodrow Wilson International Center for Scholars and Cambridge University Press, 1990.

4 The organizational approach

1 Although this analysis is concerned with terrorism against the state, terrorism by the state is also a result of organizational processes. Government bureaucracies, such as the Gestapo, and semiautonomous organizations directed and staffed by the state, such as the Anti-Communist Alliance in Argentina, could be analyzed in organizational terms.

2 The organizations under examination are referred to as "terrorist organizations" and their members as "terrorists" for the sake of convenience and because terrorism is the subject of analysis. The terms refer, however, not just to groups practicing terrorism exclusively but to organizations for which it is one strategy among several. Nor is the usage meant to imply that all members of revolutionary organizations are actively engaged in terrorist violence.

3 William A. Gamson, *The Strategy of Social Protest*, Homewood, IL: Dorsey Press, 1975, pp. 38–44.

4 J. K. Zawodny, "Infrastructures of Terrorist Organizations," in Lawrence Z. Freedman and Yonah Alexander, eds, *Perspectives on Terrorism*, Wilmington, Delaware: Scholarly Resources, Inc., 1983, pp. 61–70.

5 Gerhard Brunn, "Nationalist Violence and Terror in the Spanish Border Provinces: ETA," in Wolfgang J. Mommsen and Gerhard Hirschfeld, eds, *Social Protest, Violence and Terror in Nineteenth- and Twentieth-century Europe*, New York: St. Martin's, 1982, p. 125.

6 Manfred Hildermeier, "The Terrorist Strategies of the Socialist-Revolutionary Party before 1914," in Mommsen and Hirschfeld, eds, pp. 80–7.

7 Helena Cobban, *The Palestinian Liberation Organisation: People, Power and Politics*, New York: Cambridge University Press, 1984, pp. 146–8.

8 Richard Gillespie, *Soldiers of Peron: Argentina's Montoneros*, New York: Oxford University Press, 1982, pp. 84–5, 137, and 239–44.
9 J. K. Zawodny, "Infrastructures of Terrorist Organizations," in Freedman and Alexander, eds.
10 Bonnie Cordes et al., *Trends in International Terrorism, 1982 and 1983*, Santa Monica, CA: Rand Corporation, 1984, pp. 37–9.
11 Hildermeier, "Terrorist Strategies," p. 85.
12 See, for example, Paul Wilkinson, *Political Terrorism*, New York: John Wiley, 1974.
13 Cordes, *Trends*, p. 29.
14 Brunn, "Nationalist Violence," pp. 118–9.
15 Gillespie, *Soldiers of Peron*, p. 71.
16 Federal Republic of Germany, Bundesministerium des Innern, *Analysen zum Terrorismus*, Vol. 1, *Ideologien und Strategien* by Iring Fetscher and Gunter Rohrmoser, Opladen: Westdeutscher Verlag, 1981.
17 See Martha Crenshaw, "The Causes of Terrorism," *Comparative Politics*, July 1981, pp. 379–99.
18 See, for example, Harry R. Targ, "Societal Structure and Revolutionary Terrorism: A Preliminary Investigation," in Michael Stohl, ed., *The Politics of Terrorism: A Reader in Theory and Practice*, New York: Marcel Dekker, 1979, pp. 119–43.
19 Cynthia McClintock, "Why Peasants Rebel: The Case of Peru's Sendero Luminoso," *World Politics*, October 1984, pp. 48–84.
20 Harvey Waterman, "Reasons and Reason: Collective Political Activity in Comparative and Historical Perspective," *World Politics*, July 1981, pp. 554–89.
21 The work by J. K. Zawodny, himself a former member of the Polish underground, was an exception. See, in addition to the article cited above, note 4, "Internal Organizational Problems and the Sources of Tensions of Terrorist Movements as Catalysts of Violence," in *Terrorism: An International Journal*, 1, Nos. 3 and 4, 1978, pp. 277–85. By 2010, organizational analysis of terrorism became much more popular.
22 James Q. Wilson, *Political Organizations*, New York: Basic Books, 1973.
23 Barry E. Collins and Harold Guetzkow, A *Social Psychology* of *Group Processes for Decision Making*, New York: John Wiley, 1964, pp. 74–80.
24 Carlos Marighela, *For the Liberation* of *Brazil*, translated by John Butt and Rosemary Sheed, Harmondsworth: Penguin, 1971, p. 31. See, in general, Chapter 4, "On the Organizational Function of Revolutionary Violence," pp. 30–44.
25 Nathan Leites, "Understanding the Next Act," *Terrorism: An International Journal*, 3, Nos. 1 and 2, 1979, pp. 1–46, especially pp. 32–3. Words are regarded as an excuse for inaction.
26 Konrad Kellen, *Terrorists – What Are They Like? How Some Terrorists Describe Their World and Actions*, Rand Note N-1300-SL. Santa Monica: Rand Corporation, 1979, p. 37.
27 Hildermeier, "Terrorist Strategies," p. 85.
28 John W. Amos, *The Palestinian Resistance: Organization* of a *Nationalist Movement*, New York: Pergamon Press, 1980, p. 144.
29 Wilson, *Political Organizations*, Chapter 3, pp. 30–55. Most organizations are not combat-oriented, so violent organizations are a special case.
30 Collins and Guetzkow, *Group Processes for Decision-Making*, pp. 22–9.
31 Sidney Verba, *Small Groups and Political Behavior: A Study of Leadership*, Princeton: Princeton University Press, 1961, pp. 56–9, 122–3, and 146–53.
32 Hildermeier, "Terrorist Strategies," p. 85.
33 Federal Republic of Germany, Bundesministerium des Innern, *Analysen zum Terrorismus*, Vol. 3, *Gruppenprozesse*, by Wanda von Baeyer-Katte, Dieter Claessens, Hubert Feger, and Friedheim Neidhardt, Opladen: Westdeutscher Verlag, 1981.
34 Brunn, "Nationalist Violence," p. 126. See also Robert P. Clark, *The Basque Insurgents: ETA, 1952–1980*, Madison: University of Wisconsin Press, 1984.

35 Now we would point to their access to the internet and cell phones.
36 Kellen, *Terrorists – What Are They Like?* pp. 36–8.
37 Wilson, *Political Organizations*, pp. 49–50.
38 Cordes, *Trends*, pp. 3–4.
39 Gillespie, *Soldiers of Peron*, pp. 58–9 and 118–9.
40 There is a substantial literature on religious cults. See, for example, William S. Bainbridge and Rodney Stark, "Cult Formation: Three Compatible Models," *Sociological Analysis*, Winter 1979, pp. 283–95; and "Networks of Faith: Interpersonal Bonds and Recruitment to Cults and Sects," *American Journal of Sociology*, May 1980, pp. 1376–95.
41 David C. Rapoport, "Fear and Trembling: Terrorism in Three Religious Traditions," *American Political Science Review*, September 1984, pp. 658–77.
42 Wilson, *Political Organization*, p. 50, and in general Chapter 3, "Organizational Maintenance and Incentives," pp. 30–55.
43 Ibid., pp. 296–301.
44 Ibid., p. 201.
45 Gillespie, *Soldiers of Peron*, p. 59.
46 Ibid., pp. 47–88.
47 Cordes, *Trends*, p. 50.
48 Albert O. Hirschman, *Exit, Voice, and Loyalty: Responses to Decline in Firms, Organizations, and States*, Cambridge: Harvard University Press, 1970.
49 Gillespie, *Soldiers of Peron*, p. 139.
50 Verba, *Small Groups and Political Behavior*, pp. 172–5.
51 Hirschman, *Exit, Voice, and Loyalty*, p. 93.
52 Cobban, *Palestinian Liberation Organisation*, p. 148.
53 Hirschman, *Exit, Voice, and Loyalty*, Appendix, pp. 146–55.
54 Ibid.
55 Ibid., p. 121.

5 Subjective realities

Author's note: I wish to thank Richard W. Boyd, Khachig Tololyan, and the editors of the volume in which this essay originally appeared for their comments on this manuscript.

1 The terrorist organizations to which I refer are autonomous and clandestine groups, acting to bring about radical political change through violence against established authority. Their reliance on terrorism-symbolic violence that exceeds the limits of what society considers legitimate in order to shock and intimidate rather than to destroy is a distinguishing characteristic. I use the term "terrorist" to include all members of such organizations.
2 Brian M. Jenkins, *The Terrorist Mindset and Terrorist Decision-making: Two Areas of Ignorance*, Santa Monica: Rand, P-6340, 1979.
3 Joseph Conrad, *The Secret Agent*, Harmondsworth: Penguin, 1963 edition, p. 9.
4 Ole R. Holsti, *Cognitive Dynamics and Images of the Enemy*, in J. C. Farrell and A P. Smith, eds, *Image and Reality in World Politics*, New York: Columbia University Press, 1967, p. 18.
5 J. Sidanius, "Cognitive Functioning and Sociopolitical Ideology Revisited", in *Political Psychology*, 6, 1985, pp. 637–62.
6 Ibid., p. 641.
7 G. W. Hopple and M. Steiner, *The Causal Beliefs of Terrorists: Empirical Results*, McLean, Virginia: Defense Systems, Inc., 1984.
8 Ibid., pp. 18–9, 80–2.
9 Sidanius, *Cognitive Functioning*, p. 657.
10 Horowitz, Irving L. *The Routinization of Terrorism and its Unanticipated Consequences*, in

Martha Crenshaw, ed., *Terrorism, Legitimacy and Power: The Consequences of Political Violence*, Middletown, Connecticut: Wesleyan University Press, 1983, p. 48.

11 T. Sheehan, *Myth and Violence: The Fascism of Julius Evola and Alain de Benoist*, in *Social Research*, 48, 1981, pp. 45–73.

12 Bruce Hoffman, *Right-Wing Terrorism in Europe*, N-1856-AF, Santa Monica: Rand, 1982; and Bruce Hoffman, *Right-Wing Terrorism in the United States*, Santa Monica: Rand, 1986.

13 Jane Alpert, *Growing Up Underground*, New York: William Morrow, 1981, p. 155.

14 Harold Jacobs, ed., *Weatherman*, New York: Ramparts Press, 1970, p. 510.

15 See Holsti, *Cognitive Dynamics*.

16 D. Salvioni and A. Stephanson, "Reflections on the Red Brigades" *Orbis*, 29, 1985, pp. 494–5.

17 *Textes des prisonniers de la Fraction armée rouge et dernières lettres d'Ulrike Meinhof*, Paris: Maspero, 1977, especially pp. 63–7 and 75–82.

18 See Alex Schmid and Janny de Graaf, *Violence as Communication: Insurgent Terrorism and the Western News Media*, Beverly Hills: Sage, 1982.

19 See Hopple and Steiner, *The Causal Beliefs*, pp. 49–50; and *Textes des prisonniers*.

20 See Jacobs, *Weatherman*, pp. 509–16.

21 France Ferracuti and F. Bruno, "Psychiatric Aspects of Terrorism in Italy," in I. L. Barak-Glantz and C. R. Huff, eds, *The Mad, the Bad and the Different: Essays in Honor of Simon Dinitz*, Lexington, MA: D. C. Heath, 1981, p. 208.

22 See Hoffman, *Right-Wing Terrorism in Europe*; and Wilkinson, P., *The New Fascists*, London: Pan Books, revised ed., 1983.

23 Franco Ferracuti and F. Bruno, "Italy: A Systems Perspective," in A. Goldstein and M. H. Segall, eds, *Aggression in Global Perspective*, New York: Pergamon, 1983, pp. 308–10.

24 Menachem Begin, *The Revolt*, Los Angeles: Nash, revised ed., 1977, p. 108.

25 J. Bowyer Bell observed to the author, in response to the question of why the IRA did not seize hostages, that "armies don't."

26 Quoted in Walter Laqueur, ed., *The Terrorism Reader: A Historical Anthology*, New York: New American Library, 1978, p. 194.

27 Salvioni and Stephanson, *Reflections*, p. 493

28 Hopple and Steiner, *The Causal Beliefs*, pp. 56 and 62.

29 *Textes des prisonniers*, pp. 36–9.

30 G.J. Bereciartu, *The Political Violence in the Basque Country*, paper prepared for presentation to the International Political Science Association, Paris, France, 1985.

31 *Textes des prisonniers*, p. 188

32 Salvioni and Stephanson, *Reflections*, p. 501; also S. E. Moran, ed., *Court Depositions of Three Red Brigadists*, N-2391-RC, Santa Monica: Rand, 1986.

33 Jacobs, *Weatherman*, p. 518.

34 See H. T. Himmelweit et al., *How Voters Decide*, London: Academic Press, 1981, p. 191; K.J. Gergen and M. M. Gergen, "Narratives of the Self," in T. R. Sarbin and K. E. Scheibe, eds, *Studies in Social Identity*, New York: Praeger, 1983, pp. 254–73; and K. Tololyan, *Cultural Narrative and the Motivation of the Terrorist*, paper prepared for the American Political Science Association, New Orleans, 1985.

35 Gergen and Gergen, "Narratives," argue that in psychological terms every individual self-conception exists in terms of a narrative, but that not all narratives need be directive.

36 Tololyan, *Cultural Narrative*.

37 At the time that this article was written, students of the relationship between terrorism and religion were most concerned with Hezbollah.

38 David C. Rapoport, "Fear and Trembling: Terrorism in Three Religious Traditions," in *American Political Science Review*, 78, 3, 1984, p. 658–77.

39 David C. Rapoport, *Why does messianism produce terror?*, paper prepared for the American Political Science Association, New Orleans, 1985; and David C. Rapoport, "Messianism and Terror," *The Center Magazine*, 19, 1986, pp. 30–6.

40 Rapoport, *Messianism*, p. 36.
41 See Paul Wilkinson, *Terrorism and the Liberal State*, New York: New York University Press, revised ed., 1986.
42 See P. Billig, "The Lawyer Terrorist and His Comrades", *Political Psychology*, 6, 1, 1985, pp. 36–7.
43 G. Craig, *The Germans*, New York: Putnam, 1982, pp. 210–2.
44 Ibid., p. 12.
45 *Textes des prisonniers*, p. 37.
46 Carlos Marighela, *For the Liberation of Brazil*, Harmondsworth: Penguin, 1971, pp. 30–1.
47 Bereciartu, *The Political Violence*, p. 19.
48 Irving Fetscher and G. Rohrmoser, *Ideologien und Strategien*, in Vol. 1 of *Analysen zum Terrorismus*, Opladen: Westdeutscher Verlag, 1981.
49 Craig, *The Germans*.
50 See Martha Crenshaw, "The Psychology of Political Terrorism," in M. Hermann, ed., *Political Psychology*, San Francisco: Jossey-Bass, 1986, pp. 379–413.
51 See Ferracuti and Bruno, "Italy."
52 Jeanne Knutson, "Social and Psychodynamic Pressures Toward a Negative Identity: The Case of an American Revolutionary Terrorist," in Y. Alexander and J. M. Gleason, eds, *Behavioural and Quantitative Perspectives on Terrorism*, New York: Pergamon, 1981, pp. 105–50.
53 See also J. N. Knutson, "The Terrorists' Dilemmas: Some Implicit Rules of the Game" in *Terrorism: An International Journal*, 4, 1980, pp. 195–222; and L. Böllinger, "Die entwicklung zu terroristischem handeln als psychosozialer prozess: begegnungen mit beteiligten", in H. Jäger et al., *Lebenslauf-Analysen*, vol. 2 of *Analysen Zum Terrorismus*, Opladen: Westdeutscher Verlag, 1981, pp. 175–231.
54 Certainly Lewis Feuer, *The Conflict of Generations: The Character and Significance of Student Movements*, New York: Basic Books, 1969, felt that terrorism was a psychological reaction of sons against fathers, an inevitable part of adolescent rebellion.
55 Abraham Kaplan, "The Psychodynamics of Terrorism," *Terrorism: An International Journal*, 1, 1978, pp. 237–54.
56 Erik Erikson, *Childhood and Society*, New York: W. W. Norton, 2nd edn., 1963; and E. H. Erikson, *Identity: Youth and Crisis*, New York: W. W. Norton, 1968.
57 Böllinger, *Die entwicklung zu terroristischem*.
58 Knutson, *Social and Psychodynamic Pressures*.
59 Erikson, *Identity*.
60 J. M. Post, "Notes on a Psychodynamic Theory of Terrorist Behaviour," *Terrorism: An International Journal*, 7, 1984, pp. 241–56, especially p. 243
61 As Post, *Notes*, p. 246, also notes in the case of Italy.
62 Robert Jervis, *Perception and Misperception in International Politics*, Princeton: Princeton University Press, 1976.
63 See J. Kohl and J. Litt, eds, *Urban Guerrilla Warfare in Latin America*, Cambridge, Massachusetts: MIT Press, 1974, p. 303.
64 *Textes des prisonniers*, pp. 112–3.
65 Leila Khaled, *My People Shall Live: The Autobiography of a Revolutionary*, London: Hodder & Stoughton, 1973, pp. 133–4.
66 Irving Janis and L. Mann, *Decision-Making: A Psychological Analysis of Conflict, Choice, and Commitment*, New York: Free Press, 1977.
67 O. R Holsti, *Crisis Escalation War*, Montreal: McGill-Queen's University Press, 1972.
68 Baumann, M., *Wie Alles Anfing – How It All Began: The Personal Account of a West German Urban Guerrilla*, Vancouver, Canada: Pulp Press, 1977, p. 98.
69 D. A. Snow and R. Machalek, "On the Presumed Fragility of Unconventional Beliefs," in *Journal for the Scientific Study of Religion*, 21, 1982, pp. 15–26.
70 Kohl and Litt, *Urban Guerilla Warfare*, pp. 301–2.
71 Baumann, *Wie Alles Anfing*, p. 14.

72 I. L. Janis, "Group Identification under Conditions of External Danger," in D. Cartwright and A. Zander, eds, *Group Dynamics: Research and Theory*, New York: Harper & Row, 3rd edition, 1968, pp. 80–90.
73 Knutson, "The Terrorists' Dilemmas."
74 Ibid., pp. 213–14.
75 Ibid., pp. 214.
76 The testimony of the Red Brigades' *pentiti* provided in Moran, *Court Depositions*, deals extensively with the internal disputes that wracked the organization, especially after the kidnapping of Aldo Moro in 1978. These conflicts appeared to be both time consuming and lethal, because the contenders for power within the organization tried to demonstrate their superior revolutionary prowess by carrying out ever more sensational actions, such as the kidnapping of General Dozier in 1981.
77 Moran, *Court Depositions*, p. 87, quoting Massimo Cianfanelli.
78 See Fenzi's testimony in Moran, *Court Depositions*, pp. 121–228.
79 Jervis, *Perception*, pp. 308–10.
80 Baumann, *Wie Alles Anfing*, p. 99.
81 Richard Lebow, *Between Peace and War: The Nature of International Crisis*, Baltimore, MD: Johns Hopkins University Press, 1981, pp. 270–9.

6 The logic of terrorism

1 For a similar perspective (based on a different methodology) see James DeNardo, *Power in Numbers: The Political Strategy of Protest and Rebellion*, Princeton, NJ: Princeton University Press, 1985. See also Harvey Waterman, "Insecure 'Ins' and Opportune 'Outs': Sources of Collective Political Activity," *Journal of Political and Military Sociology*, 8, 1980: pp. 107–12 and "Reasons and Reason: Collective Political Activity in Comparative and Historical Perspective," *World Politics*, 33, 1981: pp. 554–89. A useful review of rational choice theories is found in James G. March, "Theories of Choice and Making Decisions," *Society*, 20, 1982: pp. 29–39.
2 Edward N. Muller and Karl-Dieter Opp, "Rational Choice and Rebellious Collective Action," *American Political Science Review*, 80, 1986: pp. 471–87.
3 Ibid., p. 484. The authors also present another puzzling question that may be answered in terms of either psychology or collective rationality. People who expected their rebellious behavior to be punished were more likely to be potential rebels. This propensity could be explained either by a martyr syndrome (or an expectation of hostility from authority figures) or intensity of preference – the calculation that the regime was highly repressive and thus deserved all the more to be destroyed. See pp. 482 and 485.
4 Leila Khaled, *My People Shall Live: The Autobiography of a Revolutionary*, London: Hodder and Stoughton, 1973, pp. 128–31.
5 See Martha Crenshaw, "The Strategic Development of Terrorism," paper presented to the 1985 Annual Meeting of the American Political Science Association, New Orleans.
6 See Albert Bandura, "Mechanisms of Moral Disengagement" in Walter Reich, ed., *Origins of Terrorism: Psychologies, Ideologies, Theologies, States of Mind*, Cambridge, Woodrow Wilson International Center for Scholars and Cambridge University Press, 1990.
7 William A. Gamson, *The Strategy of Social Protest*, Homewood, Illinois: Dorsey Press, 1975.
8 Manus I. Midlarsky, Martha Crenshaw, and Fumihiko Yoshida, "Why Violence Spreads: The Contagion of International Terrorism," *International Studies Quarterly*, 24, 1980, pp. 262–98.
9 See the study by David A. Newell, *The Russian Marxist Response to Terrorism: 1878–1917*, Ph.D. dissertation, Stanford University, University Microfilms, 1981.

10 The tension between violence and numbers is a fundamental proposition in DeNardo's analysis; see *Power in Numbers*, Chapters 9–11.

11 The work of Charles Tilly emphasizes the political basis of collective violence. See Charles Tilly, Louise Tilly, and Richard Tilly, *The Rebellious Century 1830–1930*, Cambridge: Harvard University Press, 1975 and Charles Tilly, *From Mobilization to Revolution*, Reading, MA: Addison-Wesley, 1978.

12 See Conor Cruise O'Brien, "Terrorism under Democratic Conditions: The Case of the IRA," in Martha Crenshaw, *Terrorism, Legitimacy, and Power: The Consequences of Political Violence*, ed., Middletown, CT Wesleyan University Press, 1983.

13 For example, DeNardo, in *Power in Numbers*, argues that "the movement derives moral sympathy from the government's excesses," p. 207.

14 Paul Avrich, *The Haymarket Tragedy*, Princeton: Princeton University Press, 1984, p. 166.

15 Seán MacStiofáin, *Memoirs of a Revolutionary*, London: Gordon Cremonesi, 1975, p. 301.

16 Waterman, "Insecure 'Ins' and Opportune 'Outs'" and "Reasons and Reason."

17 *Political Organizations*, New York: Basic Books, 1973.

18 Maria McGuire, *To Take Arms: My Year with the IRA Provisionals*, New York: Viking, 1973, pp. 110–11, 118, 129–31, and 161–2.

19 DeNardo concurs; see *Power in Numbers*, Chapter 11.

20 See Jim Hoagland, "A Community of Terror," *Washington Post*, 15 March, 1973, pp. 1 and 13; also *New York Times*, March 4, 1973, p. 28. Black September is widely regarded as a subsidiary of Fatah, the major Palestinian organization headed by Yasir Arafat.

21 John Amos, *Palestinian Resistance: Organization of a Nationalist Movement*, New York: Pergamon, 1980, p. 193; quoting George Habash, interviewed in *Life Magazine*, June 12, 1970, p. 33.

22 Jean Maitron, *Histoire du mouvement anarchiste en France (1880–1914)*, 2nd ed., Paris: Société universitaire d'éditions et de librairie, 1955, pp. 74–5.

23 "Stepniak," pseud, for Sergei Kravshinsky, *Underground Russia: Revolutionary Profiles and Sketches from Life*, London: Smith, Elder, 1883, pp. 278–80.

24 Carlos Marighela, *For the Liberation of Brazil*, Harmondsworth: Penguin, 1971, p. 113.

25 Vera Figner, *Mémoires d'une révolutionnaire*, Paris: Gallimard, 1930, p. 206.

26 *Textes des prisonniers de la "fraction armée rouge" et dernières lettres d'Ulrike Meinhof*, Paris: Maspero, 1977, p. 64.

27 *Marighela, For the Liberation of Brazil*, p. 46.

28 Schelling, *Arms and Influence*, New Haven, CT: Yale University Press, 1966, p. 6.

29 Daniel Ellsburg, *The Theory and Practice of Blackmail*, Santa Monica, CA: Rand Corporation, 1968.

30 David A. Baldwin, "Bargaining with Airline Hijackers," in *The 50% Solution*, ed. William I. Zartman, pp. 404–29, Garden City, NY: Doubleday, 1976, argues that promises have not been sufficiently stressed. Analysts tend to emphasize threats instead, surely because of the latent violence implicit in hostage taking regardless of outcome.

31 See Roberta Wohlstetter's case study of Castro's seizure of American marines in Cuba: "Kidnapping to Win Friends and Influence People," *Survey*, 20, 1974, pp. 1–40.

32 Scott E. Atkinson, Todd Sandler, and John Tschirhart, "Terrorism in a Bargaining Framework," *Journal of Law and Economics*, 30, 1987, pp. 1–21.

7 Psychological constraints on instrumental reasoning

1 See Martha Crenshaw, "The Logic of Terrorism: Terrorism as a Product of Strategic Choice," in W. Reich, ed., *Origins of Terrorism: Psychologies, Ideologies, Theologies, States of Mind*, Cambridge: Woodrow Wilson International Center for Scholars and Cambridge University Press. See also 1990 James DeNardo, *Power in Numbers: The Political Strategy of Protest and Rebellion*, Princeton: Princeton University Press, 1985.

2 See Max Taylor, *The Terrorist*, London: Brassey's, 1988.
3 Albert Bandura, "Psychological mechanisms of aggression," in *Human Ethology: Claims and Limits of a New Discipline*, edited by M. von Cranach, K. Froppa, W. Lepenies, and D. Ploog, Cambridge: Cambridge University Press, 1979, p. 338.
4 Jerrold Post, "Rewarding Fire with Fire: Effects of Retaliation on Terrorist Group Dynamics," *Terrorism: An International Journal*, 10, 1987, pp. 23–36.
5 Bommi Baumann, *Wie Alles Anjing-How it all Began: The Personal Account of a West German Urban Guerilla*, Vancouver: Pulp Press, 1977, p. 109.
6 Klaus Wasmund, "The Political Socialization of West German Terrorists," in *Political Violence and Terror: Motifs and Motivations*, edited by P. H. Merkl, Berkeley: University of California Press, 1986, p. 199.
7 M. E. Gilio, *The Tupamaros*, London: Secker and Warburg, 1972, p. 137.
8 Wasmund, "Political Socialization," p. 204.
9 Leonard Weinberg and W. L. Eubank, *The Rise and Fall of Italian Terrorism*, Boulder, CO: Westview Press, 1987, p. 83.
10 See O. R. Holsti, "Crisis, Stress and Decision Making," in *Crisis Escalation War*, Montreal: McGill-Queen's University Press, 1972, pp. 7–25.
11 See I. Janis, "Group Identification Under Conditions of External Danger," in *Group Dynamics: Research and Theory*, edited by D. Cartwright and A. Zander, 3rd ed., New York: Harper and Row, 1968, pp. 84–5.
12 See A. O. Hirschman, *Exit, Voice, and Loyalty: Responses to Decline in Firms, Organizations, and States*, Cambridge: Harvard University Press, 1970.
13 See Chapter 6.
14 A. Silj, *Never Again Without a Rifle: The Origins of Italian Terrorism*, New York: Karz, 1979.
15 Ibid., p. 115.
16 Wasmund, "Political Socialization," pp. 215 and 218.
17 See Bonnie Cordes, "When Terrorists Do the Talking: Reflections on the Terrorist Literature," in *Inside Terrorist Organizations* edited by D. Rapoport, New York: Columbia University Press, 1988.
18 David Rapoport, "Messianic Sanctions for Terror," in *Origins of Terrorism: Psychologies, Ideologies, Theologies, States of Mind*, edited by W. Reich, Cambridge: Cambridge University Press and Woodrow Wilson International Center for Scholars, 1990.
19 See G. W. Hopple and M. Steiner, *The Causal Beliefs of Terrorists: Empirical Results*, McLean, VA: Defense Systems, Inc, 1984.
20 See I. L. Janis and L. Mann, *Decision-Making: A Psychological Analysis of Conflict, Choice, and Commitment*, New York: Free Press, 1977.
21 See D. A. Snow and R. Machalek, "On the Presumed Fragility of Unconventional Beliefs," *Journal for the Scientific Study of Religion* 21, 1982, pp. 15–26.
22 Deborah Larson, *Origins of Containment: A Psychological Explanation*, Princeton: Princeton University Press, 1985, pp. 42–50.
23 J. Knutson, "The Terrorists' Dilemmas: Some Implicit Rules of the Game," *Terrorism: An International Journal* 4 (1–4), 1980, p. 213.
24 Ibid., p. 213.
25 Ibid., pp. 213–14.
26 Ibid., p. 214. Also Wasmund, "Political Socialization," pp. 218–20.
27 Baumann, *Wie Alles Anjing*, p. 76.
28 See G. R. Newman and M. J. Lynch, "From Feuding to Terrorism: The Ideology of Vengeance," *Contemporary Crises*, 11, 1987, pp. 223–42.
29 Silj, *Never Again*, p. 219.
30 Post, "Rewarding Fire," p. 33.
31 Gary Marx, "Thoughts on a Neglected Category of Social Movement Participant: The Agent Provocateur and the Informant," *American Journal of Sociology*, 80, 2, 1974, pp. 402–40.

32 Bandura, "Psychological mechanisms," p. 351.
33 Ibid., p. 356.
34 See Bandura, 1990.
35 See William Ascher, "The Moralism of Attitudes Supporting Intergroup Violence," *Political Psychology*, 7, 3, 1986, pp. 403–25.
36 As I argued in Chapter 6.
37 See Knutson, "The Terrorists' Dilemmas."
38 See K. G. Shaver, *The Attribution of Blame: Causality, Responsibility, and Blameworthiness*, New York: Springer-Verlag, 1985. See also Bandura, 1987, p. 23.
39 See Holsti, "Crisis."
40 Marid McGuire, *To Take Arms: My Year with the IRA Provisionals*, New York: Viking Press, 1973. p. 113.
41 See Janis and Mann, *Decision-making.*
42 Martha Crenshaw, "The Psychology of Political Terrorism," in M. G. Herman, *Political Psychology*, edited by M. G. Hermann, San Francisco: Jossey-Bass, 1986, p. 397.
43 See Bandura, 1990.
44 W. T. Roth, "The Meaning of Stress," in *Victims of Terrorism*, edited by F. M. Ochberg and D. A. Soskis, Boulder, CO: Westview, 1982, pp. 52–3, referring to Finz, W. D. 1975. "Strategies for Coping with Stress," in I. G. Sarason and C. D. Spielberger, eds, *Stress and Anxiety*, Vol. 2, New York: Wiley.
45 Ferracuti, 1987, p. 13.

8 Coercive diplomacy

1 See Tim Zimmermann, "Coercive Diplomacy and Libya," in Alexander L. George and William E. Simons, *The Limits of Coercive Diplomacy*, 2d edn., Boulder, CO: Westview Press, 1994, pp. 201–28. The United States had also used limited military force in efforts to apprehend individual terrorist suspects.
2 *Public Report of the Vice President's Task Force on Combating Terrorism*, Washington, D.C.: U.S. Government Printing Office, February 1986, esp. pp. 9 and 13.
3 In April 1996 Saudi authorities televised the confessions of four religious militants who claimed to be motivated by dissatisfaction with the regime. Three had fought in the wars in Afghanistan, Bosnia, and Chechnya. In May they were executed.
4 See "A False Alarm, This Time: Preventive Defense against Catastrophic Terrorism," in Ashton B. Carter and William J. Perry, eds, *Preventive Defense: A New Security Strategy for America*, Washington, D.C.: Brookings Institution, 1999, pp. 143–74.
5 See Martha Crenshaw, "The Logic of Terrorism: Terrorism as the Product of Strategic Choice," in Walter Reich, ed., *Origins of Terrorism: Psychologies, Ideologies, Theologies, States of Mind*, Cambridge: Woodrow Wilson International Center for Scholars and Cambridge University Press, 1990.
6 On the question of how to coerce terrorists, see Joseph Lepgold, "Hypotheses on Vulnerability: Are Terrorists and Drug Traffickers Coerceable?" in Lawrence Freedman, ed., *Strategic Coercion: Concepts and Cases*, New York and Oxford: Oxford University Press, 1998 and Ian O. Lesser, "Countering the New Terrorism: Implications for Strategy," in Ian O. Lesser et al., ed., *Countering the New Terrorism*, ed., Santa Monica, CA: RAND, 1999. See also Daniel Byman and Matthew Waxman, *The Dynamics of Coercion: American Foreign Policy and the Limits of Military Might*, Cambridge: Cambridge University Press and RAND, 2002.
7 Some nonstates have alternatives to terrorism, while others do not. This is an important consideration in choosing a defensive or coercive strategy.
8 Zimmermann, "Coercive Diplomacy and Libya," p. 204.
9 This account is based on David Von Drehle and R. Jeffrey Smith, "U.S. Strikes Iraq for Plot to Kill Bush," *Washington Post*, June 27, 1993; and Eric Schmitt, "Raid on Baghdad," *New York Times*, June 28, 1993.

10 The text of the president's statement on June 26 can be found in *Washington Post*, June 27, 1993, A20.
11 The Kuwaiti trial of the accused plotters had not been completed, however.
12 Text of statement in *Washington Post*, June 27, 1993, A20.
13 Richard L. Berke, "Raid on Baghdad: Poll Shows Raid on Iraq Buoyed Clinton's Popularity," *New York Times*, June 29, 1993.
14 William Safire, "Slapping Saddam's Wrist," *New York Times*, June 28, 1993.
15 Martin Walker and Michael White, "Clinton Sparks Anger Abroad," *Guardian*, June 29, 1993.
16 Stephen Hubbell, "Arab States Condemn U.S. Strike on Baghdad," *Christian Science Monitor*, June 29, 1993.
17 Paul Pillar, *Terrorism and U.S. Foreign Policy*, Washington, D.C.: Brookings Institution Press, 2001, pp. 103–4.
18 R. Jeffrey Smith, "Critics 'Wrong,' CIA Chief Says," *Washington Post*, September 6, 1996.
19 See U.S. Department of Defense, *Report to the President and Congress on the Protection of U.S. Forces Deployed Abroad* (with the Downing Investigation Report, August 30, 1996) Washington, D.C.: September 15, 1996. In June 2001 indictments returned before the U.S. District Court in Alexandria, Virginia, revealed that plans for the attack started in 1993 and that the Saudis had arrested some members of the group before the bombing.
20 Jeff Germ and Elaine Sciolino, "U.S. Takes Hard Look at Saudis with Bombing and Shah in Mind," *New York Times*, December 1, 1996.
21 David B. Ottaway, "U.S. Considers Slugging It Out with International Terrorism," *Washington Post*, October 17, 1996.
22 See Smith, "Critics 'Wrong,' CIA Chief Says." Smith also notes that Deutch's speech was remarkably lacking in detail, apparently because its contents had been strongly debated within the agency. The opponents of disclosure seemed to prevail. The CIA was apparently uncomfortable about defending the agency against partisan attacks, but National Security Adviser Anthony Lake was angry. Deutch also announced that the CIA was establishing a new "terrorist warning group."
23 Warren Christopher, "Fighting Terrorism: Challenges for Peacemakers", address to the Washington Institute for Near East Policy, May 21, 1996, in *U.S. Department of State Dispatch*, June 3, 1996, pp. 277–9.
24 Michael Dobbs, "An Obscure Chief in U.S. War on Terror," *Washington Post*, April 2, 2000. In 1994 Lake had described a moderate and nonthreatening policy toward Iran, suggesting that normal relations would be "conceivable" if Iran ceased its support for terrorism and its challenge to nonproliferation principles. He described U.S. policy as isolation and containment See "Confronting Backlash States," Foreign Affairs, March–April, 1994.
25 R. Jeffrey Smith, "Saudis Hold 40 Suspects in GI Quarters Bombing," *Washington Post*, November 1, 1996. The details of the Saudi findings and U.S. response come primarily from this reporting.
26 R. Jeffrey Smith, "Saudis Offer Data to U.S. Linking Extremists, Bomb," *Washington Post*, December 11, 1996.
27 Thomas W. Lippman and Bradley Graham, "U.S. Mulls Possible Response to Iran in Saudi Bombing," *Washington Post*, December 22, 1996. See also Robin Wright, "Iran Braces to Get Blamed for Bombing," *Los Angeles Times*, December 25, 1996.
28 R. Jeffrey Smith, "New Questions about Old Issues," *Washington Post*, January 8, 1998. Alternatively, a conclusive demonstration of Iranian complicity might persuade U.S. allies to support economic sanctions. The following April, when a German court concluded that Iran's "Committee for Special Operations" had ordered the assassinations of Kurdish dissidents, the State Department seized the opportunity to criticize the Europeans for maintaining a "critical dialogue" with Iran. The European Union was asked again to

join in U.S. sanctions in order to contain Iran. See Alan Cowell "Berlin Court Says Top Iran Leaders Ordered Killings," *New York Times*, April 11, 1997. The government was also coming under criticism at home for its policy of "dual containment" of Iraq and Iran. An impressive trio of former officials warned that although direct attacks on Americans called for retaliation, containment was not a solution to the general problem of terrorism. They urged that Iran's support for terrorism be addressed by "specific policy instruments," not the current crude and counterproductive attempt to isolate the entire country. They also advocated incentives for cooperation. See Zbigniew Brzezinski, Brent Scowcroft, and Richard Murphy, "Differentiated Containment," *Foreign Affairs*, 76, no. 3, May–June 1997, pp. 20–41.

29 Jane Perlez and James Risen, "Clinton Seeks an Opening to Iran," *New York Times*, December 3, 1999. The indictments handed down in June 2001 did not name or charge any Iranians, although the involvement of Iranian military officials was described.

30 Ibid.

31 See U.S. Department of State, Office of the Secretary of State and Office of the Coordinator for Counterterrorism, *Patterns of Global Terrorism*, for the years 1996, 1997, 1998, and 1999.

32 On U.S. awareness of the threat before the August bombings, see Vernon Loeb, "Where the CIA Wages Its New World War," *Washington Post*, September 9, 1998; Benjamin Weiser, "Saudi Is Indicted in Bomb Attacks on U.S. Embassies," and "Senior Aide Implicating Bin Laden in Terrorism," *New York Times*, November 5, 1998, and December 3, 1998, respectively; and James Risen and Benjamin Weiser, "Before Bombings, Omens and Fears," *New York Times*, January 9, 1999. Further information was revealed during the trial in New York of some of those responsible, from January to July 2001. Extensive coverage can be found in the *New York Times*, and much of the trial testimony has been made public.

33 See "Planning for Terror but Failing to Act," *New York Times*, December 30, 2001. This lengthy overview has helped inform the following discussion.

34 U.S. Department of State, *Patterns of Global Terrorism*: 1997.

35 Osama Bin Laden, interview with Peter Arnett, accessed at CNN's homepage, "CNN/Time Impact: Holy Terror?"

36 See Rohan Gunaratna, *Inside Al Qaeda: Global Network of Terror*, New York: Columbia University Press, 2002.

37 The text is available at www.fas.org/irp/world/para/docs/980223-fatwa.htm. Bin Laden also gave an interview to ABC News in May. See "Talking with Terror's Banker" on www.abcnews.com. See also the analysis of the declaration by Bernard Lewis, "License to Kill," *Foreign Affairs*, 77, no. 6, November–December 1998, pp. 14–19.

38 Details of U.S. information about Sudan and chemical weapons production are taken from James Risen, "To Bomb Sudan Plant, or Not: A Year Later, Debates Rankle," *New York Times*, October 27, 1999.

39 Thomas W. Lippman, "Clinton Imposes Sanctions on Sudan, Freezes Assets," *Washington Post*, November 5, 1997.

40 Tim Weiner and James Risen, "Decision to Strike Factory in Sudan Based on Surmise," *New York Times*, September 21, 1998.

41 Michael Dobbs, "Analysts Feel Militia Could End Anarchy," *Washington Post*, September 28, 1996.

42 See *Report of the Accountability Review Boards: Bombings of the U.S. Embassies in Nairobi, Kenya and Dar es Salaam, Tanzania on August 7, 1998*, January 11, 1999, available at www/zgram.net/embassybombing.htm. See further details from the classified report in Risen and Weiser, "Before Bombings, Omens and Fears." According to this account, the Kenyan authorities arrested a group of suspects, but the CIA station chief declined to interview them. Also see Benjamin Weiser, "U.S. to Offer Detailed Trail of Bin Laden in Bomb Trial," *New York Times*, January 13, 2001.

43 Seymour Hersh, "The Missiles of August," *New Yorker*, October 12, 1998, pp. 34–41. See also James Risen and Judith Miller, "Pakistani Intelligence Had Ties to al Qaeda," *New York Times*, October 29, 2001.

44 See Hersh, "The Missiles of August," and Risen, "To Bomb Sudan Plant, or Not" The following description of the decision-making process is based largely on these accounts, and also on background interviews with some officials. See also Tim Weiner and Steven Lee Myers, "Flaws in U.S. Account Raise Questions on Strike in Sudan," *New York Times*, August 29, 1998; and Weiner and Risen, "Decision to Strike Factory in Sudan Based on Surmise."

45 Risen, "To Bomb Sudan Plant, or Not."

46 Hersh, "The Missiles of August."

47 It appears that the aim was not so much to kill Bin Laden, although this would have been a welcome side effect, but to demonstrate U.S. knowledge of his location.

48 Former NSC staff members Daniel Benjamin and Steven Simon report that the decision was unanimous and argue that the press underestimated the importance of Al Shifa. Daniel Benjamin and Steven Simon, "A Failure of Intelligence?" in Robert B. Silvers and Barbara Epstein, *Striking Terror: America's New War*, New York: New York Review of Books, 2002. Benjamin and Simon are also the authors of *The Age of Sacred Terror*, New York: Random House, 2002.

49 See Michael Barletta, "Chemical Weapons in the Sudan: Allegations and Evidence,"' *Nonproliferation Review* 6, no. 1, fall 1998, pp. 1–37. As a counter to this view, consult Benjamin and Simon, "A Failure of Intelligence?"

50 Risen, "To Bomb Sudan Plant, or Not"; and Tim Weiner and Steven Lee Myers, "U.S. Notes Gaps in Data about Drug Plant but Defends Attack," *New York Times*, September 3, 1998. See also James Risen and David Johnston, "Experts Find No Arms Chemicals at Bombed Sudan Plant," *New York Times*, February 9, 1999, and the discussion in Paid Pillar, *Terrorism and U.S. Foreign Policy*, Washington, D.C.: Brookings Institution Press, 2001, pp. 107–9.

51 "Bombers Sent to Train on Guam,'" *New York Times*, September 3, 1998.

52 See Barton Gellman, "Clinton's Covert War" and "Terrorism Wasn't a Top Priority," *Washington Post*, National Weekly Edition, January 7-IS and 14–20, 2002, respectively. Both provide details on the 1998–2000 period.

53 *Joint Inquiry Staff Statement*, Part I, September 18, 2002, available on the House and Senate Intelligence Committee websites, intelligence.house.gov and intelligence. senate.gov., See p. 10. In 1999 only three analysts were assigned full-time to tracking Bin Laden; there were five by 2000, p. 18. The Counterterrorist Center staff doubled after September 11, from 400 to 800.

54 See Gellman, "Clinton's Covert War."

55 Wakil Ahmad Muttawakil, quoted in Pamela Constable, "U.N. Imposes Air, Economic Sanctions on Afghanistan," *Washington Post*, November 14, 1999.

56 Barbara Crossette, "U.S. Steps Up Pressure on Taliban to Deliver Osama bin Ladin," *New York Times*, October 19, 1999.

57 Gellman, "Clinton's Covert War."

58 See James Risen and Judith Miller, "Pakistani Intelligence Had Ties to Al Qaeda," *New York Times*, October 29, 2001.

59 See John Lancaster, "U.S. Pressures Pakistan to Cut Ties with Extremist Groups," *Washington Post*, January 26, 2000.

60 Among numerous press reports, see Jane Perlez, "U.S. Weighs Using Food as Support for Sudan Rebels" and "Friendly Fire: In a War, Even Food Aid Can Kill," *New York Times*, November 29, 1999, and December 5,1999, respectively. See also Mark Huband, "Debate Grows on How to Deal with Sudan," *Financial Times*, December 7, 1999. Susan Rice, the assistant secretary of state for African affairs, was said to view the Sudanese regime as "evil incarnate" and to be the main proponent of a hard-line policy.

61 Neil King, Jr., and David S. Cloud, "Casting a Global Net, U.S. Security Forces Survive Terrorist Test," *Wall Street Journal*, March 8, 2000. See also Dobbs, "An Obscure Chief in U.S. War on Terror."

62 He intended to bomb the Los Angeles International Airport, a target he chose himself, according to his testimony. See Laura Mansnerus and Judith Miller, "Terrorist Details His Training in Afghanistan," *New York Times*, July 4, 2001.

63 U.S. Department of State, *Patterns of Global Terrorism*, 1999, April 2000, p. 7.

64 Dobbs, "An Obscure Chief in U.S. War on Terror."

65 David A. Vise and Lorraine Adams, "Bin Ladin Weakened, Officials Say," *Washington Post*, March 11, 2000. However, shortly after this report Clinton canceled a visit to a village in Bangladesh during his South Asia visit, owing to threats from Bin Laden. See "Report on bin Laden Altered Clinton Plan," *New York Times*, March 21, 2000.

66 Jane Perlez, "Clinton Entreats Pakistan to Tread Lightly in Kashmir," *New York Times*, March 26, 2000. In fact, the Secret Service opposed the trip because of concerns about Clinton's safety. Extraordinary security precautions were taken, and the trip lasted only a few hours.

67 See Ambassador Michael Sheehan, "Post-Millennium Terrorism Review," speech to the Brookings Institution, February 10, 2000, as well as his testimony before the House Committee on International Relations, July 12, 2000. See also "Fact Sheet: U.S. Counterterrorism Efforts since the 1998 U.S. Embassy Bombings in Africa," August 7, 2000. The texts are available on the Office of Counterterrorism's website, state.gov/s/ct.

68 In contrast, the 1998 report referred to "forcing" state sponsors to change their behavior. The reports usually appear in the spring of the following year. This view is also corroborated by later Washington Post interviews with Ambassador Michael Sheehan (see Gellman, "Clinton's Covert War").

69 In an interview with Judith Miller, Ambassador Sheehan explained that Afghanistan was not added to the list because the United States did not recognize the Taliban government, and that Pakistan was a "friendly state" trying to improve its record, which badly needed it See "South Asia Called Major Terror Hub in a Survey by U.S.," *New York Times*, April 30, 2000.

70 However, in September Secretary of State Albright repeated the Clinton Administration's demand that the regime agree to a broad-based democratic government. Barbara Crossette, "Taliban Open a Campaign to Gain Status at the U.N.," *New York Times*, September 21, 2000.

71 Christopher Marquis. "U.S. Declares "Rogue Nations' Are Now 'States of Concern,'" *New York Times*, June 20, 2000.

72 Barbara Crossette, "Spurned Sudan, Looking for Foreign Support, Says It Has Changed," *New York Times*, June 21, 2000. See also Karl Vick, "Sudanese Leader Moves against Rival," *Washington Post*, December 15, 1999. The State Department's 2001 annual report explains the U.S. position. After the September 11 attacks, which Sudan condemned, Sudan pledged cooperation and was rewarded with the lifting of U.N. sanctions. However, U.S. unilateral sanctions remained in force.

73 National Commission on Terrorism, *Report to Congress: Countering the Changing Threat of International Terrorism*, Washington, D.C., June 5, 2000. The administration responded firmly that it was not considering sanctions against Pakistan.

74 Judith Miller, "U.S. Puts Uzbek Group on Its Terror List," *New York Times*, September 15, 2000. See also Ambassador Sheehan's testimony before the House Committee on International Relations, July 12, 2000. Afghanistan was said to be the "primary swamp of terrorism." On the other hand, Sheehan also argued that Bin Laden had no need for a state sponsor for material support. And he warned again that the Taliban would be held responsible should Bin Laden undertake any terrorist acts while based on its territory.

75 See "Planning for Terror but Failing to Act," *New York Times*, December 30, 2002.

76 John F. Burns, "Yemeni on Delicate Path in bin Laden Hunt," *New York Times*, December 15, 2000.

77 Barbara Crossette, "U.S. and Russia Ask Harsh Sanctions on Afghanistan," *New York Times*, December 8, 2000. An arms embargo might be considered an implied threat, since it would presumably handicap the Taliban in the internal struggle for power.

78 See David Johnston and James Risen, "Traces of Terrorism: The Intelligence Reports," and David E. Sanger and Elisabeth Bumiller, 'Traces of Terrorism: The Overview," in *New York Times*, May 17,2002: and Jane Perlez and David E. Sanger, "A Nation Challenged: State Department: Powell Says U.S. Had Signs, but Not Clear Ones, of a Plot," *New York Times*, October 3, 2001.

79 See the special report in Time, August 12, 2002.

80 In September 2002 a joint inquiry by the House and Senate Intelligence Committees produced an interim report. So far investigators had not found a "smoking gun" that would have alerted the government to a preventable attack. However, the government had received a stream of more general warnings, or "chatter." See *Joint Inquiry Staff Statement*, Part I, September 18, 2002, and "The Intelligence Community's Knowledge of the September 11 Hijackers prior to September 11, 2001," September 20, 2002. Both documents are available on the House and Senate Intelligence Committee websites: available at http://www.9-11commission.gov/staff_statements/staff_statement_2.pdf and http://www.fas.org/irp/congress/2002_hr/091802hill.html. The report also noted that information on what the White House and the president knew remained classified. The report states that "high government officials" were briefed repeatedly.

81 See the series of reports by Dan Balz and Bob Woodward, "Ten Days in September," *Washington Post*, January 27 February 3, 2002.

82 Siddharth Varadarajan, "Musharraf Drops Taliban to Get Kashmir," *Times of India*, September 21, 2001. He refers to "relentless pressure" from the United States. See also Farhan Bokhari and Edward Luce, "Pakistan's Choice," *Financial Times*, September 18, 2001. J. N. Dixit, former Indian foreign minister, is quoted as saying that "America's war on terrorism is the best opportunity India has had to settle the Kashmir dispute in its favour once and for all."

83 John F. Burns, "Pakistani Defends Joining with U.S." and "Pakistanis Fail in Last-Ditch Bid to Persuade Taliban to Turn Over bin Laden," *New York Times*, September 20 and September 29, 2001, respectively. Delegations traveled both to Kandahar and to Kabul and met with the Taliban for two days.

84 See John F. Burns, "New Push to Get bin Laden to Agree to Quit Afghanistan," *New York Times*, September 28, 2001.

85 See the text of the President's speech at www.whitehouse.gov/news/releases/2001/09. The Taliban had imprisoned a group of Christian relief workers accused of proselytizing.

86 John F. Burns, "Clerics Answer 'No, No, No!' and Invoke Fates of Past Foes," *New York Times*, September 22, 2001.

87 John F. Burns, "U.S. Officers Are Meeting in Islamabad on War Plans," *New York Times*, September 25, 2001.

88 John F. Burns, "Pakistan Fights U.S. Move Linked to Anti-Taliban Drive," *New York Times*, September 26, 2001.

89 See Burns, "New Push to Get bin Laden to Agree to Quit Afghanistan." Burns refers to these talks as well as the earlier set as "negotiations."

90 The following account is based on Burns, "Pakistanis Fail in Last-Ditch Bid to Persuade Taliban to Turn Over bin Laden."

91 See Michael R. Gordon and Eric Schmitt, "Pentagon Tries to Avoid Using Pakistan Bases," and Douglas Frantz, "Taliban Say They Want to Negotiate with the U.S. Over bin Laden," *New York Times*, October 3, 2001.

92 John F. Burns, "Taliban Say They Hold bin Laden," *New York Times*, October 1, 2001.
93 See Sarah Lyall, "Tough Talk from Blair on Taliban," *New York Times*, October 3, 2001.
94 Frantz, "Taliban Say They Want to Negotiate with the U.S. over bin Laden." The ambassador appeared in Quetta, Pakistan, sixty miles from the Afghan border, where the local tribal chiefs had been meeting.
95 Elaine Sciolino and Steven Lee Myers, "Bush Says 'Time Is Running Out,'" *New York Times*, October 7, 2001.
96 John F. Burns, "Taliban Link Fate of Aid Workers to U.S. Action," *New York Times*, October 7, 2001.
97 Patrick E. Tyler, "U.S. and Britain Strike Afghanistan," and "Jets Pound Taliban Sites a 2nd Night," *New York Times*, October 8 and 9, 2001, respectively. The bombing involved fifteen land-based bombers and twenty-five strike aircraft from carriers. They used precision-guided bombs. U.S. warships and British submarines fired fifty Tomahawk cruise missiles.
98 Although this attack was reported at the time, only on October 15 did the secretary of defense admit openly that the air strikes had been targeting Mullah Omar since the first day of the air campaign. See Michael R. Gordon and Tim Weiner, "Taliban Leader a Target of U.S. Air Campaign," *New York Times*, October 16, 2001.
99 Patrick E. Tyler and Elisabeth Bumiller, "Bush Offers Taliban '2nd Chance' to Yield," *New York Times*, October 12, 2001.
100 Elisabeth Bumiller, "President Rejects Offer by Taliban for Negotiations," *New York Times*, October 15, 2001. Gunaratna argues that the Taliban might have turned Bin Laden over to Pakistan had the Bush Administration given them more time, *Inside Al Qaeda*, 227.
101 Ibid.
102 John F. Burns, "Taliban Envoy Talks of a Deal over bin Laden," *New York Times*, October 16, 2001.
103 Patrick E. Tyler, "Powell Suggests Role for Taliban," *New York Times*, October 17, 2001.
104 John F. Burns, "Taliban Chief Urges Troops: Defy 'Infidel,'" *New York Times*, October 18, 2001.
105 Mullah Abdul Salam Zaeef, quoted in John F. Burns, "Don't Doubt Steadfastness of Taliban, Envoy Insists," *New York Times*, October 20, 2001. Maulvi Jalaluddin Haqqani, the commander of Taliban forces on the Pakistan border, also rejected the idea of Taliban participation in a postwar government, although Pakistan had encouraged him to consider the idea, and earlier Pakistani and U.S. intelligence agents had approached him about defecting. See John F. Burns, "Taliban Army Chief Scoffs at Report of Peace Talks," *New York Times*, October 21, 2001.
106 Michael R. Gordon, "U.S. Bombs Taliban's Forces on Front Lines," *New York Times*, October 22, 2001.
107 Access to classified information would undoubtedly yield a less tentative assessment.
108 Possibly these efforts might be interpreted as coercion at the individual rather than the group level, since militants might have been expected to lose enthusiasm for the cause once the costs of action mounted.
109 Even the 1998 cruise missile attack was meant to strike a group of senior leaders, including Bin Laden, so it might be interpreted as an assassination attempt as much as a demonstration of force.
110 Simon and Benjamin, for example, blame the press for labeling the attack on the Al Shifa pharmaceuticals a foreign policy blunder, "A Failure of Intelligence?" pp. 292–9.
111 See Chapters 11 and 12 in this volume.

9 Strategies and grand strategies

1 Stephen M. Walt, "Beyond bin Laden: Reshaping U.S. Foreign Policy," *International Security*, 26, no. 3, winter 2001–2, p. 56.
2 See Richard K. Betts, "Is Strategy an Illusion?" *International Security*, 25, no. 2, fall 2000, pp. 5–50.
3 See Michael Mastanduno, "Preserving the Unipolar Moment: Realist Theories and U.S. Grand Strategy after the Cold War," *International Security*, 21, no. 4, spring 1997, 49–88, and Barry R. Posen and Andrew L. Ross, "Competing Visions for U.S. Grand Strategy," *International Security*, 21, no. 3, winter 1996–7, pp. 5–53.
4 Christopher Layne, "From Preponderance to Offshore Balancing: America's Future Grand Strategy," *International Security*, 22, no. 1, summer 1997, p. 116. This brief mention occurs in a lengthy article, pp. 86–124.
5 Eugene Gholz, Daryl G. Press, and Harvey M. Sapolsky, "Come Home, America: The Strategy of Restraint in the Face of Temptation," *International Security*, 21, no. 4, spring 1997, p. 8.
6 Ibid., 30. The article runs from pp. 5–48.
7 Mastanduno, "Preserving the Unipolar Moment."
8 According to Richard Rosecrance and Arthur Stein, grand strategy is not just an optimal response to international pressures, threats, and power configurations but the outcome of domestic orientations, resources, constraints, and conditions. See Richard Rosecrance and Arthur A. Stein, eds, *The Domestic Bases of Grand Strategy*, Ithaca, NY: Cornell University Press, 1993.
9 Bruce W. Jentleson, "The Need for Praxis: Bringing Policy Relevance Back In," *International Security*, 26, no. 4, spring 2002, pp. 169–83. See also Peter Katzenstein, "September 11th in Comparative Perspective," paper presented to the American Political Science Association 98th Annual Meeting, Boston, August-September 2002, available at http://apsaproceedings.cup.org. Of course, much work on terrorism does involve modeling and/or aggregate data analysis.
10 Robert J. Art, "Geopolitics Updated: The Strategy of Selective Engagement," *International Security*, 23, no. 3, winter 1998–9, p. 85.
11 Ashton B. Carter and William J. Perry, *Preventive Defense: A New Security Strategy for America*, Washington, D.C.: Brookings Institution Press, 1999. The concept of preventive defense goes beyond terrorism to target the full range of threats to national security. Furthermore, the authors define "catastrophic terrorism" as acts that are an order of magnitude more severe than "ordinary" terrorism and are unprecedented outside of warfare, p. 150. Catastrophic terrorism need not involve the use of WMD.
12 Ian O. Lesser, "Countering the New Terrorism: Implications for Strategy," in Ian O. Lesser, Bruce Hoffman, John Arquilla, David Ronfeldt, and Michele Zanini, *Countering the Hew Terrorism*, Santa Monica, CA: Rand, 1999, p. 140. Lesser advocated a "core" strategy and "multidimensional" approach that would include not just direct responses to terrorism but shaping of the international environment, ibid., pp. 140–2.
13 Richard Falkenrath, "Analytic Models and Policy Prescription: Understanding Recent Innovation in U.S. Counterterrorism," *Studies in Conflict and Terrorism*, 24, no. 3, May–June 2001, 159–82.
14 Paul R. Pillar, *Terrorism and U.S. Foreign Policy*, Washington, D.C.: Brookings Institution Press, 2001, p. 223.
15 Ibid.
16 Ibid., p. 229
17 Neil C. Livingstone and Terrell E. Arnold, *Fighting Back: Winning the War against Terrorism*, Lexington, MA: D. C. Heath and Co., 1986, p. 229.
18 Marc A. Celmer, *Terrorism, U.S. Strategy, and Reagan Policies*, Westport, CT: Greenwood Press, 1987.

19 Grant Wardlaw, "State Response to International Terrorism: Some Cautionary Comments," in Robert A. Slater and Michael Stohl, eds, *Current Perspectives on International Terrorism*, London: Macmillan, 1988, p. 214.

20 Jeffrey D. Simon, *The Terrorist Trap: America's Experience with Terrorism*, Bloomington: Indiana University Press, 1994, p. 376.

21 The principle of no concessions to terrorist demands in cases of hostage seizures was developed under the Nixon Administration, primarily by Henry Kissinger. It was first applied in 1973, when American diplomats were held hostage and subsequently murdered by members of the Black September Organization in Khartoum. Its application has been inconsistent.

22 Yehezkel Dror, "Terrorism as a Challenge to the Democratic Capacity to Govern," in Martha Crenshaw ed. *Terrorism, Legitimacy, and Power: The Consequences of Political Violence*, Middletown, CT: Wesleyan University Press, 1983, p. 65. Dror also blamed social science: "This ignorance [of terrorism] principally stems from the state of the social sciences, which lack the frames of appreciation, cognitive maps, concept packages, and methodology to comprehend complex phenomena that cannot be understood through decomposition into easier-to-analyze subelements. Our generation, like earlier generations, is overwhelmed by events we cannot adequately comprehend with contemporary modes of thinking and tacit models," ibid., p. 67.

23 Ibid., p. 81.

24 See, for example, William R. Farrell, *The U.S. Government Response to Terrorism: In Search of an Effective Strategy*, Boulder, CO: Westview Press, 1982; Martha Crenshaw, "Counterterrorism Policy and the Political Process," *Studies in Conflict and Terrorism*, 24, no. 5, 2001, p. 329–38; Laura K. Donohue, "In the Name of National Security: U.S. Counterterrorist Measures, 1960–2000," *Terrorism and Political Violence*, 13, no. 3, autumn 2001, p. 47; Laura K. Donohue and Juliette N. Kayyem, "Federalism and the Battle over Counterterrorist Law: State Sovereignty, Criminal Law Enforcement, and National Security," *Studies in Conflict and Terrorism*, 25, no. 1, 2002, pp. 1–18; and Richard A. Falkenrath, "Problems of Preparedness: U.S. Readiness for a Domestic Terrorist Attack," *International Security*, 25, no. 4, spring 2001, pp. 147–86.

25 David Tucker, *Skirmishes at the Edge of Empire: The United States and International Terrorism*, Westport, CT: Praeger, 1997, p. 134. Also, Marc A. Celmer, *Terrorism, U.S. Strategy, and Reagan Policies*, Westport, CT: Greenwood Press, 1987, disagreed, however, and argued that even the Reagan Administration lacked a strategy.

26 Pillar, *Terrorism and U.S. Foreign Policy*, pp. 220–1.

27 See Falkenrath, "Analytic Models and Policy Prescription."

28 For example, Condoleezza Rice, then foreign policy adviser to the Bush campaign, wrote an article on "Promoting the National Interest" for the January–February 2000, issue of *Foreign Affairs*. Among the five key priorities the United States should focus on, she cited dealing with rogue regimes, whose threat increasingly was taking the form of potential for terrorism and the development of WMD. She devoted the most attention to China and Russia. The only specific reference to terrorism was in the context of rogue regimes, particularly Iraq, and their capacity to use chemical and biological weapons. Here she called for expanding intelligence capabilities rather than an active response.

29 Barry R. Posen, "The Struggle against Terrorism: Grand Strategy, Strategy, and Tactics," *International Security*, 26, no. 3, winter 2001–2, pp. 39–55. No mention is made of the fact that security specialists also had ignored the absence of strategy before September 11.

30 Walt, "Beyond bin Laden," especially pp. 77–8.

31 Posen, "The Struggle against Terrorism," pp. 53 and 55.

32 In this respect, the debate over the failure to predict a major terrorist attack recalls the debate over the end of the Cold War.

33 Steven E. Miller, "The End of Unilateralism or Unilateralism Redux?" *Washington Quarterly*, 25, no. 1, winter 2002, pp. 15--29.

34 Ashton B. Carter, "The Architecture of Government in the Face of Terrorism," *International Security*, 26, no. 3, winter 2001–2, pp. 5–23. Carter, however, continued to dismiss the threat of "ordinary" terrorism, failing to see the causal links between terrorism that does not cause mass casualties and terrorism that does.

35 See Benjamin Schwarz and Christopher Layne, "A New Grand Strategy," *The Atlantic Monthly*, 289, no. 1, January 2002, pp. 36–42 available at www.theatlantic.com.

36 See Audrey Kurth Cronin, "Rethinking Sovereignty: American Strategy in the Age of Terrorism," *Survival*, 44, no. 2, summer 2002, pp. 119–39. This outcome is what Dror also expected.

37 See Arie W. Kruglanski, Martha Crenshaw, Jerrold M. Post, and Jeff Victoroff. "What Should This Fight Be Called? Metaphors of Counterterrorism and Their Implications." *Psychological Science in the Public Interest*, 8, 3, December 2007, pp. 97–133. See also Martha Crenshaw, "¿Está Estados Unidos ganando la guerra global contra el terrorismo?" in Charles T. Powell and Fernando Reinares *Las democracias occidentales frente al terrorismo global*, ed. Barcelona: Ariel and Real Instituto Elcano, 2008.

38 Graduation Speech, United States Military Academy, West Point, New York, June 1, 2002.

39 It seems likely that had the Taliban surrendered Bin Ladin, he would have been tried in a civilian court.

40 *Patterns of Global Terrorism 2001*, U.S. Department of State publication 10940, May 2002.

41 White House, 17 September 2002. The report is mandated by Congress.

42 See Nicholas Lemann, "Letter from Washington: The Next World Order," *The New Yorker*, 1 April, 2002. Lemann suggested that the ideas behind the plan stemmed from officials in the first Bush Administration. See also Rice, "Promoting the National Interest."

43 Lemann, "Letter from Washington." For more discussion of pre 9/11 policy, see Timothy Naftali, *Blind Spot: The Secret History of American Counterterrorism*, New York: Basic Books, 2005. See also my review essay, "Counterterrorism in Retrospect: Chronicle of a War Foretold," *Foreign Affairs* 84, 4, July–August 2005, pp. 187–93.

44 The Clinton Administration had abandoned the term "rogue states" in favor of "states of concern."

45 See the president's address to the United Nations General Assembly, New York, 12 September 2002, available at www.whitehouse.gov.

46 Whether this new idea should be called preemptive or preventive war is open to question. Preemption assumes that the defender has almost certain knowledge of an impending attack within a short time frame.

47 See Frances FitzGerald, "George Bush and the World," *New York Review of Books*, 26 September, 2002.

48 See Marina Ottaway, Thomas Carothers, Amy Hawthorne, and Daniel Brumberg, *Democratic Mirage in the Middle East*, Carnegie Endowment for International Peace Policy Brief 20, October 2002.

49 Martha Crenshaw, "Why America? The Globalization of Civil War," *Current History*, 100, December 2001, pp. 425–32.

50 One need only look at the Department of State's annual reports on international terrorism to see that hundreds of different groups have used terrorism fitting the definition of "international," which means involving the citizens or territory of more than one country. It is not clear how "terrorism of global reach" is distinguished from international terrorism.

51 This is not to argue that underlying grievances are a direct cause of terrorism, but they motivate audiences whose support is anticipated and sought by organized radical

groups. Terrorism can be regarded as a way of soliciting and mobilizing support. Al Qaeda is by no means a mass movement.

10 Counterterrorism policy and the political process

1 Despite its significance, little systematic attention has been paid to the politics of the counterterrorism policy process. William Farrell's early book, *The U.S. Government Response to Terrorism: In Search of an Effective Strategy*, Boulder, CO: Westview Press, 1982, analyzed the organizations behind counterterrorism policy. David Tucker, *Skirmishes at the Edge of Empire: The United States and International Terrorism*, Westport, CT: Praeger, 1997, is also relevant, particularly Chapter 4, pp. 109–32. Paul Pillar's *Terrorism and U.S. Foreign Policy* presents a CIA official's view, Washington, DC: Brookings, 2001.

2 Thomas A. Birkland, *After Disaster: Agenda Setting, Public Policy, and Focusing Events*, Washington, DC: Georgetown University Press, 1997.

3 Note: The 9/11 attacks constituted an exception because of their enormous destructiveness.

4 Robert H. Johnson, *Improbable Dangers: U.S. Conceptions of Threat in the Cold War and After*, New York: St. Martin's, 1997, Chapter 2, "American Politics, Psychology, and the Exaggeration of Threat," pp. 31–48.

5 The classic work is John W. Kingdon, *Agendas, Alternatives, and Public Policies*, 2nd ed., New York: Harper Collins, 1995. See also Frank R. Baumgartner and Bryan D. Jones, *Agendas and Instability in American Politics*, Chicago: University of Chicago Press, 1993 and Deborah A. Stone, *Policy Paradox: The Art of Political Decision Making*, New York: W.W. Norton, 1997.

6 See Congressional Quarterly *Weekly Report*, January 16, 1999, p. 151.

7 See Richard A. Falkenrath, "Problems of Preparedness: U.S. Readiness for a Domestic Terrorist Attack," *International Security*, 25(4), Spring 2001, pp. 147–86. See also Martha Crenshaw, "Threat Perception in Democracies: 'WMD' Terrorism in the U.S. Policy Debate," presented to the 22nd Annual Scientific Meeting of the International Society for Political Psychology, Amsterdam, July 18–21, 1999.

8 It has 82 members and an annual budget of $8.7 million, and is expected to increase to 121 people by 2003. It is based in Virginia, as part of the U.S. Joint Forces Command. In the event of a request from local or state government authorities, it would probably take direction from FEMA. See James Dao, "Looking Ahead to the Winter Olympics, a Terrorist Response Team Trains," *The New York Times*, April 11, 2001.

9 However, the Federal Emergency Management Agency (FEMA) has jurisdiction over "consequence management," which is in effect disaster response policy in the event of a domestic attack, especially one involving mass casualties.

10 In *Terrorism & Democracy*, Boston: Houghton Mifflin, 1991, p. 39.

11 Ibid., p. 81. Brzezinski set up an NSC committee to oversee covert actions because the CIA estimated that prospects for success were low. The CIA then vetoed the list of operations the NSC suggested, but Brzezinski was reluctant to take the dispute to the president.

12 21 May 1998, p. A1.

13 See John F. Burns, "U.S. Aides Say the Yemenis Seem to Hinder Cole Inquiry," *The New York Times*, November 1, 2000.

14 April 26, 1998.

15 May 23, 1998, p. A3.

16 For the text of the speech, see http://www.defenselink.mil/news/Sep1998.

17 Richard A. Falkenrath, Robert D. Newman, and Bradley A. Thayer, *America's Achilles Heel: Nuclear, Biological, and Chemical Terrorism and Covert Attack*, Cambridge, MA: MIT Press, 1998, p. 263. See also Falkenrath, "Problems of Preparedness," p. 162, who says that the military see this role as a distraction from their core mission.

18 "Defense's Death Spiral," *Foreign Affairs*, 78(4), July–August 1999, p. 4.
19 *The New York Times*, 28 January 1999; also *The Hartford Courant*, with *Washington Post* byline, February 1, 1999.
20 See Falkenrath, "Problems of Preparedness," p. 163.
21 On this subject, see James Risen, "To Bomb Sudan Plant, or Not: A Year Later, Debates Rankle," *The New York Times*, October 27, 1999, and Seymour Hersh, "The Missiles of August," *The New Yorker*, October 12, 1998, pp. 34–41.
22 See Report of the Accountability Review Boards: Bombings of the U.S. Embassies in Nairobi, Kenya and Dar es Salaam, Tanzania on August 7, 1998, January 11, 1999, available at, http://www/zgram.net/embassybombing.htm. See further details from the classified report in James Risen and Benjamin Weiser, "Before Bombings, Omens and Fears," *The New York Times*, January 9, 1999. According to this account, the Kenyan authorities arrested a group of suspects but the CIA Station Chief declined to interview them.
23 This section relies on research assistance by Karen Millard. See press reports such as Lou Cannon, "Political Pressure for Marine Pullout Likely to Increase," *The Washington Post*, December 29, 1983; Martin Tolchin, "House Leaders Urge New Study of Beirut Policy," *The New York Times*, January 3, 1984; and John Goshko and Margaret Shapiro, "Shultz Asks for Support on Lebanon; Holds Hill Parleys as Pressure for Withdrawal Grows," *The Washington Post*, January 27, 1984.
24 See text in *The Washington Post*, January 26, 1984, p. A16.
25 See *The New York Times*, August 14, 18, and 20, 1975. Kate Whitman assisted with the research of this case.
26 Falkenrath, "Problems of Preparedness," p. 149.
27 For example, Ian O. Lesser et al., *Countering the New Terrorism*, Santa Monica, CA: Rand Corporation, 1999. The study was commissioned by the Air Force.
28 See Steven Emerson and Brian Duffy, *The Fall of Pan Am 103: Inside the Lockerbie Investigation*, New York: G.P. Putnam's Sons, 1990, especially pp. 221–5.
29 See Gideon Rose's account of the politics of the legislative process in his chapter on Libya in Richard N. Haass, ed., *Economic Sanctions and American Diplomacy*, New York: Council on Foreign Relations, 1998, pp. 129–56, especially pp. 142–4. See also Patrick Clawson's chapter on Iran, pp. 85–106.
30 See his chapter, "Taking vows: The domestication of policy-making in hostage incidents," in *Origins of Terrorism*, edited by Walter Reich, Washington, DC: Woodrow Wilson Center and Cambridge University Press, 1990, pp. 238–9.
31 Joel Rothman assisted with research on this debate. See U.S. Senate, Committee on Commerce, Subcommittee on Aviation, *The Anti-Hijacking Act of 1971*. Hearings. 92nd Cong., 2nd sess., 1972.
32 Kingdon, *Agendas, Alternatives, and Public Policies*, p. 59.
33 *The Terrorist Trap: America's Experience with Terrorism*, Bloomington: Indiana University Press, 1994, especially Chapter 7, "Media Players," pp. 261–308.
34 *Terrorism and the Media*, New York: Columbia University Press, 1994.
35 Measured by references to international terrorism in the *Readers' Guide to Periodical Literature* 1968–98. Database available upon request.

11 How terrorism declines

1 There was one exception at the time my original article was written: Jeffrey Ian Ross, and Ted Robert Gurr, "Why Terrorism Subsides: A Comparative Study of Trends and Groups in Terrorism in Canada and the United States," *Comparative Politics*, 21, 1989, pp. 405–26.
2 Alex P. Schmid, *Political Terrorism: A Research Guide to Concepts, Theories, Data Bases and Literature*, New Brunswick, NJ: Transaction Books, 1983.

3 See Ted Robert Gurr, "On the Outcomes of Violence Conflict," in T. R. Gurr, ed., *Handbook of Political Conflict*, New York: Free Press, 1980, pp. 238–94.
4 For example, see Ray S. Cline and Yonah Alexander, *Terrorism: The Soviet Connection*, New York: Crane, Russak, 1984.
5 For example, see Noam Chomsky, "Middle East Terrorism and the American Ideological System," *Race & Class* 28, 1986, pp. 1–28.
6 Since this chapter was written, there has been much more attention to the decline of terrorism, as noted in the Introduction.
7 See Robert G. Picard, "News Coverage as the Contagion of Terrorism: Dangerous Charges Backed by Dubious Science," *TVI Report*, 7, 1987, pp. 39–45.
8 Alex Schmid and Janny de Graaf, *Violence as Communication: Insurgent Terrorism and the Western News Media*, Beverly Hills, CA: Sage, 1982.
9 Paul Wilkinson, "Trends in International Terrorism and the American Response," in L. Freedman, Ch. Hill et al., eds, *Terrorism and International Order*, London: Routledge & Kegan Paul, 1986.
10 Gail Bass, Brian M. Jenkins, Konrad Kellen and David Ronfeldt, *Options for U.S. Policy on Terrorism*, Santa Monica, CA: Rand Corporation, 1981.
11 See Department of State, "Patterns of Global Terrorism: 1985," Washington, D.C.: Office of the Ambassador at Large for Counter-Terrorism, 1986. See also, U.S. Department of State, "Patterns of Global Terrorism: 1986," Washington, D.C.: Office of the Ambassador at Large for Counter-Terrorism, 1988.
12 Adrian Guelke, "Loyalist and Republican Perceptions of the Northern Ireland Conflict: The UDA and Provisional IRA," in P. H. Merkl, ed., *Political Violence and Terror: Motifs and Motivations*, Berkeley, CA: University of California Press, 1986, pp. 91–122.
13 Ibid., p. 116. Now that the conflict in Northern Ireland has ended, Guelke's predictions should be reevaluated.
14 Richard E. Rubenstein, *Alchemists of Revolution: Terrorism in the Modern World*, New York: Basic Books, 1987.
15 Harry R. Targ, "Societal Structure and Revolutionary Terrorism: A Preliminary Investigation," in M. Stohl, ed., *The Politics of Terrorism*, New York: Marcel Dekker, 1979, pp. 119–43.
16 Jean-Claude Chesnais, *Histoire de la violence en Occident de 1800 à nos jours*, Paris: Robert Laffont, 1981.
17 Ross and Gurr, "Why Terrorism Subsides."
18 Gian Carlo Caselli, "Comment nous avons vaincu les Brigades rouges," *Le Nouvel Observateur*, November 21–27, 1986, p. 30.
19 Ibid., p. 30.
20 Yet similar British policies in Northern Ireland produce different outcomes. John E. Finn, "Public Support for Emergency, Anti-Terrorist, Legislation in Northern Ireland: A Preliminary Analysis," *Terrorism* 10, 1987, p. 119 notes that IRA defendants plead guilty in order to secure more lenient sentences, but this apparent cooperation is a sign of loyalty to the IRA, not organizational disintegration. The IRA has apparently instructed its members to try to get off as lightly as possible, in order to insure group survival.
21 Sidney Tarrow and Donatella della Porta, "Unwanted Children: Political Violence and the Cycle of Protest in Italy, 1966–1972," *European Journal of Political Research*, 14, 1986. pp. 607–32.
22 Albert Legault, "La dynamique du terrorisme: le cas des Brigades Rouges," *Revue Etudes Internationales*, 14, 1983, pp. 639–81.
23 As does Sprinzak, in the original volume.
24 Legault, "La dynamique," p. 676.
25 Philippe Madelin, *La galaxie terroriste*, Paris: Plon, 1986, pp. 106–7.
26 Louis Fournier, *FLQ: Histoire d'un Mouvement Clandestin*, Montreal: Québec-Amerique, 1982.

27 Ross and Gurr, "Why Terrorism Subsides."
28 Murray J. Leaf, "The Punjab Crisis," *Asian Survey*, 25, 1985, p. 494.
29 Fernando Lopez-Alves, "Urban guerrillas and the Rise of Bureaucratic Authoritarianism in Uruguay: 1959–1972," paper presented to the American Political Science Association, 1985.
30 As'ad Abu Khalil, "Internal Contradictions in the PFLP: Decision Making and Policy Orientation," *Middle East Journal*, 41, 1987, pp. 361–78.
31 Khachig Tololyan, "Conflict and Decline in Armenian Terrorism," paper presented to the American Political Science Association, 1986.
32 Ibid., p. 19.

12 Why terrorism is rejected or renounced

1 See, for example, Peter H. Merkl, ed., *Political Violence and Terror: Motifs and Motivations*, Berkeley: University of California Press, 1986, and Walter Reich, ed., *Origins of Terrorism: Psychologies Ideologies, Theologies, States of Mind*, Cambridge: Woodrow Wilson International Center for Scholars and Cambridge University Press, 1990; exceptions are Jeffrey Ian Ross and Ted Robert Gurr, "Why Terrorism Subsides: A Comparative Study of Canada and the United States," *Comparative Politics*, 21, 1989, pp. 405–26, and Roy Licklider, ed., *Stopping the Killing: How Civil Wars End*, New York: New York University Press, 1993.
2 Bhikhu Parekh, "Gandhi's Theory of Non-Violence: His Reply to the Terrorists," in *Terrorism, Ideology and Revolution: The Origins of Modern Political Violence*, ed. Noel O'Sullivan, Boulder, CO: Westview, 1986, pp. 192–3.
3 Government of India, Home Department, Intelligence Bureau, *Terrorism in India: 1917–1936*, reprint, 1937, Delhi: Deep Publications, 1974.
4 David Allen Newell, "The Russian Marxist Response to Terrorism: 1878–1917," Ph.D. diss., Stanford University, 1981.
5 Eve Rosenhaft, "The KPD in the Weimar Republic and the Problem of Terror during the 'Third Period,' 1929–33," in *Social Protest, Violence and Terror in Nineteenth- and Twentieth-century Europe*, ed. Wolfgang J. Mommsen and Gerhard Hirschfeld, New York: St. Martin's, 1982, pp. 342–66.
6 Antoine Liniers, "Objections contre une prise d'armes," in *Terrorisme et démocratie*, ed. Furet et al., Paris: Fayard, 1985, pp. 137–224.
7 Ibid., pp. 180–1.
8 See also Alain Geismar, *L'Engrenage terroriste*, Paris: Fayard, 1981.
9 James De Nardo, *Power in Numbers*, Princeton: Princeton University Press, 1985.
10 Herbert M. Howe, "Government and Opposition Terrorism in South Africa," in *The Politics of Terrorism: Terror as a State and Revolutionary Strategy*, ed. Barry Rubin, Baltimore: The Johns Hopkins Foreign Policy Institute, 1989, pp. 153–81.
11 Ibid., p. 174.
12 Stephen M. Davis, *Apartheid's Rebels: Inside South Africa's Hidden War*, New Haven: Yale University Press, 1987, p. 210.
13 Rosenhaft, "The KPD," p. 350.
14 Ibid., pp. 355–6.
15 William O'Brien and Desmond Ryan, eds., *Devoy's Post Bag*, Dublin: C.J. Fallon, Ltd, 1953, pp. 4–10.
16 William O'Brien and Desmond Ryan, eds., *Devoy's Post Bag*, Dublin: C.J. Fallon, Ltd, 1948, pp. 143 and 323.
17 Quoted in O'Brien and Ryan, *Devoy's Post Bag*, 1948, p. 44.
18 Parekh, "Ghandi's Theory."
19 Howe, "Government and Opposition," p. 173.
20 Geismar, *L'Engrenage terroriste*, p. 51.

21 Davis, *Apartheid's Rebels*, p. 122. See also Howe, "Government and Opposition," pp. 168–70.
22 Rosenhaft "The KPD," pp. 356–60.
23 Liniers "Objections," pp. 213–23.
24 See Martha Crenshaw, "Theories of Terrorism: Instrumental and Organizational Approaches," in David C. Rapoport ed. *Inside Terrorist Organizations*, New York: Columbia University Press, 1988, pp. 13–31.
25 Liniers, "Objections," and Geismar, *L'Engrenage terroriste.*
26 Liniers, "Objections," p. 151.
27 Davis, *Apartheid's Rebels*, pp. 121–2.
28 Liniers, "Objections," p. 212, says of this reference, "Je ne vois pas quel autre mot employer."
29 Ibid., pp. 197–203, 207–213; Geismar *L'Engrenage terroriste*, pp. 49–59.
30 Howe, "Government and Opposition," p. 180.
31 Davis, *Apartheid's Rebels*, pp. 122–3.
32 Donatella, Della Porta, "Left-wing Terrorism in Italy," in Martha Crenshaw, ed., *Terrorism in Context*, University Park: Pennsylvania State University Press, 1995, pp. 105–59.
33 Franco Ferracuti, "Ideology and Repentance: Terrorism in Italy," in Walter Reich, ed., *Origins of terrorism: Psychologies, Ideologies, Theologies, States of Mind*, Cambridge: Woodrow Wilson International Center for Scholars and Cambridge University Press, 1990, p. 63.
34 For example, Arthur Campbell, "Guerillas," New York: John Day, 1968, p. 296.
35 Abou Iyad [Salah Khalaf], *Palestinien sans patrie*, Paris: Fayolle, 1978, p. 156.
36 Ariel Merari and Elad Shlomi, *The International Dimension of Palestinian Terrorism*, Tel Aviv: Jaffee Center for Strategic Studies, study no. 6, Boulder, CO: Westview, 1986, p. 99.
37 Ibid., p. 91.
38 Ibid., p. 95. See in general Chapter 5 "Conclusion: A Cost-Benefit Accounting," pp. 89–95.
39 Ted Robert Gurr, "Terrorism in Democracies: Its Social and Political Bases," in Walter Reich, ed. *Origins of Terrorism: Psychologies, Ideologies, Theologies, States of Mind*, Cambridge: Woodrow Wilson International Center for Scholars and Cambridge University Press, 1990, pp. 86–102.
40 Christopher Hewitt, *The Effectiveness of Anti-Terrorist Policies*, Lanham, MD: University Press of America, 1984.
41 Louis Fournier, *F.L.Q.: Histoire d'un movement clandestin.* Montréal: Québec/Amérique, 1982.
42 Ross and Gurr, "Why Terrorism Subsides."
43 Walker, Clive, *The Prevention of Terrorism in British Law*, Manchester: Manchester University Press, 1986, p. 175.
44 Merari and Elad, *The International Dimension*, p. 83.
45 Ross and Gurr, "Why Terrorism Subsides," see also Gurr, "Terrorism in Democracies," pp. 92–101.
46 Ross and Gurr, "Why Terrorism Subsides," p. 414.
47 Government of India, *Terrorism in India*, p. 61.
48 Khachig Tololyan, "Cultural Narrative and the Motivation of the Terrorist" in David C. Rapoport, ed. *Inside Terrorist Organizations*, New York: Columbia University Press, 1988, pp. 217–33.
49 Ross and Gurr, "Why Terrorism Subsides."
50 Hans-Joachim Klein, *La mort mercenaire: Témoignage d'un ancient terroriste ouest-allemand*, trans. Jean and Béatrice Balard, Paris: Seuil, 1980.
51 Americas Watch, *The Killings in Colombia*, New York: An Americas Watch Report, 1989, p. 12.

52 Leonard Weinberg and William Lee Eubank, *The Rise and Fall of Italian Terrorism*, Boulder, CO: Westview, 1987.
53 Ibid., p. 129.
54 Ibid., p. 130.
55 Ferracuti, "Ideology and Repentance."
56 See Donatella Della Porta, "Political Socialization in Left-wing Underground Organizations: Biographies of Italian and German Militants," in Donatella della Porta ed. *Social Movement and Violence: Participation in Underground Organizations*, ed. Greenwich, CT: JAL, 1992, pp. 259–90.

Index

Lightning Source UK Ltd.
Milton Keynes UK
UKHW03f0848260418
321546UK00004B/48/P